A Century of Sports

In Santa Clara County

1900-1999

BY JOHN E. SPALDING

Other Books by the Author:
"Always on Sunday, The California Baseball League, 1886 to 1915"
"Pacific Coast League Stars, 100 of the Best, 1903 to 1957"
"Sacramento Senators and Solons, Baseball in California's Capital, 1886 to 1976"
"Pacific Coast League Stars, Vol. 2, Ninety Who Made It In The Majors, 1903 to 1957"

ISBN 0-89745-979-2

Layout, cover design by Barry Colla Photography and Design

FIRST EDITION - by Ag Press, Manhattan, KS

Introduction

Just so we won't argue about what constitutes a century, I used the definition in *Webster's New World Dictionary*: "A century begins with a year ending in 00 and runs through 99, as . . . 1900-1999."

When you review a century of sports in Santa Clara County you may conclude that everything has changed, or possibly that very little has changed in 100 years. Back in 1900, there were no 18,000-seat arenas, no 85,000-seat stadiums, no luxury boxes, no Tartan running tracks, no softball complexes, no sports agents, and fewer idiot jocks who had to get "in-your-face" to prove their manhood. Ballparks and other facilities that existed in what was frequently referred to as the Valley of Heart's Delight were small, cozy and definitely on the primitive side. Sportsmanship instead of one-upsmanship was king and rooters spent more time cheering for their team than taunting opponents.

But, while the trappings of sports are quite different today in what some refer to as Silicon Valley, many games haven't changed much. And athletes still compete, some for money, but most just for the thrill of playing their game.

There are many more athletes and sports these days since volleyball, soccer, judo, lacrosse, field hockey, ice hockey, mountain biking, skate boarding, water polo and a few others have joined the more traditional baseball, football, basketball, track and field, swimming, golf, tennis and auto racing on the sports menu over the past 100 years. New opportunities for women in the last three decades have added even more to this interesting athletic mixture.

Some sports have evolved in ways never imagined at the start of the century. Cycling, a hugely popular spectator draw until mid-century, has turned into mainly a participant sport. Boxing, which was banned at the beginning of the period, grew into a popular local favorite in the middle of the century, then became more of a child of television as the millennium drew to a close. Wrestling remains an honorable sport in high schools and colleges, but the professional variety has deteriorated to the level of Roller Derby show biz or worse and accounts of the "matches" no longer appear in newspaper sports pages.

And, Arena football! What can be said about the bizarre, off-the-wall (and net) scoring extravaganza that draws large crowds of enthusiastic fans to the San Jose Arena?

In the following pages, no one is accorded 15 minutes of fame, just a line or two of type with three dots at the end (a la Herb Caen). That's the style I chose to produce my highlight reel history of the 36,525 days of the 20th Century. More significant stories are told in a longer, more detailed style, rather than in just a few words of text. I admit some are pretty trivial, but many are included to give a few clues about how sports have evolved in 100 years.

This isn't a record book, although there are plenty of records. It isn't a trivia book, but there's lots of trivia. It doesn't list every champion in every sport. It celebrates memorable sporting events, Santa Clara County teams that ranged from outstanding to abysmal and athletes who either played in the county or grew up here and starred elsewhere.

Primary sources for all of the information were newspapers, college and professional team media guides, record books, programs and a variety of other publications. Names are as they appeared in this material. If you detect any errors, please let me know at the address below.

Special thanks are in order to Don Nash, a former San Jose Mercury-News colleague of mine, who edited the text; Barry Colla, who helped with photos, technical expertise and designed the covers; Mark Tennis, editor of the Cal-Hi Sports Record Book, who allowed me to mention many of its records and all-state selections; Santa Clara University media relations director Jim Young and San Jose State sports information director Lawrence Fan; Stanford media relations director Bob Vazquez and his graphics designer, Don Hogue; Keith Peters at the Palo Alto Weekly and Gary Lance at the San Jose Mercury-News, and all the other people and institutions that provided photographs.

Finally, a word about the stories which appear in each chapter. I selected a lead story I thought was significant, but those that follow it are not in any supposed order of importance, but are more or less in chronological order.

I hope your favorite event, team or athlete is here. It's said that memories last a lifetime. Possibly you'll rekindle a few reading these pages. I know I did writing them.

John E. Spalding
1409 Beringer Court
San Jose, CA 95125-5993

DEDICATION

To the memory of my mother and father, who introduced me to spectator sports at an Oakland Oaks Pacific Coast League baseball game in the summer of 1940, when I was nine.

Photo Credits

Photographs are from the author's collection, except for the following:

American Basketball League: FC Azzi; **George Baljevich:** 64, 76 (left); **Bellarmine College Preparatory:** 77; **Bentley Historical Library, University of Michigan:** 10; **Campbell Historical Museum:** 17 (right), 26, 35; **Antone Chimenti:** 57 (all); **Barry Colla Photography and Design:** FC Irbe; BC Krazy George Henderson, Carney Lansford, Dave Stieb; 124 (both); 150 (both); **Mrs. Louis C. Doll:** 10; **Justin Fitzgerald Jr.:** 24; **Ron Fried:** 120 (all), 125 (right), 126, 132, 135 (left), 137 (left), 138, 140, 142, 149, 151, 155; **Don Hazelwood:** 13, 15; **Henry Honda:** 62 (both); **Japanese-American Resource Center:** 36, 42 (left); **Bea Lichtenstein:** 30; **Mark Macrae:** 49; **Marco Entertainment:** 118 (center); **Fred Matthes:** 122 (top), 136, 152 (both); **Doug McWilliams:** 73 (left); **Mountain View Historical Association:** 17 (left), 31; **Pete Nowicki:** 83; **Palo Alto Weekly:** 76 (center), 99, 108, 114, 123, 130; **Richard L. Righter:** 23; **Sarah Rosenbaum:** 119; **San Jose Giants:** BC Municipal Stadium; **San Jose Historical Society:** 11, 41, 59; **San Jose Mercury-News:** 38, 39 (both at top), 52, 58, 60, 67 (left), 70, 71, 78, 79, 80 (center), 81, 82, 86 (both), 90, 93, 95, 97, 100, 101 (left, center), 102, 103, 105 (both), 106, 107 (both), 109 (left), 111 (both), 113, 116, 118 (left, right), 121, 125 (left), 127, 128, 129 (both), 145 (both); **San Jose State University:** 67 (center), 74, 101 (right), 143; **Santa Clara Historic Archives:** 65; **Santa Clara Unified School District:** 80 (left, right); **Santa Clara University Archives:** FC Nash, 16, 53, 68, 109 (right), 146; **Rod Searcey:** 122 (bottom), 135 (right), 137 (right), 141; **Stanford University Archives:** 29 (both), 39 (all at bottom), 43, 45, 51, 54, 66 (left), 67 (right), 115, 135 (center); **R. E. Strobino:** 48, 50; **The Haggin Museum, Stockton:** 8; **University of California:** 89 (both); **Washington State University:** 85; **Bill Weiss:** 69.

Abbreviations

Initials designate organizations or familiar words and phrases. Here are the most commonly used abbreviations. When a name – i.e. (Bellarmine) or (SJS) – appears after an athlete's name, it means he or she attended that school.

AAU-Amateur Athletic Union, **AIAW**-Association of Intercollegiate Athletics for Women, **AP**-Associated Press, **CAL**-Catholic Athletic League, **CCAA**-California Collegiate Athletic Association, **CCC**- California Coast Conference, **CCS**-Central Coast Section, **CCSF**-City College of San Francisco, **CIBA**-California Intercollegiate Baseball Association, **CIF**-California Interscholastic Federation, **COP**-College of the Pacific, **Div.**-Division, **ERA**-earned run average, **ESCVAL**-East Santa Clara Valley Athletic League, **IAU**-Interurban Athletic Union, **IC4A**-Intercollegiate Amateur Athletic Association of America, **JC**-Junior College (and community college), **JV**-junior varsity, **KO**-knockout, **LPGA**-Ladies Professional Golfers Association, **MHAL**-Mount Hamilton Athletic League, **MLS**-Major League Soccer, **MVP**-most valuable player, **NASCAR**-National Association for Stock Car Auto Racing, **NASL**-North American Soccer League, **NBA**-National Basketball Association, **NCAA**-National Collegiate Athletic Association, **NCS**-North Coast Section, **NHL**-National Hockey League, **NIT**-National Invitational Tournament, **Nor Cal**-Northern California, **OT**-overtime, **PAL**-Peninsula Athletic League, **PAT**-point after touchdown, **PBT**-Peninsula Basketball Tournament, **PCAA**-Pacific Coast Athletic Association, **PCC**-Pacific Coast Conference, **PCI**-Pacific Coast Intercollegiate, **PCL**-Pacific Coast League, **PGA**-Professional Golfers Association, **QB**-quarterback, **RBI**-run batted in, **SCU**-Santa Clara University, **SCVAL**-Santa Clara Valley Athletic League, **SCVYV**-Santa Clara Valley Youth Village, **SJCC**-San Jose City College, **SJS**-San Jose State, **SPAL**-South Peninsula Athletic League, **STAL**-Santa Teresa Athletic League, **TD**-touchdown, **TKO**-technical knockout, **TOC**-Tournament of Champions, **UCSB**-University of California at Santa Barbara, **UOP**-University of the Pacific, **UPI**-United Press International, **USAC**-United States Auto Club, **USBA**-United State Boxing Association, **USGA**-United States Golf Association, **WAC**-Western Athletic Conference, **WCAL**-West Catholic Athletic League, **WSCVAL**-West Santa Clara Valley Athletic League, **WVAL**-West Valley Athletic League, **WVC**-West Valley College, **YMBA**-Young Men's Buddhist Association, **YMCA**-Young Men's Christian Association

Contents

Cover Photos

FRONT - (Clockwise from top) Arturs Irbe, Steve Nash, Millard Hampton, Luis Molina, Jennifer Azzi; (Bottom row, from left) Jim Plunkett, Ken Caminiti, Pablo Morales, Bill Walsh, Craig Morton.

BACK - (Clockwise from top) San Jose Municipal Stadium, Carney Lansford, Krazy George Henderson, Joe Leonard, Paul Child, Dave Stieb. (Center) 1930's Santa Clara University Bronco mascot.

19th Century

Santa Clara County was largely agricultural and sparsely populated in the latter half of the 19th Century, but some residents already were showing a keen interest in sports, particularly baseball, bicycling and horse racing.

Amateur baseball teams began forming in the early 1860s. By 1867, three county ball clubs were represented at the Pacific Base Ball Convention, which drew delegates from 16 teams in San Francisco and five more in Oakland. Officers from the Altas of San Jose and Originals and Eurekas of Santa Clara were at the meeting. As many as 100 teams were operating in California at the time.

Andrew Piercy, who was born in San Jose in 1856, became the first California native to play major league baseball in 1881. Piercy honed his skills as an infielder in San Francisco's fast semi-pro leagues and broke in with the Chicago National League team on May 12. After collecting two singles in eight at bats, his big league career was over and he returned to the Bay Area to play ball.

Santa Clara College (which became Santa Clara University early in the 20th Century) began fielding a team regularly beginning in the 1890s and Stanford University started play in 1892. The best teams down on The Farm went 21-2 from 1893 through 1895.

College and amateur nines received most of the fans' attention until 1891, when professional baseball began to entertain San Jose's 18,000 residents. Owner Mike "Duke" Finn moved his team to the Garden City from Stockton, where it had finished last in the four-team California League the year before. Covered wooden stands were erected near Agricultural Park at Race Street and The Alameda and Finn's "Dukes" began their 147-game schedule.

Baseball was a pitcher's game, with the mound only 50 feet from home plate, 10 feet 6 inches closer than today. San Jose won its last 12 games to take the pennant with a 90-57 record behind the league's two best hurlers, George Harper and Jacob "Nick" Lookabaugh. Harper had a 47-32 record, completed all 79 of his starts and led the league with 704 innings pitched and an 0.96 earned run average. His mound partner was 43-25 in 577 innings with a 1.74 ERA.

One of San Jose's stars was George Stallings, a catcher-outfielder who led the league with 86 stolen bases. Stallings later became a successful major league manager and guided the "Miracle" Boston Braves to the 1914 National League pennant and a four-game World Series sweep over Connie Mack's favored Philadelphia Athletics.

After the season, San Jose defeated Northwest League champion Portland in a 19-game series played mainly in San Francisco before crowds of up to 12,000.

With the series tied at nine games each, San Jose's Bill Everett stole home as Portland's players argued a close call at second base. When the umpires refused to order Everett back to third base, Portland walked off the field and the game was forfeited to San Jose.

San Jose edged Los Angeles in the won and loss percentages, .576 to .575, in the first half of the 1892 race, then fell into the cellar in the second half. Los Angeles won a disputed post-season playoff, but the teams were declared co-champions.

The team's top players were Everett (who hit .283), Lookabaugh (45-43) and Harper (37-38). San Jose hadn't done well at the box office and the team moved to Sacramento in 1893. Pro baseball wouldn't return to the Garden City for another decade.

■ GRIDIRON GLORY

Like most sports involving Santa Clara County teams, the annual football game between Stanford University and the University of California got off to a modest start.

In March, 1892, Stanford traveled to San Francisco to meet Cal in the inaugural Big Game at the Haight Street Grounds on the edge of Golden Gate Park just across Stanyan Street from the future site of Kezar Stadium.

The Golden Bears (5-1-0) had been playing football for a decade, but Stanford had only opened its doors the previous October with an enrollment of 465. Students organized a team and arranged a few games.

Cardinal became Stanford's uniform color when seven players from San Francisco Boy's High School (later Lowell) persuaded teammates to adopt their old school's color.

After disposing of Hopkins Academy, 10-6, Stanford played its next game off campus at San Jose's Agricultural Park, whitewashing Berkeley Gymnasium, 22-0. Special trains carried an estimated 150 students from Palo Alto to San Jose for the game, which drew a total crowd of about 500. The Cardinal next fell to the San Francisco Olympic Club, 10-6, and prepared for the first Big Game.

The contest was a box office bonanza as a huge crowd estimated at 9,500, 15,000 or 20,000 by different historians took in the first game of the West's greatest collegiate football series. Stanford surprised Cal and nearly everyone else by winning, 14-10. They tied, 10-10, at the same site in December before 18,753 spectators.

Until Kezar Stadium opened in 1925, there was no San Francisco facility designed exclusively for football. Major college games regularly were played on fields built for

San Jose's first pro team won 90 games and the 1891 California League title. From left (back) Joe McGuckin, manager Mike Finn and Buck Ebright; (middle) George Stallings, Carl McVey, Chick Speer, George Hanley, Charles Dooley, Bill Everett; (front) Nick Lookabaugh, mascot, George Harper.

baseball, whose popularity far exceeded the gridiron game's.

In 1896, Santa Clara College met St. Mary's College at Central Park, a cozy baseball facility at Eighth and Market streets that seated about 15,000. It was the first in the series that later became known as the Little Big Game.

The field was a muddy lake for the first encounter between the two great Catholic rivals as Santa Clara romped, 46-4. Two years later Santa Clara won again, 50-0.

Stanford and California met annually at Haight Street Grounds until 1897, when the Big Game was moved to the newer Recreation Grounds at Eighth and Harrison streets, a baseball park that could accommodate 20,000 spectators.

San Jose Normal, a teacher's school later renamed San Jose Teachers College and then San Jose State, tied Pacific in its first game in January, 1896, went 4-1-1 against mainly high schools in 1898, and 5-2-1 a year later, including a 44-0 loss to Cal.

San Jose was the first high school to play football, losing to Santa Cruz, 6-0, in 1895. By century's end, teams were fielded by Santa Clara Prep (later known as Bellarmine), Los Gatos, Palo Alto and Santa Clara high schools.

■ GARDEN CITY WHEELMEN

On the evening of Aug. 8, 1884, the seven San Jose men who owned bicycles organized the Garden City Cycling Club, soon renamed the Garden City Wheelmen.

When cumbersome "high boy" bicycles with a four to five-foot front wheel with hard tires were replaced by a safer low, two-wheel version, club membership boomed and scores of riders took part in outings along local country roads. The lack of inflatable tires didn't deter hardy riders from pedaling over the mountains to Santa Cruz.

Races were held regularly on dirt tracks along West Julian Street and South First Street. Eventually, a one-third mile concrete track and grandstand was erected at Agricultural Park.

Longer endurance races, including a 10-man, 100-mile relay from San Francisco to San Jose to Oakland, became popular in the 1880s. The Wheelmen, clad in purple and gold uniforms with a fleur de lis emblazoned on the front of the jersey, were frequent winners.

Many outstanding cyclists rode for the Wheelmen, including George Osen, Joe Desimone, Al Jarman, Joe Delmas and the relay team's anchor man, Wilbur Edwards, who was the state amateur champion in 1897.

Cycling reach its peak of popularity in the 1890s. Otto Ziegler, later a prominent building and loan executive here, won state championships from 1893 through 1895.

Riders thought nothing of cycling to San Francisco to race at Golden Gate Park, taking the ferry across the bay to Oakland, racing again at a track in San Leandro and pedaling home to San Jose.

■ HORSE RACING

Big money was at stake in the 1860s in San Jose, when thoroughbred racing was a staple of the community's meager athletic schedule.

In 1866, Santa Clara County horses competed for the Branham stakes, the best two out of three heats at one mile. The winner's purse was an astronomical $1,200. By comparison, the largest prize offered at Louisville -- site of the Kentucky Derby -- was only $500.

The Branham winner was California Ten Broeck. It won in two straight heats, defeating Derringer in the first race and Glenwild in the second. Two years later, F. Dupofsters' great chestnut colt, Lancaster, won six of eight races and took the Branham purse.

The 1900s

Baseball had been the major sporting attraction in San Jose for decades, especially in the 1890s when Mike Finn's pro team was one of the California League's best.

Since then, diamond fans had to be satisfied watching college, amateur and semi-pro games. That began to change in 1903 with the formation of a new league.

The California State League started as a modest semi-pro loop, with players sharing the gate receipts generated by games played every Sunday. Over the next seven seasons it grew into a powerful circuit that scheduled 201 games for San Jose's team in 1909, including 93 at home.

The league slowly became a serious rival to the Pacific Coast League and by 1907 was stealing away quite a few of its good players. This brought complaints from the PCL, which adhered to the National Agreement that protected player contracts, and Organized Baseball branded the State League as an outlaw organization and threatened to impose a lifetime ban on any man who played in it.

None of this fear of the upstart State League existed in 1903 when the PCL formed by adding Portland and Seattle to the four teams -- San Francisco, Oakland, Los Angeles and Sacramento -- that made up the old California League.

San Jose and Stockton were the State League's bulwarks with 21,000 and 17,000 residents, respectively. Two teams in Oakland and another in San Francisco couldn't buck the PCL brand of ball so they played almost exclusively on the road. Vallejo rounded out the six-team league that played games from March into November.

Stockton breezed to the first pennant with a 24-8 mark, six games ahead of second place San Jose. The two cities won every championship for the next five years. San Jose took the 1904 title, won the first half in 1905, but lost a one-game playoff to second half winner Stockton, and chased champion Stockton in 1906, 1907 and 1908.

Outlaw status worked to the benefit of the league. Big leaguers performed in CSL games both before and after the major league season for a number of years until the league became so strong that the majors started to enforce rules prohibiting players for accepting outlaw pay. The State League also was able to sign good players who belonged to other teams, thus elevating the level of play.

A number of fine ballplayers appeared in the league, including Santa Clara County native Harry Hooper, who went on to a 17-year Hall of Fame career in the majors. The outfielder played for Oakland and Stockton in 1907 and 1908 before the Boston Red Sox bought him.

Hooper's Boston teammate, Duffy Lewis, was in the CSL with Oakland; Ping Bodie, a powerful San Franciscan

San Jose teams played at Cycler's Park in the early seasons of the California State League. Players are unidentified except for Josh Reilly (fourth from left) and Al Erle (third from right).

and one of the first Italian-America players to reach the bigs, played in his home town and Oscar Stanage, a major league catcher for 14 years, played with Stockton. San Jose's best players included Harry Krause and Harry Wolter.

Krause graduated from St. Mary's College in 1907 and finished the season pitching for San Jose. His 7-10 showing earned him a trip to Harrisburg of the Tri-State League, where he went 17-4 and moved up the Philadelphia Athletics. Manager Connie Mack put Krause in the starting rotation in 1909 and the southpaw was the league's rookie sensation, winning his first 10 starts and finishing 18-8.

After playing several more seasons in the majors, Krause pitched 16 of the next 17 seasons in the Coast League and won more than 300 minor league games.

Wolter came off the Santa Clara College campus in 1905 and played briefly with San Jose for three seasons, spending most of his time in the PCL and getting a big league tryout in 1907.

In 1908, he ignored threats of banishment from baseball and returned to the State League, where the level of play had risen appreciably. Wolter had his best season, placing third in the batting race with a .339 average and leading the league on the mound with a 25-2 record. He went back to the majors for five seasons, then joined Los Angeles in the PCL and was batting champion in 1914 and 1915.

When his playing career ended, Wolter became the baseball coach at Stanford. He coached the Indians from 1923 to 1949, retiring with a record of 265-304-5.

Financial problems forced the State League to end its

San Jose finished two games behind champion Stockton in 1908. Among its stars were catcher Bobby Eager (standing, second from left) and (first two seated, from left) pitcher Frank Arellanes and outfielder Harry Wolter.

outlaw status and it become part of Organized Baseball in 1910. The league never achieved its previous level of popularity. It operated briefly in 1910, returned for a full year in 1913, then struggled through parts of two more seasons before going out of business forever in 1915.

■ WILLIE HESTON, ALL-AMERICAN

Stanford met halfback Willie Heston on the football field three times. All the results were blowouts.

In the first two meetings in 1900, Stanford walloped Heston and the outmanned San Jose Normal team, 35-0 and 24-0. The teachers' school dropped football until 1921.

After guiding Stanford to a 7-2-1 record in 1901, coach Fielding "Hurry Up" Yost left to become the head man at the University of Michigan. Heston, a 190-pound farm boy from Oregon who could run 100 yards in 10.2, followed Yost and enrolled at the Midwest school.

With halfback Heston scoring 72 touchdowns, playing outstanding defense and making first team All-America in his junior and senior years, Yost's "point-a-minute" Wolverines won 43 games and tied one between 1901 and 1904. One of the wins came in the inaugural Rose Bowl game with Stanford (3-1-2) as the opponent.

The Wolverines, winners of 10 straight and holding a 501-0 point spread over opponents, crushed Stanford, 49-0, on Jan. 1, 1902. Heston rushed for 170 yards in 18 carries.

Grantland Rice put Heston on his all-time All-America team in 1926, saying Willie, "could break through the line, run an end or hold his own in any broken field. For combined speed and power, Heston has never been surpassed."

■ MILE-A-MINUTE

Berna "Barney" Oldfield, whose name was synonymous with speed in the early days of the century, brought his racing car, Bullet 2, to Agricultural Park in 1903.

A crowd of 1,500 turned out on a chilly Sunday in early November to see if Oldfield -- who had become the first man to travel a mile-a-minute (60 miles an hour) earlier in the year -- could break his own world record of 55.4.

The Los Angeles race car driver was touring the Pacific Coast and thought that the San Jose oval provided an especially good opportunity to surpass his record, because it had a reputation as a fast track.

Oldfield made five tries at the mile record, but his best time was 1:00.4. His car broke down on its last trip around the track and the crowd was left to cheer for bicycle and motorcycle racers who filled out the rest of the program.

■ MINING OLYMPIC GOLD

Who was the county's first Olympic champion?

It probably was San Jose cyclist Burton "Hoots" Downing in 1904. The 19-year-old Downing was a Garden City Wheelmen cyclist in 1904, when the third Olympic summer games were held in St. Louis.

Originally scheduled for Chicago, the games were moved at President Theodore Roosevelt's request to coincide with a World's Fair celebrating the centenary of the Louisiana Purchase.

The games became a sideshow to the fair and practically all the contestants were from the United States.

Some Olympic record books don't show cycling as an event that year. But, bicycle races definitely were on the program and several Olympic histories list Downing as the all-time cycling medal winner, with six.

Downing and his cycling brothers, Lace and Hardy, grew up in San Jose and pedaled for the Wheelmen. Burton held a half-dozen records at distances ranging from one to 25 miles. While traveling to the East Coast in 1904, Burton

Willie Heston

stopped in St. Louis to compete in the races and surprised Eastern riders, who knew nothing about him.

Burton Downing had attracted attention in Bay Area cycling for some time despite his youth. In 1900, he won an 18-mile race from San Jose's St. James Hotel to Alviso and back, in 44:31. The next year, Downing broke the five-mile straightaway record at Gilroy and later showed his stamina by pedaling to the East Bay, where he won a 25-mile San Leandro race and later took a one-mile sprint several miles away at Elmhurst.

In St. Louis, Downing finished third in his first outing for a bronze medal in the 880-yard race. The next day he took silver in a 440 sprint and his first gold in a two-miler. Two days later he finished his cycling career with a gold in the 25-mile race and two more silvers at one mile and one-third of a mile. Burton continued on to New York City, became a contractor and died of meningitis in 1929.

His brother, Hardy, settled in Salt Lake City, where he rode professionally between 1904 and 1914 and promoted bouts for heavyweight boxing champion Jack Dempsey.

A contemporary of the Downings and probably the greatest Santa Clara County cyclist of them all was Floyd McFarland, another former Garden City Wheelman who rode with the pros in the late 19th and early 20th centuries.

McFarland is the only local rider named on the list of 15 all-time greats by Walter Bardgett, editor of the American Bicyclist and widely regarded as the top authority on bicycle racing in America until his death in 1953.

McFarland developed his skills by pedaling 30 miles to Gilroy every morning to deliver the Mercury-Herald newspaper to customers along the way. McFarland and his pal, Hardy Downing, rode as pros in the grueling six-day indoor races in big arenas from Salt Lake City to New York and were among the top Americans who competed in Europe, where he won a 20-mile race in Paris in 1907.

Teamed with other riders, McFarland won the Madison Square Garden six-day race in 1900 by covering 2,628 miles and in 1908 set a record of 2,737 miles. The most serious of his many injuries in this dangerous sport occurred in 1907. He fell during a Salt Lake City race and was hospitalized for 10 days after a five-inch splinter from the board track ripped a hole in his chest near his heart.

A Cycler's Park crowd of 3,000 watched a pair of Garden City Wheelmen (right) and two Sacramento Capital City Wheelmen riders line up for the start of a 50-mile relay race won by Garden City in 1905.

■ BIG GAME ON CAMPUS

Football's annual Big Game between Cal and Stanford came to Santa Clara County for the first time in 1905.

The Golden Bears and Cardinals had been playing their traditional annually since 1892, but the first 12 games were contested at ballparks in San Francisco, where crowds of up to 20,000 could watch the action.

Neither university had a facility on campus that could handle a large crowd until 1904, when California Field was built at Berkeley. Stanford's powerful and experienced team was 5-2-1 coming into the game against the Bears, who were undefeated and unscored upon in six games.

Stanford ruined the dedication for the Bears, dealing California its only loss, 18-0, before 20,000 fans. Stanford rooters celebrated their first Big Game victory since 1900 with a torchlight parade up San Francisco's Market Street.

The following season, the Big Game moved to the new Stanford Field for the first time and 13,000 turned out to see two undefeated teams. The Bears' record was marred only by scoreless ties against Willamette and Oregon to go with four shutout wins. Stanford was undefeated in seven games and was favored because it had downed Willamette, 12-0, and Oregon, 10-4.

Stanford marched 50 yards in five plays for one touchdown and staged another 75-yard drive that ended with a 15-yard scoring run by Ted Van Dervoort as Cal fell, 12-5.

■ DEATH ON THE GRIDIRON

The death of a Santa Clara High School football player was one of many in 1905 that helped change the course of American Football at all levels of competition before the year had ended.

Clarence Van Bokkelen, an 18-year-old halfback for Santa Clara, died as the result of a skull fracture near the base of his brain sustained in the second half of the game against arch rival San Jose High in November.

Van Bokkelen was hurt early in the annual game, won by San Jose, 8-2, but refused to leave the lineup. Once removed from the game, a player couldn't return.

Van Bokkelen talked to his father during the halftime intermission and was back on the field when play resumed. After being knocked unconscious, he was carried to a nearby drug store where he was examined by two doctors who sent him to O'Connor Sanitarium. He died several hours later.

None of the players wore helmets and there was one report that the Van Bokkelen had been kicked in the head by an opposing player while lying on the ground.

Reaction to the death came quickly. The next day, a *San Jose Mercury-Herald* editorial titled, "Football -- An Abomination," noted that 45 American players had died and more than 300 had been seriously injured in the previous five seasons. It called on school principals to ban the game.

"In football, a man may be tripped, thrown, pounced upon, kicked and even killed . . . It is brute strength against brute strength, the only skill required being that which enables one the more effectively to use his brute strength against a less muscular man."

Two days later, Santa Clara College dropped football, followed quickly by Santa Clara High. By the end of the month, officials at San Jose and Los Gatos high schools banned the sport. Gilroy officials announced a ban, but apparently rescinded it before the following season.

Because of the high number of deaths and injuries, President Theodore Roosevelt threatened to abolish football if college authorities failed to reform the game. Delegates from 62 universities met in December and formed an organization which eventually became the NCAA.

They adopted new rules effective in 1906 eliminating the mass plays that had created many of the injuries. Six men were required on the line of scrimmage, the forward pass was authorized and playing time was cut by 10 minutes to 60. Hurdling, tripping and crawling with the ball were prohibited. The distance needed to advance the ball for a first down was increased from 5 to 10 yards in three downs and foul rules were tightened against punching, kneeing or kicking an opponent. Even with these and other changes, the carnage continued and 87 players died and hundreds more were seriously injured through the 1910 season.

Not all coaches favored the revised rules. Stanford's Jimmy Lanagan said, "if you try to cut out this so-called roughness you will kill the game or turn it into (soccer) . . . There is no other game that allows a man to show what kind of character there is in him . . . "

The rule changes came too late to save football in the Bay Area. Stanford and Cal switched to rugby in 1906. Playing mainly Canadian and local club teams, Stanford went 34-9-1 for the rest of the decade, beating Cal in the Big Scrum three years out of four.

In 1915, the Golden Bears returned to football, which was the game of choice for most universities outside of the region. Stanford fielded rugby teams through 1917. Santa Clara didn't play either game in 1906 or 1907, but competed in rugby from 1908 to 1917. San Jose, Santa Clara and Palo Alto high schools began playing rugby in 1906.

■ LUNA PARK

San Jose sports fans got their first real baseball park in 1907, when the proprietors of a new amusement facility north of town added a baseball diamond and grandstand.

The $50,000 Luna Park was built by Lewis E. Hanchett on the north side of what today is Hedding Street between North 13th and North 17th streets. In addition to the enclosed diamond, park attractions included a roller coaster, devil's slide, merry-go-round and carnival games.

Hanchett, who developed the residential area near The Alameda and Race Street that bears his name, located Luna Park far away from downtown, forcing patrons to ride his San Jose and Santa Clara Railroad Co. trolleys to get there.

The ballpark's primary patron was the San Jose team in the outlaw California State League. After playing in the cramped facilities at Cyclers Park -- a bicycle velodrome -- the Prunepickers were pleased to move into the new digs.

The covered double deck grandstand with two parapet towers seated 3,500 and another 2,000 spectators could be accommodated in bleachers that extended down the first base line. The ballpark had a dirt infield, but grass covered the outfield. It was converted to an all-grass facility in 1914.

■ FOR THE RECORD

In a 1903 state prep record that has been tied, but never surpassed, Palo Alto High's Charley Swain returned a kickoff 105 yards against the Stanford Frosh.

Stanford pole vaulter Norman Dole set a world record at 12-1 8/25 in 1904.

In 1906, G. Tomasini of Palo Alto High produced a state record toss of 178-0 in the hammer throw.

■ 100 MILES ON A BIKE

Several seasons after the popular around-the-bay 100-mile relay race from San Francisco to the East Bay had been abandoned, the Garden City Wheelmen scheduled their own 100-miler in San Jose in 1908.

The race ran over a course that took the riders on a 10-mile loop from San Jose through Campbell and back to the start at Race Street and The Alameda. Racers would complete the circuit 10 times. Ten-man teams from two San Francisco cycling clubs joined the Wheelmen on May 31, but the race was stopped by a tragedy before the competitors had completed the second circuit.

Edward Treacy, an 18-year-old rider for San Francisco's Golden City Wheelmen, was pedaling hard south along Race Street in pursuit of a San Jose cyclist who had a half-mile lead. As Treacy and another San Francisco rider approached the street car tracks running along Park Avenue, their view was blocked by a barn and an orchard and they failed to see a westbound trolley car speeding toward the intersection.

The street car was only 20 feet away when the cyclists saw it. The other rider made it across the tracks ahead of the trolley, but Treacy was struck and dragged under the car. One of his legs had been nearly cut off, toes on his other foot were gone, one arm was shattered and his head was lacerated. Treacy was taken by auto to nearby O'Connor Sanitarium, where doctors amputated his mutilated leg.

The race was canceled when word of the accident reached officials at the starting point. A spokesman for the Interurban Railroad said he would have ordered street cars to stop at Race Street if he had been told that riders would be crossing the trolley line. Treacy survived his injuries, but the *San Jose Mercury-Herald* editorialized against resumption of urban racing, saying, "The streets of a city are no proper place for a race under any circumstances."

California Associated Cyclists, which sanctioned all events, said future races wouldn't be approved unless a map was provided that showed the route crossed no rail lines. The race was rerun over to a rolling five-mile course in San Jose's rural Berryessa district six weeks later. Garden City Wheelmen took it in 4:14.47.

■ HOME COURT ADVANTAGE

The women's basketball team at San Jose Normal rolled over most of its opposition in the 1908-09 season, losing only to Chico State, 11-10.

The team defeated Stanford twice, University of

Many members of the 1902 Santa Clara College varsity team played pro ball. From left, (top) Win Cutter, Bob Kennedy, Ben Healy; (middle) Steve Nichols, Charley Strub, Bob Keefe, Tom Feeney, Harry Sullivan; (bottom) Fran Farry, Bill Whalen, Pierre Merle.

Pacific, and finally took on Nevada at Reno.

The future teachers handled Nevada, 19-6, but the *San Jose Mercury-Herald* reported the victory didn't come easily. "The game was played on a slippery dance floor," the newspaper said. "As the Normal team is used to an open air court, it was at a decided disadvantage."

■ LITTLE BIG BEEF

After several years with no athletic competition, Santa Clara and St. Mary's reached an eligibility agreement in 1909 that cleared the way for them to play each other again.

Along lines similar to an understanding between Stanford and Cal, the two Catholic institutions agreed to limit play to students who took at least three class hours daily and met the national amateur association standards.

No student could play more than six seasons and anyone leaving one of the schools couldn't compete at the other for one year. Graduate students could play for only one season and teachers at both schools were ineligible.

But in 1911, after St. Mary's beat Santa Clara, 5-3, in rugby, relations were severed on the field when the Gaels were accused of using non-student "ringers." The teams didn't meet again in football until 1922, when the Little Big Game series resumed with a 9-7 victory by St. Mary's.

■ FIRST STATE PLAYOFF

The first prep team from Santa Clara County to reach a state championship game was the Santa Clara High rugby squad in 1909.

Santa Clara had five wins, including a 57-0 blowout against Mountain View, and losses to the Pacific freshmen and SCU varsity as the regular season neared its end.

Arch rival San Jose High (3-6-1) gained a scoreless tie and Santa Clara tied powerful Palo Alto High (5-2-2) in the final league game, 3-3.

Santa Clara and Palo Alto met again for the Academic Athletic League title with Santa Clara winning in decisive fashion, 11-0. In the Northern California title game in late November, Santa Clara downed San Francisco Lowell, 9-3, to move on to the state championship game.

Santa Clara expected to play Los Angeles Poly, but Poly officials refused to sanction the game because Santa Clara demanded $500 to cover the costs of traveling to Southern California. Redlands High accepted the challenge and guaranteed $400 in travel expenses. Poly fans claimed the championship, since their team had tied and defeated Redlands during the regular season, but the title game went on as scheduled on Christmas Day.

Although outweighed by the much larger Redlands fifteen, expectations were high. But, Santa Clara lost the state playoff on a muddy field, 6-0.

■ TRIVIAL PURSUITS

William Roth, Stanford tennis star at the turn of the century, later became a steamship magnate with the Matson Navigation Co. and bred thoroughbred race horses.

In the 1905 game in which a player suffered fatal injuries, San Jose High scored a safety when Santa Clara's Heinie Harrison ran the wrong way with a punt and was tackled in the end zone. A game account years later said Harrison was humiliated by his mistake, jumped a fence, ran home and didn't return to school for several days.

■ 1900 ■

George Keffel wins San Jose Rifle Club first place medal in what may have been county's first 20th Century athletic event . . . Catcher Charley Graham -- future Pacific Coast League club owner -- captains SCU baseball team . . . Palo Alto High girls blank San Jose Normal School women's basketball team, 12-0 . . . SCU tops Sodality Club, 28-1, with future big leaguers Bobby Keefe on mound, Jack Sheridan of San Jose as umpire . . . Outfielder Mouron belts grand slam as San Jose Normal beats St.

Matthews, 8-6 . . . San Jose Normal nine defeats SCU twice, 12-11, 11-4 . . . Los Gatos High falls to San Jose High, 21-4 in baseball . . . Garden City Wheelmen whip Olympic Club cyclists in 25-mile race on Cyclers Park oval . . . San Jose town nine, 11-0 against Bay Area opposition, claims Pacific Coast amateur title . . . Six days of trotter, pacer races for $500 purses draw fans to San Jose's Agricultural Park . . . Cyclist Jack Wing of San Jose beats H. D. Bean by two furlongs in Centerville 10-mile match race . . . Garden City Wheelmen's 10-man team downs Olympic Club in 50-mile relay . . . Golfer Guy Vacell shoots 102 for first men's title at Linda Vista Golf Club in East San Jose . . . Pitcher Charles "Demon" Doyle of San Jose goes 19-18 for Sacramento of California League . . . SCU gridders fall to Lowell High, 12-0 . . . Boxer Kid Williams of Los Angeles whips Jack Kane at Rose Carnival Pavilion . . . Scoring on long runs, Santa Clara High beats San Jose, 23-5 . . . Palo Alto High edges Santa Clara, 6-0, claims county football championship.

■ 1901 ■

San Jose Normal women's basketball team dumped by Stockton High, 4-0 . . . Stanford nine drops San Jose Normal, 11-10, in 10th when catcher Al Erle loses ball in February darkness at 6:30 p.m. . . . Loaded with many pro diamond stars including Demon Doyle, Sodality defeats SCU, 13-8 . . . Garden City Wheelmen's team wins 100-mile race from San Francisco through San Jose to Alameda in record 4:42:30 . . . Semi-pros organize four-team Central California baseball league with clubs in San Jose, Salinas, Watsonville, Santa Cruz . . . San Jose's Hardy Downing takes 15-mile Massachusetts pro cycle race . . . Garden City Wheelmen lose 50-mile Reno race . . . San Jose native Aurelio Herrera, early Mexican-American boxer (52-13-4), KO'd in five rounds by featherweight champion Terry McGovern in San Francisco title bout . . . Southpaw third baseman Hal Chase makes three errors in four chances in 6-3 San Jose win over Santa Cruz at Cycler's Park . . . Demon Doyle goes 20-12 for California League's Sacramento team before hurting arm . . . 30-yard field goal by Bill Magee gives SCU win over Lowell High, 5-0 . . . Santa Clara High (3-0-1) posts 24-0 football win over San Jose High (0-1-0). Palo Alto preps lose three games, gain 6-6 tie with Cal Frosh . . . Winter baseball brings big leaguers George Van Haltren, Nap Lajoie, Jake Beckley to San Jose with All-Americans, Nationals.

■ 1902 ■

Garden City Bowlers lose second straight match to Eugene team of San Francisco, who claim Northern California title . . . Getting good pitching from Win Cutter, Bobby Keefe, SCU tops Stanford, Cal, St. Mary's, San Jose Normal, but loses to California League pros from San Francisco. After college, Cutter turns pro, is 13-24 with Sacramento in California League . . . San Jose semi-pros whip San Francisco's Olympic Club, on six-hit, 1-0 shutout by star pitcher-manager Mike Steffani . . . SCU's all-around athlete Win Cutter wins three sprints, hammer throw, shot put, pole vault in meet against San Jose High . . . Rudy Kocher takes pole vault, shot put, hammer throw, but San Jose High finishes second to Santa Clara in annual Pacific Athletic League track meet . . . SCU nine ends year 10-3-1. Bob Kennedy leads hitters at .394 . . . Future PCL pitcher Walt Nagle of Oakland Heeseman's team stops San Jose townies on one hit, 2-0 . . . Garden City Wheelmen capture around-the-bay 100-mile race from San Francisco to Oakland in 4:48:0 . . . San Jose High cyclists take 25-mile San Leandro prep relay race second straight year . . . 2,500 spectators pack Agricultural Park for July 4th horse races . . . Reno cyclists drub Garden City Wheelmen in Nevada 50-mile relay race, but club wins return engagement at home . . . San Jose beats So Differents, touring black baseball team, 18-5 . . . Garden City Alleys curtains off two lanes so prying eyes can't watch ladies of Pioneer Bowling Club . . . Late score by Louie Magee gives SCU 6-0 victory over Hastings Law College . . . University of Pacific in San Jose defeats Palo Alto High in football, 11-6 . . . Stanford gridders beat Oakland's Reliance Club three times . . . Pair of PAT miscues by Andrews Military Academy give UOP 12-10 win . . . Touring "Big Three" team brings 25-0 record to San Jose, whips Garden City Bowlers best in five matches, 2,880 pins to 2,748 . . . UOP Academy closes grid season with 22-0 win over Hollister High . . . San Jose High whitewashes Santa Clara High, 11-0, in grid traditional . . . San Jose nine has four hits, downs Northwest League pros, 3-1.

■ 1903 ■

SCU baseball coach is Joe Corbett, ex-big leaguer, brother of heavyweight champ "Gentleman Jim" Corbett . . . Stanford cagers, "not yet recognized (as official team) by student body," lose to San Francisco YMI, 32-12, whip Oakland YMI, 31-21 . . . Cal downs Stanford, 11-9, in what *San Francisco Chronicle* calls, "first intercollegiate men's basketball game on the Pacific Coast." Game isn't listed in either school's records . . . Portland PCL team trains in San Jose, loses 2-1 to local State League entry, then tops error-prone Prunepickers, 22-9 . . . Oakland High scores 73 points to combined 59 by San Jose, Santa Clara preps in Agricultural Park track meet . . . SCU hurler Bobby Keefe stops several teams, but is blasted by San Francisco of PCL, 16-4 . . . Future major league star pitcher Orvie Overall leads Cal to 8-3 win over SCU . . . Baseball pros from Butte of Pacific Northwest League train in San Jose, defeat SCU, Stanford . . . Roy Smith wins both hurdle races, pole vault as SCU Frosh swamp San Jose High, 73-49 . . . Hunter of Santa Clara High sets mile record at 4:41.2 as team finishes fourth in north state prep meet . . . Garden City Wheelmen's Johnny Berryessa loses pedal near end, enabling Oakland Wheelmen to register 10-second win in 100-mile Hayward test . . . Garden City wins even closer race, taking annual around the bay 100-mile bike race by six inches at tape . . . Wind makes it "exceeding difficult to throw a goal" when Mountain View High girls tip Campbell on outdoor hoops court, 5-4. In return match Campbell High's Alice Joy, "astonished both sides by making her free throws," in 8-2 win over Mountain View . . . Garden City Wheelmen in rare back-to-back losses at Sacramento, Reno . . . 5,000 attend Admission Day motorcycle, bike races at Agricultural Park . . . SCU lineman Tom Leonard is 6-foot-6, 250-pounds . . . Santa Clara Prep gridders split with Hoitt's Academy, losing 11-0, winning 16-0 . . . Jim and Judd McClatchy, Louie Magee score two TDs each in SCU's 39-0 win over Pacific Coast Business College . . . Los Gatos High opens football season with 11-10 win over San Jose . . . Stanford Frosh down SCU, 12-0 . . . Santa Clara High's Roy Titus scores TD, kicks two field goals to top San Jose, 15-0.

■ 1904 ■

Stanford trustees authorize building baseball, football fields on 40 acre on-campus site . . . Former Garden City Wheelmen star

Floyd McFarland, who has $30-a-week endorsement deal with Boston wheel company, makes $10,000 racing in Australia . . . Nick Williams, ex-Cal star, future San Francisco Seals' manager, is SCU baseball mentor. Loose eligibility rules allow him to pitch in several games . . . Hal Chase home run gives Mayer Bros., top local semi-pro team, 1-0 win over SCU. Southpaw Chase shows versatility at catcher, second, third, shortstop, then hurls SCU to one-hit, 11-0, win over Stanford . . . San Jose Normal falls to Campbell High girl's basketball team, 12-2 . . . Demon Doyle quits Stanford baseball coaching job to return to pro baseball . . . San Jose YMCA hoops squad falls to Oakland Y, 14-7 . . . UOP Academy tops San Jose High, 72-58, as Harry Smith wins high hurdles, broad jump, 880; Sam Smith takes 100, mile . . . Thistles, California soccer league champs, beat league all-stars, 2-0, at Cyclers Park . . . Sam Titus wins both hurdles as Santa Clara cops county prep track title . . . Never headed, Garden City Wheelmen win 100-miler around bay in record 4:40:43 . . . Wheelmen lose by mile in 50-miler at Reno, later win San Francisco 50-mile race . . . San Jose's Carl Limberg takes 20-mile New York City amateur bicycle race . . . Clarence Letcher of San Jose wins four races in his Cadillac racing car . . . SCU gridders shut out Mission High, 22-0, Stanford Frosh, 10-0 . . . Swichard, Edwards run back kickoffs for San Jose High scores in 18-0 victory over Los Gatos . . . Palo Alto High star fullback G. Tomasini plunges for only TD in 6-0 win over San Jose . . . Fort Baker bows to SCU in game ended early by players' rhubarb, 12-9 . . . Santa Clara High gridders blank rival San Jose, 24-0 . . . San Jose Normal women down Palo Alto High in basketball, 9-7.

■ 1905 ■

Harry Wolter, future big leaguer, Stanford baseball coach, fans 15, pitches no-hitter for SCU against Stanford . . . San Jose High's Edna Corbalay scores seven free throws in 11-7 win over Palo Alto girls . . . Powerful SCU nine wins majority of games against Stanford, Cal, others . . . Santa Clara High boy's cagers down Alameda High, 9-7 . . . Unbeaten Watsonville YMCA tops UOP five, 18-17 . . . San Jose High's sensational soph Bruce Bothwell wins 440, 880 to lead team over Santa Clara High. Bothwell sets records in mile (4:41.0), 880 (2:06.4) as team wins PAL meet before 1,500 at Stanford . . . SCU diamond reserves (possibly Santa Clara Prep) win 24 of 25, losing only to Palo Alto High, 4-2 . . . Palo Alto High sprinter Pomeroy is area's lone winner at Northern California meet at Berkeley . . . Campbell High defeats Redwood City High in girl's basketball, 10-4 . . . 100-mile race circling San Francisco Bay won by Bay City Wheelmen, but protest over foul gives Garden City Wheelmen title . . . San Jose's Johnny Baumgartner roars to five-mile motorcycle win in 6:30.6 . . . Cycler's Park crowd of 3,000 sees Garden City Wheelmen defeat Capital City Wheelmen of Sacramento in 50-mile relay race . . . Red Bradbury's 30-yard TD scamper gives San Jose High 8-2 win over Santa Clara High in game in which Santa Clara player fatally injured . . . Tacoma hurler Bobby Keefe (SCU) stops Oakland, 3-0, at San Jose's Cycler's Park in only PCL no-hitter pitched at neutral site. He misses perfect game on error, later compiles 16-21 record in major leagues.

■ 1906 ■

All scoring by free throws as San Jose High loses to San Mateo Girl's Athletic Club, 6-2 . . . Lella Montgomery scores 10 points

Bobby Keefe (left) warmed up in 1907 for New York Highlanders manager Clark Griffith.

in San Jose Normal women's basketball win over San Francisco Poly High, 11-7 . . . Seven-man team with big leaguer Hal Chase on mound defeats Garden City Wheelmen, 27-17, in indoor baseball game at Rose Carnival Pavilion . . . 1,000 spectators pay 15 cents each to watch celebrated pro roller skater Harley Davidson top Pacific Coast champ L. M. Morgan for $100 16-lap race at Varsity Rink. Davidson, self-styled "Champion Skater of the World," later covers two miles in six minutes to outrace Milton Bernard by a yard . . . SCU baseball team beats San Jose pros in three of four, then topples St. Mary's twice, claims Pacific Coast collegiate title . . . UOP cagers win on road at Watsonville, 19-15, Santa Cruz, 28-23 . . . Stanford women cagers lose, 16-2, to Cal in rain storm on Berkeley's outdoor, tan bark court . . . Powerful April 18 earthquake disrupts Bay Area sporting events for nearly a month until San Jose's State League baseball team resumes play May 13 with 6-0 win over Alameda. Stanford-Cal track meet is canceled . . . San Jose High tops Santa Clara, 54-53, as five-school PAL track meet moves from earthquake-damaged Stanford campus to San Jose's Agricultural Park. Palo Alto High does not participate . . . William Hines of San Jose High wins 4.5-mile YMCA cross-country run in 27:05 . . . Seven Palo Alto High students who play in Palo Alto Athletic Club's 6-0 grid victory over Lowell expelled by school trustees, who banned game . . . Raines of Santa Clara High captures hurdles, high jump in victory over San Jose . . . Garden City Wheelmen take 10-mile relay race, sprints at Golden Gate Park . . . Olive Reid's five points tops San Jose Normal women in 10-5 hoops win over Stanford Frosh . . . Hardy Downing's team second, Floyd McFarland's team third in six-day Madison Square Garden bicycle races.

■ 1907 ■

UOP hoops team stops YMCA, 35-9, 41-32 . . . Stanford adopts gray uniforms for all sports because red dye on jerseys makes athletes' skin break out in rash . . . Fans hiss Hal Chase with San Jose's State League team because he coaches St. Mary's College nine . . . Harry Wolter breaks leg sliding in semi-pro game, but recovers to debut with Cincinnati Reds in April . . . Stanford downs Cal, 65-57, at Berkeley before 4,900 fans, largest Pacific Coast track crowd to that time . . . San Jose High girls defeat Campbell, Centerville in basketball . . . SCU trails by two in top of 12th, tallies three runs to down Stanford, 4-3 . . . Garden City

Going home from spring training in 1909, the Chicago White Sox stopped in San Jose to play Santa Clara College at Luna Park, home of the city's State League club.

Wheelmen's Emile Agraz manages bike track in Mexico City . . . SCU takes odd game in five-game baseball series against Stanford, 1-0 . . . Campbell High loses to Centerville in high-scoring girl's hoops, 17-12 . . . Poor trolley service forces some of 3,600 spectators to walk two miles to Luna Park to see San Jose's State League win against Oakland . . . Stanford four-oar crew wins in San Diego . . . SCU captures baseball series with third victory over Cal, 4-2 . . . Dressed in street clothes, Santa Clara High's Frank Cilker takes shot put at 44-4 1/2 in win over San Jose. Santa Clara defeats San Jose again in PAL meet . . . Palo Alto Rifle Club downs San Jose Rifle Club, 4,397 to 4,367 . . . San Jose High's Cyril McGraw pitches three-hit win over Stockton, 9-0 . . . Led by Morton Fraser's 27:21 win in five-mile PAL cross-country race, San Jose High takes team title . . . Johnny Berryessa of Garden City Wheelmen captures Sacramento 10-mile race . . . L. DuBois scores 13 field goals in San Jose High's 43-22 basketball romp over Lick of San Francisco . . . Dan Murphy won't return as Stanford rowing coach unless paid $1,200 for five-month season . . . Garden City Wheelmen lease 13 acres near Monterey Road, Phelan Avenue for cycling facility . . . Stanford crew in two length loss to Washington . . . Neptune Swim Club organizes at Vendome Baths, plans meets with major San Francisco, Oakland clubs . . . San Jose jockey Johnny Reiff wins $32,500 purse in prestigious Epsom Derby in England . . . Ernest Lion of San Jose wins $100 silver cup at Alum Rock Road hill climb . . . Frank Arellanes of San Jose whiffs 15 in 1-0 shutout win over San Francisco then celebrates July 4th by pitching San Jose's only State League no-hitter against Alameda, 11-0 . . . San Francisco Olympic Club downs Oakland, 14-6, in Luna Park lacrosse exhibition . . . When San Jose plays State League crucial contest at Sacramento, Mercury-Herald takes 456 phone calls from fans, who learn Prunepickers won, 2-1 . . . Roller skating fans mourn passing of Princess Rink, destroyed by fire . . . Carl Showalter of Garden City Wheelmen takes 27-mile Berryessa race . . . Lacrosse league opens at Luna Park with San Mateo beating San Jose, 14-11 . . . First rugby game between prep rivals sees San Jose blank Santa Clara, 25-0 . . . Playing mostly college teams, San Jose High ruggers go 2-6-0 . . . San Jose High girl's cagers top San Mateo, 19-4, fall to San Jose Normal, 14-11. Boys whip San Mateo, 23-14 . . . Hardy Downing, partner fourth in New York City six-day bike race.

■ 1908 ■

Ex-SCU gridders tie San Jose All-Stars at Luna Park, 6-6 . . . Hardy Downing, back at Campbell ranch for winter, beats roller skater William Jones in one-mile match race at Auditorium Rink . . . Stanford, Cal joint committee agrees schools won't play teams -- including SCU, St. Mary's -- which allow pros in lineup . . . San Jose High nine whips Santa Clara High, 7-2, Pacific Business College, 13-0 . . . SCU nine splits four with Cal, takes four of seven against Stanford . . . Touring world champion Iowa Muscatine hoops squad drubs San Jose YMCA, 62-10 . . . Mountain View High girls trounce Palo Alto High, 31-1, for third straight basketball victory . . . California defeats UOP in basketball, 31-28 . . . Lacrosse league with teams in San Jose, San Mateo, San Francisco, Oakland opens 24-game schedule. San Francisco Olympic Club tops San Jose in first Luna Park match, 11-4 . . . Santa Clara High girl's cagers top UOP, 15-6 . . . Larry Hanchett of San Jose High takes long jump, high jump, but Santa Clara wins meet, 80-56, at UOP's new College Park district track . . . SCU downs Cal in baseball, 5-3, claims Pacific Coast intercollegiate title . . . Stanford block sweaters go to 19 track athletes, nine baseball players, nine crewmen . . . Golden City Wheelmen defeat Garden City Wheelmen in 50-mile San Francisco race . . . Campbell, Los Gatos, Mountain View, Morgan Hill highs band together as Interurban Athletic Union . . . With Horton winning 220 hurdles in 26.0, taking shot put at 41-9, Stanford downs Colorado at Boulder . . . Twenty members organize San Jose Motorcycle Club . . . Pole vaulter Sam Bellah, first Stanford athlete to compete in Olympic Games, finishes sixth . . . Paced by motorcycle driven by Plinn Maginni, Johnny Berryessa cycles 30 miles to Gilroy in 60:01.46, breaking Maginni's mark by 74 seconds . . . J. B. Clayton of San Jose covers mile in 1:39 to win Alum Rock Road auto hill climb in 1908 runabout . . . Santa Clara Prep (3-1-0) wins three rugby games against San Jose High . . . Palo Alto High (4-4-0) downs San Jose ruggers twice . . . San Jose High (2-7-0) trips Santa Clara High (4-4-0), 8-5 . . . SCU nine battered in 20-4 loss to Agnews Hospital . . . San Jose YMCA defeats San Jose High, 34-16, at indoor track meet offering events such as fence vault, standing broad jump . . . Thousands of enthusiastic spectators

Girl's prep basketball teams were more common than boy's early in the century. Left is Mountain View High's 1908 team, from left, Agnes Urban, Mary Eastwood, Henrietta Bar, Annette Stuart, Isabelle Morton, Pearl True, Fanny Distel, Edith Higgins, Fannie Razek. Seated is Campbell's 1903 squad, from left, (back) Lyle Foster, Francis Fablinger, Anna Ross; (middle) Vera Fablinger, Maud Farley, Della Kennison, Ellen Wakeman; (front) Mabel Ross, Nina Davison, Alice Joy.

line route as San Francisco YMCA whips San Jose in 50-miler.

■ 1909 ■

San Francisco YMCA makes it two wins in a row over San Jose, taking 50-mile indoor relay race at Auditorium Rink before 2,500 . . . Stanford sells 20-game baseball season tickets for first time . . . UOP cagers in 39-27 win over Watsonville YMCA . . . SCU baseball star Art Shaffer signs with New York Giants . . . San Jose Normal women's basketball team whips Stanford, 11-4, 6-2 . . . Agnew Hospital nine finishes season with 51 wins, 14 losses . . . Needham of UOP Academy wins 50, 100, 220, 880, high jump, broad jump against Gilroy High . . . Chicago White Sox down SCU, 3-0, in Luna Park baseball exhibition . . . Campbell High handles SCU in hoops, 25-20 . . . Santa Clara High girl cagers drop Sequoia, 17-8 . . . Cal takes two of three baseball games from Stanford, last one in 17-inning, 4-3, nail biter . . . Mountain View wins IAU track meet . . . Stanford crew comes from behind to top Washington for Pacific Coast title, then drops sport . . . San Jose High's Stillwell stops Palo Alto with three-hitter, 6-0 . . . Stanford has record win in first track meet against USC, 104-18 . . . Charlie Friene's two-hit, 3-1, win over St. Mary's gives SCU series, two games to one . . . In its first ever track meet, SCU tops St. Ignatius, 68-43 . . . Garden City Wheelman Charles Chaboya covers 10-mile leg in 25:40 as team takes 100-miler over hilly Berryessa course . . . A. E. Curtner of San Jose drives his Mitchell up one-mile Alum Rock Road course to win in 1:15 3/5 . . . Six-man Garden City Wheelmen team takes 50-mile San Leandro race . . . UOP ruggers drop opener to Olympic Club, 23-0 . . . Mountain View High loses all six rugby games . . . 10,000 see auto, motorcycle races at new Monterey Road Driving Park, one-mile dirt track banked seven feet on turns . . . Brooklyn's John Hummel triples, scores on Franklin "Home Run" Baker's error to give National League Stars 3-2 win over Philadelphia Athletics at Luna Park . . . Mountain View High girls split in basketball, losing to Santa Clara, 19-15, topping Palo Alto, 19-11.

The 1910s

Hal Chase was the first great baseball star to rise from the county, going from Santa Clara College to the Pacific Coast League to the American League in one year.

A left-handed second baseman and pitcher in college, the Los Gatos native made three hits against St. Vincent's College early in 1904 and was seen by Los Angeles owner James Morley, who signed Hal for $75-a-month. After batting .279 with 39 stolen bases in the PCL, Chase was drafted by the New York Highlanders for $750.

Called "Prince Hal" by the press, Chase was one of the era's leading players, hitting .291 over his 15 big league seasons, but at the end no one would hire him because of repeated accusations that he offered bribes to other players and threw games.

Chase was idolized by the fans, who were awed by his catlike quickness, his ability to field bunts in front of the mound, tag the batter and throw out the lead runner.

While he was one of the most graceful first basemen in history, Chase habitually posted sub-par fielding averages, led the league in errors six times and showed frequent fielding lapses. His critics said these were clues that Chase was crooked and in the pay of gamblers. Opposing bench jockeys often shouted at Chase, "what are the odds today?"

Manager George Stallings accused Hal of trying to throw a game in 1910. Stallings was fired and replaced by Chase, who ended the season with a 10-4 managerial record and was 76-76 the following season. Chase was traded to the Chicago White Sox, but jumped to the outlaw Federal League in 1914 and hit .347 in 75 games with Buffalo. In 1915, he led the Feds with 17 home runs and batted .291.

Reinstated in 1916, Chase went to Cincinnati and hit a league-leading .339. In August, 1918, Cincinnati manager Christy Mathewson suspended him for indifferent play.

At hearings on the suspension, players testified that Chase offered them bribes. Chase denied the allegations, saying he had bet on only two games in his life, one an exhibition and the other as a spectator. League President John Heydler ruled Chase had acted carelessly, but said the evidence and record of the games refuted the accusation.

The Redlegs traded Chase to the New York Giants, where he hit .284 in 1919. Chase didn't return to Organized Baseball the following season. During the furor over the conspiracy of Chicago White Sox players to fix the 1919 World Series against Cincinnati, New York manager John McGraw revealed he had released Chase when Lee Magee reported that Hal had bribed him to throw games.

In California, Chase was banned by local leagues and from Pacific Coast League ballparks after being accused of trying to bribe Salt Lake City pitcher Spider Baum.

Hal Chase

After reports of the Black Sox scandal came out, Chase was indicted by a Chicago grand jury. Pitcher Rube Benton testified that Chase and Heinie Zimmerman offered him $800 to throw a game when all three were with the Giants.

Benton said Chase told him about the Black Sox fix in advance and won $40,000 betting against Chicago. California authorities refused to extradite Chase, who never stood trial. Chase later played outlaw ball in the Southwest and finally was hospitalized with beriberi in Colusa, California.

In a 1941 interview, Chase said his life had been, "one big mistake after another." He denied any part in the Black Sox fix, but admitted, "I am an outcast and I haven't got a good name. I'm a loser, just like all gamblers are."

■ RUGBY RULES

American football continued to live in the dog house in the years before World War I as local high schools and universities stuck with rugby.

Stanford had the best record through 1917, but lost its top opponent when officials on The Farm and at Berkeley couldn't agree about the freshman rule in 1915 and Cal returned to playing football. Stanford officials insisted freshmen should be eligible because Cal's enrollment was six times larger than their school's 1,000. The schools resumed athletic relations after Stanford banned first year students from playing on varsity teams in 1919.

Stanford ruled the rugby roost from 1910 through 1916, compiling a 59-11-2 record with undefeated teams in 1914 and 1915. Stanford was unbeaten again in 1916 until it met Santa Clara University in the season's final game.

Playing a less demanding schedule, SCU produced a 33-17-5 record from 1908 through 1914, including a startling 15-10 upset of Stanford in 1912.

Both were unbeaten, with a single tie, when they met in 1915's final game on Nov. 13. The contest had replaced the Cal-Stanford affair as the big game on the schedule and Ewing Field in San Francisco was packed with 15,000 fans, including California Governor Hiram Johnson.

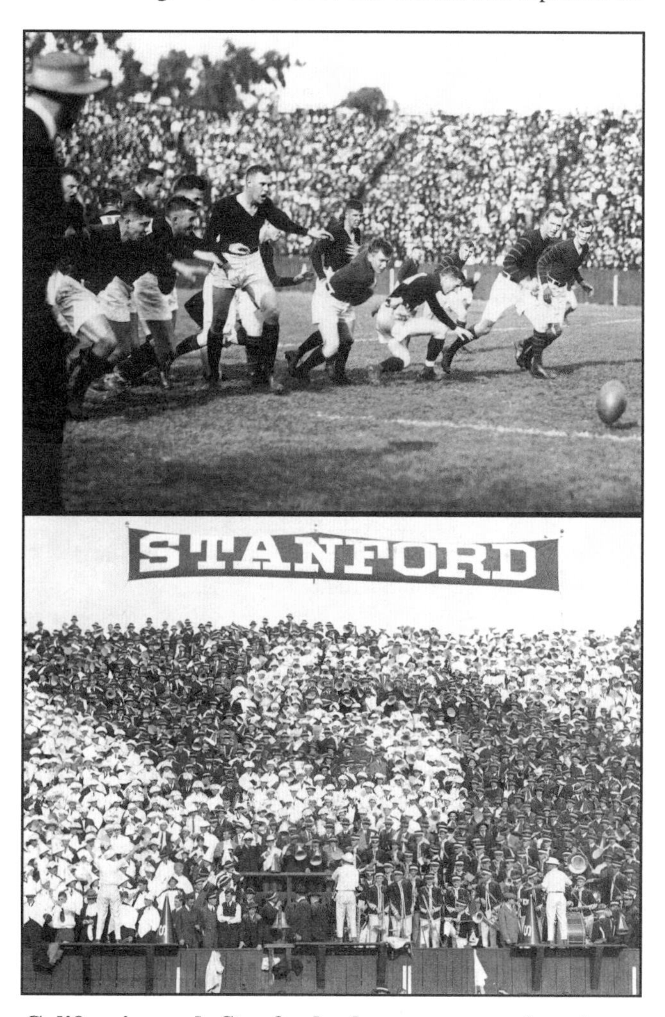

California and Stanford players pursued a loose rugby ball during 1911's Big Game at Stanford Field. The Golden Bears won, 21-3, as Cardinal rooters and the band formed a white "S" on a field of red.

Santa Clara played well in the first half, trailing 10-0, but after intermission it was all Stanford. Joe Urban raced 70 yards to score, Rick Templeton made the third of his six conversions and the Cardinal was on its way to a 30-0 win.

The Broncos (9-0-0) gained revenge in 1916, outscoring opponents 294-8. SCU beat Stanford, 38-5, snapping a 34-game Cardinal unbeaten streak stretching back to 1913.

Because of World War I's restriction on its athletic program, Stanford played only one rugby game in 1917. It was payback time as the Cardinal handed SCU its only loss of the year, 15-11.

Both schools dropped rugby after 1917 and returned to football two years later. Stanford compiled a 4-3-0 record in 1919, losing the Big Game to Cal, 14-10.

■ TOPPING THE PREPS

Palo Alto High's rugby team made five straight appearances in the postseason playoffs early in the decade.

In 1910, they suffered the same fate as Santa Clara had the year before, falling to Los Angeles High, 10-0. Led by Bert Risling, the team racked up a 9-2-1 record before the state final, losing twice to the Stanford Frosh and tying San Jose High, 0-0, before beating them in the playoffs, 6-0.

The next year's team was more impressive, grinding out 11 wins in 15 tries with two of the losses to the Stanford Freshmen. Six prep opponents were blanked.

Although Paly lost to Berkeley in the final game of the Academic Athletic League playoffs, it continued to play in the postseason and gained some measure of glory by beating Porterville in the last game of the year, 9-5.

In 1912, Palo Alto produced its best rugby team, finishing 18-3-0 with losses to the freshmen teams of Cal and Stanford and 8-5 to Berkeley High in the AAL final. Again the team continued in the playoffs, topping Pomona for the state title, 11-6. In another postseason contest, Paly beat Central Section champion Porterville, 11-6.

The school ran its victory streak to 20 games by winning the first 16 in 1913 before dropping the California championship to Pomona, 27-10. The 1914 squad (10-4-2) played two ties with Woodland before losing a third contest, 3-0, for the Northern California title. Palo Alto had one more good year, losing the regional crown to Berkeley in 1915, but didn't have another winning season until 1921.

■ GIRL'S BASKETBALL

YMCA and women's teams helped spread the game of basketball across America after it was invented in 1891 by Dr. James Naismith in Springfield, Mass.

Girls and women played at many schools before the game became popular with male students. Stanford and Cal played the first women's intercollegiate game in 1895.

One of Santa Clara County's best early female teams represented San Jose High School in 1911-12.

The school had the advantage of size in selecting athletes since San Jose had 1,248 students, the sixth largest high school enrollment in California. Santa Clara County's next biggest high school was Palo Alto with 272.

Sadie Langford and Marjorie Leffler began showing their skills for San Jose High in 1911. Typical was a 59-3 win over San Mateo with the Langford-Leffler tandem producing 27 of San Jose's 29 first half points. The 1912 team was even better. In one game, Langford dropped in 39 and Leffler 28 as San Jose thumped Live Oak, 67-7.

San Jose went on to defeat Palo Alto for the Peninsula Athletic League championship and met mighty San Francisco Lowell for Northern California honors. Lowell was undefeated over two seasons and had handed San Jose its only loss in 1911. San Jose beat Lowell, 25-18, to finish the season undefeated in seven games.

The winning streak continued. By March, 1914, it was reported at 23 straight against prep teams after Langford hit 32 against Mountain View in a 46-10 blowout that nailed down the Peninsula title again. Their only loss during the period was to the Stanford women, 21-18.

■ HIGH JUMP CHAMPION

No one ever learned that necessity is the mother of invention better than George Horine.

The great Stanford high jumper is credited with inventing the western roll style of jumping and setting the first recognized world record in his event.

Using the traditional scissors style and approaching the bar from the right side, Horine managed a leap of 5-1. Then his family moved to a Channing Street home in Palo Alto, where the back yard's alignment forced him to approach the bar from the left. Taking off from his left foot, Horine learned to roll over the bar and the new style was born.

He leaped 6-1 1/2 in 1910 and 6-4 the following year. Horine set the record at 6-7 in an Olympic trial meet at Stanford when the bar jiggled up and down for several seconds, but stayed on the standard. The mark eventually was recognized as the first world record for the event.

Horine's leap of 6-2 1/4 in the 1912 Olympics at Stockholm earned him a bronze medal.

■ GIMMIE AN 'S'

Male cheerleaders are the exception in high school today, but that wasn't the case before World War I.

When San Jose girls led cheers at a rally in 1913 to bolster school spirit for a baseball game against Los Gatos High School, it was big news.

"GIRLS LED YELL AT HIGH SCHOOL," proclaimed one bold headline in the *San Jose Mercury-Herald*, followed by another head which said, "Novel innovation is introduced by fair sex and enthusiasm is aroused."

"Considerable difficulty was experienced by the girls in getting their yell team together, but when the team did appear the results were surprising to every student present," the story said of the team composed of cheerleaders Marie Goff, Florence Hunter and Dortha Ball.

"The girls have contemplated organizing a girls' yell team for some time, but yesterday was the first time in the history of the school that a yell was conducted entirely by girl yell leaders."

■ IN PASSING

John F. "Jack" Sheridan, 18-year big league umpire from San Jose, died at his sister's home in the Garden City in 1914. He was the first umpire hired by American League president Ban Johnson when the circuit formed in 1901.

Wallace Bray, better known as "Happy Hogan," died of pneumonia at age 39 in 1915 in Los Angeles. Santa Clara native Bray used the pseudonym so his parents wouldn't know he was playing Sunday ball against their wishes. He turned pro after playing at UOP and USC. Never a great player, Bray's leadership qualities were impressive and he became manager of the Pacific Coast League's Venice team in 1909. A testament to his popularity was the turnout of 3,000 mourners at his funeral.

Russell Downing of Los Gatos, an outfielder on the Stanford baseball team that was playing a series of games in Hawaii during the summer of 1915, died of a broken neck suffered diving into the ocean at Waikiki Beach.

County singles tennis champion Donald Walker of San Jose passed away in a San Jose hospital after an operation for appendicitis in 1915. He was 20.

K. L. "Kenny" Fenton, Stanford rugby kicking star and third baseman in 1906 and 1907, died in 1917 of injuries suffered in a fall from his home's roof in Portland, OR.

■ THE PAC-10

The Pacific Coast's strongest collegiate conference, now known as the Pac-10, formed in 1915. Called the Pacific Coast Intercollegiate Athletic Conference, original members were California, Washington, Oregon and Oregon State. Stanford and Washington State joined a year later.

The United States' entry into World War I curtailed varsity competition until 1919. USC entered the conference in 1922 and UCLA joined in 1927. Because of the travel distances after USC's entry, the conference split into north and south divisions in all sports except football.

World War II also hampered the sports program in the organization then known as the Pacific Coast Conference. Stanford dropped sports from the fall of 1943 through 1945. In 1959, the Oregon schools and Washington State dropped out of the league, but all were readmitted by 1964.

With the entry of Arizona and Arizona State in 1978, the conference was renamed the Pac-10.

■ WRASSLERS

A pro wrestling match in the early days of the century was much more of an actual athletic contest than today.

There was still quite a bit of what passes for "showmanship," but bouts usually were staged without costumes, female assistants and planned outcomes. It was basically a couple of guys trying to see who was the fastest, strongest and possessed the best technique.

San Jose got its first taste of big time wrestling in 1916, when promoter Charles Daubert matched heavyweight contender Charlie Cutler of Chicago against St. Paul's George Costello, famous as the "Belgian Tiger."

Costello put up a great battle in the match at the Garden Theater, but lost a chance to win when Cutler slipped out of a toe hold and dodged when Costello tried to jump on his back and hit the floor instead.

The 230-pound Cutler took both falls. When Cutler extended his hand to the loser, Costello turned on his heel and headed for his corner as the crowd hissed.

"I am sorry that the quick temper of wrestlers sometimes destroys their better judgment," Cutler said. "(I regret) wrestlers do not all work to keep the sport clean and free of reproach," he added, as the crowd roared its approval.

■ TRIVIAL PURSUITS

The first card stunts appeared in the California rooting section in the 1910 Big Game at Berkeley.

The *San Jose Mercury-Herald* insisted on calling Santa

Clara University baseball coach Joe Aurreocoechea, "Joe Sneeze" in headlines.

■ THAT UNOFFICIAL BIG GAME

Teams representing Cal and Stanford met in football in 1918, but the result isn't listed among the 100-plus Big Games played between the Bay Area rivals. California won easily, 67-0, but fans found little joy in the victory because the opponents were only an "unofficial" team put together on The Farm by the Student Army Training Corps.

When the SATC was organized, students were ordered to play football, not rugby, which had been on Stanford's fall schedule since 1906. The team, which included players who weren't students, wasn't very talented, losing to Mare Island Navy, 80-0; Mather Field, 70-0, and USC, 25-8.

SATC officials accepted an invitation to play Cal, with the receipts going to a war relief fund. Nineteen thousand spectators turned out at California Field to see the first game between the teams since the Golden Bears dropped rugby and returned to American football in 1915.

Stanford's unofficial eleven was no match for Cal and halfback Pesky Sprout, who scored seven TDs. Stanford netted minus 10 yards rushing and didn't complete a pass.

■ FOR THE RECORD

In 1910, well-named Leland Stanford Scott pole vaulted 12-6 1/8 for a new Stanford mark before 6,000 in the Big Meet win over California and raised the world pole vault standard to 12-10 7/8 in a dual meet against Colorado.

Stanford set a school rugby scoring record in 1913 with an 88-3 win over the Barbarians club team.

It was baseball, not football in 1915, when San Jose High shut out Montezuma Academy of Los Gatos, 32-0.

In 1919, Mountain View lost a CIF Northern California football playoff game to Berkeley, 116-0. It is the most points ever scored against a county high school grid team.

■ WAR AND PESTILENCE

Sports played second fiddle to a war and a virus in 1918. World War I's effects began to be felt a year earlier with America's entry into the conflict.

The nation's attention was diverted from less important pastimes in 1917. The next year, a widespread draft of young men and a "work of fight" order that curtailed pro baseball schedules everywhere and closed down the Pacific Coast League in mid-year proved even more damaging.

In the fall of 1918, the second catastrophe struck on the home front. A virulent Spanish influenza epidemic swept across Europe and America, killing about 40 million people around the world, including 650,000 Americans. In San Jose alone, thousands were stricken in a four-month period and health officials said the final death toll was 239.

Public schools in the county were closed for weeks and citizens were required to wear gauze masks in public to help prevent spread of the disease.

The most prominent athletic figure to die in the county was Frank Arellanes, a former major league and minor league pitcher who succumbed on Dec. 13.

Arellanes was one of San Jose's top California State League pitchers in the early part of the century.

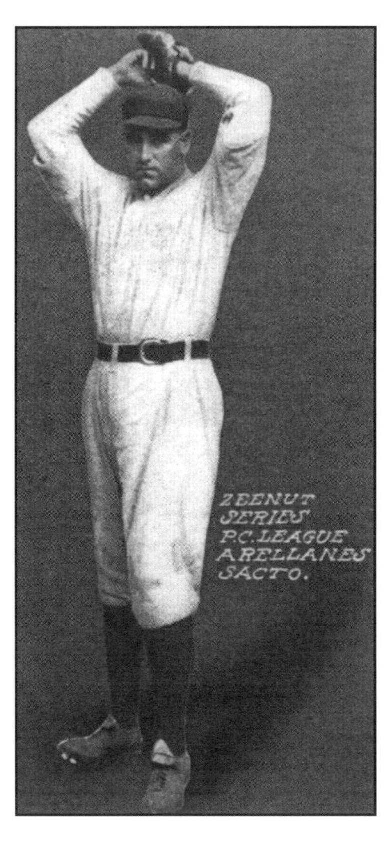

Frank Arellanes died in the 1918 flu epidemic.

He went 22-10 in 1907 and was off to a 10-3 start the following year when the Boston Red Sox shelled out $1,200 for his contract.

The Santa Cruz native won four of seven decisions for the BoSox that season and 16 more the following year before pitching seven seasons in the Pacific Coast League.

Most sporting events, including the college and prep rugby seasons, fell victim to the epidemic. It was nearly December before officials allowed any games.

Instead of the dozen played in 1917, San Jose and Palo Alto high schools played only two. Palo Alto and San Mateo beat San Jose and San Mateo took the league title with a win over Palo Alto.

Santa Clara University ruggers beat Stanford three times and the Cardinal won over Palo Alto A.C. and Cal.

■ 1910 ■

U. S. Army district cycling champ Joe King defeats Olympic Games runner-up Dorando Pietri in 12-mile race at Luna Park that ends when the Italian quits in a downpour after two laps . . . SCU's new basketball squad, "not well versed in rules," commits numerous fouls in 29-26 loss to UOP . . . Officials abolish San Jose High baseball squad after first game when players lie, report road win over Manzanita, when they actually lost . . . H. E. Reed of Stanford sets school record 10.0 in 100 in track meet at Provo, Utah . . . Stanford stops SCU's 14-game baseball win skein, 4-3 . . . San Jose State men's basketball team (7-3) loses to San Jose, Chico Teachers, UOP . . . Santa Clara High girl's cagers down San Jose, 25-7, to win Academic Athletic Sub-League championship . . . IAU winners are Los Gatos High (tennis), Mountain View (track) . . . Thomas of San Jose High wins 100, 220 as team takes league track title . . . St. Mary's wins two straight over SCU nine, which finishes 21-5 . . . New Century Wheelmen edge Garden City Wheelmen by 47 seconds for San

Leandro trophy . . . San Jose Rose Carnival motorcycle races attract 8,000 . . . Stanford is second to Notre Dame in national intercollegiate track meet . . . Chicago Bloomer Girls baseball team whips San Jose's top semi-pro nine, 5-4, at Luna Park . . . Garden City Wheelmen win 100-mile relay at San Jose Driving Park. Charles Chaboya posts best time . . . *Bicycling World and Motorcycle Review* criticizes cyclists, including locals Johnny Berryessa, Hal McCormick, Robert Diefenbacher, for posing as amateurs while making living as riders . . . Jake DeRosier fails by five seconds to match world motorcycle record of 47 seconds for mile at Driving Park . . . Garden City Wheelmen shine in state title races, taking all but one . . . Ex-San Jose Police Chief Thomas Carroll hits 73 of 75 targets, wins state marksmanship title at San Jose Rifle Club . . . San Jose High loses first three rugby contests, including games against Stanford Frosh, Cal Frosh, rallies for 4-4-1 finish. Mountain View (1-4-1), Santa Clara (2-2-0), Gilroy (2-2-1) are also-rans.

■ 1911 ■

R. P. Geissler of Stanford runs 75-yard dash in 8.0 at San Francisco indoor meet . . . UOP cagers whip Sequoia High, SCU, St. Mary's, St. Ignatius (now USF), San Jose Normal . . . San Jose Normal's baseball team compiles 2-3 record . . . University of the Pacific renamed College of the Pacific, UOP Academy becomes College Park Academy . . . St. Mary's downs SCU cagers, 14-10, to take what becomes traditional series . . . San Jose Normal tramples Nevada, 39-23, in men's hoops . . . Stanford defeats Sacramento in soccer, 3-0 . . . SCU's Leo Girot pitches two-hitter, but loses to PCL Vernon Tigers, 1-0 . . . San Jose High downs St. Mary's College in track as Thomas runs 100 in 10.2, 220 in 23.2 . . . Boston Red Sox reserves defeat SCU at Luna Park, 3-2 . . . Stanford's Kenyon Lee sets school mile mark at 4:28 2/5 against USC . . . Rick Templeton of Palo Alto High takes high hurdles, high jump, ties for first in pole vault, but San Jose wins league track meet . . . SCU's Justin Fitzgerald signs with New York Yankees, hits .315 in 12-year pro career, mainly in PCL . . . Waseda University of Japan loses baseball games to Stanford, 11-2, SCU, 10-1 . . . Harris Smitherum runs 10 2/5 to set 100 record as Stanford wins PCC track title . . . COP overcomes San Jose Normal in tennis . . . Palo Alto High wins statewide prep track title . . . San Jose High's Archie Stewart fans 17 batters in 11-1 win over St. Mathews . . . SCU tops Berkeley High, St. Mary's College in track . . . San Leandro 100-mile cycling trophy goes to Garden City Wheelmen in 4:29:30 . . . Cal, Stanford faculties cancel women's events between schools, citing "too much rivalry for the championships and rough play" . . . SCU swimmers bow to San Jose Albatross club at Vendome Plunge . . . 5,000 see San Jose's C. H. "Bud" Northrup win motorcycle races in San Jose Speed Carnival . . . Sheriff checks reports of illegal Guadalupe Mines boxing match between San Jose's Kid Herman, Harry Davis of England.

■ 1912 ■

SCU cagers down Palo Alto High, 52-30, behind Voight's 13 field goals . . . Crew of British gunboat Algerine bows to Stanford soccer team, 4-0 . . . Future big leaguer Johnny Couch strikes out 12 in Stanford win over Olympic Club . . . Mountain View High's Leroy Morton wins district cross-country race . . . Roy Needham's 10.3 win in 100, 23.4 victory in 220 leads San Jose High to easy victory over Berkeley High . . . Baseball out draws auto races, 5,000 to 4,000, as St. Mary's whips SCU, 3-1 . . . Louis Disbrow drives 100 horsepower racer 25 miles at dusty Driving Park, breaking three Barney Oldfield world record lap times . . . San Jose High topples Palo Alto, 14-5, 8-5, to win Peninsula division baseball title . . . Palo Alto High beats San Jose in track, 91-40 . . . Brown pitches San Jose High to 2-0 win over Stockton in semifinal, but locals lose Northern California title to San Francisco Mission, 7-5 . . . Jockey Johnny Reiff wins England's Epson Derby aboard Tagalie . . . San Jose High tennis team slips past San Jose Normal, three matches to two . . . Barney Oldfield and his 300 horsepower, front-wheel drive Christie fail to break world dirt track record, but crack San Jose standard with 47.6 finish. Earl Cooper defeats Oldfield in 50-mile race . . . San Jose High rugby team wins last five to finish 5-2-1 . . . SCU opens new baseball field with 5,000-seat grandstand . . . San Jose fans transported to Sweden as Empire Theater shows films of Olympic Games.

■ 1913 ■

Brilliant rugby player, ex-Palo Alto High captain Bert Risling drops out of Stanford after two seasons to take haberdashery job . . . San Jose State quintet loses pair to Monterey High . . . San Jose High tips San Mateo, 24-19, for Peninsula hoops title . . . San Jose High baseball team loses both ends of unusual morning-afternoon twin bill against St. Mathews Military Academy, Heald's Business College . . . Oakdale High defeats San Jose, 23-22, at COP gym in Northern California hoops final . . . Stanford downs St. Mary's, 4-3, for ninth consecutive win on way to 15-5-1 baseball record . . . Floyd Snook of SCU allows Stanford no hits in 5-0 win called after six innings because of darkness . . . Palo Alto High takes PAL track title as Swain breaks mile record in 4:52 2/5 . . . Stanford downs USC, 75 1/5 to 45 4/5, with Cardinals' Don Dawson smashing broad jump mark at 23-10 3/4 . . . Blondy Haskamp of SCU wins both sprints, 120 high hurdles, high jump against Nevada . . . Campbell High edges Los Gatos, 11-10, to take league baseball playoffs . . . San Jose Albatross captain Rudy Caspers wins 50 freestyle in 29.0 against Santa Cruz Neptune Club . . . County tennis singles champs are Stanford's Laura Herron, Lin Murray . . . doubles winners are San Joseans Mrs. S. C. Maynard, Alice Lewis and Harvey Broderick, Donald Walker . . . Santa Clara Prep ruggers blank only opponents, San Mateo High, 15-0; St. Ignatius, 20-0 . . . San Francisco YMCA beats San Jose by 11.5 minutes in 50-mile race between cities in 5:14.00 . . . Campbell High cagers top Los Gatos for IAU title, 43-20 . . . SCU's Bert Hardy upsets Stanford's Dick Grant in 100-yard dash, but Stanford wins Mercury-Herald's Thanksgiving track meet . . . Sadie Langford's 25-foot shot thrills crowd as San Jose High opens Peninsula hoops race with 39-4 win over San Mateo . . . Outfielder Hazel Carter, 14, first girl on local boy's team, gets two hits in Moreland Grammar School's 5-4 win over Campbell Grammar School.

■ 1914 ■

Already reported as disbanded because students more interested in training for outdoor sports, SCU basketball team loses to Nevada, 34-32 . . . Men barred as spectators when Stanford women beat Nevada, 28-13, in basketball. Referee Sprig Marden is only man on premises in Stanford's next outing, a 28-12 win over San Jose Normal . . . Stanford men's hoops team gains official status, wins opener against St. Ignatius College, 22-20 . . . SCU's Pinky Leonard whitewashes Chicago White Sox reserves, 7-0, at Luna Park . . . San Jose High's Elgin Worley tosses nine inning no-hitter against Belmont Military Academy . . . Hillman Lueddemann of San Jose High runs record 23.2 in 220, but Santa Clara High wins meet, 61-60 . . . Bill Noonan's three hits, four RBIs lead Stanford over Cal, 6-5 . . . Palo Alto High scores 41 points to win Northern California track title on muddy track. San Jose's Roland Thompson speeds to record 26.1 in 120 low hurdles . . . Stanford, Cal fall to Washington's eight-oar crew on Oakland Estuary . . . Palo Alto High's Ken Johnson ties 100 record in 10.1 as team wins state prep track meet at Stanford . . . San Jose Country Club's 18-hole layout near Alum Rock Park opens to members . . . Clarence Farmer of San Jose High wins 50, 100, but Belmont Military takes swim meet . . . Lowell High stops Palo Alto, 2-1, for Northern California baseball title . . . Santa Clara High captures IAU track crown . . . Ben Torres of San Jose wins 100-mile motorcycle race at Driving Park . . . Ken Johnson of Palo Alto High captures 100 in 10.2 at Cherry Carnival track meet in San Jose won by Olympic Club . . . Fred Hanchett, Donald Walker of San Jose lose to Roland Roberts, H. Van Dyke Johns in Pacific Coast junior doubles title match at Naglee Park . . . Santa Cruz Neptune Club handles San Jose Albatross, 36-24, at Vendome plunge . . . San Jose YMCA's Russell Hart edged at finish line, but illegal substitution in final leg of 100-mile around-the-bay foot race disqualifies winning San Francisco team . . . Lin Murray (Stanford) returns to area from eastern tour where he won 91 of 96 tennis matches . . . Donald Walker defeats Hillman Lueddemann in five sets for county tennis title . . . San Jose High ruggers beat St. Mathew, 14-0, before 800 spectators in first game at Reed Field at Sixth and Virginia streets . . . Santa Clara Prep ruggers down San Mateo, Santa Cruz, tie Stanford Frosh . . . When San Jose Country Club caddies strike for $1-a-round, golfers carry own bags and price stays at 50 cents . . . COP bows to San Jose High in rugby on late passing rush by Art Dorr, Les Leake plus Ted Moore's conversion . . . Darkness ends 10-inning, 4-4, tie between American, National League baseball all-star teams before 1,000 at Luna Park . . . Anne Baxter's 16 tops San Jose Normal women's 26-8 hoops win over Stanford.

■ 1915 ■

College Park Academy's Dick Wright pumps in 30 in 60-27 hoops win over San Jose Normal . . . A. J. "Gus" Hoever gives up only one hit in five-inning Stanford win over SCU . . . Morgan Hill High girl's cagers drub Campbell, 53-4 . . . San Jose Normal men, women win basketball twin bill against Pacific Grove High . . . COP's Allen Ham is whole show with 11 for 19 free throws as Tigers lose to Nevada, 29-26 . . . Future Black Sox World Series conspirator Lefty Williams pitches five innings for PCL Salt Lake City in 5-3 win over Chicago White Sox in Luna Park exhibition . . . Stanford's A. S. Hayes is shelled for 14 hits in 11-1 loss to Chicago White Sox . . . SCU basketball team ends season 9-1 with only loss to Olympic Club, 35-30 . . . Los Gatos High's pitcher Taylor strikes out dozen in 2-1 win over San Jose High . . . Losing only to San Mateo, 31-19, Campbell High cagers finish 14-1 . . . Stanford's Rick Templeton takes third place with 22-foot broad jump in final event of Big Meet to edge Cal, 62-60 . . . San Jose High's Art Forward takes 880, mile, teammate Roland Thompson wins high, low hurdles in first North Coast Section meet . . . Stanford crew defeats Washington by less than a length on Oakland Estuary . . . Although San Jose High's Bill Paull strikes out 15 Alameda batters, locals lose, 7-3

The 1914-15 Campbell High basketball champs went 14-1. From left, (back) Eric Byderkarken, C. E. "Swede" Righter, James Fablinger, coach D. H. Cramer; (front) James Huntley, Leland Lancaster, Clare Bryant, Ed Kennedy. Righter won seven letters at Stanford and became the school's first All-Pacific Coast Conference basketball player in 1920.

. . . Running for Olympic Club, Milton Samis of Stanford wins San Francisco indoor mile in 4:37 . . . San Jose High sweeps PAL track, baseball crowns . . . Stanford's Reg Caughey, who earns eight letters in five sports, wins shot put with record toss of 46-6 1/2 at San Francisco Pan-Pacific Exposition. Feg Murray of Stanford wins both hurdles, surpassing world records, but loses marks to excessive wind . . . San Jose High nine topples Oakland Tech, 7-5, San Rafael, 3-1, for north state title . . . Cornell noses past Stanford crew by inches to win four-mile Intercollegiate Rowing Association's regatta . . . Palo Alto High's rugby team (8-4-0) edges San Jose, 9-5, for Peninsula title, loses to Berkeley in Northern California playoff, 24-3 . . . San Jose ruggers dropped first five games, finish 5-7-0 . . . Santa Clara Prep loses to Santa Clara High on way to 4-1-0 grid record . . . Earl Cooper, who grew up in San Jose, wins 301-mile Illinois race averaging 74.97 miles an hour . . . In all-Stanford final, Herbert Hahn tops H. Van Dyke Johns for Pacific Coast tennis singles title.

■ 1916 ■

With Dick Wright pouring in 36, College Park Academy beats San Jose High in basketball, 40-31 . . . Stanford officials elevate basketball to major sports status, give players their block "S" . . . Interstate Trapshooting Association says five-man San Jose team led by O. N. Ford has state's top scoring average, 92.45 of 100 . . . Vic Herrera tops George Locatel, 50-40, to defend county three-cushion billiards title . . . Stanford Frosh defeats San Jose High nine, 7-6 . . . San Jose High girl's cagers whip San Mateo, 44-13, for fifth straight win . . . COP cagers fall to St. Mary's, 41-40, but contend score actually 42-41 in their favor . . . Olympic Club's Oliver Millard wins eight-mile race from Evergreen School to downtown San Jose YMCA . . . Bill Paull pitches San Jose High to 4-2 win over Palo Alto . . . Los Gatos

Justin Fitzgerald (sliding in Portland uniform) left Santa Clara University in 1911 to start a 12-year pro baseball career in which he averaged .315 at the bat and nearly 30 stolen bases annually.

High defeats SCU Day School, 8-2, on Will Darling's two-run homer . . . Andy Phillips pitches well but San Jose High's nine errors lead to 3-2 loss to Alameda . . . San Francisco Seals hold spring training in San Jose. Record Luna Park crowd of 3,500 sees Seals down SCU for third straight time . . . Art Forward breaks own mile record with 4:41.1 as San Jose High wins Northern California track crown. Forward later lowers mile mark to 4:38 3/5 as San Jose falls to Palo Alto, 62-60 . . . International balk line billiards king Willie Hoppe defeats Japanese champ Koji Yamada in San Jose Union Club exhibition . . . Ben Torres navigates 200-yard Alum Rock Road motorcycle hill climb course in 8.5 seconds . . . San Jose High's 9-3 win over Campbell clinches PAL title without loss in eight games . . . Stanford crew speeds to eight length victory over California on Oakland Estuary . . . San Jose High pitcher Bill Paull defeats Oakland Tech, 7-1, in semis, stops Hitchcock Military Academy in Northern California final, 3-2 . . . Garden City Wheelmen's George Semondi takes Stockton one-mile race . . . IAU prep titles go to Campbell High (boy's basketball, baseball, tennis), Los Gatos (track), Live Oak (girl's hoops) . . . Laura Herron of Palo Alto wins Pacific States tennis title at Del Monte . . . San Jose's largest paid crowd of 20,000 jams city trolley lines, Luna Park for Independence Day Round-Up rodeo, other events. San Joseans among winners: Joe Flores (bull riding), Tim Sullivan (chariot race) . . . Dr. Fred Schumacher averages 180 pins to take Mercury-Herald bowling medal . . . San Jose YMCA team wins 50-mile San Francisco to San Jose relay . . . San Jose city tennis title taken by F. A. Parton . . . After three straight rugby losses, COP defeats Stanford Reserves, 8-6 . . . Mrs. S. C. Maynard wins county women's tennis singles . . . San Jose High girls defeat Los Gatos in hoops, 27-8 . . . Olympic Club ruggers whip Palo Alto AC, 18-5, for Northern California club title . . . Gilroy High five tops King City, 26-21 . . . Stanford's Norman Ross breaks 220 freestyle world mark in 2:21 3/5 . . . Ora Forman, Delmar Dooley annex county bowling title over Frank Arnerich, B. S. Slettedahl by 31 pins . . . IAU hoops title won by Los Gatos High . . . Santa Clara Prep's Ferraro tallies 11 baskets in 59-21 win over Los Gatos.

■ 1917 ■

SCU increases hoops seating to 750, "so this very strenuous game can be witnessed in safety from any angle" . . . San Jose Normal eliminates women's basketball against Chico State, because severe tension before and during games has been "detrimental" to players' health . . . Match between wrestlers Nick Daviscourt, Cyclone Jenkins draws 500 to Garden Theater . . . SCU beats USC cage team, 63-13 . . . Charles Payne of San Jose High tops 11 feet for pole vault record in loss to SCU . . . Pitcher Elmer Pearson of San Jose High stops Centerville, 4-2 . . . Ben Fitzpatrick of SCU decisions Stanford in 14 innings, 4-3 . . . COP women defeat Mills College in hoops, 39-34 . . . Bill Paull of San Jose High shuts out Stanford Frosh, 9-0 . . . Hal Rhyne goes four for six, Al Saxe pitches one-hit ball as San Jose High tramples South San Francisco, 26-0 . . . Stanford crew falls to Washington by four lengths . . . William Zettle wins motorcycle hill climb up Alum Rock Road's 70 percent grade . . . Walter Tweedle wins 880, mile as San Jose High takes Peninsula title . . . Lin Murray (Stanford) wins U. S. tennis singles . . . Ernie Spurway runs record 10-flat 100 to lead San Jose High over Palo Alto, 88-34 . . . Los Gatos High wins IAU track and field title . . . Lorraine Waters goes nine for nine with four home runs, strikes out 11 in 52-13 win over Campbell as undefeated San Jose High girls win title . . . Lorraine Waters, Roberta Terry of San Jose High capture PAL tennis doubles . . . San Jose's Earl Cooper takes 250-mile Chicago auto race . . . O. N. Ford comes home to San Jose with 27 trap shooting trophies after two-month national tour . . . Dr. D. C. Walters of San Jose wins state amateur golf title . . . Glen Neville of Garden City Wheelmen pedals from San Jose to Los Gatos and back in 59:25 . . . A. H. Hubbard defeats C. G. Clute for county tennis singles title. Clute and wife beat Mrs. S. C. Maynard, E. Jackson in mixed doubles . . . San Jose High falls to San Mateo, 11-0, in football game called in second half after ammonia fumes from nearby hospital sicken San Jose players . . . Curtis of Los Gatos scores 30 points in 63-13 basketball win over Campbell . . . Palo Alto High's once powerful ruggers fall on hard times, beat Sequoia for only win in 11 games . . . San Jose High ruggers drop last three, finish 6-6-0 . . . Marion Curtis of Los Gatos hits 38 points in 40-24 girl's basketball win over Mountain View . . . New gymnasium ends hoops play on San Jose High's outdoor dirt court . . . Live Oak High, 74-20 loser in first meeting, upsets IAU cage champion Los Gatos, 28-21.

■ 1918 ■

Camp Fremont 8th Infantry downs San Jose High hoops squad, 45-36 . . . Stanford nine finishes 2-1, including 10-8 loss to SCU . . . Ernie Spurway's 30 leads San Jose High to 70-18 basketball win over Campbell . . . Future Hall of Famer Eppa Rixey fans 12, pitches Camp Fremont Hospital to 7-5 win over SCU in 10 innings . . . COP women lose to Nevada, 12-10, in basketball . . . Mountain View High runs wild, stealing 17 bases in 9-8 win over Palo Alto . . . San Jose High quintet beats Lick-Wilmerding, Commerce in CIF prelims, falls to Oakland Fremont, 43-12, in Nor Cal final . . . Orlo Hayes takes both hurdles in San Jose High's 103-35 victory over Berkeley . . . SCU's Gus O'Connor hits double, two homers in 15-4 win over Camp Fremont's 12th Infantry . . . San Jose's Frank Cisternino captures Meteor Rock Hill motorcycle climb . . . Stanford baseball captain Ken Lilly injures ankle in morning game against Cal, wins 100-yard dash in Big Meet against Bears in afternoon . . . Hal Rhyne pitches San Jose High to 4-3 victory over San Mateo for PAL title, defeats Oakland Tech, 5-2, in NCS championship game . . . Bill Tilden bows to Lin Murray (Stanford) for national tennis singles title . . . San Jose High girls defeat Stanford, 16-13, with Myra Waterman fanning 11 batters . . . Garden City Wheelmen's Frank Russ wins 25-mile stakes race in 1:04.57 . . . G. H. Hartman of San Jose, Sam Parks of Milpitas top steer-ropers at Fourth of July roundup . . . Flu epidemic eliminates most late year sporting events.

■ 1919 ■

San Francisco Seals hold spring training on SCU diamond . . . San Jose High takes Sequoia, 79-23, for PAL hoops crown. Lick-Wilmerding falls to San Jose, 69-6, in NCS playoff, but locals lose, 26-23, to Oakland Fremont for section title . . . Palo Alto High's Kendrick Shedd pitches two no-hitters against Stanford Frosh . . . Santa Clara Prep nine unscored on after first three games . . . Mountain View High boy's quintet ends season 17-1, losing only to San Jose. Mountain View girls are PAL champs . . . San Mateo High downs San Jose, 13-8, to take two of three for PAL baseball title . . . San Jose's H. L. Burt wins Pacific Coast bowling crown, rolling 1,818 for nine games . . . IAU track title goes to Mountain View with 82 points to runner-up Santa Clara's 38 . . . Stanford's eight-oar crew falls to Washington, California on Oakland Estuary . . . San Jose letter carrier J. J. Payne wins Del Monte tennis tournament . . . Stanford (6-2) beats Cal twice in only conference baseball outings . . . San Jose Bears whip all-black Shasta Limited nine, featuring Jimmy Claxton, who pitched for Oakland Oaks in 1918 . . . Stanford second to Cal in first PCC track meet . . . Pitcher Tom Hickey (SCU) fans 23 batters in San Jose Bears' 12-inning victory over USS Boston . . . Don Carlos Hines of San Jose loses to Ashton Stanley at Del Monte in first state junior golf final.

The 1920s

Rugby wasn't held in high esteem on the Pacific Coast until colleges and high schools began playing it in 1906 as a substitute for the more popular American football. One of the most important results of the switch was a pair of gold medals for the USA Olympic team.

Many local high schools, as well as Stanford and Santa Clara University, stuck with rugby after Cal and others went back to the American game.

Most of the men on the USA rugby team in the 1920 Olympics were Californians. They included C. E. "Swede" Righter and Robert "Dink" Templeton, who went on to successful coaching careers after leaving Stanford, Righter at College of the Pacific and Templeton at his alma mater.

Other Stanford men were Dan Carroll, Charles Doe, Jack Patrick, Hector Wrenn and sprinter Morris Kirksey, one of only two Americans to win Olympic gold medals in two sports. He ran with the champion 400-meter relay team in 1920. Santa Clara's John O'Neil, Bill Muldoon and Rudy Scholz also were on the squad.

When it was discovered there were no money to fund the trip, a group of prominent rugby fans donated $20,000 to send the team to Europe.

The team was lightly regarded by most Europeans, who believed the game belonged to them. But, the Americans stunned the world by defeating the highly-favored French team in the final, 8-0.

In 1924, the 22-man USA rugby squad again was loaded with players who were either Santa Clara County residents or ex-Stanford and SCU players. Among them were 1920 holdovers Muldoon and Scholz of Santa Clara plus Patrick and Doe from Stanford.

Also from Stanford were Phil Clarke, Norm Cleaveland, Linn Farrish, Bob Devereaux, William Rodgers, Dick Hyland, who went on to a long career as a celebrated Los Angeles sports writer, and Dud DeGroot, who later became San Jose State's most successful football coach.

Other Santa Clara University players were Hugh Cunningham, Ed Graff and Caesar Mannelli. The team was coached by Charles Austin, who had been the rugby head man at both Stanford and SCU.

This time, travel expenses were covered by a variety of

USA's rugby team defeated France for the 1920 Olympic title. From left, (back) Dink Templeton, Bill Muldoon, Hector Wrenn, Morris Kirksey, Rudy Scholz, George Davis, Dan Carroll, Swede Righter, George Fish, Jack Patrick, M. E. Hazeltine, Tilden, Colby Slater, Jim Fitzpatrick, Wallace; (front) Charles Doe, Joe Hunter, Harry Von Schmidt, Charles Meehan, John O'Neil.

sources, including money donated by the players.

Again, the Americans made it into the final, where the odds were 20-1 they wouldn't repeat against another powerful French team. Despite injuries and illness, Uncle Sam's defending champs surprised 50,000 spectators by defeating France, 17-3, for their second gold medal.

The United States remains the Olympic Games' defending rugby champion. After the stunning 1924 victory, competition in the sport was discontinued.

■ LITTLE BIG GAME

It had been a decade since Santa Clara and St. Mary's broke off athletic relations in a dispute over player eligibility when the schools renewed their gridiron rivalry in 1922. The first of what would become known as the "Little Big Game" was a thriller. Trailing 9-0 in the fourth quarter at San Francisco's Ewing Field, the Broncos scored on a 60-yard pass.

After the ensuing kickoff, Santa Clara recovered a fumble and drove to the two with the clock running down. On fourth down, St. Mary's held Santa Clara at the six-inch line to preserve the win. The Broncos gained revenge in 1923, winning 10-9, to take a three game to one lead in the series. It was their last win over the Gaels until 1936.

One of the best games was in 1926 when SCU was an underdog against the Gaels in their first Kezar Stadium meeting. St. Mary's coach Slip Madigan and Santa Clara's Adam Walsh were Notre Dame graduates and devoted to the Rockne system, which was at the height of its popularity.

Notre Dame coach Knute Rockne's teams lined up in the T formation, then shifted the backfield into a box formation. The rules allowed players to come to a complete stop momentarily. Since "momentarily" was not defined in the rules, Rockne system teams had a distinct advantage over defenders.

More than 15,000 fans came to Kezar to see the first all-college game played at the two-year-old stadium. The weather was dry, but an earlier storm had filled the field with thick mud. The Broncos subbed for every player except Len Casanova, their captain and star halfback. Eight St. Mary's men played the entire 60 minutes. The slippery footing helped both teams, which were strong defensively.

Late in the final period after several punts, St. Mary's drove 60 yards and scored. The extra point kick made the final 7-0 and gave St. Mary's an unbeaten season and a trophy for three straight wins in the series.

■ HOLD THAT TIGER

Before College of the Pacific moved out of San Jose to Stockton in 1924, head coach C. E. "Swede" Righter had turned a truly dismal football program around.

The Tigers, who drew their nickname and school colors of black and orange from Princeton University, had played rugby for a few seasons before World War I, but football was a new sport in 1919.

COP was 1-4-0 that first year and the Tigers' first three games were losses to Cal Frosh, 79-0; Nevada, 132-0, and Stanford reserves, 38-0. The loss to the Wolfpack was the worst ever sustained by a Santa Clara County football team at any level of play.

COP improved to 1-2-1 in 1920, and Righter, a Campbell High graduate, arrived a year later fresh out of Stanford, where he had won seven football and basketball letters and was the school's first all-conference hoops player in 1920.

Righter emphasized defense and his team produced a remarkable 13 shutouts in 18 games over the next three seasons. The Tigers were 3-1-0 in 1921, blanking Fresno, San Jose and Chico Teachers Colleges and losing only to the Stanford Frosh, 49-6.

In 1922, COP ran off a string of five shutout wins, including victories over Chico and San Jose Teachers Colleges and beat Modesto JC, 19-7, before bowing to Fresno, 12-7, in the finale of a 6-1-0 season. The Tigers' last season on the College Park campus in San Jose was the best. They went 7-0-0, outscoring opponents 171-12.

Righter coached the Tigers in Stockton until 1932. His position at COP was filled by another able coach, Amos Alonzo Stagg, who had guided Chicago University for 41 seasons before being forced to retire and move to Pacific. Righter became Burlingame High's football coach in 1934.

■ BIG GAME, BIG STADIUM

Stanford Stadium, the country's largest privately owned college stadium and Santa Clara County's oldest major sports facility, has been Stanford's football home for nearly 80 years.

It is one of three major Bay Area stadiums built in the 1920s. Stanford Stadium came first in 1921, followed two years later by Berkeley's Memorial Stadium and in 1925 by Kezar Stadium in San Francisco.

Football crowds had outgrown 15,000-seat Stanford Field and in 1919, work began on the $573,000 Stanford Stadium. Mule power was used to excavate the site near the main entrance to the beautiful campus. Its 60,000 seats were filled for the 1921 Big Game. Although Stanford scored first, California spoiled the show by winning, 42-7.

California dedicated its own 73,000-seat stadium -- funded by $1 million in private subscriptions from loyal Golden Bear backers -- on Nov. 24, 1923, with a 9-0 victory over Stanford.

The original configuration of Stanford Stadium was U-shaped, 65 rows high. Between 1927 and 1929, it was expanded to its current 85,429-seat capacity by the addition of 25 rows upward and the large section in the south end zone. The stadium now ranks as the eighth largest college facility in the nation.

■ JIMMY O'CONNELL

Who knows what Jimmy O'Connell might have accomplished as a major league baseball player if he hadn't made one stupid mistake.

The popular O'Connell starred in center field at Santa Clara University in 1919 and showed such remarkable hitting prowess that the San Francisco Seals signed him. He went on the season's last road trip with the PCL club and batted .313 in 32 times at bat.

O'Connell was an atrocious fielder, but the Seals wanted his bat in the lineup so they played him at first base in 1920. He hit a mediocre .262 and led the league in errors.

Jimmy O'Connell starred on Santa Clara's 1919 baseball team, then joined the San Francisco Seals. The Bronco squad, from left, (back) coach Joe Aurreocoechea, Bill Griffith, Les Perasso, Vic Larrey, John Chase, Eddie Varni, Jack O'Neil, James O'Connor; (front) Paul O'Neil, O'Connell, Tom Hickey, Ken Berg, Caesar Mannelli.

In 1921, he topped the Seals with a .337 average, 17 homers and 101 runs batted in. The New York Giants paid an unheard of $75,000 for his contract, a record at the time for a minor league player. He stayed with the Seals in 1922, hitting .335 with 62 extra base hits and 39 steals.

O'Connell was a bust with the Giants in 1923. The following year he showed signs of becoming a capable big leaguer by hitting .317 in 52 games up to the last weekend of the season as the Giants fought off Brooklyn in the race for their fourth straight National League pennant.

But, before the Giants-Phillies game on Sept. 27, O'Connell offered Philadelphia infielder Heinie Sand $500, "if you don't bear down too hard against us today." Sand rejected the bribe and reported the offer to his manager.

The Giants clinched the pennant by beating the Phillies, but Baseball Commissioner Kenesaw Mountain Landis investigated the incident. O'Connell admitted his bribe attempt, but said he was acting on orders from New York coach Cozy Dolan.

Dolan said he didn't recall talking to O'Connell. Three Giants' stars that O'Connell had implicated -- Frank Frisch, George Kelly and Ross Youngs -- denied any knowledge of the fix. Landis banned O'Connell and Dolan for life.

"I didn't think it was wrong when I did it," O'Connell said. "I thought Dolan was representing the New York club and I was obeying orders. I was surprised when Landis sent for me (and) I didn't think of denying what had happened for I didn't realize there was any harm done."

■ RACE RELATIONS

The Cal-Stanford boxing matches were canceled by Stanford officials in 1923 rather than allow their students to appear in the ring with African-American opponents. Stanford had defaulted whenever Cal sent a black man into the ring until 1922, when a Stanford boxer won such a bout.

W. H. Barrow, Stanford physical education director, said the UC graduate manager apologized after the match and blamed a misunderstanding for the black's participation.

"This year," Barrow said, "California . . . signified its intention of entering two Negroes in the Friday bouts. We do not feel that a bout between a white man and a Negro engenders race prejudice. Although it is our desire to place all students in both universities on an equal footing . . . mixed bouts do stir up race feeling rather than accomplish anything in establishing an equal status for the colored man."

The boxing teams didn't meet again for four years.

■ STANFORD FOOTBALL GIANTS

How good was Stanford fullback Ernie Nevers? Asked to compare Nevers with the great Jim Thorpe, who he'd coached a decade earlier at Carlisle Indian School, Stanford head coach Glenn S. "Pop" Warner didn't hesitate.

"Of the two, I guess Nevers was the finer player," responded Warner, whose Stanford teams went 71-17-8 between 1924 and 1932 and played in three Rose Bowls.

Nevers was a two-way star in the days of the 60-minute man. As a junior in 1924, the 6-foot-1, 205-pounder known as "Big Dog" carried Stanford to a 7-0-1 record.

The Cardinals were matched against Notre Dame in the Rose Bowl. Nevers played the entire game with tightly wrapped ankles. One had been broken in preseason, the other in the Montana game the week before the Big Game. Despite the handicap, Nevers gained 114 yards, out rushing Notre Dame's entire Four Horseman backfield. Stanford out gained Notre Dame, 316 yards to 186, but three Cardinal errors were turned into scores and the Irish won, 27-10.

Nevers closed his career in 1925 for the 7-2-0 Cardinals by rushing for 117 yards and a pair of scores in a 27-14 win over Cal -- Stanford's first Big Game win since 1914.

A three-sport athlete at Stanford (football, baseball, basketball), Nevers played pro baseball, pitching for the St. Louis Browns and in the Pacific Coast League for several seasons. To cash in on his football reputation, he signed late in 1925 with a group of Florida promoters who guaranteed him $25,000 for five games plus 5 percent of the gate. He was deprived of a huge payday when the team folded after

Pop Warner (right) said that Stanford fullback Ernie Nevers was the best football player he had coached, including his legendary Native American star, Jim Thorpe.

only a few games.

In 1926, Nevers joined the Duluth Eskimos of the NFL. Counting on Nevers' name to pack the stands, the league sent Duluth on the road to bigger cities. Between Sept. 6 and Feb. 5, the Eskimos played 29 league and exhibition games and Nevers' weight fell to 185. He continued playing with Duluth and the Chicago Cardinals until 1931.

Warner, inventor of both the single and double wing formations, saw his 1926 team go undefeated in 10 games and tie Alabama in the Rose Bowl, 7-7. Stanford won the Rissman National Trophy, given annually to the nation's top team based on a mathematical rating system devised by University of Illinois professor Frank Dickinson.

The following season, Warner closed his Stanford bowl career, guiding the Cardinals to a 8-2-1 season that included a 7-6 Rose Bowl victory over Pittsburgh. He coached for 44 seasons with an overall record of 313-106-32.

■ ANOTHER BRAND OF BIAS

Santa Clara County high schools offered girls a chance to play basketball, volleyball and baseball against other schools during the first two decades of the century.

That ended late in 1925 when school officials decided interscholastic competition was unfair since it was available only to the most athletically proficient girls.

A new athletic policy for female athletes went into effect late that year, when teams in the Peninsula Athletic League normally would have been preparing for varsity basketball games. Instead, girls were allowed to meet only informally in what were called "play days."

The first one took place on Dec. 12, when San Jose High girls hosted their counterparts from Santa Clara and Campbell high schools. "The new policy is to furnish competitive sports for all girls (who) wish to play, and not the few (who) are proficient enough to win places on the school teams," explained the *San Jose Mercury-Herald.*

The play day was held on a Saturday. The program opened with a "posture parade" in the school's gymnasium and was followed by singing, tennis, hockey, speed ball, basketball, hit pin baseball and captain ball before a 90-minute lunch break. (The young ladies had to bring their own). After lunch there was a round of "stunts, school songs and yells," followed by dancing and swimming.

Three years later, two students who participated in amateur events outside San Jose High were barred from even these activities. Mildred Simpson was dropped from an inter class baseball team for running in the Western girl's track and field championships held at Reed Field. Evelyn Raymond wasn't allowed to swim in play day events after competing in a junior swimming meet in San Francisco. Only tennis players and golfers were exempt from the bans.

Nearly half a century would pass before federal Title IX legislation mandating equal treatment for male and female athletes would take effect, giving local high school girls another chance to represent their schools in interscholastic athletic competition. In 1974, the Central Coast Section established track and field as the first high school sport for girls on an equal footing with boys under the new law.

■ A RECORD ROUND

The first major professional golf tournament held in the county was the 1926 Santa Clara Valley Open at San Jose Country Club, an event added to the tour by the Professional Golfers Winter Tournament Association.

The total purse of $2,000 may seem small in today's inflated terms, but it was large enough to draw such top pros as 1924 U. S. Open champ Cyril Walker; Bill Mehlhorn, the 1924 Western Open winner; Al Watrous, runner up to Bobby Jones in the 1925 British Open, and former Scottish amateur champion Tommy Armour.

The 54-hole tournament was played on Christmas Day (18 holes) and the following day. Mehlhorn trailed Armour by four shots at the 36-hole luncheon break. He caught the leader and made the turn at the ninth hole with a two-under par 33 to Armour's 37. On the back nine, Mehlhorn shot a three-under 32 for a course record 65 and a 54-hole total of

207 to take the $500 first prize. Armour finished with 211, good for $350 and Johnny Farrell was third at 214 for $225.

■ FOR THE RECORD

State high school records were set in 1920 when Santa Clara Prep's Isaac Whitfield scored seven touchdowns and Ed McEneany converted 14 of 15 PATs in a 104-0 pasting of the Fort Funston 14th Balloon Company team.

Stanford's Old Pavilion -- the nation's largest facility used exclusively for basketball at the time -- opened in 1922 with the Cardinal whipping COP, 30-21.

In 1926, San Jose Country Club caddies Pierre Oscamou and Marion Thatcher averaged 79.9 strokes per 18 holes while playing 102 holes between sunup and sundown to break a 1923 course record of 90 holes in one day.

Mountain View High's 1926 football team (0-3-5), failed to score a single point and played five scoreless ties.

Stanford graduate Emerson "Bud" Spencer lopped four-tenths of a second off the world 440 record, running 47.0 in May, 1928. He won a gold medal with the USA 400-meter relay team at the Amsterdam Olympics later that year.

In 1928, Garden City Wheelmen's Tom Silvera rode 10,853 miles in five months at a San Leandro track to break the record set by Englishman in a 12-month period.

■ BAD BLOOD

Stanford and St. Mary's met on the football field in 1927 in a game so violent that it sullied the reputations of both teams and ended their gridiron relationship forever.

Slip Madigan's Gaels arrived on the Farm on the first Saturday in October for the Bay Area's first important collegiate battle. It was a game marked by the number 16. Stanford made 16 first downs to just one for the Gaels, but fumbled 16 times as St. Mary's won, 16-0.

The Gaels scored the easy way, on a field goal and two touchdowns on fumble recovery returns by center Larry Bettencourt and tackle Homer Hicks. The score may have been the least important aspect of the game.

In his St. Mary's football history, *They Did It Every Time*, Randy Andrada said the game was a class and religious war that pitted big, rich, Protestant Stanford against poor, working class Catholics from tiny St. Mary's.

Given the level of animosity between some Catholics and some Protestants in the 1920s, there was a measure of truth to that statement. But, it seems a stretch to condemn the game as simply a class and religious struggle. While newspaper accounts describe the game as being marked by "savage and hard play," neither the *San Francisco Chronicle* nor the *San Jose Mercury-Herald* mentioned anything dirty.

Stanford athletic publicity director Don Liebendorfer had a different view. In his history of Stanford Athletics, *The Color of Life Is Red*, Liebendorfer describes the contest as the "most bitter, most inexcusably vicious football game these eyes have ever seen." The Gaels started the rough stuff, he said, and Stanford players eventually paid them back in kind.

The worst incident involved Ike Frankian, who had a reputation as a rough and often overly aggressive player. St. Mary's fans applauded his hard play, but opposing rooters booed Frankian and branded him a thug.

Andrada said Frankian's action was retaliation for a series of injuries inflicted earlier on his teammates. But, it appears Frankian's late hit on a Stanford player may have triggered the violence, since it occurred in the first quarter.

Stanford end Theodore "Spud" Harder was rising to his feet after catching a pass and falling out of bounds when Frankian -- unnamed in Liebendorfer's book, but described by him as a "gangster" -- landed on Harder's face with both knees. Harder suffered a broken cheekbone and was out of action for five weeks.

The incident did nothing to ease the animosity between Catholics and Protestants and St. Mary's was off the Stanford football schedule from then on.

■ OLYMPIANS

Margaret Jenkins and Henry "Cocky" O'Brien were two Santa Clara County hopefuls in the 1928 Olympics.

Jenkins was the first woman from the county to qualify for the Games, going to Amsterdam in 1928 as a discus thrower. It was the first year women were allowed to compete in track and field events at the Olympics.

A San Jose State graduate and Santa Clara school teacher, Jenkins' trip was financed by local businessmen and fans who had high hopes for her success, because Jenkins was the American champion in both the javelin and baseball throw.

In 1926, Jenkins finished sixth on both AAU events, while San Jose Teachers College teammate Aurelia Brown was third in the shot put. At the 1928 nationals, Jenkins hurled the javelin 112-5 5/8. That was short of her record toss of 127-3 1/2 the previous year at Eureka, where she won the baseball throw with a mark of 233-11 1/2.

Neither of her events were on the Olympics schedule, so Jenkins trained in the discus, placing third to qualify for the team. Jenkins was eighth in the discus in Amsterdam, but threw less than 100 feet in the 1932 Olympic Games

Margaret Jenkins

preliminaries and didn't make the finals at Los Angeles.

She continued competing successfully in the discus and baseball throw in women's meets into the early 1930s. Jenkins was a successful tennis player, teaming in 1922 with Fred Coolidge to win the county mixed doubles title and with Helen Lathrop to take the San Jose women's doubles. She was county singles champion in 1922, 1923 and 1924.

O'Brien, the son of a San Jose laundry man, was the area's best amateur cyclist during the 1920s and 1930s.

As a 16-year-old in 1926, O'Brien won the California junior title. He came back a year later and, in a busy five weeks during the summer, took a 116-mile around-the-bay race, swept the San Jose title races and won the state crown. He went on to Louisville to finish fourth among senior riders in the Amateur Bicycle League of America nationals.

O'Brien made the USA cycling team in 1928. He qualified in a 100-mile race from San Francisco to San Jose and back in 4:56:19, just four minutes and 19 seconds off the world record. He finished 15th in the finals at Amsterdam.

In 1929, O'Brien was first in every race and lapped the field in the 10-miler to take the state cycling title at San Jose Speedway. He achieved national recognition as a pro racer after finishing his amateur career in sixth place at the 1932 Los Angeles Olympics Games.

■ IN PASSING

Bobby Eager, 46, a catcher with the 1908 and 1909 San Jose teams in the outlaw California League after a career in the PCL, died of pneumonia in 1926.

Patrick Higgins, SCU rugby coach in 1912 and 1914, died of pneumonia in Paris in 1926.

Lawrence Hibasco, 27, of Palo Alto, was killed in 1929 when his speedboat collided with another driven by Bud Speegle of San Jose during a race on Alviso Slough.

Santa Clara Bronco football guard Hank Luoma died in O'Connor Sanitarium in San Jose in 1929 two weeks after surgery for a ruptured appendix. He was 22.

■ HOME AT LAST

The 1928 football season wasn't a particularly notable one in the win-loss column as Santa Clara University won five and lost four decisions.

But, there was one aspect of the schedule that is worth mentioning: four of the wins came at Varsity Field and it was the last time more than one contest would be played on campus in a single year for three decades.

Santa Clara was whitewashed by Cal, 22-0, and Stanford, 31-0, on the road in 1928. The school had a 1-2-0 record at Kezar Stadium, the neutral site in San Francisco that would become the Broncos' primary home away from home for the next quarter century. They beat St. Ignatius (later University of San Francisco), but fell to the Olympic Club and St. Mary's.

At home, SCU whipped Nevada, West Coast Army and COP before gaining 644 yards in a 83-0 blowout over Fresno State, the biggest victory margin in Bronco history.

Fans would see the Broncos on campus only once more, a 27-0 win against Portland at Ryan Field in 1936, before the football program was dropped after 1952. The program was resurrected on a small college scale in 1959. The first on campus game of the new era came against UC Davis in 1962, when Buck Shaw Stadium was opened.

Mountain View High's 1920 baseball team, from left, (back) Robert Wright, Paul Cameron, Leon Couch, coach W. E. Hester, unknown, Jess Regli; (front) Mason Butz, Stanley Hawkins, Jack Ehrhorn, Robert Bowers, John Manfredi. Regli is the only four sport member of San Jose State's Athletic Hall of Fame.

■ TRIVIAL PURSUITS

Feg Murray, Stanford hurdler who won a bronze medal in the 1920 Olympics, became a nationally syndicated newspaper cartoonist about sports and Hollywood.

Stanford retired Ernie Nevers' jersey Number 1 in 1925. It was issued the following season to team captain Fred Swan, who relinquished it when the error was discovered.

The all-dirt era ended when Fremont High School became the first prep team in the county playing on a grass football field in 1928.

Hurdler Hugo "Swede" Leistner of Stanford stowed away aboard the SS President, which carried the American Olympic team to Amsterdam in 1928. Leistner was freed from the brig when friends put up $130 for his passage.

■ BOX OFFICE BONANZAS

Frank and Angelo Boitano were always on the lookout for ways to bring new money into their Garden City Billiards parlor in downtown San Jose.

In 1928, they offered several exhibition matches that drew good crowds. The first was the famous George Sutton, who owned the record of balk line billiards runs and once clicked off 3,009 straight in spite of having no hands.

Sutton didn't use any artificial devices to grip his cue, explaining that, "it's a demonstration of doing something with nothing."

Later in the year, the Boitanos brought in Welker Cochran, former 18.2 balk line billiards champion, and Jake Schaefer, the present title holder. Cochrane won the majority of the afternoon and evening matches.

■ HONORS

Stanford's first All-Americans were football end Jim

The Carroll and Bishop cigar store team won the 1927 San Jose Winter League title. From left, (back) Walt Williams, Peeney Oliver, Warren Canfield, Mart Cunningham, Swede Harper, Roy Chittick, Johnny Narvaez, Ted Stawetski, Eddie Lyons, Nick Giandria, Diaz, Gus Lyons; (front) manager Charley Bishop, mascot Charley Bishop Jr., bat boy Gussie Lyons.

Lawson in 1924 and nine-letter man Harlow Rothert (track, football, basketball), in basketball in 1929.

Guard Jack Nolan was the first Santa Clara player to gain All-America football recognition when he made honorable mention on a 1924 team selected by coaches Pop Warner of Stanford, Knute Rockne of Notre Dame and Tad Jones of Yale. He also was the first Bronco to play major league professional football, joining Los Angeles in 1926.

■ 1920 ■

San Jose High wins PAL girl's basketball . . . Paced by Ora Forman's 745 series, San Jose Chamber of Commerce team sets Pacific Bowling Association records against Bachelor's Inn at Oakland . . . Record 800 spectators watch San Jose High cagers crush Lodi, 46-16 in boy's game, 22-8 in girl's. In unusual move to cover Lodi's travel expenses, San Jose charges 25 cents admission to game . . . Cage star A. Driscoll scores 30 as San Jose High tops Campbell, 52-23. Driscoll pours in 28 more in 56-11 win over Palo Alto . . . Caesar Mannelli leads way with 11 as SCU basketball squad beats COP, 17-14 . . . Hal Rhyne, future major leaguer called San Jose High's greatest athlete, joins Gilroy in semi-pro Mission League . . . Stanford cops PCC basketball title at 9-1 . . . Jess Wells takes both hurdles races, is third in 100 as Stanford tops USC, 61-52 . . . Luna Park is torn down to make way for axle plant . . . San Jose whips Watsonville Pippens, 2-1, in first baseball game at renovated Sodality Park . . . San Jose High nine defeats Palo Alto, 7-3, for PAL pennant . . . George Veit conquers field in Garden City Wheelmen's 21 1/4-mile race in 52:34 over Berryessa course . . . Sprinter Morris Kirksey (9.8 in 100, 21.4 in 220) is Stanford track captain, gains Olympic gold medal with 400-meter relay team, takes silver behind USC's Charlie Paddock in 100 . . . Every mark eclipsed as Stanford wins second annual PCC track meet . . . Mountain View High's Bob Bowers sets league record with 128-1 3/4 discus throw . . . Santa Clara High girls are Interurban Athletic Union (small school) hoops champs . . . San Jose freshman Mint Howell victor in Stanford pentathlon with 3,207 points . . . Frank Arnerich bowls Dream Alleys record 268 . . . Stanford swimmer Norman Ross captures three Olympic Games gold medals, diver Clarence Pinkston wins another . . . Crowds gather in front of Mercury-Herald building to see World Series results posted on huge outdoor scoreboard . . . San Jose High tips Palo Alto, 12-10, in grid battle of big local rivals . . . Stanford's L. S. Fish beats Fred Hanchett for county tennis title . . . Ty Cobb doubles, steals base, is jeered off field for lackluster play as all-stars fall to San Jose . . . Stanford gridders top SCU, 21-7, in only game of series played at Santa Clara . . . Ed "Strangler" Lewis, who lives in San Jose, gets nickname from devastating head lock, pins Joe Stecher to win world heavyweight wrestling title.

■ 1921 ■

San Jose's Art Forward is third in 41:28.2 in San Francisco Bulletin race across San Francisco -- early version of modern "Bay to Breakers" . . . Bernie Burchfiel drops in 17 points as COP downs Nevada, 38-25 . . . Unbeaten San Jose High girls defeat San Mateo, 28-27, to take PAL basketball title . . . Art Forward wins Evergreen eight-mile race in 47:49 . . . William Storie of San Jose High surprise winner over college 440 runners in YMCA track carnival . . . Campbell High five, which plays on outdoor dirt court, downs Sequoia, 35-12, for PAL title, loses to Berkeley in regionals . . . Error-prone SCU nine falls to Cal, 10-5, on nine miscues, to PCL Sacramento, 8-7, on eight more . . . San Jose Normal renamed San Jose Teachers College . . . Stanford cagers (15-3) down Cal in last two games of season to tie Bears for league title . . . Harry Dolen's grand slam gives St. Joseph's High of San Jose victory over Santa Clara Preps, 13-5 . . . Defending champ Palo Alto High girls withdraw from PAL baseball after other teams complain about team's ability . . . Cyclist Clyde Arbuckle of San Jose bucks strong wind to take gold watch in record-setting 2:43:54 2/5 for 60-mile San Jose-Gilroy-San Jose run . . . San Jose High's Kenneth Jordan fans 11 in 13-0 win over Mountain View . . . Hugo "Swede" Leistner captures both hurdles, broad jump to lead Palo Alto High to North Coast Section track title . . . Brick Muller's 16 points in broad jump, discus, high jump, javelin too much for Stanford as Cal wins Big Meet in downpour . . . Santa Clara High nine clinches PAL with win over Campbell High, competing in sports for first time since 1916 . . . Morgan Hill's Paul Walker wins YMCA's strong man contest . . . San Jose High girls defeat Santa Clara, 9-0, in first field hockey game on Ninth and San Fernando

Babe Ruth and Ty Cobb (inset) were just two of the big league baseball stars who played at San Jose's Sodality Park.

streets field. Team wins PAL without giving up goal . . . Phil Neer of Stanford first Westerner to capture NCAA lawn tennis singles title . . . E. H. Thomas earns $50 for bowling first perfect game at Dream Alleys . . . Ed "Strangler" Lewis pins Nick Daviscourt at San Jose's Victory Theater in benefit match seen, *Mercury-Herald* notes, "by many prominent society women" . . . San Jose Teachers College (1-4-0) returns to gridiron for first time since 1900 . . . Fans view films of boxers Jack Dempsey, Georges Carpentier at Victory Theater for 50 cents, $1 for loge . . . Powerhouse Santa Clara Prep (later renamed Bellarmine Prep) gridders go 7-0-0, outscore foes 344 to 7 . . . Roy Pitzer, driving car built by Sunnyvale's Otto Raines, smashes West Coast dirt track record, navigating mile at Pleasanton in 49.5 . . . San Jose High girls win PAL hoops title over San Mateo, 29-22 . . . Led by Chinese-American halfback Bing Moy, Palo Alto High's PAL grid champs (9-1-0) dump Lick-Wilmerding in Nor Cal playoffs, lose to Berkeley, 42-0.

■ 1922 ■

SCU cagers win four of six on Southern California trip . . . San Jose High girls chalk up 10th straight hoops victory, 50-10, over COP . . . Charles Draper of Live Oak High scores 12 points in 20-16 victory over San Jose . . . Stanford's Phil Neer, James Davies capture NCAA tennis doubles championship . . . Campbell High's Albert Gross tallies 27, 24, 22 in hoops wins over San Jose, Santa Clara, Palo Alto as team (13-4) wins IAU title . . . Peter Klyo, pacer owned by C. H. Angevine of San Jose, clocks 2:06 1/4 at Sacramento, West Coast's fastest mile of year . . . Garden City outdoor golf driving range opens in East San Jose . . . Ed "Strangler" Lewis regains world wrestling title in two falls over Stanislaus Zybazko . . . Santa Clara High takes PAL girl's volleyball championship . . . Santa Clara High's Wilhelm hits two home runs in 7-6 win over San Jose . . . San Jose High finishes second to Berkeley in Nor Cal CIF track meet . . . 20,000 see Stanford, California tie 65 1/2-all in Big Meet. Stanford's Flint Hanner (San Jose) sets javelin mark at 182-7 1/2 . . . Three-man Mountain View High track team wins seven events, finishes second to San Jose in PAL meet . . . Los Gatos defeats Santa Clara High for baseball crown . . . Helen Howell of San Jose High tosses baseball 195-6 to lead team to first PAL girl's athletics meet title . . . All-PAL includes Campbell outfielder Verne Sawyer (.454 average), Palo Alto catcher Clarence Dirks (.450), San Jose shortstop Buddy Leitch (.406), pitcher Duke Cleghorn (12-1) . . . City women's tennis singles title goes to Sue Maynard over Marjorie Postelthwaite . . . Stanford nine has 7-8 mark against military, town teams in Hawaii . . . San Jose High girl's field hockey team downs San Mateo, 2-1, for PAL title . . . COP gridders visit Stockton -- where school moves in 1924 -- to dump USS Camden, 13-0 . . . Genevieve Arnerich leads San Jose High girls to 43-4 hoops win over Campbell . . . Large gallery sees British Open golf champion Walter Hagen, Joe Kirkwood defeat Eddie Traube, Willie McEwan at San Jose Country Club, 3 and 1.

■ 1923 ■

Local golf pros Abe, Al Espinosa each shoot 72 at San Jose Country Club to take golf match from international stars Jock Hutchinson, 73; Gene Sarazen, 74 . . . Chuck Stevens of COP hits 20 in 29-19 hoops win over Fresno State . . . Live Oak High is IAU cage champ with 34-23 victory against Los Gatos . . . Undefeated San Jose High soccer team loses, 2-0, to Half Moon Bay for PAL title . . . San Jose High girls' string of PAL basketball titles ends at seven with 27-25 loss to South San Francisco . . . SCU's high scoring forward John Vukota nets 19 in 47-40 victory over San Jose American Legion . . . San Jose Asahi bows to All-Hawaiian baseball team, 1-0 . . . San Jose High starting five -- Al Biaggini, Johnny Minshall, Larry Ward, Lester "Fat" Woods, Dick Worden -- on all-league team. PAL champ San Joseans top Monterey, fall to Berkeley, 27-16, in CIF playoffs . . . COP nips Fresno State, 25-24 in three OTs, to take California Coast Conference title series . . . San Jose High baseball win streak ends at 16 with 7-2 loss to Santa Cruz . . . St. Mary's College downs SCU, 12-8, 7-0, in first diamond meetings between Catholic rivals in dozen years . . . William Storie of San Jose Teachers College captures 100, 220, 440 as Spartans topple Modesto JC, 66 1/2 to 55 1/2 . . . Lane Falk of Stanford sets records of 15.1 in 120 low hurdles, 22.7 in 220 high hurdles, but Cardinal loses Big Meet to Cal . . . Santa Clara High girls drop hoops title game to San Mateo, 11-4 . . . Jess Regli of Mountain View High wins 100, sets NCS discus record with 127-1 3/8 throw . . . San Jose Teachers College nine claims CCC championship with pair of playoff wins over Fresno State . . . Campbell High track team wins IAU title . . . City tennis singles won by Hal Overfelt (men), Marjorie Postelthwaite (women), Ernie Renzel (juniors). Overfelt, Renzel repeat in same county divisions . . . Horse, auto races dedicate new County Fairgrounds Speedway at Alum Rock, King roads . . . G. K. McDaniels defeats San Jose's R. D. Syer, 1 up, at Del Monte for California junior golf title . . . Charlie Barclay of San Jose wins California senior cycling title at Fresno, Amateur Bicycle League of America crown at Chicago . . . Driving Adolph Giusti's Ford Special, Jack Hayes of San Jose takes 30-lap race at Speedway . . . Injuries force Mountain View High (1-6-0) to forfeit last four football games . . . Santa Clara Prep (4-2-0) handles St. Mary's of Berkeley, 9-7 . . . Gilroy High (6-1-0) gridders lose only to Monterey in league play . . . Powerhouse Palo Alto High (9-1-1) wins PAL, but loses in playoff, 31-0, to Lick-Wilmerding of San Francisco . . . Fresno State refuses to meet COP in football playoff when Tigers guarantee travel expenses for only 12 of 18 players, offer to split gate receipts for others . . . San Jose Mercury-Herald names COP backs Eddie Spoon, Pete Knoles to All-CCC.

■ 1924 ■

Stanford top scorers John "Nip" McHose, Ernie Nevers can't prevent three straight basketball losses to California at season's end to finish 10-5 . . . Campbell High prospers in new gym, wins IAU hoops . . . SCU dedicates Seifert Memorial Gymnasium with 18-17 loss to Olympic Club. Ex-lightweight champion Willie Richie thrills 1,100 fans with three-round boxing exhibition against featherweight Fred Murphy . . . San Jose High cagers snap Campbell's 10-game win streak, 27-14, lose to San Mateo to force playoff game. San Jose defeats Campbell, 28-26, in two OTs for PAL title . . . Ernie Renzel hits 22 as San Jose High whips Lick-Wilmerding in CIF hoops semifinal . . . San Jose All-Stars defeat Pittsburgh Pirates, 9-5, in Sodality Park exhibition . . . San Jose's five-man bowling team -- Ora Forman, Charles Behr, Cyril McGraw, J. B. Konz, "Dad" Meek -- finishes eighth in American Bowling Congress tournament in Chicago . . . COP loses to Fresno State, 32-21, to drop CCC hoops title series in three straight . . . San Jose High (14-5) falls to Berkeley, 28-13, in NCS hoops final . . . With Ernie Nevers as top starting pitcher, Stanford (14-10) has first winning season since 1919 . . . San Jose High finishes second in NCS track competition, takes PAL meet with Aylett Sparks setting 880 record in 2:03 1/5 . . . Russell Hinaga strikes out eight as San Jose Asahi nine whips touring Meiji University of Japan, 6-3 . . . Outfielder Tommy Randazzo leads SCU baseball team with .455 average in dozen games . . . Cyclist Charlie Barclay finishes first in 116.8-mile Olympic preliminary race from San Jose to Tracy and back in 6:41:00. Illness prevents him from competing in Olympic final trials . . . Kenneth "Slim" Wright goes 6-2, strikes out 99 for Santa Clara Prep (9-2) . . . Ila Wilcox leads unbeaten Santa Clara High girl's tennis team to PAL title, teams with Henry Willard to snare county mixed doubles title . . . Stanford Olympic Games medalists: Al White wins gold in springboard, platform diving, Glenn "Tiny" Hartranft silver in shot put, Arthur Austin, Elmer Collett, Reggie Harrison bronze in water polo . . . PAL girl's track title goes to San Jose High . . . San Mateo High girls down Santa Clara for PAL baseball pennant, 15-11 . . . Hal Overfelt, Vivian Arnerich win San Jose tennis singles . . . San Jose's Adolph Giusti speeds to 15-lap win at Fairgrounds Speedway, breaks shoulder, hip in crash six weeks later when 18,000 turn out to watch national racing star Ralph De Palma take four firsts in his straight-eight Miller Special . . . Helen Wills turns tables on Phil Neer for 1923 defeat, takes tennis exhibition, 6-4 . . . George "Red" Earl wins Michigan amateur cycling crown . . . Palo Alto (5-2-0) loses to San Mateo for PAL grid title, 34-14 . . . Mountain View High's chance for league grid crown ends in 14-6 loss to South San Francisco . . . Stanford tennis team returns from Australia with 9-3 record . . . Harry Lawless nets 16 as San Jose Teachers top Hollister, 49-8 . . . Palo Alto High nips San Jose in basketball, 29-27.

■ 1925 ■

SCU halfback Jimmie Needles, Stanford backs Scotchy Campbell, Norm Cleaveland, Jack Patrick, tackle Harry Shipke play in first East-West Shrine football game at San Francisco's Ewing Field. West wins, 6-0 . . . Promoter Ora Forman brings high class boxing to San Jose under new state boxing law allowing 10-round bouts. Matches formerly limited to four rounds . . . Ed "Strangler" Lewis loses world heavyweight wrestling title to Wayne "Big" Munn . . . Defense-minded Stanford basketball team, coached by Andy Kerr, fashions 10-3 record averaging 20 points while giving up only 15-a-game . . . Stanford plans 25,000-seat enlargement of football stadium . . . San Jose High falls to Contra Costa County champ Alhambra, 29-28, in overtime with Bob Riordan, Lester "Fat" Woods scoring 11 apiece . . . Stanford, San Jose Teachers College in 1-1 soccer draw . . . Palo Alto High quintet wins PAL crown . . . PCL's Portland Beavers hold spring training at Sodality Park . . . SCU, St. Mary's sign new peace treaty as old three-year pact expires . . . San Jose Teachers College quintet (18-3) takes third game from Fresno State, 17-14, to win CCC championship series . . . Santa Clara High girls down San Jose, 35-31, for PAL southern division volleyball crown, dump Sequoia for PAL title, 30-20 . . . Lanky San Jose High pitcher and future PCL home run king Arthur "Mike" Hunt strikes out 13, but loses to Santa Clara, 5-4 . . . Bernice Jordan singles to send Louise Blanchard home with winning run as San Jose High edges Santa Clara, 11-10, for PAL division crown . . . Portland nine beats San Jose Asahi, SCU, St. Mary's in exhibitions. Stanford relay team wins Big Meet's final event to nip Cal, 66 1/2 to 64 1/2 . . . Tiny Hartranft of Stanford sets world discus record of 157-1 5/8 . . . Henry Schmidt takes 100, 220, broad jump as San Jose High wins PAL meet . . . Stanford's Ernie Nevers hits home run in each game, pitches pair of victories over Cal . . . Live Oak High nine whips San Jose, 11-3, for PAL pennant, but forfeits crown when ineligible Acorn player is found . . . Montezuma School's Bill Hubbard throws 7-1 win over former San Jose High teammates . . . San Jose Teachers College takes second in final relay to win CCC track title by one-fifth point over Modesto JC . . . Los Altos Golf and Country Club opens . . . Hugo "Swede" Leistner of Stanford takes 120 hurdles in 14.6. Cardinals win NCAA for first time . . . San Jose High girls beat Campbell to win PAL baseball crown . . . Mike Hunt of San Jose High defeats Tamalpais pitcher Tony Freitas, 7-0, for NCS "B" division title. Freitas goes on to win 367 pro games as all-time best minor league southpaw . . . San Jose Asahi baseball team wins 12 of 18 games on three-month tour of Japan . . . Vivian Arnerich successfully defends city women's tennis title. J. J. Payne takes men's, junior's singles, Violet Miller tops junior girl's singles field . . . Carl Stevenson of San Jose wins U. S. one-mile junior swim on Russian River at Healdsburg . . . Hal Toso ends four years at SCU, earns 11 letters in football, basketball, baseball . . . San Jose Teachers College students select "Spartans" as team nickname . . . County tennis winners: Ernie Renzel, Ila Wilcox (singles); Henry Willard, Hal Overfelt; 16-year-old twins Ruth, Naomi Koehle (doubles) . . . "World's Greatest Bowler" Jimmy Smith beats all comers in six-game Dream Alleys exhibition . . . Palo Alto High's Nelson Smith scores on 75-yard run in 28-0 romp over San Jose . . . Three Stanford students lose future Big Game ticket rights after trying to scalp $5 ducats for $25 each on the San Francisco Stock Exchange . . . Santa Clara High (3-2-1) only grid team with winning record. Winless teams are Los Gatos (0-5-5), Gilroy (0-6-0), first year Fremont (0-2-2).

■ 1926 ■

Andy Kerr quits Stanford staff to become head football coach at Washington & Jefferson . . . Bob Fatjo scores 12 as Santa Clara Prep cagers down Serra Club, 27-8 . . . Back from riding indoors in the East, Red Earl of Garden City Wheelmen sets record cycling from San Jose to Oakland in 1:25:25.4 . . . Palo Alto High's Steve Payson hits 14 in 34-12 trouncing of San Jose . . . San Jose Winter League players each get $3.50 as share of baseball season's receipts. Leading batter Art Hunter (.538) given choice of spikes or glove at San Jose Hardware . . . PAL officials split high schools into Santa Clara, San Mateo county groups . . . Livermore Cowboys, with five McGlincey brothers in lineup including former Bronco, Jim, down SCU, 35-26. George Malley leads SCU with 11 . . . Crowd of 2,500 sees Tiger Johnny Cline decision Charley Long in 10-round main event at opening of Foreman's Arena in San Jose . . . Santa Clara Prep's Marv Owen goes five for five in 12-0 win over St. Ignatius . . . Floyd Hudson head pro at new Commercial Club golf course (renamed Hillview in 1927) on land now covered by Eastridge shopping center.

The 1925-26 Campbell High basketball team, from left, (back) coach Ralph Noddin, Harold Cramer, Art Sundquist, Leo Hedegard, Warren Eddleman, Pat Abanate, Peter Heingren; (front) Elbert Clark, Aldrich Kalas, Breck Reid, Richard Shelley, Swede Nelson.

Architect is Sam Whiting, who designed San Francisco's Olympic Club, Harding Park layouts . . . USC defeats Stanford in track for first time since 1912 . . . Stanford's Cranston Holman, U. S. junior tennis champ, bows to Bud Chandler of Cal, but Cardinal wins Big Match, 3-2 . . . Stanford captain Bill Richardson defeats ex-880 record-holder Elmer Boyden of Cal by four yards, cracks record with 1:53.8 before 20,000 Big Meet spectators . . . Palo Alto High takes PAL track meet . . . Jess Regli wins 100, 220, low hurdles shot put, discus, anchors winning relay team as San Jose Teachers College whips Sacramento JC . . . Palo Alto High's Warner Wilson wins 100 (in record 10.1), 220 as Vikes edge Berkeley, 27-26, for NCS track title . . . Mountain View High nine downs Half Moon Bay, 6-2, for PAL division crown. IAU title goes to Santa Clara High . . . Philip Niederaur, Wilbur Cox of San Jose High win NCS tennis doubles, finish second in state prep tourney . . . Jess Regli's 10.0 record 100 top mark in San Jose Teacher College's CCC track title win . . . Palo Alto High tops Mountain View, 4-1, for PAL baseball crown . . . Ted Miller (440), Bill Richardson (880), Chuck Harlow (javelin) set meet marks as Stanford takes PCC track and field . . . Theron Connett of San Jose wins three-mile bike race at Speedway . . . Stanford finishes second to USC in IC4A track meet . . . Bernice Cottrell wins city junior girl's tennis singles . . . Marion McCoy of San Jose clips 14.5 minutes off Red Earl's San Jose-Oakland cycling mark . . . Henry Willard takes Emery Abbott in five sets for San Jose singles title . . . San Jose Asahi opens its new baseball park with 8-5 loss to Stockton . . . Red Berti is San Jose cycle champ with wins in mile, five mile races . . . In unprecedented twin win, Wilbur Cox, Phil Niederaur take county junior, senior tennis doubles . . . Joe Stecher retains world heavyweight wrestling crown, beating Cowboy Jack Taylor at Forman's Arena . . . San Jose's Carl Stevenson captures Golden Gate, San Diego's Silver Gate swim races . . . Tom Work picks off Occidental pass, returns it record 95 yards in 19-0 Stanford win . . . PAL "B" Division champ Gilroy High gridders, undefeated (7-0-0), unscored upon, forfeit playoff to San Mateo, which wins state title . . . Four San Jose semi-pro football teams play round-robin winter schedule at San Jose State College field.

■ 1927 ■

Barbara Burnham of San Jose wins contest to name Los Gatos golf course, receiving lifetime membership at La Rinconada . . . San Jose Teachers College track star Jess Regli plays baseball to fulfill teacher training requirement . . . Earl Goodell goes for 20 as San Jose High obliterates Monterey cagers, 42-3 . . . Montezuma, undefeated two years, claims it has best small private school basketball team in state . . . Carroll & Bishop nine downs Consolidated Laundry, 4-2, for San Jose Winter League crown. Each player gets $175 for season . . . Santa Clara High undefeated champion of PAL "B" division hoops . . . Cook Sypher raps three hits as Stanford nine tips SCU, 9-5 . . . Palo Alto High takes PAL "A" division basketball playoff with 38-16 win over San Mateo, beats Santa Clara, 34-21, for league title behind Emile "Frenchy" LaCombe's 20 points. Vikes (16-4) fall to Dinuba in state hoops final, 19-14, as LaCombe drops in seven . . . Modesto JC downs San Jose Teachers College in deciding game of three-game CCC hoops playoff, 28-25 . . . San Jose twins Ruth, Naomi Koehle win county tennis titles in adult, junior doubles . . . Stanford downs Olympic Club as Bob King high jumps 6-6 1/4 . . . Palo Alto High's Harry Plymire takes

The 1929 San Jose Asahi team, from left, (back) Kay Miura, Tosh Takeda, Henry Tsuruda, Tosh Santo, George Ikeda, Nurmi Honda; (front) Handa, Chick Hinaga, Jim Uyemura, Jim Uyejo, Mike Yamada, Linc Tokunaga. They played at Asahi Park near Sixth and Younger streets.

state tennis singles . . . Shades of 1990s: SCU nine downs Cal, 21-11, in 3-hour, 20-minute contest . . . Triple winner Charles Kaster (both hurdles, high jump) leads San Jose Teachers College over Fresno State, 66-55 . . . PAL track title goes to Palo Alto High . . . Stanford track team whips USC, 75-56, before 15,000 . . . Abe Espinosa wins Northern California PGA golf at San Jose Country Club . . . Paul Yager takes 100, 220 as San Jose Teachers College nabs CCC track title . . . San Jose Teachers College (11-5) whips Sacramento JC, 3-2, for CCC baseball crown . . . Palo Alto High wins NCS baseball crown over Fort Bragg, 7-5 . . . Joe Haskins shoots 227 to capture first 54-hole county golf championship at San Jose Country Club . . . Wilbur Cox pairs with Cecil Moellering to take county junior tennis doubles, then beats partner for singles crown. Ruth Koehle tops twin sister, Naomi, for junior girl's title, but Naomi decisions sibling in county tournament . . . Carl Stevenson (San Jose High, Stanford) wins San Diego Silver Gate swim, but fails to defend 1925, 1926 titles in one-mile race at Healdsburg . . . Fleishhacker Swim Club flash Gloria Scigliano moves to San Jose, wins 50-yard freestyle at Del Monte, 440, 880 ocean swims at Santa Cruz . . . Jim Leddy of San Jose is state junior cycling champ, finishes fourth in nationals . . . Oakland Oaks whip Consolidated Laundry, 7-2, but PCL pitching no mystery for Peeney Oliver, who rips four hits with pair of doubles . . . Gene Arnold's 90-yard fumble recovery TD earns San Jose High (0-5-1) 6-6 tie with Sequoia . . . Babe Ruth wallops Sodality Park homer as "Bustin' Babes" beat Lou Gehrig's "Larrapin' Lous," 15-3 . . . Stanford coach Pop Warner thinks so little of SCU he spends day scouting Cal. Broncos score 13-6 upset . . . Clarence Dirks (Palo Alto) is Washington football captain . . . San Jose Teachers College football shows signs of life (4-5-0) with first four-win season since 1899.

■ 1928 ■

Jack Gough of SCU hits 18 in 40-29 loss to YMI . . . Grid star Red Grange at PAL awards ceremony at San Jose High, hands MVP gold footballs to Edward Riley (San Jose), Norm Weller (Palo Alto) . . . California State League organizes with San Jose as one of eight semi-pro baseball clubs . . . Palo Alto, Sequoia Highs briefly refuse to meet San Mateo, Burlingame in dispute over reports northern schools recruit players . . . PAL champ Palo Alto High (13-3) loses Nor Cal basketball crown to Stockton, 23-20 . . . San Jose Teachers College, whose 16-game win streak fell nine days earlier to Chico State, gains revenge with 29-28 victory for CCC basketball title behind Hal Hawley's 12 points . . . Roland King hits home run, strikes out 10 for San Jose High in 6-0 win over Palo Alto . . . Speedway fans angry as Barney Klopfer wins $1,000 first place money in 400-lap auto race that ends after only 250 laps . . . Stanford wins first PCC men's tennis championship . . . Gordon Graves takes 220 freestyle in 2:52 as San Jose High downs Sequoia . . . NCAA tennis doubles winners are Ralph McElvenny, Alan Herrington of Stanford . . . Chick Boysol wins shot put, high hurdles, sets discus mark at 127-5 as San Jose tops PAL field. Boysol later wins NCS discus . . . Jess Regli gets four hits, scores four runs as San Jose Teachers College defeats Modesto JC for CCC crown, 17-7 . . . PAL champion San Jose High (17-5) wins NCS baseball pennant against Tamalpais, 5-3 . . . Stanford wins NCAA track and field championship . . . Palo Alto High swimmers dominate NCS . . . Phil Niederaur of San Jose Teachers College wins CCC singles . . . Ralph Hoffman takes county golf . . . Stanford's Bob King captures Olympic Games high jump at 6-4 3/8 . . . San Jose High coach Bill Martin runs first football training camp two weeks before school opens in fall . . . Gloria Scigliano wins Santa Cruz ocean swim mile, 100 freestyle races . . . San Jose's Les Driesbach captures 15-lap motorcycle race at Speedway . . . Red Berti (senior), William Creamer (junior) win state bicycle championships. Creamer, a Roosevelt Junior High student, finishes second in nationals . . . County junior girl's tennis titles go to Claire Coolidge of Santa Clara High, who wins singles, pairs with Jean Hawley in doubles . . . Tackle George Norton picks up fumble, runs 80 yards for touchdown in San Jose High's 12-0 win over Watsonville . . . Mountain View, Fremont, Gilroy, Los Gatos, Santa Clara form Santa Clara Valley Athletic League.

Mountain View beats Los Gatos, 27-0, in playoff for league title . . . SCU's George Barsi reaches end zone twice in Broncos' 33-0 win over St. Ignatius . . . San Jose Teachers College football fans celebrate first winning season (5-2-1) of 20th Century . . . San Jose Teachers College quits CCC, joins tougher Far West Conference.

■ 1929 ■

Middleweight contender Jack Malone decisions Tom Pratt in San Jose 10-rounder . . . Joe Milia's 14 points leads San Jose High in 37-9 hoops trouncing of San Mateo . . . SCU whips Cal, 32-26, as Tom Connelly contributes 16 . . . Al Nelson topples Dream Alleys six-game record 1,316 pins in annual Mercury-Herald bowling tourney . . . Soph Marshall Leahy leads way with eight as SCU breaks St. Ignatius' 15-game hoops win streak, 26-13 . . . Palo Alto High nine forfeits game to San Jose because most of its players are involved in regional hoops play . . . SCU nine wins 10 in a row before tie with Cal . . . Woolworth's, Telephone Co., Secretarial School, Blum's back women's industrial basketball squads in San Jose . . . Tom Maloney high with 22 points as San Jose Teachers College downs Chico State, 33-32, in overtime in deciding game of CCC playoffs. . . San Jose High slugger Ray Peterson hits home runs in three straight games . . . Stanford swimmers win first of five straight conference crowns . . . Stanford's Eric Krenz unleashes world record discus throw of 163-8 . . . Palo Alto's Harry Plymire ranks fifth in U. S. among tennis juniors . . . Bill Hubbard wins 100, 440 as San Jose Teachers College takes meet at Sacramento JC dedicating new $200,000 Hughes Stadium, later sets 440 record (49.5) in conference meet . . . San Jose High wins Mission Relays at San Francisco's Kezar Stadium as Fred Saunders hurls discus 120-3 . . . Renauldo Wren wins broad jump, 100 (meet record-tying 10.1), as San Jose High takes PAL track . . . Santa Clara High beats Mountain View, 12-4, behind pitcher Dick "Lefty" Freitas' 14 Ks . . . Ward Edmonds pole vaults 13 feet, highlight of Stanford's record win over Cal . . . Stanford takes IC4A track title for third straight year . . . Ernie Pieper wins county, state junior golf titles . . . Gordon Graves of San Jose High captures 100, 220 freestyle, 50 backstroke against Sequoia . . . Gilroy High wins relay to edge Mountain View for league track title . . . Red Berti of San Jose wins 85-mile cycle race over King's Mountain in San Mateo County . . . Lucille McCann, John Gordon take city junior singles . . . Bill Nilli, Al Bariteau capture San Jose handball doubles . . . Wilbur Cox takes city, county tennis singles, pairs with Phil Niederaur in both tourneys for doubles wins . . . Los Altos assistant pro Ben Coltrin wins Northern California PGA golf . . . San Jose Bees' owner Sam Battaglia fined $25, banned from attending games after assaulting umpire . . . J. C., Bud, Alice Speegle win Alviso speedboat races in benefit for racer killed earlier in year . . . Ed Sabatte bowls 1,250 in Mercury-Herald sweepstakes tournament. Prize is sparkling new 1929 Ford sedan . . . Henry Schmidt (San Jose) named SCU trainer . . . Peeney Oliver celebrates "day" with three hits, three steals in 19-0 San Jose Bees romp over Modesto. Fans give $200 to team's most popular player . . . Ruth, Naomi Koehl top teenagers Alice Marble, Ida Cross for San Jose-All Comers tennis doubles crown . . . Bill Bratte scores four TDs as Mountain View High trounces Los Gatos for SCVAL title, 28-0.

The 1930s

College football was king of the county sports scene in the 1930s. Stanford and Santa Clara University entertained fans with five bowl teams and by the end of the decade San Jose State's high-scoring, but defensive-minded teams were among the nation's best small colleges.

The Indians went to the Rose Bowl as Pacific Coast Conference champions from 1933 through 1935. The 1937 and 1938 Broncos took a pair of Sugar Bowls and the Spartans won 46 games between 1937 and 1940 while giving up fewer than five points per game.

When USC beat Stanford, 13-0, in 1932, members of the Indians' freshman team declared they would never lose to the Trojans. True to their word, the "Vow Boys" took the first of three straight over USC in 1933 and rolled into the Rose Bowl the following January with an 8-1-1 record.

Behind a line boasting Bob Reynolds -- who played every minute in three bowl games -- Keith Topping, Bill Corbus and Monk Moscrip, the Indians out gained Columbia 272 yards to 104, with future All-America Bobby Grayson racking up 152. But Columbia won, 7-0, on a hidden ball play known as KF-79.

Back in Pasadena on Jan. 1, 1935, Stanford (9-0-1) fell to unbeaten Alabama, 27-13, with future Green Bay Packers' star Don Hutson catching six passes for 164 yards and two scores. The "Vow Boys" ended the bowl jinx a year later by winning a defensive struggle against SMU, 7-0.

The Associated Press instituted rankings in 1936 and Santa Clara finished in the top 20 in five of seven seasons before World War II. Ranked sixth in the poll's first season, the Broncos joined the bowl parade on Jan. 1, 1937.

Coach Buck Shaw's team had won seven of eight games, losing only to TCU, 9-0, when the Horned Frogs' Sammy Baugh kept SCU deep in its own territory with his booming punts. SCU topped No. 2 LSU in the Sugar Bowl, 21-14. Nello Falaschi, an outstanding signal caller and blocking back, and center Phil Dougherty became the first Broncos to achieve first team All-America honors.

Santa Clara won nine straight and set an NCAA record the following year by holding opponents to 69.9 yards per game rushing. The defense surrendered only one touchdown (to Stanford) and the team was tied with Notre Dame for No. 9 in the AP poll on the eve of the Sugar Bowl game. Santa Clara beat LSU, 6-0, to collect $38,033 in receipts.

There were no national polls or bowl games for small colleges in the 1930s, but if there had been, San Jose State would have been high on both lists.

Stanford grad Dud DeGroot arrived in 1932 to build a football program. It was a big job, considering the Spartans were 22-50-7 in the previous 11 years against high schools, junior colleges and other small colleges.

Santa Clara University football coaching staff (from left) Al Ruffo, Buck Shaw, Len Casanova.

DeGroot's first team went 7-0-2. To celebrate, the San Jose Elks Club sponsored a postseason contest matching the Spartans against Weber State. The locals won, 20-0, before a crowd of 3,000. The next four seasons produced break-even records as DeGroot dropped the JCs to schedule tougher opponents. SJS had its first great team in 1937, an 11-2-1 year, and followed with an 11-1-0 record marred only by a one-point loss to Hawaii in the last game.

The best Spartan eleven took the field in 1939 with tailback Leroy Zimmerman as its star and former Stanford mentor Glenn S. "Pop" Warner as an advisor. For the first time, the Spartans' prospects were reviewed by *Illustrated Football Annual*, whose on-the-money prediction was that San Jose State was ready, "to lick the schedule clean."

The Spartans did just that, ripping through 13 opponents without a loss, scoring 324 points and setting a small college defensive record by allowing only 71.3 total yards per game. Captain Ken Cook kicked six field goals, an NCAA record that wasn't surpassed for 20 years.

Zimmerman made Little All-American and became the first SJS player to gain full All-America honors when selector Paul Williamson picked him along with backs from Iowa, Texas A&M and Clemson. End Lloyd Thomas had been the first Spartan named Little All-American in 1938. Zimmerman played nine seasons in the NFL as a quarterback and punter and was picked on the 1944 United Press all-pro team. After football, he was an outstanding fast pitch

San Jose State football coach Dud DeGroot's 1939 team went 13-0-0 and featured All-America tailback Leroy Zimmerman (right).

softball pitcher who led teams to 10 world titles.

■ VICTORIOUS VIKINGS

Palo Alto High put together back-to-back North Coast Section basketball titles in 1928-29 and 1929-30 with a great team that won 33 straight games.

The 1929 Vikings (19-0) toppled Piedmont, 25-21, for the NCS crown, but had nowhere to go for further glory when the CIF dropped the state playoffs against the Southern California champion. Perennial PAL title holder Palo Alto also lost in the 1927 state finals to Dinuba.

In 1930, every member of the Vikings' starting five of Frenchy LaCombe, Wilho Erickson, Lloyd Sublett, Jack Misenhimer and Gordon MacLachlan was named to the all-PAL team by the *San Jose Mercury-Herald*. The *Palo Alto Times* left Misenhimer and MacLachlan off its all-star squad only because the players were mid-season graduates.

The league champion Vikings topped Burlingame in a PAL playoff and disposed of Pacific Grove, 35-12, before taking the NCS title from Berkeley, 33-16.

The team's biggest star, LaCombe, went on to letter in basketball at Stanford.

■ MARV OWEN

Marv Owen played baseball at Santa Clara University before going on to a long and distinguished career in professional baseball.

Named the most valuable player in his college league in 1929, the soft-spoken Owen was looking forward to being captain of the 1930 team. But, he made a grievous error before his senior year, agreeing in writing to join Seattle of the PCL, which had ties to the Detroit Tigers.

Owen had been assured his college eligibility wouldn't be jeopardized so long as he didn't actually sign a contract. When officials disagreed and barred him from playing in 1930, Owen coached the SCU team.

After graduation, Marv played with the Coast League team. Detroit shelled out $25,000 and two players in 1932 and he became the Tigers' third baseman for five years. He hit .317 in his best season in 1934, when he batted in 96 runs and later drove in 105 and batted .295.

Owen played with other American League teams until returning to the PCL with Portland in 1941. He became the Beavers' manager in 1944.

The following season, the Beavers won their first pennant since 1936 with Marv batting .311 with 40 doubles and 83 RBIs. Owen was hurt before the next season began and he was fired when the Beavers fell to last place.

Marv wasn't out of work long. The Red Sox added a

Stanford "Vow Boys" Rose Bowl heroes (from left) Monk Moscrip, Bobby Grayson, Bones Hamilton.

Hal Rhyne (left) and Marv Owen were great fielders. Rhyne topped PCL third basemen a record three times in fielding average and headed the American League once. Owen was an outstanding major leaguer and has the PCL fielding mark for third basemen.

San Jose farm club in the California League and Owen was its manager. The team finished in the first division four of five years before he retired and became a Detroit scout.

■ UNLOVED CUP

In 1909, New York Giants teammates gave a beautiful silver loving cup to Hal Chase, who they regarded as "the greatest first baseman of all time." Chase fell on hard times after leaving baseball and played outlaw baseball in Arizona for several years.

CHASE, N. Y. AMER.

The state of Chase's financial distress was revealed in September, 1931, when a newspaper learned that Chase had pawned the cup in Los Angeles the previous February. Photos of the cup and the pawn ticket were used in many newspapers, including the *San Jose Mercury-Herald*. Chase had received $35 for the cup, signing the pawn ticket under the pseudonym, "H. Charles," but listing his home town correctly as Douglas, Arizona.

The pawn dealer said the loving cup -- pictured on a 1910 tobacco card being held by Chase -- was not for sale.

■ SPLITSVILLE

Bellarmine Prep and San Jose High ended their football relationship forever in 1931 in a dispute over the eligibility of one of the Bells' players.

The schools met for the first time on the gridiron in 1930 in a greatly-hyped contest billed as a game for the "city championship." More than 3,500 spectators packed Reed Field to watch the Bulldogs take a hard-fought contest, 12-6, on Al Sievers' two touchdown runs.

In 1931, the teams played for a trophy donated by the Victory Theater and Roos Brothers, a major Northern California men's clothing store chain. Sam Lima's three-yard run and a conversion gave San Jose another win, 7-6.

San Jose officials protested the use of quarterback Joe Sullivan, who was removed from the game after San Jose threatened to take its team off the field. San Jose principal Raymond B. Leland contended Sullivan was a ninth semester student and ineligible to play under state rules. However, other CIF officials disagreed.

The teams never met again on the gridiron and severed athletic ties in all sports until 1949, when San Jose stopped the Bells in basketball, 39-31.

■ THREE FOR THE CROWD

Although the Great Depression meant tough economic times, three major sports facilities -- a football stadium, a downtown auditorium and an outdoor velodrome -- all were built in San Jose in the 1930s.

San Jose State's football program got a boost in 1933, when the team moved into Spartan Stadium at Seventh and Alma streets, just south of Phelan Field, where the Spartans formerly played their home games.

The new stadium was created at a cost of $20,000 by excavating a large hole 14 feet deep and pushing the dirt into 50-foot high mounds on either side of the field. Seating was on wooden benches.

The first game was played on Oct. 7. The Spartans, with halfback Ray Arjo running for two scores and passing to Wesley "Bud" Hubbard for a third touchdown, crushed San Francisco State, 44-0.

A week later, SJS entertained 8,000 fans with a 12-6 win over College of the Pacific in the game that formerly dedicated their new home. The winning score came with three minutes to go. John Hines passed to Arjo, who was supposed to lateral to a teammate. When he couldn't spot the other player, Arjo ran 25 yards to score.

The initial night game was played on Sept. 20, 1937. Morris Manoogian had the first score under the lights on a 38-yard run as the Spartans demolished Idaho, 59-0, before 10,000 spectators. SJS piled up 421 yards while holding the Vandals to minus 30.

These photographs show Spartan Stadium shortly after it opened in 1933. Since only eight Spartans are lined up at the right, the picture on the left probably was taken after the kickoff.

The stadium's capacity was expanded from 12,500 to 17,000 in 1948 and to more than 31,000 in the 1980s.

The next important home for sporting events was San Jose Civic Auditorium, which opened in April, 1936. No venue in the county has provided a wider variety of sports attractions, over a longer period of time than the Aud. The popular building has been a home to basketball, boxing, roller derby, wrestling, tennis and volleyball. San Jose State and Santa Clara University basketball teams called it home before their present on-campus facilities were built.

The first attempt to finance a multi-use auditorium was mounted in 1921, but city voters rejected a $500,000 bond issue. Another bond measure for $750,000 lost in 1926.

In 1933, T. S. Montgomery and his wife donated the site at Market and San Carlos streets. The PWA, a federal depression era agency set up to create jobs, added $117,000 for the project and in February, 1934, San Jose voters approved $375,000 in bonds.

Cyclists were thrilled when Burbank Velodrome opened in May, 1936, on a former spinach field at Olive and Wabash streets now the site of Lincoln High School's football field. The 3,500-seat facility, officially known as the Garden City Velodrome, was built with federal financial aid.

Martin Deras and Sammy Rinella won the first one-hour team event and Bobby Echeverria sped one lap in 12.8 seconds on the day the first races were held at the $25,000, one-eighth mile oval board track.

Enthusiastic crowds packed the stands to watch the weekly competition in six to a dozen races. By 1937, Burbank residents began to complain about noise from spectators and occasional motorcycles races.

Later they demanded school officials eliminate the velodrome, calling it a public nuisance and a hindrance to area development. The track was torn down after the 1941 season to make way for construction of Lincoln High in 1942.

■ CAN YOU SPARE A DIME? (PART I)

Times were tough in 1932, when San Jose cyclist Red Berti qualified for a place on the USA pursuit team at the Olympic Games in Los Angeles.

Other athletes were housed at the Olympic Village, but pursuit team members were on their own after the U. S. Olympic Committee exhausted its $450,000 fund.

A *San Jose Mercury-Herald* editorial pleaded with business men and cycling fans to contribute between $75 and $100 to cover Berti's expenses. The newspaper put it in practical terms, saying the city, "stands to cash in on the glory, prestige and publicity of its home-town boy who's making good in the fastest company in the world."

Starting off the fund with its own $15 contribution, the paper asked for donations of "any amount, from a penny up." Within a day, readers had sent in $116.

There was no happy ending to the story. The USA team was eliminated early in the competition.

■ CAN YOU SPARE A DIME? (PART II)

When Fresno State's track and field team visited San Jose State in 1934, they brought along Walter Marty, who had set a world record in the high jump at 6-8 5/8.

On the chance that he might do it again, Spartan officials asked the AAU what they had to do to obtain certification if Marty set another world mark.

To his dismay, track coach Erwin Blesh learned the school had to pay for the attendance of four AAU officials plus a surveyor or civil engineer to take measurements. SJS was required to publish an official program for the event and the high jump standards had to meet detailed requirements that meant extensive work on the high jump pit, bar and standards. SJS spent $50 -- no small change in the depths of the Great Depression -- to meet the requirements.

Marty won the meet with a jump of 6-6, but knocked off the bar when he attempted a record height of 6-9.

■ ON THE ROAD AGAIN

Back in the days before local colleges rarely traveled outside of California, Stanford coach John Bunn took his Stanford basketball teams on a pair of ambitious road trips.

In the 1932-33 season, the Indians (9-18) didn't rest during Christmas vacation, but boarded the train for a two-week swing through the Rocky Mountains and Midwest that saw them win three and lose eight against teams in Nevada, Utah, Colorado, Kansas, Nebraska and Wyoming.

Bunn wasn't disappointed with the results, and two seasons later the Indians went on another extended excursion. Stanford was off to an 0-1 start with an upset 28-25 loss to San Jose State as the dozen varsity players boarded the train Dec. 19 for the trip that would cover nearly 3,000 miles and put them on the court 10 times in 16 days.

The Indians traveled to Ogden, where they split a pair

Russell Hinaga (above) won a 3-2 victory over the Tokyo Giants, shown as they arrived for their 1935 tour of the United States.

of games with Utah. They were scheduled to play Rocky Mountain Conference champion BYU on Dec. 22, but the game was snowed out so the Indians hopped on a Pullman and moved on to Kansas City. White Eagle Oil Co., a fast AAU team, pinned a 19-point loss on the Indians. More defeats came against Notre Dame, Michigan State, Marquette and Iowa.

After catching their collective breath on New Year's Day, Stanford went to Omaha, where it beat Nebraska and split with Creighton to close out the trip with a 3-7 record. The Indians ended the year 10-17, not counting wins over San Jose YMCA and the USS Tennessee, which don't appear on the university's official record.

■ GOOD MORNING SUN

Japanese-American teams played baseball in San Jose for a half century, but no game achieved greater significance than a contest against the Tokyo Giants.

The Giants, composed of many of Japan's best players, toured America in 1935. Fans who jammed Asahi Park near N. Seventh and Younger streets for the March game weren't disappointed as pitcher Russell Hinaga drove in the winning run in the ninth inning for a 3-2 victory. Noted white Russian pitcher Victor Starfin struck out 13 for the losers.

The Asahi, whose name comes from the Japanese words for morning sun, was the most successful of local Japanese-American teams that began playing in 1903.

In 1924, they won 12 of 18 games on a three-month tour of Japan and returned home to continue their success against other Japanese-American teams in California. After World War II, a new team called the Zebras was organized and played in Japanese-American and Caucasian leagues until it disbanded in 1963.

■ BULLDOGS ON THE PROWL

San Jose High's best football teams won all 10 games in 1936 and nine more the following season before tasting defeat in the final game of the 1937 season.

The star of both of Coach Walt Williams' clubs was Pete Kmetovic, an elusive single-wing tailback with sprinter speed who later starred at Stanford. Other top Bulldog players included back Chuck Taylor, who played guard, coached football and was athletic director at Stanford, and tackle Willis Boyarsky, who starred at COP.

The Bulldogs had won their last game in 1935, so the win streak grew to 20 games before Eureka snapped it with a narrow 14-7 win on a muddy field in November, 1937. San Jose had four one-touchdown shutouts in 1936, outscoring its opponents 147-25, with Kmetovic accounting for 11 TDs, several on runs of 55 to 92 yards.

The 1937 team dominated the opposition, giving up touchdowns to only Salinas and PAL opponent Burlingame in taking their second straight league title. They defeated Berkeley, 28-20, before losing to Eureka. Kmetovic passed for several scores and tallied 10 TDs on runs as long as 90 yards to lead all California preps in scoring with a total of 60 points.

■ THE GREATEST OF THEM ALL

No local player dominated his game to the same extent as Stanford basketball legend Angelo "Hank" Luisetti, who is known to historians as the game's first "modern" player and the best-known pioneer of the one-handed shot.

When Luisetti began playing at San Francisco's Galileo High, basketball's primary offensive weapons were the layup and the two-handed set shot. Luisetti didn't invent the one-hander that's become a staple of every player's repertoire today, but his outstanding play at Stanford from 1936 through 1938 popularized it.

Even as a slender 6-foot-2 freshman, Luisetti was a great shooter, superb passer and tremendous jumper. He averaged a remarkable 20 points a game with the frosh and moved to the varsity in 1935-36, joining a team that would win three straight Pacific Coast Conference titles.

In his first varsity game, he made all nine shots and the Indians were off to a best ever 22-7 record as Hank scored a school record 416 points. Stanford beat Northern Division champion Washington twice for the PCC title with Luisetti pouring in 32 and 21 points.

Stanford won 25 of 27 games in 1936-37. During a seven-game Eastern tour, the Indians took Madison Square Garden by storm, beating Long Island University, 45-31, to snap the Blackbirds' national record 43-game win streak. The fans were amazed as Luisetti dribbled and passed behind his back, appeared to shoot without glancing at the basket and faked out defenders with his quick moves.

On another tour a year later, Stanford won a pair at the Garden and went to Cleveland for the game of Luisetti's life. The Indians drubbed Duquesne, 92-27, as Hank scored a national record 50 points.

Hank wound up his career with 1,596 points to set a national four-year standard. He established other Stanford records with 465 points for the year and 232 in the conference as a senior. Stanford retired his Number 7 after Luisetti made the All-America team for the third straight season and was chosen player of the year twice.

With no pro basketball league available after graduation, Luisetti lost his amateur standing when he signed a $7,500 contract with Paramount Pictures to make a movie, "College Confidential." Luisetti was reinstated in 1940 and starred for the San Francisco Olympic Club until World War II. Luisetti and Santa Clara University's Ralph "Toddy" Giannini led the club in the 1941 national AAU tournament, losing to 20th Century Fox of Hollywood in the title game, 47-34. Both were AAU All-Americans.

Luisetti was one of first four players inducted into the National Basketball Hall of Fame in 1959.

■ SAN JOSE SPEEDWAY

Fire destroyed the 5,000-seat grandstand at San Jose Speedway in early August, 1939, just 30 minutes after a Sunday auto racing crowd of 1,000 had departed.

California's first dirt auto racing track had been built near Alum Rock and King roads in 1927 at a cost of $10,000 by San Jose realtor Bart Logan and San Franciscan Henry Vowinkle.

At first, they promoted racing under the auspices of the American Automobile Association. In the early 1930s, they began leasing the track to free-lance promoters who brought in many top racing drivers, including Babe Stapp, "Wild Bill" Campbell, Stubby Stubblefield and Ernie Triplett.

The eight-acre property later became the site of the area's first ice skating rink. In the late 1940s, a new speedway was located at another East San Jose site near Reid-Hillview Airport.

■ FOR THE RECORD

The fastest pro wrestling pin recorded in San Jose took place in 1931 when Red Thomas stopped Dick Raines in seven seconds in the final fall at Forman's Arena.

San Jose's Hoover Junior High cagers shut out Burnett Junior High, 1-0, on a free throw by Hartman in 1932.

Season leader Ambrose Alves scored all of Santa Clara High's points on six field goals and a free throw in a 1932 double overtime, 13-11, basketball win over Live Oak.

Hank Luisetti, Stanford's hoops scoring king.

In 1932, Ben Eastman of Stanford set a 440 record of 46.4 and followed with a 1:51.3 in the 880 a week later. After being bed-ridden with a sinus infection, Eastman took the Olympic silver medal in the 400 meters at Los Angeles.

Hal Rhyne (San Jose) tied a Pacific Coast League record in 1936 by leading all shortstops in fielding for the third time in his career in the league. He also topped American League shortstops with the glove once during his 18-year pro career.

Lowell Todd became San Jose State's first NCAA title winner in 1937 with a javelin toss of 214-9 3/8.

Bob Fontaine (Bellarmine) fanned eight batters in three innings, Johnny Nelson (San Jose) added 17 more for a combined county record of 25 strikeouts as Turner Plumbing downed Sunnyside Market, 15-2, in 1939.

Campbell High, which had posted only six points the year before in an 0-5-1 football season, failed to score at all while losing seven games in 1939. The streak grew to 10 before the team scored in its second game in 1940.

■ IN OTHER FIELDS

1930s San Jose football linemen included future county supervisors Wesley "Bud" Hubbard and Ed Levin at San Jose State and Sam Della Maggiore at San Jose High. Spartan guard Bart Collins was San Jose's chief of detectives for many years. Football linemen at SCU included A. P. "Dutch" Hamann, later San Jose's influential city manager, and Emery Delmas, an attorney and San Jose councilman.

Ray Blackmore, long time San Jose police chief, was a capable amateur and semi-pro catcher in the 1920s and

1930s. Amateur golf champ Don Edwards of Stanford had a long career as a congressman from San Jose and star SCU basketball center Ed Nelson became a Superior Court judge.

■ IN PASSING

Eric Krenz, 25, Stanford's record-setting discus man, drowned in 1931 at Lake Tahoe while trying to save a child.

In 1931, Lester "Fat" Woods, the only San Jose High basketball player to make all-PAL twice in the mid-1920s, died of tuberculosis in Banning.

Champion cyclist and trainer Johnny Berryessa, 52, died of kidney disease in 1936. He was among the nation's top riders until 1915, when one kidney was removed. Later, he trained many of the area's top riders.

Gordon Graves, 21, San Jose High and Stanford water polo captain and swimmer, died of a ruptured appendix in San Francisco in 1935.

■ TRIVIAL PURSUITS

San Jose State pitcher Dario "Si" Simoni, who was 18-0 from 1932 through 1934, said his proudest moment was when he struck out future Hall of Fame outfielder Chick Hafey twice in a local game against a pro all-star team after Hafey won the National League batting title.

Santa Clara University was the county's first team to appear in a postseason game that wasn't sanctioned by the NCAA. The Broncos beat Hawaii, 26-7, on New Year's Day, 1934. Stanford was the only other team to appear in such a game, trouncing Hawaii, 74-20, on Jan. 2, 1950.

Jackie Coogan, 1920s child movie star who later played Uncle Fester on TV's "The Addams Family," was a member of Santa Clara University's 1934 golf team.

Water polo player Wally O'Connor of Stanford carried the American flag during opening ceremonies in the 1936 Olympic Games at Berlin.

■ 1930 ■

Future welterweight boxing champ Young Corbett III defeats San Jose's Babe Anderson in Forman's Arena 10-rounder . . . $125,000 Stanford University golf course opens with grad Gary Bennett as "director of golf" rather than head pro . . . Justin Fitzgerald resigns as SCU head baseball coach in wake of eligibility scandal . . . Undefeated All-USA women's field hockey team downs San Jose Teachers College, 15-0, on West Coast tour . . . Jack Gough scores on long shot with three seconds left as SCU tips Cal, 33-31 . . . With only four players eligible, San Jose High forfeits hoops game to Palo Alto . . . Stanford's Richard Stevenson stops USC's Bud Thompson, 1-up, after 36 holes for Pacific Coast college crown . . . Former major leaguer Bill Cunningham replaces Paddy Siglin as San Jose Bees manager . . . Bellarmine crushes Santa Clara High, 19-2, holding Panthers to single basket by Ambrose Alves . . . Milt Axt drives in both runs as SCU shuts out Stanford, 2-0, behind pitcher Bob Gaddy, who later signs with Seattle of PCL, hits .264 in 37 games in outfield . . . Campbell High's 16-15 win over Fremont clinches SCVAL hoops title . . . Tim Connolly's 16 paces SCU (15-5) to 34-25 win over St. Mary's in last game . . . San Jose Bees mascot Frankie Battaglia inks contract, but outfielder Peeney Oliver holds out for more cash . . . Stanford student body leaders adopt Indian as school's athletic mascot . . . Santa Clara High's Lefty Freitas fashions consecutive no-hitters over Los Gatos, Live Oak, fans 20 Fremont batters, signs with Seattle . . . USC wins state meet at Stanford, but Indians' Eric Krenz raises discus world record to 167-5 3/8 . . . Harlow Rothert of Stanford wins third NCAA shot put crown with 51-1 3/4 heave . . . Mountain View High nabs SCVAL track title. Attilio Manfredi tosses discus 115-8 . . . It takes five extra holes before Jim Rea of San Jose wins county golf over Ward Dwight . . . Mary Callender of San Jose defeats Gracyn Wieler of Los Angeles for California under-16 tennis title . . . Ex-Cincinnati Reds player Sammy Bohne bats in winning run with triple as San Jose Bees defeat Santa Cruz, 7-6, to knot CSL first half standings. Bees win title playoff . . . Record 4,000 fans jam Forman's Arena when ex-heavyweight king Jack Dempsey referees main event . . . Former Garden City Wheelman Norman Hall finishes in money in 11 straight Eastern pro races to earn $1,000 . . . San Jose's Les Driesbach races to 10-lap motorcycle victory at Speedway . . . Cocky O'Brien wins city senior cycling crown. R. Gorman, Bobby Echeverria tie for junior title . . . Ernie Pieper cops state junior golf over A. S. "Slim" Dreier, 5 and 3 . . . Ora Forman opens Garden City Recreation, $60,000 bowling, boxing emporium in downtown San Jose . . . Led by A. R. Bodenschatz, Frank Laine with 191 each, Mountain View Rifle Club wins third straight National Rifle Association title in postal contest . . . Ex-Stanford tennis star Johnny Doeg teams with George Lott to win U. S. doubles . . . San Jose's Babe Stapp eighth in Italian Grand Prix auto race . . . County tennis singles titles go to Harry Plymire (men), Naomi Koehle (women), Lucille McCann (junior girls) . . . Sid Bastian's 70-yard punt return TD gives San Jose High 7-0 win over Lodi . . . Los Gatos High's Jack Anti scores twice, passes for another TD as Wildcats humble Fremont, 26-0 . . . Jimmy Mills of Garden City Billiards is second in Western tourney at Hollywood . . . Santa Clara High forfeits 27-0 win over Los Gatos for using ineligible player . . . Ray Fellows has three TDs, including 90-yarder, as Mountain View beats Los Gatos, 19-0, for SCVAL crown.

■ 1931 ■

Phelan Field tennis courts replace those lost when Hotel Vendome is torn down . . . Jim Arnerich is double digit hoops scoring star for San Jose High . . . Mrs. Brent Potter of San Jose wins first Northern California women's golf crown at Mount Diablo Club, later takes Northwest title with win in Tacoma . . . Tom Aitken scores 13 as Palo Alto High cagers topple San Jose, 29-19 . . . Scoring king Earl Goodell leads San Jose Teachers College (14-3) to Far West Conference basketball title, joins Don Kerchan on all-conference squad . . . SCVAL hoops champion Los Gatos High defeats Gilroy, 26-11 . . . Jimmy Nicholas drops in 12 as SCU's best-ever quintet downs USF after police stop players' fight on floor . . . Vince Philippi's three-run homer in last of ninth gives Stanford 8-7 win over Santa Clara in first game played at $25,000 Sunken Diamond. Indians (18-5) tie USC for first PCC baseball crown, win CIBA outright . . . Fred Hauck has record 757 series at Jose Bowl . . . Alameda High beats San Jose in track meet, but Chad Ralston runs 120 high hurdles in record 16.0 . . . Don Edwards of San Jose High registers rounds of 76-78-154 at San Jose Country Club to take first county junior golf tourney, later falls by one stroke to Ernie Pieper for county title . . . Jack Wool of San Jose Teachers College pole vaults 13-0 in win against COP . . . Nino Bongiovanni goes five for five as Santa Clara High drops Live

Oak for SCVAL baseball crown, 19-0 . . . PAL baseball pennant belongs to San Jose High . . . Stanford's Hec Dyer defeats USC's Frank Wykoff in 220 in 21.3 . . . Stanford mile relay team clocks record 3:12.6 at Fresno . . . Centerville High, coached by ex-San Jose Teachers College star Jess Regli, whips San Jose nine, 9-5, for NCS title . . . NCAA tennis singles title goes to Stanford's Keith Gledhill . . . San Jose High wins PAL track crown over Palo Alto, whose athletes compete in underwear after track suits stolen . . . Bespectacled Ben Eastman of Stanford races to world record 47.4 quarter mile . . . Larry Hall downs Harry Plymire in county singles tennis final . . . Ernie Basquez of Garden City Wheelmen wins Palo Alto to Santa Cruz road race by seven seconds over Cocky O'Brien, who is delayed by flat tire . . . Cracking SCVAL records in six field events, Mountain View High wins league track and field crown . . . Ruth Koehle succeeds twin sister, Naomi, as county women's singles tennis champ . . . San Jose High foursome of Bill Eakin, Don Edwards, Bobby Richardson, Henry Duino score 337 to beat Jefferson by three strokes in PAL golf tourney . . . Palo Alto High's Henry Goodman leads way with wins in 50, 100 freestyle as school takes PAL swim championship . . . Century Road Club's Pat McDonough takes 23-mile Fiesta de las Rosas race . . . Bruce Risley of San Jose wins 25-mile Sunnyvale dirigible base (later Moffett Field) cycle race in 1:08:05 . . . Portland baseball club officials learn Sodality Park will be torn down after 1932 so Southern Pacific Co. can reroute rail line across land . . . San Jose's Oyster Loaf team -- Frank Arnerich, Ora Forman, George Mitchell, Delmar Dooley, Cyril McGraw -- wins Pacific Coast Bowling Congress title at Forman's new Santa Clara Street pin palace . . . World champ motorcyclist Joe Petrali wins all three races he enters at Speedway . . . Austin Clapp of Stanford beats 119 entrants, knocks 27 seconds off Golden Gate swim record . . . Al Kyte leads San Jose Bees with .500 average in 15 games . . . Morgan Hill's R. W. Liston pilots runabout "Swede" to victory in national outboard motorboat championships at Oakland's Lake Merritt . . . Freddie Hanks scores on 85-yard punt return, 55-yard pass from Sam Lima as San Jose High upsets San Mateo, 20-18 . . . Menlo football guard Mel Hornbeck (San Jose) makes JC All-Northern California . . . Small crowd turns out to see Babe Ruth ref two bouts at Forman's Arena . . . Santa Clara High (8-0-0) gives up year's only score in 20-7 victory over Los Gatos for SCVAL title . . . Stanford divides hoops team, splits twin bill with Olympic Club . . . Los Gatos Mail-News publisher Hyland L. "Hy" Baggerley elected president of the Pacific Coast League.

■ 1932 ■

San Jose Teachers College opens $180,000 Spartan Gym with 25-21 victory over COP before 2,800 spectators . . . Emile "Frenchy" LaCombe (Palo Alto) consistent high scorer for Stanford five . . . SCU cagers (14-4) hit season low winning points total, topping USF, 20-10 . . . Santa Clara High dumps Mountain View, 34-31, to clinch SCVAL hoops title. Ambrose Alves scores 19 . . . Hillview becomes public golf course . . . San Jose's Bob Church covers 51.7-miles between San Jose, San Francisco to win bicycle race in 2:14:36.2 . . . SCU pitcher Attilio Manfredi beats Cal, 8-3, as Tony Judnich goes three for four with home run . . . Young Men's Buddhist Association, (28-0), San Jose nine, takes state Japanese-American baseball title . . . Stanford 400 swim relay team sets U. S. college mark of 3:38.1 against Cal . . . Nino Bongiovanni of Santa Clara High

Stanford distance running ace Ben Eastman.

hits two triples, homer, walks in ninth, steals second, third, home to nip Los Gatos, 5-4 . . . Coach Walt Williams abolishes San Jose High football camp at Big Basin saying players seem to lose interest in game when season starts . . . San Jose High tramples Half Moon Bay, 32-5 . . . Pole vault record goes to Stanford's Bill Miller at 14-1 7/8 . . . San Jose's Al Chasteen wins 16-lap Speedway motorcycle main event . . . Stanford's Charlie Seaver wins Northern California amateur golf title at San Jose Country Club, 1 up, over Charley Ferrera . . . Santa Clara High retains SCVAL baseball crown . . . Les Powers leads SCU nine in batting with .360 average . . . Ernie Dalmon wins San Jose Mercury-Herald bowling, 1,228 pins to runner-up Delmar Dooley's 1,220 . . . After 224-stroke tie in 54 holes with Colin "Scotty" Heron, Ernie Pieper takes nine-hole playoff for county golf crown . . . Mountain View High's Alan Cranston runs 10-flat 100 . . . Stanford's tennis doubles team of Keith Gledhill, Joe Coughlin wins NCAA title . . . Uncrowned featherweight king Fidel LaBarba KOs Bobby Gray in eighth at Forman's Arena . . . Ohio State's Jack Keller sets world record 14.4 in 100-meter hurdles at Stanford. It is the first world mark timed with an official wind speed reading . . . Declining membership because of Great Depression forces San Jose Tennis Club to go public . . . San Jose's Bill Halla, 16, takes county junior golf title at La Rinconada . . . Olympics gold medal in pole vault goes to Stanford's Bill Miller with vault of 14-1 7/8 . . . Les Spangler wins 100-lap race at rebuilt San Jose Speedway where straightaways, turns are resurfaced, banked curves widened for higher speed . . . Olympians Attilio Pavesi, Mario Cemetti of Italy defeat Cocky O'Brien, Red Berti in Pasadena match races . . . Jerry Kestley's four TDs give Palo Alto High 33-6 win over Santa Cruz . . . Santa Clara High's Gene Elam runs for three, passes for two TDs in Panthers' 33-6 win over Montezuma . . . Ex-SCU star and International League MVP Marv Owen of

Newark belts homer to beat Minneapolis, 7-6, in Little World Series final . . . Mountain View's 25-0 win over Fremont clinches SCVAL football crown . . . County tennis titles go to Larry Hall (men's singles); Hall, John Gordon (men's doubles); Marjorie Postelthwaite (women's singles); Postelthwaite, Naomi Koehle (women's doubles); John Law (juniors) . . . Palo Alto High eleven downs San Jose, 15-12 for PAL title . . . Cocky O'Brien-Red Berti team travels 1,812 miles in Los Angeles six-day bike race to edge fellow San Joseans Ted Snaveley, Ernie Basquez by eight-tenths of a mile . . . Norman Hill of San Jose, partner William Grimm, among five teams tied with 2,482 miles plus nine laps in Madison Square Garden six-day bike race. Team loses title on lap points . . . Junior Hansen, Jean de St. Cyr, Tom Meredith, each score twice as San Jose Polo Club downs San Mateo at Speedway, 6-5 . . . Light heavyweight champion Maxie Rosenbloom decisions Tony Poloni at Forman's Arena . . . SCU gridder Frank "Hands" Slavich is named All-America, picked at end by International News Service (second team), Hearst (third).

■ 1933 ■

Hands Slavich contributes dozen points in SCU's 32-17 hoops win over Cal . . . In Forman's Arena wrestling twin bill, Ed "Strangler" Lewis defeats Sam Leathers in 37 minutes, then disposes of Red Thornton in 15 . . . Thirteen riders including Red Berti quit Los Angeles six-day bike races in dispute over prize money . . . Athens Club tops San Jose Teachers College cagers despite Martin Mathiesen's 17 points . . . Bad economic times force Hillview to cut Sunday, holiday green fees from $1.50 to $1 . . . Ernie Nevers' All-Stars surprise Green Bay Packers at San Francisco's Kezar Stadium, 13-6, with Nevers completing 14 of 19 passes . . . Henry Martinez tops Mountain View High with 17 in 38-23 win over Campbell . . . Bobby Grayson scores on 60-yard run as Stanford ruggers topple Barbarians, 9-0 . . . Norman Hill teams with Reggie McNamara to capture Cleveland six-day bicycle race, joins Dave Lands for win at Boston . . . Boxer Fidel LaBarba quits ring to return to studies at Stanford . . . 6-foot-3 soph center Murray "Red" Cook leads Campbell High to SCVAL basketball title with scoring average of 20-plus points-per-game . . . Cal defeats SCU nine, 3-2, with Milt McIntyre (Santa Clara) going three for four for Bears . . . Stanford (9-18) closes books on season with 41-23 loss to Cal as Keith Topping tallies 14 . . . Willie Radunich hits 12, but St. Joseph High loses Catholic championship to Stockton St. Mary's, 25-20 . . . Stanford's Joe Coughlin wins second straight NCAA tennis doubles title with partner Sam Lee . . . Doug Taylor runs wind-aided 9.6 100 for San Jose Teachers College in win over USF . . . Gus Meier of Stanford tops 120-yard hurdles world record in 14.2 to take NCAA . . . SCU downs St. Mary's as Frank Sobrero gets double, home run . . . Jack Idiart leads SCU batters with .375 average . . . San Jose's Japanese-American Young Men's Buddhist Association nine (18-2) is runner-up for state crown . . . Bert Delmas of Stanford tops CIBA batters with .525 mark . . . Frank Cunningham of San Jose Teachers College breaks conference javelin mark at 212-2 . . . Bowler Ed Hoeninghause wins Mercury-Herald tournament . . . Charlie Seaver retains his Northern California amateur golf title, wins state amateur . . . San Jose High withdraws from PAL track meet after coach-principal Raymond B. Leland, 49, dies of heart attack . . . Ernie Pieper's record 54-hole, 218 score wins county golf . . . $100,000 Alviso track open six nights a week for greyhound racing . . . Ingleside Co. buys Hillview golf course, pays off debts . . . Local teams in State League are A's and Bees . . . Mrs. A. Camnitz of San Jose takes 880-yard bicycle race in 1:42 . . . Louis Duino, Walt Williams, Lyle Decker, Court Randolph represent county in National Public Links golf . . . San Jose High's John McGuire comes off bench to tackle Hollister back at 30-yard line, preventing TD in 13-0 loss to 'Balers. Referee rules "illegal intrusion," gives Hollister ball at 15 . . . Jim, Harry Bailey each score two TDs as Bellarmine tops Serra of Hollister, 38-0 . . . County tennis champions: Ben Day, Naomi Koehle (singles), Larry Hall, John Gordon, Naomi, Ruth Koehle (doubles) . . . Nameless San Jose High teams (called "Terrors" by Mercury-Herald) become "Bulldogs" by student body vote . . . Don Edwards downs Jim Rea on 36th hole in city golf final . . . Mountain View High takes SCVAL grid title over Fremont, 6-0 . . . Palo Alto High captures PAL water polo crown with 11-0 win over Mountain View . . . Golden Gloves champs from San Jose are flyweight Tommy Cobb, lightweight Earl Brooks . . . Red Cook scores 23 as Campbell High creams Live Oak in hoops, 42-4 . . . Norman Hill wins U. S. pro cycling all-around championship.

■ 1934 ■

St. Joseph High handles Hollister, 36-14, behind Willie Radunich's 23 . . . Undefeated San Jose YMBA hoops team defeats Santa Clara High, 32-28, as Harry Yoshioka nets 11 . . . Viad Taranik, Jim Benet score three goals each in undefeated Stanford's 9-4 water polo win over Athens Club . . . Jimmy Mills of San Jose wins Pacific Coast pocket billiards title . . . Bobby Grayson belts triple, homer in Stanford's 7-6 loss to Athens Club . . . Bob Kinsley of San Jose Teachers College tops divers as Stanford wins meet, 66-27 . . . Campbell High retains SCVAL hoops title. Red Cook averages 19.1 in league with high of 42 in practice game . . . SCU drops baseball for year . . . San Jose Teachers College trails 16-3 at half, rallies for 42-35 win over Chico State quintet for conference title with David Biddle scoring 16 . . . Lawson Little of Stanford wins PCI golf crown . . . Stanford ruggers stop Cal, 13-0 . . . Howard "Lefty" Blethen doubles, homers as San Jose Teachers College nine beats Cal, 6-5 . . . Ed Fitzgerald sets San Jose Teachers College 440 freestyle mark against San Francisco State . . . Sprinter Louis Salvato wins 100 in 9.6, 220 in 21.2 for San Jose Teachers College against Fresno State . . . Every Stanford player scores in 19-1 baseball win over St. Mary's . . . County golf title taken by Jim Rea . . . Despite presence of ex-pro Dutch Ruether on mound, San Jose Bees bow to Modesto, 11-3 . . . World record falls when Stanford's Ben Eastman races half mile in 1:49.8 . . . Nina Westbrook rolls record 279 at San Jose Bowling Palace . . . Stanford wins NCAA, IC4A track titles . . . Portland's Nino Bongiovanni (Santa Clara) hits in 43 straight PCL games . . . Teacher Iva Liston takes county women's golf . . . Walt Williams wins playoff over Court Randolph, Ernie Pieper in first tourney at Hillview's nine-hole, par 24 pitch and putt course . . . After player strike sours him on baseball, San Jose Bees owner Bill Neibel sells team to his sister, Margaret, for $1 . . . San Jose's Don Edwards falls to Don Hawley in state amateur golf final, 1 up . . . SCU halfback John Storm joins Philadelphia Eagles to become school's first player in modern NFL . . . Campbell High's first football team since 1926 loses only games played to Los Gatos JVs, 6-0, 7-6 . . . Two TD passes by Glenn Sinnott defeat Sequoia High, 12-6, in early season game which gives San Jose league title . . . Buddy Baer engages Benny Gersey in three-

Santa Clara High's Nino Bongiovanni played baseball in the Pacific Coast and major leagues.

round exhibition bout at Forman's Arena with brother Max Baer as ref . . . Bellarmine's Tommy Wall keeps Jefferson in hole averaging 50 yards on punts, including 70-yarder, but Bells lose, 6-0 . . . Future Cal football standout Dave Anderson scores all 14 TDs for Los Gatos (2-3-2) . . . Ernie Pieper nips Don Edwards, 3 and 2, in city golf final . . . Playing both ways, back Bobby Grayson rushes for 124 yards, intercepts four passes, returning two for TDs in 24-0 Stanford rout of Washington . . . Tackle Dario "Si" Simoni only San Jose Teachers College player on all-FWC team as Spartans (2-0-3) tie Fresno State (3-0-1) for title. Coach Dud DeGroot declines playoff invitation because players taking final exams . . . Rule requiring center jump after every basket eliminated in Pacific Coast Conference games, year before rule goes national . . . Red Cook outscores opponents with 16 as Campbell High overwhelms St. Joseph, 40-11.

■ 1935 ■

Although he represents San Francisco Olympic Club, end Bill Hubbard is first ex-San Jose Teachers College player to appear in East-West Shrine contest. SCU's Frank Sobrero throws TD pass in West's 19-13 win . . . San Jose Teachers College renamed San Jose State College . . . Larry Arnerich hits 15 as SJS beats Pacific, 38-34 . . . Bill Ambrose swims record 56.4 in 100-yard freestyle in SJS win over San Jose High . . . Scarlet fever epidemic forces postponement of SJS at Cal Aggies basketball contest . . . Mountain View High five (18-3) wins SCVAL . . . San Mateo JC downs SJS boxers despite wins by Carlyn Walker, Richard Mathews, Glenn Tucker . . . Merv Martin's 18 leads St. Joseph High over Bellarmine, 26-22 . . . Stanford whips Cal, 20-13, to capture California Rugby Union title . . . Montezuma School's Leroy Kirkpatrick runs record 14.7 low hurdles in Pacific AAU . . . YMBA five has three-year record of 124-7 . . . 317-pound wrestler Man Mountain Dean defeats Pat Fraley at Forman's Arena . . . Earl Booker, Harold Tousaint take Pacific AAU boxing crowns at San Francisco . . . Al Skelton of San Felipe wins $400 in calf roping contests at Gilroy Rodeo . . . Bill Dutton's two-run homer gives SCU 7-6 win over Cal . . . Stanford nine (2-13) struggles to worst record in history . . . USF sprinter Elmo Ferrari (San Jose) takes 100, 220 in win over SJS . . . SJS pitchers Burt Watson, Marv Olson win twin bill against San Francisco State as Spartans end baseball season 17-6 . . . Cal defeats Stanford in track for first time in 11 years . . . Les Steers of Palo Alto High high jumps 6-2 3/4 for PAL meet record . . . San Jose Tech High downs St. Joseph to finish first baseball season 14-1 . . . Sam Klopstock of Stanford (San Jose) lowers world 120-yard hurdles record to 14.1 . . . Ex-heavyweight wrestling champ Jim Browning stops Mike Mazurki . . . Stanford's Don Edwards wins county golf title in pair of nine-hole playoffs with Mark Macklin . . . In meet's last event, Los Gatos relay team's win gives Wildcats league title . . . County women's golf title goes to Mrs. J. C. Moore, who shoots 179 for 36 holes at Stanford . . . San Jose's J. B. Konz is Mercury-Herald bowling champ . . . Running for San Francisco Olympic Club, Leroy Kirkpatrick (Montezuma) clocks world record-tying 14.2 high hurdles at AAU meet in Nebraska. Record is disallowed for excessive wind . . . Lefty Blethen wins Pacific Northwest tennis singles title . . . Large gallery sees British women's champion Joyce Wethered shoot course record 76 in San Jose Country Club exhibition . . . Ernie Pieper fires low amateur score 297 in California Open at Pebble Beach won by pro Cam Puget with 286 . . . Irma Dutra gets four hits, whiffs nine as National Shoe beats Valley Auto Wreckers, 9-2, in all-San Jose final for state women's softball title . . . Ronnie "Lefty" Edwards of Los Gatos High beats Jack Gurley in Pacific Coast under-15 tennis final . . . SJS fullback Bull Lewis intercepts two passes to set up his TD runs of 35, 80 yards in 19-0 win over McKinley of Hawaii . . . Brooklyn end Bud Hubbard, first SJS player in NFL, runs 56 yards with deflected pass against Pittsburgh for deciding TD in 13-7 win . . . Mountain View High blanks Fremont for SCVAL title, 25-0 . . . Jack Mortenson's pass tipped by defender to Frank Bonanno, who catches it for score with two minutes left as San Jose High beats Palo Alto, 6-0 . . . SJS guard George Cannell blocks field goal try, two punts in 25-6 win over Humboldt State . . . Golden Gloves KO winners at San Francisco: George Freitas of Mountain View, Earl Booker . . . Record over-capacity crowd of 94,000 jams Stanford Stadium to watch Indians dump Cal, 13-0 . . . Babe Didrikson out drives men on several holes, fires 82 as she, Eddie Duino (70) lose, 3 and 2, to Eugenia McClay (81), Ernie Pieper (68) in San Jose Country Club exhibition.

■ 1936 ■

SJS basketball team upsets Utah State, 40-34, at Spartan Gym . . . Coach Dario "Si" Simoni's San Jose Tech High team downs Montezuma in basketball, 48-34 . . . Drafted by Pittsburgh Steelers, Stanford All-American halfback Bobby Grayson declines to sign professional contract . . . SJS faculty member Earl Atkinson named American Trapshooting Association's 1935 champ, scoring perfect 100 for 100 . . . Associated Oil Co. sponsors Stanford, Santa Clara University basketball games on radio stations KQW, KSFO, KLX . . . Sophomore Hank Luisetti rips nets for 14 as Stanford five topples UCLA in conference opener, 44-30 . . . 227-pound home town favorite Al Perry defeats Gino Garibaldi in year's first wrestling main event at

Forman's Arena . . . Nick Radunich's last second shot from half court gives SCU stunning 42-41 victory over San Francisco YMCA at Seifert Gym . . . San Jose High's Dick MacGregor ruled ineligible under CIF's new rule reducing maximum age of prep athletes from 21 to 20 . . . Stanford backfield coach Ernie Nevers named head football coach at Lafayette (Pa.) College . . . 14-year-old Ronnie Edwards top ranked junior in Northern California Tennis Association . . . San Jose pro cyclist Cocky O'Brien teams with Chicago's Cecil "Rabbit" Yates, San Jose's Bobby Echeverria to finish near top of six-day bike races at San Francisco, Oakland . . . Pro golf great Walter Hagen, actor Richard Arlen down locals Eddie Duino, Ernie Pieper, 4 and 2, in San Jose Country Club exhibition . . . Leaky roof in four-year-old Spartan Gym makes hoops play treacherous . . . DeWitt Portal's SJS boxing team whitewashes Cal, 9-0 . . . Stanford's Don Edwards upset by USF's Mat Palacio for Pacific Coast college golf championship . . . Sunnyvale teacher Norman Bright wins 5,000-meter race in 15:02.0 at San Francisco indoor meet . . . Hank Luisetti goes two for 12 from floor as Oregon State defeats Stanford in Olympics trials . . . Hal Lowe belts three triples as San Jose High beats Balboa, 6-4, for tenth straight baseball win . . . Cook Sypher, who coached Mountain View High to fourth consecutive baseball title, 30 straight SCVAL wins, leaves for Santa Rosa JC coaching job . . . Jim Hall pitches no-hitter over Sequoia in San Jose High's 14th straight win. Bulldogs, losers only to Mountain View in opener, finish season 16-1 . . . Gilroy takes CCAL-B track championship . . . San Jose High, Palo Alto tie for second place in NCS track meet. Bulldogs' Harvey Brooks (100), Frank Ferrana (discus), relay team grab firsts . . . San Jose

Nello Falaschi was Santa Clara University's first All-American backfield star.

Asahi baseball team bows to Waseda (Japan) University, 6-4 . . . Ben Day, Bill Seward of Stanford take NCAA tennis doubles . . . Barbara Beach Thompson of Los Altos wins county women's golf crown . . . Cocky O'Brien takes 50-mile New Jersey motorcycle race, quits bicycling to sign up for 25 more East Coast events . . . Joe Jio of San Jose Asahi bats .444 in Northern California Japanese Baseball League . . . John Gordon defeats Larry Hill for city tennis championship . . . San Jose Merchants' 25-game win streak stopped, 7-6, by former PCL spitball pitcher Pudgy Gould of Oakland's Golden Glow team . . . Campbell High's dirt football field in rough shape from hay crop grown in winter and spring . . . San Jose's Mark Macklin downs Bill Higgins of Oakland, 8 and 7, in city golf final . . . Gilroy High joins SCVAL for football . . . Pete Spily has three TDs including 65-yard punt return as Mountain View High blasts Gilroy, 53-0 . . . San Jose polo field at east end of San Antonio Street opens as 1,000 see San Jose down Menlo College, 7-6 . . . Mountain View (7-0-0) wins SCVAL football title, outscores five league opponents 233 to 6 . . . Bellarmine gridders (0-6-1) fail to score a point . . . Stanford starts hoops reserves against SJS, falls behind 16-6 at half time, takes game, 31-24 . . . San Jose boxers Delino Ontiveras, Stan Griffin win California Golden Gloves championships.

■ 1937 ■

SJS scoring leader Ivor Thomas hits 16 in 42-19 hoops win over COP . . . San Jose High blasts Live Oak cagers, 72-17, behind Bill Helbush's 19 points . . . Following five straight KO wins, San Jose featherweight Johnny Pacheco is knocked out by Jack LaSalle . . . After 13-2 start, SCU quintet drops last five games . . . San Jose pro cyclist Norman Hall breaks vertebrae, retires . . . SJS boxers George Latka, Dale Wren, Bob Harris, Pete Bolich, Don Walker win PAAU titles . . . Stanford tops Cal, 36-32, takes annual hoops series for first time since 1921 . . . Pitcher Burt Watson of SJS tops PCL's Mission Reds, 9-4 . . . Sixteen cyclists including San Jose's Tony Zulim, George Antrobus suspended for breaking pact with Oakland six-day bicycle race promoter . . . Howard Withycombe of SJS wins PAAU 100 backstroke . . . Future middleweight champ Ceferino Garcia KOs Jack Wade in first round at Civic Auditorium . . . Heavyweight wrestling champion Dean Detton takes Ivan Managoff in two straight falls . . . Wayne Richardson converts 15, 20, 35-yard penalty kicks as Stanford ruggers whitewash Cal, 9-0, for California Rugby Union, PCC titles . . . Stan Griffin of SJS, Julio Chiaramonte of SCU are college boxing champs . . . Coach John Bunn's Stanford five (25-2) named national champion by Helms Athletic Foundation . . . San Jose Tech High joins SCVAL after three years as independent . . . SJS heavyweight Don Walker loses to Mississippi State's Harry Mullins in NCAA boxing final . . . Don Edwards of San Jose defeats Mat Palacio, 6 and 5, for Northern California amateur golf title . . . Gus Ricard's 1,136 pin total gives him Mercury-Herald bowling crown by 24 pins over Clarence Leese . . . Frank LaForte doubles, triples, homers for Tech High in,4-2 win over Chaminade . . . Three-round total of 212 strokes gives county golf title to Ernie Pieper over Stanford's Art Doering, 214 . . . SJS tennis team beats San Mateo JC to finish 13-0 . . . Charles Smith of San Jose wins Class C speedboat race at Calero Lake before 12,000 fans . . . Bill Lyons pitches well, but San Jose High falls to Jefferson for PAL title, 2-1 . . . Undefeated Ray Bottini leads Santa Clara High to SCVAL tennis crown . . . Les

The 1938 San Jose State baseball team, from left, (front) Dino Morati, George Haney, Harvey Rhodes, Haven Smith, James Luque, Manuel Sanchez, Jack Riordan; (back) student J. Stull, Arthur Carpenter, Bob Freitas, Walt McPherson, Elbert Garcia, Leroy Zimmerman, student G. Walsh; (inserts, left) Tony Martinez, (right) coach Gil Bishop.

Carpenter tops SJS (9-5) batters at .349 . . . Mrs. W. H. Pabst Jr. beats Eugenia McClay by stroke in county women's golf . . . State amateur boxing title goes to Bill Radunich of SJS in three-round decision over John Henschen of Ontario . . . San Jose city tennis winners are John Gordon (singles), Victor Ehle (juniors), Jim Rea, George Rotholtz (doubles) . . . Buck Davidson defeats ex-world heavyweight wrestling champ Joe Stecher . . . Garden City Wheelmen's Vince Gatto captures 13-mile Watsonville race . . . Bobby Rodriguez hits two doubles, homer as San Jose Memory Post scores 10 runs in last three innings for 16-11 win over C. C. Thomas Post of San Francisco to take American Legion district title. San Jose loses playoff to Berkeley . . . Pacific Greyhound ends Franco Market's 15-game win streak, 14-8, at Washington Park in county's first night baseball game . . . Frank Kovacs retains singles title at San Jose All-Comers tennis tourney . . . Locals players lead PCL: Portland's Nino Bongiovanni (Santa Clara) in runs (136), hits (236); Seattle outfielder Arthur "Mike" Hunt (San Jose) in homers (39) . . . Punt by Palo Alto High's Hank Norberg soars 68 yards in the air for 83 yards including roll against San Jose High . . . Guard Glenn Dubose, out of SJS football lineup with knee injury, becomes professional wrestler after recovery . . . Stanford's Art Doering whips Brown Cannon, 7 and 6, for city golf crown . . . Bellarmine beats Sacred Heart, 12-0, to end string of 12 straight scoreless games . . . SJS grid squad tops Redlands on Thursday, 12-0, travels to Humboldt for rain-soaked Saturday win, 13-2 . . . Tackle John Aimonetti is Los Gatos High's MVP . . . Hal Stoefen's 20 points leads Stanford to 45-38 win over SJS . U. S. handball singles champ Joe Platak downs San Jose's Art Toste in YMCA exhibition.

■ 1938 ■

Tech High's Dick Bastian scores 18, but Craftsmen fall to Los Gatos, 44-33, in school's first SCVAL game . . . State bantamweight champ Pablo Dano floored twice as Tomboy Romero gains 10-round decision at San Jose . . . SJS loses to Olympic Club, but Martin Wempe breaks Spartans' 220, 440 freestyle records . . . Ellsworth Vines defeats Fred Perry in tennis exhibition on Civic Auditorium's hardwood floor . . . Pitcher Art Carpenter of SJS decisions Stanford, 12-1 . . . SJS quintet ties SCU for league title, downs Broncos, 50-44, in playoff to end year 19-4. Invitation to national tournament in Kansas City rejected when school officials rule players must stay home to study for final exams . . . SJS 165-pounder Steve Bolich wins 17th straight bout as Spartan boxers fall victim to Washington State, 5-3 . . . Mountain View High's Pete Spily averages record 17 points per game in SCVAL play. Campbell, Los Gatos deadlock for title . . . . Former Sunnyvale teacher Norman Bright of Olympic Club duals Sullivan Award-winning distance star Don Lash of Indiana in series of East Coast races . . . SCU cancels first boxing bouts against SJS because of hoops playoff "incidents," apparent reference to fights before game, garbage strewn over Broncos' campus . . . Heavyweight wrestler George Zaharias takes Glen Wade in two of three falls . . . Stanford wins first of four NCAA golf titles in five years under coach Eddie Twiggs . . . SJS wrestlers John Jones, Mel Rush, Art Winglen win as Spartans finish second in PCC . . . Sandor Szabo quits Civic Auditorium ring after 34 minutes in loss to heavyweight wrestling champ Bronko Nagurski . . . National Junior Davis Cup Team member Ronnie Edwards leads Los Gatos High to league title . . . Ed Morihiro pilots "Miss San Jose" to runabout win in Santa Clara Valley Speedboat Association races at Calero Lake . . . Santa Clara High's Earl Pemberton recovers from mumps to pitch title-clinching win over Live Oak, 23-2. Bill Benevich leads 16-hit attack with triple, home run . . . Undefeated Stanford quarter miler Ray Mallot is NCAA champ in 46.8 . . . San Jose High takes PAL track meet with Bulldogs' Pete Kmetovic (100, 220), Palo Alto's Hank Norberg (discus, shot put) top performers . . . Ernie Pieper blows five-hole lead, loses Northern California amateur golf title to Mat Palacio, 2 and 1, at Pasatiempo . . . San Jose High's 880 relay team (Pete Kmetovic, Al Mathis, Bob Shottenhamer, Al Wool) wins NCS . . . Don Edwards wins county golf title by four strokes over Stanford teammate Art Doering . . . South San Francisco High deals San Jose only PAL loss, but Bulldogs win baseball crown . . . SJS student Barbara Wallace wins Santa Cruz ocean swim women's title . . . Bill Radunich wins TKO over Vic Lindskog of Los Angeles in defense of Northern California amateur heavyweight boxing crown . . . Sam Arena takes national 200-mile motorcycle title . . . Barbara Beach Thompson shoots record 78 on final 18 at

Stanford for winning 161 total in county women's golf tourney . . . Boxing champion Henry Armstrong throws four shutout innings as Champion Colored Dynamiters lose, 4-1, to Jerome C. Bean nine . . . Southpaw Dick Freitas fans county semi-pro record 17 batters as Franco's Markets whips Bear Photo, 9-0 . . . Ronnie Edwards of Los Gatos wins Pacific Northwest tennis over U. S. boy's champ Robert Carruthers . . . Leo Perez, Gene Echeverria set Burbank Velodrome record, racing 28 miles plus one lap in one hour . . . E. A. McLean of San Jose wins five-mile outboard runabout race at Modesto . . . Merta Longley of San Jose produces record 1,092 points to win National Archery Association's junior girl's title . . . San Jose Progressive Optical loses in first round at national women's softball play in St. Louis, later edges Tennessee champs, 4-3, on pitcher Willie May Turner's two-hitter . . . Joe Colla holds off Sammy Rinella on final night to win Burbank Velodrome title by 10 points . . . Joe LoCurto scores TDs on 15-, 82-yard runs, passes to Pete Ghiorso for another as Bellarmine stops Salinas, 19-7 . . . Stanford's Dick Wright whips teammate Warren Berl in rainstorm in city golf final, 2 and 1 . . . Ex-big league baseball player Art "The Great" Shires loses wild wrestling match to LaVerne Baxter . . . Bill Cashen's field goal gives Palo Alto High 9-6 win over San Jose . . . Soph Bob Feerick guns in 20 as SCU downs Athens Club, 68-42 . . . San Joseans John Perry, Byron Lamphear, Bill Radunich win regional Golden Gloves championships. Lamphear, Radunich capture Pacific Coast crowns.

■ 1939 ■

SCU drops 33-31 decision to Marquette as 6-foot-5 center Ed Nelson scores 13 . . . Bearded heavyweight Ivan Rasputin falls to champion Jim Londos before record Civic Auditorium crowd of 2,678 wrestling fans . . . Ex-lightweight title holder Tony Canzoneri knocks out Everett Simington in third round at Civic Auditorium . . . Bruce Hale's 14 points gives SCU 48-35 win over St. Mary's plus league title . . . Campbell High tops Los Gatos, 45-36, as Dave Farley scores 20 . . . Grey McConnell of SJS upsets defending Northern California champion Knute Pederson in school's first wrestling tourney . . . San Jose tennis fans see Ellsworth Vines down Don Budge, 6-1, 3-6, 6-2 . . . Sacred Heart High's 32-17 whipping ends Bellarmine (14-3) 12-game hoops win streak . . . SCU nine blows 16-0 lead, loses to California, 22-19 . . . Campbell High five wins SCVAL title . . . SJS wrestlers Sam Della Maggiore, Mel Bruno win national AAU titles . . . Nick Lazaneo of Fremont High tosses no-hit victory against Santa Clara . . . Owen Collins sets SJS 440 record of 49.5 in Fresno State meet . . . Art Carpenter fans 16 Nebraska batters as SJS ends season with 8-7 win . . . Light-heavyweight boxer Pete Bolich is only SJS winner against Wisconsin, defeating national champ Truman Torgerson . . . Stanford repeats as NCAA golf champion . . . Fremont High's Al Ariza belts pair of homers, knocks in five runs as Indians clinch SCVAL with 8-2 win over Campbell . . . Earl Pemberton of Santa Clara High throws no-hitter at Sequoia . . . Stanford's Art Doering breaks 12-year San Jose Country Club monopoly by taking county golf title . . . After bowling only 18 months, SJS student Mitch Ucovich wins Mercury-Herald championship by two pins over Carl Endeward . . . Stanford's Pete Zager takes third straight NCAA discus title with 164-0 1/4 toss . . . Stanford track coach Dink Templeton retires after 18 years, three NCAA, four IC4A titles . . . San Jose High nine is second in round robin, wins four straight playoff games for PAL title . . . Don Presley wins shot put, discus to lead SJS to CCAA title . . . San Jose High's Jim Peterson takes 100, 220 (in record 21.9), Tommie Higgins captures shot put as school snares first NCS track title in two decades. Palo Alto's Lyle Taggert ties for first in pole vault . . . Jack Bariteau Jr. of San Jose High wins PAL golf with 74 on Crystal Springs course. Bulldogs take team crown . . . Gilroy High breaks nine-year Los Gatos hold on league track title as Herman Heilman wins 440, 880 . . . Paul Herron of Stanford takes one-mile Santa Cruz ocean swim in 24:29 . . . San Jose YMCA's Ralph Bernardo wins 148-pound weight lifting event at Golden Gate International Exposition on Treasure Island . . . Mrs. W. H. Pabst Jr. of San Jose overcomes Mrs. Roy Bozeman at Stanford to take county women's golf by two strokes . . . San Jose's Art Toste retains county handball title, defeating Jack Black . . . Vince Gatto-Leo Perez team ends Gene Echeverria-Jack Hennessy national record string of five straight one-hour cycle race wins at Burbank Velodrome . . . San Jose Memory Post wins American Legion district title over Salinas, falls to San Francisco's Rincon Hill Post, 8-5 . . . Kansas City Monarchs break 17-game Franco's Markets winning streak, 8-7. Monarchs' pitchers Jack Matchett (11 strikeouts), future Baseball Hall of Famer Satchel Paige (8) fan 19 on following night in 11-inning, 4-3 victory . . . San Jose officer Bill Young ties record with perfect 30 for 30 hits in Alameda Police Department's shooting competition . . . Record 4,700 paid customers plus 1,000 fence hoppers see San Francisco Seals defeat Franco's Markets (40-10), 9-8 . . . Jim Kincaid, Charles Kerwin, Don Taylor, Conrad Lacey, Bill Sellers of SJS go on boxing tour in Japan . . . TD receptions by Bobby Green, Frank Holmes, Bill Hennessy give Bellarmine 21-0 victory against formerly unbeaten, unscored upon Berkeley St. Mary's. Bells finish with 6-0-0 mark . . . Hal Sonntag races 25 yards for deciding score in 14-7 Los Gatos win over Washington for Wildcats' first SCVAL football crown . . . Bellarmine joins California Catholic Athletic League for basketball . . . SJS tops UCLA, 40-31, as tallest Spartan, 6-foot-2 Dick Urhhammer, pours in 15 points.

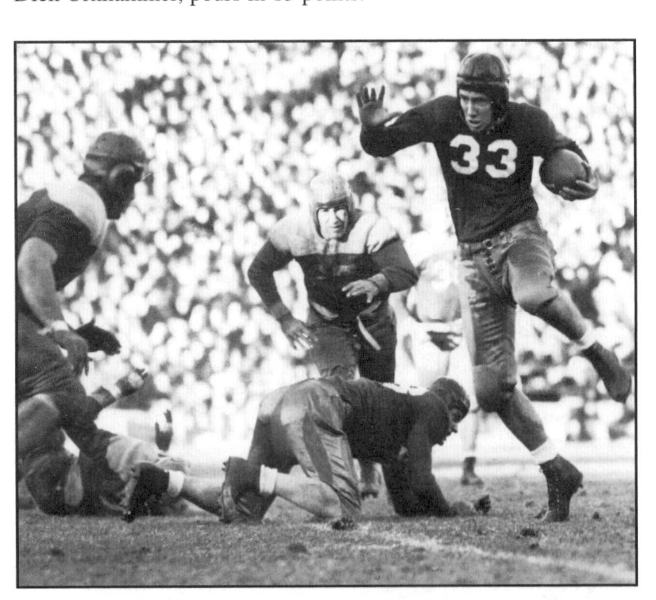

Halfback Joe Hoyt (33) of Santa Clara heads for the nine-yard line, where he was tackled by St. Mary's Jerry Dowd (left) in the 1938 Little Big Game, which was won by the Gaels, 7-0.

The 1940s

Stanford unveiled a "new" football formation in 1940 that would change the school's gridiron fortunes and help to alter the look of American football.

Before the year was over, Stanford's "Wow Boys" would be one of the most talked about college squads in the nation. Before the decade had ended, teams across America would convert to the Indians' modern T formation.

Stanford's football win-loss records had gone down hill since 1935, sinking to a dismal all-time low of 1-7-1 in 1939. Head coach Tiny Thornhill was fired and Clark Shaughnessy was brought in as his successor.

Shaughnessy had coached the University of Chicago since 1933. The Maroon was a former Big Ten powerhouse that dropped football after 1939, when it finished 2-6-0 and lost its three conference games by a combined 0-192 score.

Shaughnessy also worked for the Chicago Bears, helping coach George Halas analyze NFL teams and tinkering with the unusual formation the Bears had used since 1930. The T dated back to the 19th Century, but Halas had moved the quarterback up under the center, instead of making him take a short snap from the pivot man to start each play. The Bears also employed a man in motion and split ends.

Shaughnessy refined the T, spreading the linemen even wider, putting a back in motion in one direction and splitting an end on the other side in a system that was unique among the pros. The T's popularity soared after Chicago steamrolled the Washington Redskins, 73-0, for the 1940 NFL title and Stanford won the Rose Bowl 24 days later.

Shaughnessy saw that the Stanford players could make the T's quick opener runs and passing effective. The quarterback was a key and the Indians had Frankie Albert, who had alternated with Pete Kmetovic at single wing tailback in 1939. Frankie wasn't fast enough as a runner and Kmetovic was a poor passer, but the left-handed Albert was an ideal candidate for quarterback and became one of the best.

Shaughnessy described him as, "a magician with the ball, a gifted field general, wonderfully observing and courageous to the point of almost foolhardiness." The QB called all the plays in the 1940s and Albert was a daring gambler during his days with Stanford and the San Francisco 49ers.

Observers didn't know what to expect before the Indians opened against favored USF in the second game of a rare Kezar double-header. The game program predicted fans would watch, "a razzle dazzle wide open attack, the like of which has never been seen before on the Pacific Coast."

Most of the attention was directed at the Santa Clara-Utah opener, won by the Broncos, 34-13, but Stanford's 27-0 win over the experienced Dons was impressive. With Albert passing, Kmetovic and Hugh Gallernau zipping off tackle or around end and 245-pound fullback Norm Standlee pounding the middle, Stanford went undefeated in 10 games.

Frankie Albert, Stanford's T formation wizard.

Not all the wins were easy. Santa Clara was edged by a point, 7-6, and the Indians trailed Washington 10-0 before rallying for a 20-10 victory. But Stanford downed USC, undefeated in 17 straight, 21-7, and represented the Pacific Coast Conference against Nebraska on New Year's Day.

The Indians were ranked No. 2 behind Minnesota, which was prohibited by Big Ten rules from playing a bowl game. Stanford beat No. 7 Nebraska, 21-13, icing the win with Kmetovic's scoring 40-yard punt return, a zigzag run

World record sprinter Hal Davis of Morgan Hill dominated the dashes in the 1940s.

described as one of the finest plays in Rose Bowl history.

Albert, a brilliant defender as well as an offensive star, made most of the All-America teams. He repeated as an All-American in 1941, when the 6-3-0 Indians started strong, but were hit by injuries and dropped their last two games.

The Stanford T was such an innovation that the 1941 NCAA Football Guide devoted 12 pages of text and photos to it. Within 20 years, almost all college and pro teams had switched to the more versatile T from the traditional wing and box formations that had dominated football for decades.

There were doubters in the beginning. Some thought the T was too fancy compared with old fashioned smash mouth football. In his "Ballad of the T Formation," (to the tune of McNamara's Band) *San Francisco Chronicle* sportswriter Dick Friendlich wrote:

"Oh, the ends they crash and the tackles smash and the guards they submarine;

"The halfbacks lunge, the fullbacks plunge, the center stoops between;

"But, lo, the cerebral quarterback, standing all serene;

"He merely gives the ball away and keeps his jersey clean."

■ JACKIE JURICH

Jackie Jurich fought in San Jose more than 20 times in the 1930s and 1940s, held the U. S. flyweight title and battled for the bantamweight crown in his 82-fight career.

His first big local bouts came late in 1937 when he drew with former flyweight champ Small Montana at Civic Auditorium and took a 10-round decision from Montana in a return bout seven weeks later.

In 1938, Jurich fought five times in England. He lost to Benny Lynch on a 12th round technical knockout, but Lynch was stripped of the world flyweight title for being overweight. Jurich then lost to Peter Kane in 15 rounds for what the British recognized as the world flyweight crown.

The U. S. flyweight title was in dispute between Jurich and Montana. Jackie won it in Hollywood in March, 1939, when he knocked out Montana in seven rounds and beat him again in Oakland later in the year.

Three thousand boxing fans produced Civic Auditorium promoter Babe Griffin's biggest gate of $2,428 in 1940 as Jurich lost to former world flyweight champ Little Dado in 12 rounds. Jurich continued to fight in the early 1940s, with nearly two years out for Army service.

In 1946, Jurich won a 10-round decision over fourth ranked lightweight Luis Castillo to earn a shot at world bantamweight king Manuel Ortiz. When Ortiz knocked him out in the 11th round, Jurich retired from the ring with a record of 61-14-7.

■ ON THE GROUND AND IN THE AIR

Two of America's greatest track and field men of the era just before World War II -- sprinter Hal Davis and high jumper Les Steers -- came out of Santa Clara County high schools in the late 1930s.

There had never been a world class prep sprinter in the county until Davis arrived on the scene in 1938. Before his college career ended, the man known as "The California Comet" was recognized as one of the world's best.

The 17-year-old Live Oak High junior raced into the headlines in April, 1938, when he ran a 9.7 in the 100-yard dash and 22.0 in the 220 against Gilroy. Running unattached a month later in a San Jose State-Cal Poly meet, Davis clocked 9.9 in the 100 and 21.5 in the furlong. He bettered both times in an AAU meet at Spartan Stadium and set records of 9.7 and 21.4 in his high school league.

As a senior in 1939, Davis couldn't compete in prep section or state meets because Live Oak didn't belong to the California Interscholastic Federation. Stanford's Clyde Jeffrey nipped him at the tape in the 100 at 9.5 at the Pacific AAU meet, but Davis won the 220 in 21.0.

Son of a Morgan Hill barber, Davis went to Salinas JC in 1940, where he was coached by Bud Winter, later San Jose State's great track and field mentor. Davis, who was known for his abysmal starts and remarkable finishes, set U. S. junior college marks and took the national AAU 100-meter (10.3) and 200-meter (20.4) races.

In 1941, Davis equaled Jesse Owens' 100-meter world record of 10.2 at Compton and had wind aided victories at 100 yards (9.4) and 220 (20.2) at Fresno. He failed to repeat his previous win in the 100 at the AAU nationals, but successfully defended his 200 title.

After transferring to the University of California at Berkeley in January, 1942, Davis raced to a double win in the NCAA meet in the 100-yard (9.6) and 220-yard (21.2) dashes. He took the National AAU 100-meter crown (10.5) and won again at 200 meters (20.9).

Davis repeated as NCAA sprints champion in 1943, won his third AAU 100-meter crown with a wind-aided 10.3 and took his fourth straight AAU 220-yard title in what would have been world record time but for excessive wind. He also sped 100 yards in 9.4 at the Fresno Relays.

Sadly, the 1940 and 1944 Olympic Games were canceled by World War II or Davis would have been favored to lead the USA's sprinters in their quest for gold medals. Instead, he spent several years as a Marine Corps enlisted man. After the war, he sustained a severe hamstring injury and never regained his previous form.

Steers won the state high jump for the first time as a Palo Alto High sophomore in 1935, leaping 6-2. He didn't equal that mark a year later, but still took the California title and won it for a third straight time in 1937 with a jump of 6-4, three inches below his best height of the year.

Using the straddle style, Steers continued jumping at the University of Oregon. He won the AAU title in 1938 and 1939 and tied for the 1940 championship at 6-9 3/4.

The world record was 6-10 and 3/8 when Steers surpassed it twice. His marks were recognized by American officials, but not internationally, so for a time the U. S. high jump record was higher than the world record.

Steers eliminated the difference in June, 1941, when he jumped a world record 6-11 at the PCC-Big Ten meet in Los Angeles. The following February, Steers became the first man to clear seven feet in a meet that was never recognized as an official competition.

■ COME FLY WITH ME

San Jose State's football team took to the air for six of its seven away games in 1940, a move university officials believed was unprecedented among college squads.

In this era, almost every other athletic team, including major league baseball, traveled by train.

While schools in other parts of the country had made an occasional flight, SJS officials said no Pacific Coast team had flown to a game and none had booked space on an airliner for a majority of the away games on its schedule.

The Spartans chartered two Douglas Mainliners, each capable of hauling 21 passengers, to fly about 5,000 miles on trips to Montana State, Utah State, Willamette, Santa Barbara State, Loyola of Los Angeles and Fresno State. The only road game not on the "Flying Spartans" itinerary was against USF since it was played at Kezar Stadium, 50 miles north of the Washington Square campus.

Air travel agreed with the Spartans, who fashioned an 11-1-0 record. Their only defeat came in the home opener against Texas A&I, 10-0.

■ MAGICIANS OF THE MAPLEWOOD

The official name was Santa Clara University, but basketball teams that wore the crimson and gold from 1939 through 1941 often were called the "Magicians of the Maplewood" for their quick movements and fancy passes.

Four of the school's top prewar players played for coach George Barsi during the era, Toddy Giannini, a senior in 1939-40 and future pros Bob Feerick, Bruce Hale and Marty Passaglia on all three squads.

The clubs compiled a record of 47-15, with the best record coming in 1940 (17-3), when they lost to DePaul by a basket, to USF by a point and split a pair with Cal. The Broncos took the Northern California intercollegiate league title the previous season, winning seven of eight games.

East Coast writers first saw the Magicians in 1939-40. Giannini scored 20 as they beat LaSalle and CCNY in Madison Square Garden, where huge crowds saw 15 double-headers matching New York teams against college quintets from across America. Giannini was voted to the Garden's second team and became the first SCU player to receive All-America mention. Hale was a second team Garden pick in 1940-41 as the Broncos took CCNY again, 49-41.

Feerick became a pro star. Playing for Washington, he was named to the 1947 first team all-league in the Basketball Association of America, which became the National Basketball Association. Feerick led the NBA in field goal and free throw percentages in 1948 and was all-

Santa Clara's 1939-40 varsity went 17-3. From left, (front) Bob Feerick, Marty Passaglia, Toddy Giannini, Jim Rickert, Bruce Hale; (center) Joe Felipe, Dick Morrisey, Wallace Mandler, Leo Murphy, Dick Mangan, manager Scholk; (back) trainer Henry Schmidt, Bob Nico, Dale Case, coach George Barsi.

Stanford's 1941-42 NCAA basketball champs (from left) Bill Cowden, Howie Dallmar, Ed Voss, Jim Pollard, Don Burness, head coach Everett Dean.

league again. He later coached SCU and the San Francisco Warriors.

Passaglia played two seasons in the league and Hale, later known locally as Rick Barry's father-in-law and coach of St. Mary's College and the American Basketball Association's Oakland Oaks, was a pro for three seasons.

■ STANFORD'S NCAA CHAMPS

The county's only NCAA basketball champion was the Stanford men's team in 1941-42. The towering Indians, whose starters ranged from 6-foot-3 to 6-foot-5, compiled a 28-4 record and were ranked No. 1 in two major polls.

Paced by All-Americans Jim Pollard and Don Burness, the Indians romped through the Pacific Coast Conference Southern Division with an 11-1 record and moved into the three-game playoff series with Northern Division winner Oregon State. Stanford whipped the Beavers in two of three with Pollard leading the way with 16 markers in the final and headed for the NCAA western regional in Kansas City.

Eight teams made it to what was sometimes referred to as the World Series of Basketball. The fourth annual tournament was significant because it came on the 50th anniversary of Dr. James Naismith's invention of the game

More than 12,300 cash customers saw the regional where Colorado polished off Kansas, 46-44, and the Indians beat Rice, 53-47, with Pollard scoring 26 in the semifinal. Pollard led the way again in the regional championship game with 17 points as Stanford defeated Colorado, 46-35.

When the final against Dartmouth (22-3) rolled around a week later in Kansas City, 6-foot-5 sophomore Pollard sat on the bench in street clothes after suffering through two days of high temperatures with the flu. Burness, who missed the regionals because of an ankle injury, hobbled onto the floor along with the other starters.

Coach Everett Dean's Indians led by two at the half, but pulled away to win the title, 53-38, behind tournament MVP Howie Dallmar's 15 points. Three years later while attending University of Pennsylvania as a Navy pre-flight student, Dallmar made the consensus All-America team.

■ SPARTANS BOMBED, LITERALLY

San Jose State's football team fell on hard times late in 1941. The Spartans had posted a 46-4-1 record the previous four years to rank among the nation's top small colleges.

The 1941 Spartans were off to a good start with five wins and two ties, but saw their string of 18 games without a loss snapped when future Cleveland Browns star Marion Motley led Nevada to 20-19 win with TDs on a 64-yard run and 100-yard kickoff return. They played a scoreless tie with Fresno State and dropped a pair to USF and Moffett Field.

The players hoped their luck would change when they took their annual excursion to Honolulu to play Hawaii. After all, Spartan teams had fared well on previous trips to the islands, winning four of five games since 1935.

The team flew to Honolulu looking forward to catching some rays and watching the hula dancers. Their bad luck continued when games against Hawaii and Willamette were canceled after the Dec. 7 Japanese attack on Pearl Harbor. The team volunteered for police duty and when it returned home after Christmas, seven players stayed behind to continue working for the police department.

■ OWLS AND JOSOX

Professional baseball, missing here since the California State League folded because of bad weather in the soggy spring of 1915, returned to San Jose in 1942.

In addition to a new team, the city had a sparkling new ballpark, Municipal Stadium. The 2,900-seat, all concrete facility was built for $90,000 by the federal Works Progress Administration and remains the oldest ballpark in California where professional baseball is played.

The Pacific Coast League's Portland Beavers trained in San Jose and played in the stadium's first game, a March 7 exhibition against the San Francisco Seals. More than 2,000 turned out to see the Seals beat the Beavers, 15-8. A week later the San Jose Owls opened the California League season with a 13-1 win over defending champion Fresno.

The California League was in its second year, but down to four teams from 1941's eight due to the onset of World War II. Poor attendance caused it to fold in late June with San Jose (35-32) in second place. Under owner Bob Ripley's low budget operation, players rode regularly-scheduled Greyhound buses on road trips. The batter with the lowest average was forced to carry the team's bats and the pitcher with the highest ERA was responsible for transporting all the baseballs. Outfielder Sal Taormina (San Jose) was the team's star, leading the league with a .357 batting average.

The league returned in 1947 with San Jose as a Boston Red Sox farm club, an affiliation which produced such major leaguers as Albie Pearson, Marty Keough, Norm Zauchin, Ken Aspromonte, Dick Gernert and pitchers Tex Clevenger, Frank Sullivan and Earl Wilson.

A record crowd of 4,091 attended the 1947 opener, filling temporary bleachers and spilling onto the outfield grass. The Red Sox lost to Stockton, 6-4, and ended the season in third place under manager Marv Owen.

After finishing seventh in 1948, the 1949 Red Sox rose to fourth as record attendance exceeded 113,000. The team dumped second place Fresno in the playoff's opening round. Zauchin hit his seventh postseason homer and 26th of the year as the Red Sox won their fourth straight over Ventura, 4-3, to take the title and split the $1,250 pot.

■ ULTIMATE INSTANT REPLAY

College of the Pacific football coach Amos Alonzo Stagg didn't ask for instant replay of the touchdown play that cost his Tigers a loss against San Jose State in 1941. He wanted the entire game to be played over.

Nearly a week after the Spartans won at Stockton, 7-0, on fullback Allen Hardisty's short plunge, Stagg was on the telephone to SJS athletic director Tiny Hartranft.

Stagg asked for the replay after he saw a newspaper photograph showing that Hardisty didn't cross the goal line and because there was concurrence by eyewitnesses and "dissatisfaction" among COP players. Hartranft politely declined the unprecedented request from the 79-year-old Stagg, who had been coaching college football since 1892.

The Spartans had a full schedule, he said, and game officials had decided Hardisty scored on the play in question. Referee Joseph Canella said the ball rested on the goal line before Hardisty was thrown back out of the end zone and that the play was called properly.

■ MOFFETT FIELD FLYERS

A new football program shared the county with Stanford, Santa Clara and San Jose State in 1941, when the Moffett Field Army Air Corps base fielded a team the 1942 NCAA Football Guide described as, "the greatest service football team since the gridiron era of World War I (and) the mythical national service champion."

Moffett Field's Flyers had played several games against junior college elevens and the California junior varsity team the previous year, but offered a stronger schedule in 1941.

The Flyers' roster was loaded with ex-college players, including former Stanford All-Coast center Tony Calvelli, San Jose State QB Jack Sarkisian and kicker Ken Cook, USF backs Bill Telesmanic and Marty Mosconi, Cal back Bill Huters and player-coach Ray "Butch" Morse, an end from Oregon who played five years with the Detroit Lions.

San Jose State football coach Ben Winkelman ran the program before stepping down to an advisory role after several games. The team went 7-1-0, beating Chico State, 28-0, the Cal Ramblers, 26-6, and San Jose State, 22-13, while losing only to St. Mary's, 6-0.

Other games were against the region's best military teams. The Flyers drew 40,000 to Berkeley's Memorial Stadium on Armistice Day for a game in which they beat the 12th Naval District, 20-7. Other games were played at Spartan Stadium and San Francisco's Kezar Stadium.

The Flyers were in Seattle preparing to meet Fort Lewis for the West Coast championship on Dec. 7, but the game was canceled when the Japanese attacked Pearl Harbor.

■ FOR THE RECORD

Indiana's Archie Harris set a discus world record in 1941 with a toss of 174-9 in the NCAA meet at Stanford.

Howie Dallmar of Stanford stole home twice in a 13-run inning against St. Mary's in 1943.

Glen Wilson of Mountain View High ripped the nets for 42 points in a 99-26 win over Live Oak in 1946. He led the SCVAL with a record 132 points in eight games.

San Jose's Marv Owen (Bellarmine, SCU) made only six errors and fielded .985 with Portland in 1946, still the Pacific Coast League record for third basemen playing in at least 150 games.

■ CASUALTIES OF WAR

In a two-week period in August, 1943, county football fans were dealt a trio of severe blows. World War II killed off all three college gridiron programs as San Jose State, then Stanford and finally Santa Clara all dropped the sport.

San Jose State abolished football for the duration of the war because of a lack of players and a fear there wouldn't be enough opponents to fill the Spartans' schedule.

Before the military draft accelerated, up to 2,000 male students attended classes on San Jose State's Washington Square campus. Fewer than 250 were expected to enroll in October for the 1943 fall semester.

Spartan Athletic Director Tiny Hartranft said if football continued, it would have to rely on 17-year-olds and men classified 4F (physically unfit for military service).

Stanford and Santa Clara also lost many students to the military, but both operated training programs for the Army. Unfortunately, while the Navy, Marines and Air Corps allowed on-campus trainees to play college football during the war, the Army didn't.

Stanford coach Marchie Schwartz said he would stay at The Farm to train soldiers in physical fitness, but school officials felt they couldn't continue football. Santa Clara coach Buck Shaw echoed Schwartz and noted 94 percent of SCU's all-male student body was in the armed forces.

None of the schools fielded varsity football teams again until 1946, although in 1945 both San Jose State's freshman team (3-3-0) and Stanford's unofficial squad (1-1-0) played

The backfield for Santa Clara's 1942 football team -- the last before the program went into hibernation during World War II -- was (from left) Pete Davis, Pat Higgins, Paul Vinolla and All-American tailback Jess Freitas.

against junior college and service teams.

Stanford dropped basketball and baseball until 1946, while SJS played baseball throughout the war and fielded an unofficial cage team in 1943-44. Santa Clara did not play baseball during the war or basketball in the 1943-44 season.

San Jose State's 1943-44 basketball team went 4-12 against college and military opponents, but isn't mentioned in the school's media guide. Lack of recognition apparently stems from the fact that all the players on coach Bill Hubbard's squad were freshmen, although both collegiate opponents, San Francisco State and College of the Pacific, list the SJS results in their records for the season.

The 1944-45 Broncos basketball team coached by varsity mentor George Barsi started one letterman, Fred Lautze, and lost all 11 games, mainly against service teams.

■ BIG BONE PRELUDE

The Big Bone trophy came later, but the cross-town rivalry was just as intense when Lincoln and San Jose high schools met on the football field for the first time in 1943.

Lincoln High opened in the fall of 1942. It began playing football in the Santa Clara Valley Athletic League, which had smaller schools than the Peninsula Athletic League, where San Jose was a dominant force.

The following fall, Lincoln was admitted to the PAL, setting up the first meeting in the traditional series which continues to this day as a major end-of-the-season attraction for backers of the Lions and Bulldogs.

Coach Lee Cox had guided his Lions to a 3-1-0 start going into the Armistice Day game against Walt Williams' 1-2-1 Bulldogs at Spartan Stadium.

With local college football programs sidelined for the duration of the war, prep football was the only game in town. Eleven thousand turned out to root for their favorites to gain bragging rights as San Jose's best team. The game's intensity was heightened because many of Lincoln's students attended San Jose before their new school opened.

With the score tied at 7-7 in the third quarter, San Jose recovered a fumble on the Lion's 27. George Boehme ran 22 yards to the five and took the ball into the end zone three plays later for San Jose's 13-7 win.

The Big Bone trophy appeared the following year. A group of San Jose lettermen found the bone, painted one end with Lincoln's colors (blue and gold), the other with San Jose's (red and gray) and put the score in the middle. The Big Bone goes to the winning school each year.

■ MINOR LEAGUE FOOTBALL

Although the San Francisco 49ers located their training facility in Santa Clara in the 1980s, they weren't the first play-for-pay football team to call the county home.

That honor falls to the San Jose Mustangs, member of the minor league Pacific Coast Football League in 1944 and 1945. The league had operated along the Pacific Coast since 1940, with most of the teams located in the San Francisco-Oakland and Los Angeles-Hollywood areas.

Rosters were full of former West Coast college players, including a few who went on to stardom in the NFL and All-America Football Conference or in other fields.

Among the best known were former Stanford QB Frankie Albert, Kenny Washington -- a black halfback and Jackie Robinson's running mate at UCLA -- kicker Ben Agajanian and future Washington Redskins star back Steve Bagarus. Actor Woody Strode of UCLA was all-league at end with Hollywood in 1941.

San Jose joined the league in 1944 when ex-SCU star Frank Sobrero, the nominal owner of the Alameda Mustangs, merged his club with the Richmond Boilermakers, who listed former Stanford football coach Tiny Thornhill as an advisor.

Sobrero had tested the San Jose market in 1943, when a crowd of 1,500 turned out to see Alameda lose to Richmond at Spartan Stadium, 16-13.

Sobrero, who played halfback, rented the stadium for 1944 and the Mustangs opened with a 14-7 loss to the San Francisco Packers before 3,000 fans. San Jose played only six of 10 scheduled games, finishing 3-3-0.

Players with local ties included QB Stu McCullough of Stanford, backs Bob Boucke and Ernie Hesse of SJS, and Sobrero, back Red Perkins, end Burns Campbell, and guards George Cosgrove and Bob Debenedictis of SCU.

Sobrero's brother, Jack, joined the team in 1945 and punted for an average of 40.7 yards. The Mustangs (0-5-0) needed his toe to get them out of trouble, since they were outscored 162 to 58. Home crowds averaged 4,500 and the team folded after the season.

The Pacific Coast Football League continued to operate through 1948, when it collapsed because fans were more interested in watching the AAFC's San Francisco 49ers and Los Angeles Dons and the NFL's Los Angeles Rams.

■ RAISINS AND MORE RAISINS

With World War II over, San Jose State returned to the gridiron in 1946. The Spartans expanded their schedule to include more powerful football schools, including St. Mary's, Santa Clara and Stanford, and won three-quarters of their games through the end of the decade.

The first postwar head coach was Bill Hubbard, who had won 12 letters at San Jose State and was all-conference

San Jose attracted cyclists to the Burbank (above) and San Jose Velodromes in the 1940s and 1950s. Burbank was on the present site of Lincoln High School's football field and San Jose was next to the Speedway on Tully Road. Among the riders were (from left) Dominic Lavardi, Percy Smith and former Olympian Cocky O'Brien.

in football and basketball in the 1920s.

Blessed with teams that included many returning war veterans and 17 players who eventually would reside in the school's athletic Hall of Fame, Hubbard molded a potent offense that averaged nearly 30 points per game during his four years at the helm. The teams won 36 of 48 games and made two postseason bowl appearances.

In 1946, the 9-1-1 Spartans lost only to undefeated Hardin-Simmons. They beat Fresno State, 13-2, in the mud for the CCAA title when Pete Denevi ran for one touchdown and passed for the other. SJS polished off Utah State in its first Raisin Bowl game in Fresno, 20-0.

San Jose State went 9-3-0 in each of the next two years, stepping up in class in 1948 when they lost close games to Stanford and St. Mary's but were embarrassed by powerful Nevada, 39-0.

Although they were shelled 49-0 by Stanford and 45-7 by Pacific, the 1949 Spartans fashioned a 9-4-0 mark and a school record 477 points. The Spartans had 702 offensive yards, intercepted seven passes for 171 more and rolled over University of Mexico in the opener, 103-0. They returned to the Raisin Bowl and beat Texas Tech, 20-13.

Little All-Coast first team honors went to quarterback Gene Menges, who threw 15 touchdown passes, and halfback Harry Russell. Tackle Harley Dow and end Billy Wilson won All-Coast honorable mention.

■ TRIVIAL PURSUITS

Len Casanova, a Santa Clara University football player and coach, was the brother-in-law of Joe Oeschger, who -- along with opponent Leon Cadore -- pitched the longest game in big league history (26 innings) in 1920.

Stanford champion golfer Sandy Tatum could hit the books as well as the ball, earning membership in the Phi Beta Kappa honor society.

The first San Francisco 49ers team in 1946 was loaded with local players: QB Frankie Albert, guard Bruno Banducci, end Hank Norberg, back Norm Standlee (Stanford); guard Dick Bassi, end Alyn Beals, back Ken Casanaga, center Ed Forrest, QB Jesse Freitas, guards Visco Grgich and Rupe Thornton (Santa Clara); end Bob Titchenal (San Jose State).

■ IN PASSING

San Jose amateur cycling star Tony Vallerga, 20, was struck and killed by an automobile on Stevens Creek Road near Doyle Road in 1940 while training.

Harlan Dykes, 47, former Santa Clara University law professor and 1927-35 basketball coach (101-48), died in a San Francisco hospital in 1940 after a long illness.

Joseph "Chick" Amaral, 35, former baseball player and Hillview golf champion, died of a heart attack in 1943.

Dick Edmonds, 31, Sacramento Union sports editor who led the fight to keep the PCL franchise in the state capital in 1944, died of pneumonia a year later. The city's ballpark was renamed in honor of Edmonds, a San Jose State graduate and former Mercury-Herald sportswriter.

Wartime casualties included Bellarmine athlete Richard Minear, killed on the USS Arizona in the Japanese attack on Pearl Harbor in 1941; Lt. Fred Dittman, 22, Santa Clara University football player, killed in a 1942 plane crash near Las Vegas that took the lives of 21 others, including Clark Gable's actress wife, Carol Lombard; Lt. William Gunther, 21, Palo Alto High basketball star, killed in a bomber crash in San Francisco Bay in 1942, and paratrooper Dave Hines, San Jose State wrestling champ, killed in Belgium in 1945.

■ UNWANTED BRONCOS

Santa Clara University's basketball players turned down an offer from the eight-team National Invitational Tournament at the end of the 1946-47 season in hopes they would be chosen for the NCAA postseason competition.

Today that wouldn't be big news. But, in the 1940s, the four-night NIT at New York's Madison Square Garden was every bit as prestigious as the NCAA tournament.

Unfortunately, the NCAA invited only eight teams and the Broncos, 21-4 after playing a strong independent schedule under new coach Ray Pesco, were ignored in favor of champions from four major western conferences.

Santa Clara won 17 of its first 18 games, bowing only to a strong Washington State team. Big center Frank Laney set a school scoring mark of 325 points as he led the Broncos to victories in five of six games against other PCC teams, losing only to Stanford.

Other loses came against USF, who they beat in the rematch, and to the Oakland Bittners, a powerful AAU team led by former Stanford All-American Jim Pollard.

■ BUCKING THE BEAR

If you visit Toso Pavilion on the Santa Clara University campus, you can inspect the large and impressive trophy the Broncos collected for winning the 1950 Orange Bowl football game.

The Broncos kept their own bowl record perfect at three straight victories by beating Kentucky, 20-13, and handing coaching legend Paul "Bear" Bryant his first bowl loss.

The No. 11 Wildcats were solid favorites because they had led the nation in total defense and only SMU had scored more than one touchdown against them. Oddsmaker Jimmy "The Greek" Snyder later said he lost the largest sum of money in his career when he bet $250,000 on Kentucky.

Santa Clara hadn't been in a postseason game since 1937, when it beat LSU in the Sugar Bowl for the second consecutive season. Coach Len Casanova's 1949 Broncos were a typical post-war team, a mixture of teenaged sophomores and military veterans back from World War II.

It was the era of one-platoon football, so everyone played both offense and defense. The team's star was halfback Hall Haynes, who was third in the nation with a 44.0 punting average for the 8-2-1 Broncos.

SCU might have spent New Year's Day at home but for Oklahoma head coach Bud Wilkinson. The Broncos had whipped his team in 1948 at Kezar Stadium, 20-17, the last loss before the Sooners went on a 31-game winning streak.

Santa Clara nearby beat the Sooners again in 1949 at Norman, Okla., losing 28-21. When Oklahoma accepted a

Admiring the 1950 Orange Bowl trophy were (from left) Johnny Justice, John Pasco, Buster Wraith, Ed Rotticci, Jim Cozad, Bob Dominick. Santa Clara beat Kentucky, 20-13, in the game.

Graham Field was home for San Jose semi-pro baseball in the 1930s and 1940s. Cars beyond the bleachers were parked on Willow Street between Almaden Avenue and First Street. After the stands were destroyed by fire, Graham street was cut through the property.

bid to the Sugar Bowl, Wilkinson recommended the Orange Bowl extend an invitation to the Broncos.

The Broncos trailed Kentucky at halftime, 7-0, but tied the game on John Pasco's quarterback sneak in the third period and went ahead on Haynes' touchdown run.

The Wildcats came back to score, but missed the extra point and trailed 14-13. Late in the game, Santa Clara iced the win with a 61-yard drive that ended with Bernie Vogel's 17-yard scoring scamper.

■ 1940 ■

Fifty cents admission lets fans watch Fred Perry top Bill Tilden in tennis exhibition at Civic Auditorium . . . Al Long pins opponent in 44 seconds as San Jose High wrestlers defend north state AAU prep title . . . San Jose High's Sam Alaimo hits 15 points, Abel Rodriguez 13 in Bulldogs' 40-22 PAL title clincher over Sequoia . . . Gene McFadden scatters 11 hits as SCU beats St. Mary's on diamond for first time in half dozen seasons, 8-3 . . . Plans announced for $60,000 West San Jose ice rink plus second $120,000 facility at Gish Road, N. Fourth Street . . . Los Gatos High's Hal Sonntag hits school record 25 against Washington to finish SCVAL hoops season with record 119 points. Tech, Mountain View tie for league title . . . Seattle outfielder Bill Lawrence (SCU) ties PCL record with 11 putouts against Los Angeles . . . Stanford's Clyde Jeffrey equals 100-yard record in 9.4 . . . Eddie Lyons of Tech High pitches perfect seven-inning win over Jefferson . . . Bill Bolich of SJS, Joe Lacey of SCU win Pacific Coast college boxing titles . . . Stanford's Larry Dee, Jimmy Wade win NCAA tennis doubles . . . Jim Fahl, Roy Diedricksen of SJS all-league for 7-0-1 soccer champions . . . Paul Moore of Stanford sets world mark of 2:58.7 at 1,320 yards . . . SJS school records fall to pole vaulter Tony Sunseri (13-9), miler Vin Ruhle (4:27.2) against San Diego State . . . Ernie Pieper beats Don Edwards by a stroke for sixth county golf title . . . Grant Denmark takes shot put, discus as Palo Alto High wins PAL . . . Former SJS grid star Lloyd Wattenberger pitches 32 straight no-hit, no-run innings for Hester Dairy in five softball games . . . Pitcher Tony Rose overcomes seven errors by Santa Clara High teammates, Bill Benevich whacks two doubles to drive in four in Panthers' 8-5 win against Mountain View for league title . . . Ken Hoernlein shoots 70-78-148 for medalist honors as SJS wins CCAA golf . . . SJS track records shattered: Don Presley puts shot 48-3, Ed Vasconcellos broad jumps 23-6 1/2 . . . Abe Acquistapace wins Mercury-Herald bowling championship . . . San Jose's Vic Sundberg takes inboard runabout speedboat race at Calero Lake, averaging 38 miles an hour . . . San Jose High tennis duo of Lloyd Clark, Victor Morton captures NCS doubles . . . Jimmy Mills, Pacific Coast billiards titleholder, undefeated in San Jose matches for 15th straight year . . . Ex-Stanford ace Larry Hall wins city tennis . . . Pitcher Bud Bosque, said to throw blistering 100 miles an hour, tops Knights of Columbus, 6-3, as Keystone Coffee wins third straight San Jose Softball Association title . . . Movie star George Raft buys San Jose lightweight contender George Latka's contract . . . Satchel Paige gives up two hits, fans eight in five frames as Kansas City Monarchs down Franco's Markets, 12-5 . . . Mountain View takes Gilroy, 12-6, for league title, but gives up first TD of year on 28-yard run by Mustangs' Billy Pirizzola . . . 5,000 see SJS crush South Dakota, 40-7, in Elks Lodge charity Prune Bowl at Spartan Stadium.

■ 1941 ■

Stanford's Bobby Blatt wins best individual skier award at Sun Valley, Idaho . . . San Jose High wrestlers topple Santa Clara, 27-21, for top places in Nor Cal tourney . . . Notre Dame High of San Jose defeats Moreland Academy of Watsonville, 27-22, in girl's hoops . . . Frankie Albert scores eight points in Stanford's 17-6 rugby win over Olympic Club . . . 6-foot-7 reserve center Bob Siebert goes for 20 in SJS victory over USF, 56-47 . . . Wheel length separates winner Trini Perez from Joe Colla, Dick Anderson in 50-mile Peninsula bicycle race . . . Frank Jelincich (San Jose) tops city Winter League hitters with .460 average . . . San Jose High's Mel Gomes dumps in 23 in 68-17 win over Half Moon Bay . . . 1,300 watch Sacramento JC, Southern Pacific draw, 4-4, in Alum Rock ice arena's first hockey game . . . Dick Uhrhammer leads SJS with 24 as Spartans clinch CCAA basketball title tie with 39-36 win over Fresno State . . . San Jose High's 24-game hoops winning streak ends with 35-34 loss to Burlingame . . . Tech High downs Santa Clara, 43-27, to tie Washington for SCVAL title. Marvin Neal tops Craftsmen with 15 . . . SJS boxer Bob Webber wins PCI 120-pound crown . . . SCU knocks USC out of CIBA first place with Bill Mustanich homering among four hits . . . Miler Bob Ingram of San Jose High breaks league record with 4:40.6 against Sequoia . . . SJS wrestlers Ivan Olsen, Vic Govin, Dave Hines, Bob Riddle take Pacific Coast titles . . . No-hitter by freshman Tony Janovich gives Mountain View High 11-0 win over Palo Alto . . . San Jose High's Larry Stewart wins PAL tennis singles. Bulldogs take team title . . . Bill Avellar grabs state handicap trapshooting crown . . . Omar Cowles of Palo Alto High sets state meet 120-yard high hurdles record of 14.3 at Spartan Field. San Jose's Bob Ingram tops milers in 4:32.8 . . . Tech High's 5-foot-5 Henry "Lefty" Honda whiffs 21 in 13-inning tie with Santa Clara High. Panthers win replay for league crown, 2-1 . . . Don Johnson (broad jump, high jump), Woody Linn (shot put, discus) lead Santa Clara High to SCVAL track title . . . George McGraw takes Mercury-Herald bowling with 1,219 pins . . . Ray Watson of Stanford tops Bert Stamps on fifth playoff hole for county golf title . . . San Jose High nine falls to San Mateo in PAL playoff final. Nick Baggese, Bulldogs' top batter, hits .422 . . . San Jose's Nash Garrison loses to No. 10 heavyweight boxer Tony Musto . . . Hester Dairy's Leroy Zimmerman (SJS) throws 12 no-hit softball games. Team loses in state playoffs after he reports to Washington Redskins . . . Pete Felice pitches 17 strikeouts in Franco's 9-5 win over Longshoremen . . . Barbara Beach Thompson of Los Altos repeats as county women's golf champ . . . Gus Kettman downs Dr. Leo Abate in county handball final . . . Eddie Booker of San Jose wins state middleweight boxing title from Shorty Hogue at San Diego . . . Cycle team of Joe Colla, Bob Stauffacher wins record seven straight one-hour races at Burbank Velodrome. Streak ends when they travel to state road races . . . Jerry Cantell's three hits with home run pace Permanente nine to 14-8 win over Fresno for American Baseball Congress regional title. Permanente takes state crown over Century Gasoline of Long Beach, 9-8 . . . State amateur golf title goes to Ernie Pieper, 4 and 2, over Bobby Gardner of San Diego. Pieper also wins San Jose title, 8 and 7, over Elmer Anderson . . . Dick Anderson scores twice, Bill Kievover once, passes for second TD as Palo Alto High dominates traditional rival San Jose, 26-0 . . . End Alyn Beals paces SCU with 10 TDs . . . Miffed by opponent's tactics, boxing champ Joe Louis KOs George Giambastiani in four-round exhibition bout at Civic Auditorium . . . First round pick Norm Standlee (Stanford) scores twice in Chicago Bears' 37-9 NFL title game romp over New York Giants . . . San Jose's fight dates produce third best revenues in state after Hollywood Legion Stadium, San Francisco Coliseum, but Babe Griffin quits promoting bouts until war ends.

■ 1942 ■

Dutch Boysen hits 14 points as SJS ends San Francisco State's nine-game basketball win streak, 59-44 . . . Palo Alto High dumps San Jose, 42-33, behind Hugh West's 16, goes on to win PAL hoops title in 18-0 season . . . San Jose High wrestlers tops in Nor Cals sixth straight year . . . Bruce Hale (SCU) leads Moffett Field with 37 in 67-45 win over Olympic Club . . . With

Woody Linn (center), 285-pound San Jose State weight man, clowns with distance runners Murray Collins (left) and Merle Cox.

Phil Griffin contributing 20, John Williams 18, Campbell High cagers crush Fremont, 47-8 . . . Tech High is SCVAL hoops champion, but Los Gatos High's Bob Pourey leads league with 125 points in eight games . . . Soph Stan Patrick sets SCU season basketball record, scoring eight in win over USF to close with 246, seven more than Bruce Hale's 1941 mark . . . SJS wrestlers Dave Hines, Ivan Olsen capture Pacific Coast titles . . . Duane Pillette pitches SCU to win over Cal after six straight losses . . . SJS boxers Dick Miyagawa, Charles Townsend are Pacific Coast champs . . . SCVAL cancels spring sports because of wartime transportation problems . . . Frank Minini (shot put, discus), Bill Smith (100, broad jump), double winners as SJS clips Stanford in track for first time, 85-46 . . . World champs Welker Cochran, Willie Hoppe attract 450 billiards fans to Civic Auditorium matches . . . Stanford's Frankie Albert (Chicago Bears), Pete Kmetovic (Philadelphia) go in NFL's first round . . . Gas rationing cuts attendance, forces closure of Ice Bowl skating rink . . . Best U. S. broad jumps recorded by SJS teammates Bill Smith (25-0), Willie Steele (24-8 1/2) at Fresno. Steele wins broad jump, triple jump at Junior AAU in New York, is second in senior broad jump . . . Joe Antuzzi's double, triple, four RBIs lead Bellarmine (9-3) to 14-6 win over Half Moon Bay . . . Walt Williams is county golf champion by stroke over Don Edwards . . . Sandy Tatum of Stanford leads NCAA individuals as Indians defend 1941 golf title . . . Stanford's Ted Schroeder wins NCAA tennis singles, teams with Larry Dee for doubles title . . . Murray Collins (mile), Bud Mortenson (both hurdles) lead San Jose High to NCS title . . . Frank Vizza's single drives in game winner as San Jose High defeats South San Francisco in PAL playoff, 2-1 . . . Larry Quetano wins Mercury-Herald bowling tourney . . . Former heavyweight wrestling champ Ed "Strangler" Lewis beats Cy Williams in comeback . . . Everett Goulart, golf pro at Crystal Springs and ex-San Jose caddy, tops Harry Bassler of Los Altos Country Club, 5 and 4, for Northern California PGA title . . . Mrs. A. A. Boldon of San Jose wins county women's golf . . . Bantamweight champ Lou Salcia whips Nat Corum in San Jose 10-rounder . . . Abel Rodrigues has three hits with homer as San Jose Creamery beats Santa Clara Merchants for city title, 6-5 . . . Army order to dim lights forces SJS to move six night football games to afternoon . . . San Jose boxer Eddie Booker beats Shorty Hogue for state middleweight crown . . . Eli Bariteau Jr.

tops Bobby Harris in two matches for under-14 golf title . . . San Jose High drops lightweight basketball after Japanese-American students are interned in prison camps . . . Palo Alto High dumps San Jose, 12-0, on pair of scores by George Fuchs, one a 96-yard punt return . . . Only 12 players have football experience, but new Lincoln High wins first game, 7-6, after center Charles Johnson falls on Mountain View fumble in end zone . . . Converted track star Willie Steele romps 74 yards with pass from Charley Cooke as SJS tops Alameda Coast Guard, 9-0 . . . Averaging 14 yards in 10 carries, Bob Barry scores twice in Mountain View High's 26-7 win over Campbell . . . SCU wins Little Big Game over St. Mary's, 20-7, before 50,000 at Kezar Stadium as Bill Prentice races 86 yards to end zone . . . John Felix tallies once, throws 33-yard pass to Frank Gonzales for second TD in Santa Clara High's 14-0 SCVAL title win over Campbell . . . Bellarmine quintet tops Burlingame, 38-33, behind Jack Cody's 16 points.

■ 1943 ■

With ex-Stanford star Jim Pollard scoring 17, Coast Guard downs SCU, 55-53. Sam Alaimo leads Broncos with 20 . . . Norm Keeler scores 12 as Palo Alto High wins 36th straight game, 25-24, over SJS Frosh. Burlingame ends string at 37 games, 33-32 . . . Manuel Ortiz TKOs Santa Clara's George Freitas in 10th round of bantamweight title fight at Oakland . . . Wrestler Jim Casey can't continue after Swedish Angel smashes him to mat at Civic Auditorium . . . SJS athletic department down to three coaches when DeWitt Portal, Bud Winter leave for Navy duty. Spartan boxers defeat Stanford with senior P.E. student Brent Riley as new coach . . . Basket by Ray Heatherington for Santa Clara High beats Lincoln, 31-29, to take SCVAL . . . Pitcher Earl Escalante tops Livermore Navy Reserve, giving Permanente Cementers Winter League playoff . . . Palo Alto High bests San Jose for PAL hoops title, 32-17 . . . Clara Mortensen defeats Rita Martinez to retain women's wrestling title, Sandor Szabo stops Sockeye McDonald in main event before 4,000 at Civic Auditorium . . . Ex-Stanford track coach Dink Templeton takes over same post at St. Ignatius High, USF . . . Coach Sam Della Maggiore's San Jose High wrestlers take PAL . . . SJS finishes third straight unbeaten soccer season (17-0-4 during period) . . . Frank Cleary wins city bowling . . . Swede Hensley's 25-second KO of Bob Poe gives SJS boxing win over Cal . . . Lincoln High's Murray Collins beats college runners, wins San Francisco indoor mile in 4:32.8 . . . SJS sports program hit hard when 200 reservists called to military duty including Bill Perry, Bert Robinson (football); Hal Sonntag, Pete Felice (basketball); Hal Souza, John "Bud" Urzi (baseball); Bill Smith, Thelmo Knowles (track) . . . Unbeaten Stan Smith of SJS loses narrow decision to Myron Miller of Wisconsin for NCAA boxing title . . . Don "Monk" Taylor swipes six bases as San Jose High steals 17 in 6-2 win over Santa Clara . . . Eldon O'Brien fans school record 15 as Bellarmine powders Lincoln, 11-1 . . . Soph Al Marciel throws two-hit, 2-0, win over Fremont High in first prep start for San Jose Tech . . . Lincoln High's George Wright KOs 16 Campbell batters . . . Freshman Hal Capers sets SJS high jump record at 6-8 against Fresno State . . . Bellarmine (16-0) plays independent baseball schedule . . . California tops Stanford, 85-46, in 50th Big Meet . . . San Jose High (22-3) defeats Sequoia twice in playoffs -- with Ralph Romero's no-hitter gaining one win -- to take third straight PAL title . . . Lincoln High's Murray Collins wins West Coast Relays mile in 4:29.7 . . . Ernie Pieper wins seventh county golf title by 10 strokes over runner-up Bert Stamps, who tops Mark Macklin in city golf final, 12 and 11 . . . Bowler Bob Nelson grabs Mercury-Herald title . . . Nash Garrison flattens Len Marshall in second round at Civic Auditorium . . . George LeDeit's two-run homer gives Davis Shell 3-2 win over Hendy's for city softball crown . . . Twenty-one yard Carroll Pugh to Ed Harvison TD pass leads Palo Alto High to 13-13 tie with San Jose . . . Shut out in first three games, playing with two days rest, Bellarmine gridders whitewash St. Vincent's of Vallejo, 19-0, end season 5-3-1 . . . Mountain View High students tear down goal posts after Los Gatos beats Eagles, 18-12. When school officials refuse Los Gatos' request for apology, relations break off. Teams don't meet again in football, basketball, baseball until 1946 . . . Scoreless in previous five games, Santa Clara High defeats Fremont, 6-0, stopping Indians from winning league, leaving Los Gatos, Mountain View in title tie . . . With 13 freshmen averaging 5-foot-8, SJS opens hoops season against Moffett Field Flyers, loaded with ex-college stars including Loyola's Pete Newell. Spartans are crushed 52-20.

■ 1944 ■

SCU hoops scoring star Stan Patrick transfers to Illinois . . . Twenty points by Ed Maggetti pace San Jose High over Palo Alto, 42-25 . . . Heavyweight wrestling champ Steve "Crusher" Casey retains title over Harry Kent . . . Harlem Globetrotters thump San Jose All-Stars, 49-34. Lou Colla tops locals with nine . . . Pete Denevi's 19 leads Los Gatos High to 53-29 win over San Jose Tech . . . San Jose High wrestler Tom Fama unbeaten for second year in 145-pound class . . . Mountain View High sets hoops records in 79-17 win over Fremont. Tony Janovich pumps in 34 . . . Tie among Lincoln, San Jose, Sequoia ends with Lions taking hoops playoff. Center Don McCaslin leads Lincoln to PAL title in playoff with Half Moon Bay . . . Leo Righetti tallies 15 as Bellarmine (13-1) wins 13th straight over Washington. Bells' lone hoops loss was to Palo Alto, who they beat in rematch . . . Pete Denevi steals home with winning run in Los Gatos High's 2-1 win over San Jose Tech to clinch SCVAL championship . . . Lincoln High wins PAL track crown as Fred Frevert sets mile record in 4:30.8. Lions later take NCS title . . . Los Gatos High's Bob Chambers captures NCS 880 in state record 1:55, later lowers mark to 1:54.4 . . . Bellarmine baseball team wins 13 of 15 games. Leo Righetti closes out his senior season with four straight one-hit wins plus no-hit game against Santa Cruz, signs with New York Yankees for $10,000 bonus . . . Ernie Pieper captures eighth county golf trophy with 54-hole record 209, wins state amateur title over Bobby Rosburg, 5 and 4 . . . Bud Bosque of Davis Shell pitches perfect game with 15 strikeouts to end Redwood City Eagles' 20-game softball win streak. Merced eliminates Davis Shell in state tourney . . . Officer Mitch Ucovich (SJS) quits Highway Patrol to play tackle for Washington Redskins . . . Jim Ferrier captures Northern California Open golf at San Jose Country Club . . . Fremont High's Walt Gachina keeps Los Gatos at bay with four punts of 45 to 65 yards in 0-0 tie . . . Warren Dawson holes eight-footer on 36th hole to edge Bert Stamps in city golf final, 1 up . . . Bellarmine stops undefeated CCAL champ Hollister, 21-6 . . . With future 49ers' All-Pro Billy Wilson at one end, Campbell High wins first SCVAL grid title . . . Lincoln High steamrolls South San Francisco, 34-0, to clinch PAL grid title tie . . . San Jose High hits only pass for 45 yards to set up George Boehme's

The San Jose Zebras at Municipal Stadium, from left, (back) George Yoshihara, John Horio, Shig Tachibana, Frank Horio, Fuzzy Shimada, coach Sam Della Maggiore; (middle) Ralph Horio, Tom Okagaki, Frank Shimada, Ikeke, Babe Nomura, Ernie Inouye, George Hinaga; (front) Sumito Horio, Russell Hinaga, Henry "Lefty" Honda, Chi "T-Bone" Akazuki, Morey Shimada, Jim Nagahara. At right is Honda, who once fanned 21 batters in 13 innings for San Jose Tech High.

TD run in 7-7 tie with Palo Alto that gives archrival Lincoln PAL title outright . . . San Jose High's Dick Finnegan, QB in school's new T formation, is top vote getter for All-PAL . . . Bellarmine's Bud Dowling racks up 123 yards in 13-0 triumph over St. Ignatius.

■ 1945 ■

Bellarmine's 14-game hoops win streak ends in 22-17 loss to Campbell High, led by Jack Wilson's 13 . . . Vic Bellomo of Mountain View High scores 27 in Eagles' 47-41 win over Santa Clara . . . SJS ends 10-game loss string on Don McCaslin's school record 32 points in 47-28 win over San Francisco State . . . Unbeaten San Jose High wrestler Lynn Robey wins Nor Cal 145-pound title . . . Grace Madriago is city all-events bowling champ . . . Santa Clara, Mountain View, share league hoops crown with 6-1 records . . . Babe Didrikson Zaharias, Betty Jameson lose golf exhibition to Ernie Pieper, Dick Richmond . . . Lincoln High's Elgin Martin adds 10 feet to previous best to take discus at 126-5 as Lions win PAL title . . . Marvin McDole pitches Santa Clara High to 6-3 win over Live Oak for title . . . Bill Rodrigues wins city, county golf . . . Lincoln High takes PAL on pitcher Archie Cassingham's 1-0 three-hit playoff win over South San Francisco . . . Jim Cunningham of Campbell High sets only record of 21-4 1/2 in broad jump as Santa Clara cops league track title . . . Lincoln High of San Francisco defeats Bellarmine boxers in Civic Auditorium matches . . . Eli Bariteau Jr.'s 77 leads Lincoln High to PAL golf crown . . . Angelo Pasin topples 1,291 pins for Mercury-Herald bowling title . . . Jesse Owens loses 100-yard race to horse, Harlem Globetrotters beat bearded House of David nine before record 2,500 at Municipal Stadium . . . Bay Meadows Blues nine trips San Jose A's, 5-3, to win semi-pro tournament . . . Lightweight Jess Flores, undefeated in 17 bouts, KOs Mike Villanova in sixth . . . Bellarmine tramples Campbell, 29-6, on Friday with Wayne Buck scampering 80 yards for TD, downs St. Mary's on Monday, 25-0, before 6,000 at Spartan Stadium . . . Triple-threat Don Panighetti of SCVAL champ Los Gatos (7-0-0) is unanimous all-league . . . Free admission crowds of 10,000, 17,000 watch Stanford's unofficial football team in win, loss against service teams . . . Ex-Stanford shortstop Bobby Brown signs with New York Yankees for $50,000 bonus.

■ 1946 ■

Los Gatos, Mountain View prep teams end feud . . . Ed Maggetti drops in 26 in SJS victory over San Francisco State, sets school season record at 338 points . . . Chuck Crampton's 50-footer rolls off rim at final gun as Lincoln High (21-1) falls to San Jose, 23-21. Loss ends 21-game win streak, creates PAL title tie between Lions, Sequoia . . . Playing with San Diego, Jim Pollard is national AAU cage tourney's MVP . . . Lincoln High's Gabe Padilla holds San Francisco Mission to two hits by future major leaguers Jim Baxes, Gus Triandos in 4-2 win . . . Tom Cruza's last minute field goal gives Bellarmine 36-34 win over St. Mary's for Catholic crown. Cruza (15.4 average) is all-league . . . San Jose High's Bob Maruca pitches one-hitter, but San Mateo wins, 1-0. PAL champ Bulldogs finish 17-2 . . . Eli Bariteau Jr. defeats Bobby Harris, 2 and 1, in north state junior golf final . . . Al Freitas, Pete Mesa lead Santa Clara High to SCVAL championship . . . Tom Kelly hits two doubles, triple, bats in three as SCU finishes with 8-6 win over St. Mary's . . . Head coach Larry "Moon" Mullins quits SCU grid job after spring practice saying he can't find house in area . . . Wanda (Gerrard) McGraw bowls record 267 game, 692 series at Jose Bowl . . . Future SCU baseball coach Al Endriss gets St. Elizabeth High's only hit in 10-1 loss to Bellarmine . . . Record 54-hole low 205 gives county golf to Ernie Pieper . . . Swede Lindskog wins first 20-lap midget main event at new San Jose Speedway. Clouds of dust from track, Tully Road gridlock mar evening for 5,000 fans . . . Chuck Bedolla (Bellarmine) gets three hits, Bill Ashley (Santa Clara) two as West Bay All-Stars top East Bay . . . Stanford wins NCAA golf title . . . San Jose motorcyclist Sam Arena takes Hall's Valley hill climb . . . Stanford grads Frankie Albert, Norm Standlee score as new San Francisco 49ers entertain 10,000 at Spartan Stadium with first intrasquad game

. . . Howie Dallmar skips senior season of basketball at Stanford to join pros . . . San Jose Tech High goes 3-3-1 in first football season . . . Palo Alto High beats Lincoln, 19-7, as Buddy Traina scores one, throws for two TDs . . . Joe Filice's three second half runs, including 90-yard kickoff return, give San Jose High 19-13 win over Palo Alto . . . San Jose's Pete Dixon wins Grand National Rodeo bareback bronc riding contest at Cow Palace . . . Ex-featherweight champ Jackie Wilson decisions Luis Castillo in 10 . . . Marte Formico of Bellarmine scores three times as Bells (8-0-0) close season with 43-6 win over Sacred Heart . . . League's best back Bob Cassell scores three TDs as Mountain View (7-1-0) wins SCVAL, 52-6, over Gilroy. League's top lineman is Eagles' tackle John Pear . . . Palo Alto High lightweight basketball team hands Santa Clara first defeat after 35 straight wins.

■ 1947 ■

San Jose High wrestler Karl Jensen wins 25th straight for Nor Cal title . . . Overflow crowd jams Civic Auditorium to watch Goose Tatum in Harlem Globetrotters' win over House of David, 49-44 . . . Poly High of San Francisco ends Lincoln's 13-game victory string, 38-30 . . . All-American Redheads women's cagers stop in San Jose, tip Moffett Field, 35-30 . . . Jim Bell, 6-foot-10 reserve, breaks San Jose High mark with 34 against Campbell in 37-27 win . . . Lorin Myers' half court shot as time runs out gives Lincoln High 29-27 win over San Jose for PAL title. Myers loses league scoring race to Palo Alto's Paul Watson by one point . . . Los Gatos takes SCVAL hoops. Wildcats' star Don Panighetti all-league third straight time . . . Bob Anderson, Wayne Fontes win Pacific Coast boxing titles for SJS. Fontes loses first bout in NCAA tourney to John Lendenski of Wisconsin . . . Sam Arena, winner of 45 of 48 motorcycle races, is champion of the year at first San Jose Banquet of Champions . . . San Jose Zebras' Chi Akizuki makes 15 points as San Jose Zebras win state nisei hoops over Los Angeles . . . Bobby Harris (SJS) downs Al "Fritz" Andrade (Tech) for Northern California junior golf crown, 7 and 6. Andrade later takes county junior title . . . Morgan Fottrell of SJS tops Stanford's Ernest Kellburg, 6 and 4, in north state college golf final . . . Mountain View High's Pete Mesa no-hits Washington, but loses, 1-0 . . . Grand slam by Lincoln High's Jim O'Connor defeats Burlingame in final inning, 10-7 . . . Woody Linn tops SJS discus mark against COP at 156-2 . . . Bob Barkhimer wins Speedway 25-lap main event . . . USC star half miler Bob Chambers (Los Gatos) falls, breaks leg . . . Ed Rutherford's grand slam against San Mateo puts San Jose High in PAL playoff final, where Bulldogs lose to Sequoia . . . Los Gatos High takes SCVAL tennis without losing set. Roy Mullins wins singles, Bradley Osborn, Dick Harris take doubles . . . County golf title goes to Jack Bariteau . . . Bellarmine's Marte Formico wins 100, 220, broad jump as Bells take 13 of 15 events in first Catholic League track meet . . . Washington, Santa Clara deadlock for SCVAL baseball crown. Panthers' all-leaguers Bob Parsons, Dan Hruby share batting title at .417 . . . Stanford's Bob Anderson wins 50, 100 freestyle races in PCC swim meet . . . Robert Likens of SJS retains NCAA javelin title with 209-1 throw . . . Julie Menendez, ex-SJS boxer who won national Golden Gloves title against Chuck Davey, turns pro. Menendez 17-1 in pro bouts when hand injury ends career . . . Willie Steele transfers to San Diego State because of housing problems at SJS, wins NCAA broad jump at 26-0 . . . Gus Gatto of San Jose tops field in three races for California bicycle crown . . . Wally Yonamine scampers to two TDs as Reds down Whites, 33-28, in 49ers intrasquad game at Spartan Stadium . . . Sam Arena wins motorcycle hill climb east of Milpitas, traveling 425-foot slope in 14.22 . . . Claire Lobrovich of San Jose hits .209 with Kenosha and Rockford in All-American Girls Baseball League . . . Bellarmine's grid win streak stopped at 14 by 7-6 loss to Sequoia . . . Freddie Agabashian's 25-lap Speedway win gives him Northern California point lead . . . Lincoln High's first unbeaten football team (8-0-0) inflicts Palo Alto's only loss in PAL opener, 19-7 . . . Baseball clowns Max Patkin, Johnny Price delight 3,000 at Municipal Stadium, where Bob Feller's big leaguers edge PCL stars, 4-2 . . . Pacific defeats SJS for first time since 1931, 14-0, before Spartan Stadium crowd of 14,693 . . . Jerry Piper captures San Jose Speedway's first 150-lap California Championship before 10,000 . . . St. Elizabeth tops Bellarmine, 13-6, at Townsend Field in fog so thick punts are eliminated, ball automatically advanced 35 yards . . . Ernie Jordan passes for two, runs for third TD as Los Gatos topples Campbell, 20-12, in battle of league undefeateds for SCVAL title . . . PAL player of the year Buddy Traina (Palo Alto) scores 17 TDs . . . Stanford's first winless football team nearly upsets powerful Cal, losing late, 21-18, on 80-yard Jackie Jensen to Paul Keckley pass play . . . San Jose's Al Scaffone takes state amateur motorcycle title.

■ 1948 ■

SCU opens year with Frank Laney pumping in 19 in 62-60 win over Temple . . . New seats, $50,000 lights for Washington Park in Santa Clara . . . Palo Alto High's Jim Loscutoff, future Boston Celtics star, scores 37 in 67-40 win over Lincoln . . . Bobby Harris (SJS) shoots nine birdies, nine pars for La Rinconada course record 61 . . . Record 12,206 fans turn out for Cow Palace doubleheader featuring Stanford over SCU, 53-41, Cal over St. Mary's, 70-53 . . . Ahead 45-40 against COP, Stanford stalls last five minutes for 45-43 win . . . Eddie Ingram's 24 points leads Lincoln High to win over Jefferson, 43-36 . . . Wayne Belardi (Bellarmine) tops Winter League with 24 RBIs . . . Bernard Bernheisal of San Jose captures novice class in 400-mile Oakland to Santa Cruz to San Francisco motorcycle race . . . San Jose Tech's Johnny Fredericks has record 145 points in eight league games, is SCVAL player of the year . . . Stanford freshman crew overturns shell in San Francisco Bay, all eight oarsmen rescued by passing boat after half hour in frigid water . . . San Jose High's PAL hoops winners finish 22-2, grab third place in Tournament of Champions . . . Stu Inman, Bob Hagen lead SJS (23-9) to first postseason hoops appearance in NAIA tourney, losing to Indiana State, 59-52 . . . 6-foot-5 San Jose High center George Clark is All-Northern California . . . SJS boxers Kenny Cayocca, Pete Franusich take PCI bouts . . . San Jose Zebras retain regional nisei hoops title . . . Northern California junior golf champ is San Jose Country Club caddy Chris Sgambati . . . Ray Eckert defeats Billy Hanson at Civic Auditorium for West Coast pro wrestling crown . . . Otis Chandler heaves shot put 53-2 as Stanford beats SJS, 70-61, for first track and field win since war . . . Herm Daz is San Jose Mercury-Herald bowling king . . . Ralph Romero fans 16 as SJS defeats San Diego State, 6-4 . . . Stanford high hurdler Bill Kreitz runs Big Meet record 14.4, but Indians fall to Cal, 76-55 . . . Jane Robb of San Jose captures California Bowling Proprietors tournament . . . SJS wins CCAA track title as Don Smalley sets meet records in 100 (9.7), 220 (21.4) . . . San Jose High pitcher Joe Carbonaro blanks Palo Alto with no-hitter, 15-0, goes three-for-three at plate . . . Lincoln High's Herb Cohen wins NCS 880 in 2:01.3 . . . Fremont High's Charles Gonzales runs low hurdles in record 24.3 as Indians take SCVAL title . . . Eric Pedley wins 880, mile for Catholic track champ Bellarmine . . . Wayne Belardi of Bellarmine is MVP in North-South All-Star baseball games at Muni Stadium . . . SJS wins NCAA golf at Stanford with Bobby Harris 1 up winner over Ed Hopkins of Texas for medalist honors . . . Ben Hogan shoots 64 in San Jose Country Club exhibition . . . Sam Arena second to Windy Lindstrom at U. S. motorcycle hill climb. Top amateur is Sunnyvale's Cliff Ricker . . . In one of state amateur golf tourney's greatest comebacks, Eli Bariteau Jr. rallies from four down with six to play to beat Bobby Rosburg on 37th hole at Pebble Beach . . . Earl Peters of Los Gatos sets records in Salton Sea hydroplane races . . . Bobby Harris wins city golf title over Vern Brown, 6 and 5 . . . Three Ellery Williams TD receptions give SCU 25-13 win over USF . . . Tied at 12 with two minutes left, Palo Alto High's John Bettencourt runs back pass interception 75 yards for 19-12 win over San Jose . . . Palo Alto High's hoops team downs San Jose, 59-32, with Hod Ray Jr. hitting 18 . . . Behind champs Tommy Adams, Frank Padia, Bill Saia, San Jose High wins Nor Cal wrestling . . . Al Talboy drops in 18 as Palo Alto High whips San Jose Tech, 51-29 . . . Mal-Suns, San Jose's entry in amateur American Basketball League, lose opener to Idaho, 52-50. Team folds at end of season . . . Bob Keeler hits record 66 goals for National AAU junior champion SJS water polo team (12-1-3). Freshmen squad, led by George Haines' 48 goals, goes 12-0-1.

■ 1949 ■

Johnny Fredericks pops for 27 in San Jose Tech High's 46-31 victory over Mountain View . . . Stanford tops future NIT champ USF, 65-55. George Yardley scores 20, leads Indians with 345 points . . . Al Talboy's 27 not enough as Palo Alto High falls to San Jose, 51-44. Talboy leads PAL in scoring (117 in eight games), is league's top player. San Jose's Vern Wilson also on All-PAL . . . Primo Carnera, ex-heavyweight wrestling champ, puts Tommy O'Toole down in straight falls before 4,200 at Civic Auditorium. Ticket sales produce record $4,845 . . . Fremont High deals San Jose Tech first league loss, 45-42, as Bob Poen hits 14 . . . Missing flu-ridden top scorer Don Dolen (221 points), Bellarmine falls to St. Mary's in CAL playoff, 46-33 . . . Soph Andy Collins leads SCU cagers with 189 points . . . Fremont High wins SCVAL hoops, but San Jose Tech's Johnny Fredericks paces scorers (119 points), is only unanimous all-star . . . Stu Inman's school record 521 points helps SJS reach second NAIA basketball tourney. Spartans lose to Eastern Illinois, 81-75 . . . San Jose's J. T. Ross (26 KOs in 36 bouts) stopped in five by middleweight contender Steve Belloise at Madison Square Garden . . . Five SCU homers, with two by Bill Renna, beat USF, 8-6 . . . San Jose's Gus Gatto takes 23.5-mile Lake Merced cycling race third straight year . . . Motorcycle champ Sam Arena captures 275-foot Dublin hill climb in record 6.98, adds Hall's Valley climb to win list . . . SJS takes CCAA track title as Bob Crowe clocks 9.7 in 100 and 21.1 in 220 . . . Gay Bryan's 23 points (wins in 100, 220, low hurdles, second in broad jump) leads Stanford to Big Meet win over Cal . . . Home water at Palo Alto Yacht Harbor not enough as Cal whips Stanford crew by two-plus lengths . . . George Mattos first from SJS to top 14 feet in pole vault . . . Wayne Fontes of SJS wins NCAA boxing title . . . Bob Wuesthoff cracks four hits with double, home run, four RBIs as SJS (16-10) handles Fresno State, 21-6, in CCAA playoff opener. Pete Mesa pitches 13-8 title game victory . . . Don Straub of Los Gatos High wins SCVAL tennis . . . Eleventh county golf trophy rests on Ernie Pieper's mantle . . . Fremont High registers record 143 points to take SCVAL track. Johnny Mesa wins 100, 220, triple jump . . . Ted Schroeder (Stanford) takes Wimbledon tennis . . . Stanford's Otis Chandler breaks PCC meet record with 54-9 1/2 shot put . . . SCU's Bill Renna hits .369, leads CIBA in hits, RBIs. Teammate Hal Toso (5-2) tops in innings pitched . . . Pioneer Investors Savings and Loan bowlers win state team title. San Jose's Vern Hoffman, Gerry Swanson take doubles . . . Memory Post 399 (Bellarmine, Lincoln players) loses to Bill Irwin Post of Oakland in American Legion baseball. Irwin wins national title . . . San Jose's Tom Easton, John Darendinger win Speedway's first 24-hour endurance race, covering 1,128 miles . . . Cyclist Gus Gatto takes north state title . . . Eli Bariteau Jr. crowned Northern California amateur golf champion . . . County tennis champions: Frank Pisale (singles), Earle Alderman, Dick Steinhauer (doubles), Steinhauer (junior singles), Lorraine Steinfeld (junior girl's singles) . . . Mimi Arnold of Los Gatos wins national hard court under-11 girl's tennis title . . . Bud Bosque hurls Western Gravel to 5-0 win over East Oakland Merchants for state softball title . . . SCU edges SJS, 14-13, as Broncos' Marte Formico runs back punt 50 yards for score . . . Ken Ravizza races 209 yards in 12 carries as Bellarmine plasters Washington, 40-12 . . . Manuel Rocha scores four TDs on short runs, adds 50-yard TD reception from Johnny Leal in San Jose High's 32-12 victory over Palo Alto . . . Fremont High (7-1-0) wins first SCVAL grid title. San Jose High (9-0-0) takes PAL with end Bud Wichert voted top player . . . Santa Clara High halfback Bill Gil all-league third straight year . . . San Jose High quintet beats Bellarmine, 39-31, with Vern Wilson scoring 16 in first meeting since Bells, Bulldogs cut athletic ties in 1931 . . . City golf won by Ernie Pieper over Bill Ogden, 10 and 8 . . . Palo Alto beats Sequoia, 49-43, with 24 from Larry Ramm, who transfers to Sequoia next semester.

Former Bay Area grid stars Norm Standlee of Stanford and USF's swift little Forrest Hall, left, clowned at the 49ers' training camp.

The 1950s

Before its heyday was over, stars of the Santa Clara Swim Club were among the biggest names in international swimming -- Chris von Saltza, Don Schollander, Donna de Varona and Mark Spitz, to name just a few

But in 1954, the club that eventually produced scores of world class swimmers, took its first tiny step toward national recognition by sending coach George Haines and a four-girl team to the AAU women's indoor swimming championships in Daytona Beach, Fla.

The team finished a remarkable fifth with Carol Tait, a 15-year-old Menlo-Atherton High School student, winning both the 250- and 500-yard freestyle events. Other members of Haines' historic foursome were Susan Doll, Anne Howry and Pat Mahaney. The swim club had produced age group champions for several years, but its first venture into the big time brought a huge payoff.

"Those victories were a tremendous boost to the program," Haines said later. "A lot more kids turned out because of (Tait)." Tait won the 500-yard freestyle in 1955 and joined the USA team in the Pan American Games.

In 1956, the club was fifth in the national women's indoor meet and third outdoors. Tait was joined by Doll, Jane Wilson, Mary Mahaney and a 12-year-old phenom from Saratoga Elementary School named Chris von Saltza, who broke the women's record for the 400-yard freestyle.

The following year it seemed that von Saltza or other club members broke an age group, AAU, national or U. S. citizen record every time they jumped into the pool. The club won its first AAU senior women's title with von Saltza accounting for more than one-third of its 62 points.

Von Saltza was 14 when she appeared on television's "To Tell The Truth" in 1958. She stumped all the panelists except Conrad Nagle, who correctly picked her from among three girls claiming to be Saratoga's champion mermaid.

The success continued through the rest of the decade with von Saltza breaking several marks and joining with Wilson, Doxie Ransom and Susan Honig for an American 400-meter medley relay mark.

Von Saltza closed out the 1950s by taking five gold medals in the Pan American Games and began to look ahead to the 1960 Olympics, where her name would become known around the world.

Santa Clara Swim Club coach George Haines talks to Olympic champion Chris von Saltza.

■ BOB MATHIAS

Bob Mathias was one of the world's best known athletes when he arrived on the Stanford campus in the fall of 1949 to play a little football and run some track.

As a 17-year-old the previous year, Mathias had become the youngest person ever to win an Olympic medal, taking the decathlon in a heavy downpour at London.

It was an amazing achievement for the youngster from Tulare High School, who had never run a distance race, pole vaulted, long jumped or tossed the javelin until the spring of 1948, when his coach suggested he try the 10-event decathlon. Mathias won the Pacific AAU meet in Los Angeles and took the Olympics in only his third try at the event on his way to a perfect 11 for 11 career record in decathlons.

Mathias set two world records, the first in the 1950 AAU championships in his hometown -- one of his four AAU titles -- and another in 1952, when he defended his

Bob Mathias

Olympic crown in Helsinki with a 7,592 points total.

Mathias was a star fullback on the Stanford football team in 1951 and 1952. His 96-yard kickoff return for a score helped beat USC, 27-20, in 1951 as the 9-2-0 Indians went to their first Rose Bowl in more than a decade.

The No. 7 Indians were no match for No. 4 Illinois, who blew the game open with four fourth quarter touchdowns on the way to a 40-7 victory. Mathias was held to minus eight yards rushing and two catches for 42 more.

Washington took Mathias in the 30th and final round of the 1953 NFL draft, but he didn't play with the pros. He opted instead to make movies, playing himself in "The Bob Mathias Story." His other films were "China Doll" and "It Happened in Athens" with Jayne Mansfield.

■ EDDIE CHAVEZ

Eddie Chavez could bring out the boxing fans in the 1950s. The popular San Jose junior lightweight drew Civic Auditorium's largest crowd in four years early in 1950 when 3,750 watched him beat Chico Rosa in 10 rounds.

In May of the same year, Jackie McCoy won the nod over Chavez, ending his 25-bout winning streak. But, Eddie came back in June with a 10-round decision over McCoy.

Chavez drew the largest fight crowd in county history when an estimated 8,000 fans paid a record $21,000 in late September to see him decision Maxie Docusen easily in the first professional bout ever held at Municipal Stadium.

It was San Jose's first outdoor fight since the early 1920s, when a bout between Joe Dunn and Mason Griffin at the old San Jose Speedway raised money for the widow of a policeman who had been killed by a gunman.

In 1951, Chavez won a 10-round decision over Manuel Ortiz in the first boxing match in Santa Clara since the sport was legalized in California decades earlier. The bout drew 2,685 at Washington Park.

Chavez, a popular amateur who produced a 47-1 record before turning pro in 1948, fought some of the best during his career. He lost a split 10-round decision to former world featherweight titleholder Willie Pep at the Cow Palace in 1951 and decisioned future lightweight king Jimmy Carter in 10 at San Francisco in 1953. He lost to future lightweight champ Paddy DeMarco at Madison Square Garden in 1951 and fought him to a draw in San Francisco in 1952.

Chavez won six of seven bouts in 1953, including a split decision win over lightweight champ Carter in a non-title bout in San Francisco. He achieved another milestone by beating Henry Davis in a July 4 bout that was the first ever televised nationally from San Jose.

He retired several years later, but made brief comeback in 1957 only to be outclassed and suffer an eighth round TKO by Willie Morton.

Eddie Chavez

■ FOR THE RECORD

Gus Gatto of San Jose won the 1951 national seniors amateur cycling championship at Columbus, Ohio, setting a 10-mile record of 23:22.2.

Using a javelin of his own design that later was banned from international competition, Stanford's Franklin "Bud" Held posted a world record throw of 268-2 in 1953.

San Jose High's Ben Gonzales had a league strikeout mark of 18, including the first nine batters, in a seven-inning, 5-1, win over Palo Alto in 1954.

Stanford's Ron Tomsic broke the PCC Southern Division single-game hoops scoring mark with 40 against USC in 1954. He ended his four-year career with 1,416 points, surpassing Hank Luisetti's three season total of 1,291.

Carroll Williams of San Jose State was 16-for-16 from the free throw line against Loyola in 1955.

Pitcher Roger Osenbaugh (Stanford) gave up nine home runs for Sacramento in a 22-5 loss to Los Angeles in 1957 to set the Pacific Coast League record.

In 1957, QB Chon Gallegos of Lick High set a state mark by completing his first 16 passes in a 35-19 win over Los Gatos. He went 17 of 20 with three TDs.

QB Dick Norman of Stanford set the NCAA standard

Basketball stars were (from left) Santa Clara's Ken Sears, San Jose State's Stu Inman and Stanford's George Yardley. Sears and Yardley played in the NBA and Inman was the Spartans' coach.

for completions (34), yards (401) and passing percentage (.872) in a 20-17 loss to Cal in 1959.

■ THE BIRD

George Yardley might have been the best late bloomer to come out of Santa Clara County.

An inconsistent basketball player in his first two varsity seasons at Stanford, the skinny Yardley, who carried only 195 pounds on a 6-foot-5 frame, starred as a senior.

Nicknamed "Bird" because of his physical appearance and an incredible jumping ability that allowed him to seemingly hang in the air, Yardley averaged 16.9 points in the 1949-50 season, the nation's 27th best average, and made third team All-America.

The Indians lost to Cal, 64-55, in the season finale, but the big story was Yardley's effort to surpass Hank Luisetti's PCC Southern Division scoring record of 232. Yardley racked up 26 points to break the mark by five. But down south, USC's Bill Sharman hit 21 second half points against UCLA to take the scoring crown with 238.

The Fort Wayne Pistons offered Yardley a chance to turn pro, but he turned it down because he hoped to play in the 1952 Olympic Games.

Yardley joined San Francisco's powerful amateur quintet, Stewart Chevrolet, scoring 33 against Fort Collins as his team won the national AAU championship. Yardley continued to play with Stewart, but broke his hand in the 1952 Olympic trials and failed to make the USA team.

Yardley joined the Detroit Pistons in 1953 and nearly quit after a so-so rookie season when he averaged only nine points. But, he returned to the team and raised his scoring steadily over the next three years.

His best year was 1957-58 when he set the Boston Garden scoring record with 51 against the Celtics and scored 2,001 points for a 27.8 average to become the first NBA player to exceed the 2,000 point mark for a season.

Traded to Syracuse, Yardley averaged 21.0 points and ended his six-season NBA career with a 19.0 average. He moved on to the American Basketball League in 1961 with the Los Angeles Jets. His career ended when the league collapsed midway through the following season.

■ NOW BATTING FOR THE COMETS

Mario Lococo wasn't Eddie Gaedel, the famous major league midget who drew a walk for the St. Louis Browns in 1951. Lococo, Lick High's 15-year-old bat boy in 1957, stood only 37 1/2 inches, while Gaedel was 43 inches tall.

But, with the bases loaded and his Comets down by a run in the last of the sixth, Lick coach Wil Concklin used Lococo as a pinch hitter. Mountain View coach Tony Calvelli protested and Concklin argued with umpire Dick Mattlock for 10 minutes before the arbiter ruled that Lococo could bat because his name was on the official roster.

The Eagles countered by moving 5-foot-2 third baseman John Shimizu to the mound, but another 10-minute rhubarb ensued when Calvelli complained that Lococo was out of uniform because he wasn't wearing spikes. Lick assistant coach Tom Ryan placed his own spikes in the batters box and Lococo returned to take his cuts facing a two balls and one strike count.

Lococo's appearance would have had a perfect Gaedel-like ending if he'd walked. Instead, Shimizu bore down and treated Lococo to a Mighty Casey finish, striking him out on the next two pitches. The Comets got their revenge in the final inning, scoring twice for a 4-3 victory.

■ A TITLE CONTENDER

Santa Clara's Bob Feerick took advantage of expansion of the NCAA's postseason field from eight to 16 teams to become the first head basketball coach from the West to take teams to three straight tourneys in 1952 through 1954.

The Broncos weren't the first local team to win an NCAA at-large berth under the new format. That honor fell to San Jose State's 1950-51 five -- led by Dean Giles' 12.9 average -- who bowed to BYU in the opening round, 68-61.

Santa Clara had a 15-10 record when the 1951-52 regular season ended and didn't even expect a tournament bid. The team was loaded with freshman and sophomores who thought they might not advance and took along only enough laundry for a weekend at the Corvallis regional.

Santa Clara's 1952-53 starting lineup (from left) Dick Garibaldi, Ken Sears, Dick Soares, Herb Schoenstein and Jim Young. The Broncos went 20-7, but lost in the NCAA's Western regional.

Instead, they made it to the Final Four, beating UCLA, 68-59, behind Herb Schoenstein's 18 point outburst and taking Wyoming, 56-53, with Ken Sears and Jim Young hitting 14 apiece. These wins produced another problem when the Broncos moved on immediately to Seattle

The players now had been on the road beyond the time allowed by the university. They had to attend two hours of classes at Seattle University before meeting Kansas in the semifinal that night. They lost to the champion Jayhawks, 74-55, then dropped a third place game to Illinois.

Feerick's 16th ranked youngsters rolled to a 20-7 record in 1952-53 and defeated Hardin-Simmons and Wyoming to reach the NCAA's Western final. Sears hit 23 against Washington, but Santa Clara lost, 92-70.

Young and Sears led the Broncos (21-7) again in 1953-54. After beating Texas Tech and Colorado A&M, Santa Clara fell to USC, 66-65, in double overtime. Trailing by one as the second extra period began and with three starters fouled out and Sears playing with four, the Broncos held the ball for more than four minutes to get the last shot. The ball went to Sears with eight seconds left, but the ball was batted away and the Broncos great NCAA run was over.

Sears had an outstanding senior year, but the Broncos were a mediocre 13-11. He set league and school records for points (41) and rebounds (30) in his final game against COP and ranks as SCU's fifth all-time scorer.

The 6-foot-9 Sears averaged 22.3 points, was mentioned for All-America and was the New York Knicks' first draft choice. "The Big Cat" averaged 16.5 points in six seasons with the Knicks and jumped to the American Basketball League for the 1961-62 season with the San Francisco Saints. He finished his career in 1963-64 back in the NBA with the San Francisco Warriors.

■ TRIVIAL PURSUITS

When Bellarmine beat St. Mary's of Berkeley, 31-18, in 1951, singer Bing Crosby's son, Dennis, scored three Bells' touchdowns and the son of bandleader Phil Harris played for the Panthers.

Renowned flagpole sitter George "Ozzie" Osborne vowed to live above Municipal Stadium's press box until the Red Sox sold out a game in 1953. He came down after 42 days when 4,312 turned out to see a win over Stockton.

Football players appeared on both offense and defense in 1953, when Stanford's Bob Garrett topped the NCAA in passing as a QB and pass interceptions as a defensive back. He was taken by Cleveland as the NFL's first draft pick.

Willow Glen High's mid-1950s basketball super scorer Wayne Marion was the son of John "Red" Marion, manager of the San Jose Red Sox baseball team.

■ RED SOX TO JOSOX TO NO SOX

San Jose romped to its first modern California League pennant in 1953, going 93-47 in the regular season to finish 18 games ahead of second place Bakersfield. Manager Red Marion's men also won the playoffs.

The Red Sox were led offensively by outfielders Ed Sobczak (.337, 142 RBIs), Albie Pearson (.334, 108 walks) and Marty Keough (.330, 28 steals). On the mound, Tex Clevenger went 16-2 and led the league with a 1.51 ERA. Clair Parkin added 18 wins, Ed Mayer 17 and Bo Palica 15.

Clevenger, Keough and Pearson all had successful major league careers. Albie hit .275 with Washington in 1958 and was the American League Rookie of Year.

Sobczak coached the San Jose State baseball team from 1957 through 1969, finishing his career with a record of 223-252.

After the 1955 Red Sox finished 98-48 but failed to make the playoff between first and second half champions, Boston sold the franchise to a group headed by Chuck Mallory, a local public relations and advertising executive.

The team was renamed the JoSox and finished third in 1956 under player-manager Dick Whitman, who led the circuit with a record .391 average and was named MVP. The JoSox drew only 41,886 and before the season was half over there was talk of bankruptcy. Mallory sold his interest and Eddie Duino became club president and signed a working agreement with Pittsburgh.

The San Jose Pirates finished a game under .500 the following season as attendance fell to 36,000. The team was in deep financial trouble before the 1958 season even opened. When only 7,114 passed through the turnstiles in the first 14 games, the team was moved to Las Vegas.

■ A TRIP TO OMAHA

Stanford's baseball team had a banner year -- actually a pennant year -- in 1953, tying USC with a 10-6 record for the CIBA title and making its first trip to the College World Series at Omaha, Neb.

The CIBA was composed of the four Pacific Coast Conference Southern Division schools, plus Santa Clara and St. Mary's. Stanford had only won the league twice since it formed in 1928, first in 1931 and again in 1950.

The 1953 team was Stanford's greatest, taking the north-south playoffs for the first time from Oregon and traveling to the big postseason tournament.

The Indians were paced to a school record 29 wins by four future Stanford Hall of Famers, shortstop Warren Goodrich, power-hitting outfielder Chuck Essegian, 11-win MVP pitcher Bob Murphy (later the radio voice for Stanford football and basketball), and catcher Jack Shepard, who hit a school record .379.

While the Indians were knocking off Oregon, 9-3 and 8-1 in the playoffs, the Trojans beat San Diego State and Seattle. When no playoff for the World Series berth could be arranged because of final examinations, the Indians won a coin toss to represent the West in Omaha. They finished in fifth place, beating Houston, but falling to Lafayette and champion Michigan.

■ BARRIER-BREAKER

When San Jose's Don Bowden cracked the four-minute barrier in the mile in 1957, it took America off the hook where it had been hanging for three years, two months and 26 days.

Seventeen sub-four-minute miles had been run since Roger Bannister achieved the previously unattainable record in 1954, when he ran 3:59.4. It seemed that America might never catch up with the rest of the world.

The 20-year-old Bowden was an unlikely candidate to do the catching. The 6-foot-3, 150-pounder wasn't even a full-fledged miler. His primary event was the half mile and

The 1953 champion San Jose Red Sox, from left, (back) Jerry Nebron, Ed Mayer, Norm Luoni, manager Red Marion, Cliff Allmon, Bill Zonner, Jim Ollis, Ed Sobczak, Tex Clevenger; (middle) trainer Lloyd Boussie, Ed Irons, Bo Palica, Jerry Zimmerman, Clair Parkin, Hal Toso, Marty Keough, Harv Toso, business manager Bob Freitas; (front) mascot Wayne Marion, Bob Turk, Leo Alarid, Nino Spatafore, Albie Pearson, Bill Whitson, bat boys Monte McCuston, Ken Corneilson.

Don Bowden

had been since he first stepped on the track at Lincoln High.

Bowden, who worked out regularly at the Municipal Rose Garden near his home, won the 880-yard title in the Peninsula Athletic League meet in 1953 with a 1:57 clocking. He went on to take the NCS title and was the state champion at 1:57.1 despite arriving late and running without warming up.

Bowden ran 1:54.1, the second fastest high school 880 in history, in a meet at Lincoln in 1954. He broke the record two weeks later with a 1:53.2 at the league trials at Fremont High and lowered it to 1:52.3 in the state meet.

As a University of California freshman in 1955, Bowden learned that track coach Brutus Hamilton thought he had great potential as a miler. Bowden continued his record breaking efforts at the new distance, setting a national college freshman mark of 4:11.7 in the mile.

Although he concentrated on the half mile, Bowden ran 4:08.2 in only his second mile race in his sophomore year. Bowden qualified for the 1956 Olympics in Melbourne in the 1,500 meters, but contracted mononucleosis and was eliminated from competition in the first heat.

As a junior, Bowden set an NCAA record of 1:47.2 in the half mile and ran 4:01.6 in the mile anchor lap of a medley relay. Hamilton decided he should try for the record at the Pacific AAU meet at the end of the 1957 season.

On the day of the race, Bowden completed an exam at Cal in the morning and drove the 75 miles to Stockton. Having run only a handful of mile races in his life, Bowden was 40 yards ahead of the mediocre field as he entered the last lap. He raced the final quarter in 58.1 seconds to finish at 3:58.7 for the American record.

The record gave him a trip to New York City, where he appeared on television and received a huge silver trophy from the AAU. Col. Hans Lagerloef had donated the cup in 1941 to be presented to the first American miler to crack the four minute barrier.

Bowden continued to run and in 1958 sustained his first 880 loss to Stanford's Ernie Cunliffe, but then posted a 1:49.1 half mile to help Cal's sprint medley relay team set a world record 3:19.8 at the Texas Relays. Later, he ran 3:52.2 in the 1,500 meters in Sweden. In 1960, Bowden tore his Achilles tendon and missed the Olympics.

■ FLU BUG STRIKES

Responding to one of the worst influenza epidemics in decades, Santa Clara Valley Athletic League officials canceled an entire week's sports schedule in October, 1958.

More than 300 deaths were reported nationwide and the federal government estimated that one million Americans had been laid up by the virus.

Officials forbade practice sessions and canceled football, water polo and cross-country schedules at all 10 member schools, including nine in Santa Clara County.

Football teams were allowed to reschedule the missing round later in the year. Since none of the results would have counted toward the league championship, the coaches decided not to play the games.

■ READY FOR SOME FOOTBALL?

Santa Clara University returned to the football wars in 1959 after an absence of six seasons.

When the announcement was made in March, lots of San Jose Mercury-News customers got the word elsewhere, because newspaper employees were on strike.

The strikers' San Jose Reporter put the story on top of Page 1 with a gigantic headline announcing: "SCU WILL PLAY FOOTBALL AGAIN! NO BIG LEAGUE"

"In no way does this minor return to the game of football imply that Santa Clara again will be playing major football teams," explained university vice president, the Rev. James E. Sweeters, S.J.

The program would be simple and inexpensive, he added, with no scholarships, no cross-country travel, no recruitment of high school athletes and no spring drills.

SCU had dropped football in 1953, following the lead of Catholic rivals St. Mary's, which abandoned the gridiron game after the 1950 season, and USF, which quit in 1952.

All three played home games at Kezar Stadium in San Francisco. They had found that competition from the professional San Francisco 49ers and mounting costs that outstripped revenue were too much to keep their programs viable. Santa Clara's final nine-game schedule sent the Broncos to nine stadiums with only one game at Kezar.

A direct link between the 1959 and 1952 teams came with Pat Malley's hiring as the Broncos' new head coach. He had played guard and was co-captain of the last SCU team and spent the intervening years coaching at Fort Hood, Tex., during military service and at San Francisco's St. Ignatius High School.

Santa Clara launched its small college "play for fun" program with a 28-8 loss to McClellan Air Force Base at Townsend Field. The Broncos won their other four games, including two over a resurrected USF eleven.

Malley compiled a 141-100-3 record before his death at age 54 in 1985. He was succeeded by his son, Terry, who coached until SCU dropped football in 1993 after the NCAA voted to require Div. 1 schools to play at that level in all sports. Football was the Broncos' only Div. 2 sport.

IT'S A TEAM GAME

Stanford proved in 1959 that football is a team game. The Indians benefited from some great individual efforts during that season, when:

- QB Dick Norman led the nation in passing with 152 completions and nearly 2,000 yards.
- End Chris Burford topped the U. S. in pass receiving with 61 catches.
- Back Skip Face was second in scoring with 100 points on 11 touchdowns, 25 conversions and 3 field goals.

Despite all this success, the Indians couldn't put up enough big numbers on the scoreboard and finished 3-7-0. Stanford averaged 23.2 points per game in 10 contests, but gave up 261 and lost games to Oregon, Wisconsin, USC and Cal by a total of eight points.

HONORS

Three Stanford athletes were among the leaders in a 1950 Associated Press sports writers' poll for the best of all-time. Bob Mathias ranked 12th among all athletes, Hank Luisetti was Number 2 in basketball and Ernie Nevers was fifth in football.

Stanford end Bill McColl was consensus All-America in 1950 and 1951 and a unanimous pick in the latter year.

In 1952, players in the NBA since its start in 1946 voted Jim Pollard (Stanford) as the period's best player.

Pitcher Joe Chez became Stanford's first All-American on the diamond in 1952.

San Jose Mercury-News sportswriter Wes Mathis was honored in 1952 as the San Jose Chamber of Commerce man of the year for leading the campaign to organize Little League baseball in San Jose and building its first stadium.

In the 1950s, four Stanford players joined the National Football Foundation Hall of Fame: backs Ernie Nevers, Bobby Grayson and Frankie Albert and guard Bill Corbus.

IN PASSING

Pit crew member Russell Margalati, 36, was injured fatally at San Jose Speedway in 1950. While trying to wave off drivers after cars stalled on the track, Margalati was hit by a car that had spun out of control.

Howard "Hod" Ray (162-78-27), whose Palo Alto High football teams had only five losing seasons during his 30 years as head coach, died of a heart attack in 1952 at age 57. His last two teams were undefeated in 18 straight games and outscored opponents 602 to 109.

DeWitt "Dee" Portal, 47-year-old San Jose State boxing coach, was crushed to death by a bulldozer blade at his Mount Hamilton ranch in 1953 while working on the tractor. In 19 seasons at SJS, his boxers won five individual NCAA titles and 17 Pacific Coast championships as well as numerous league and regional team crowns.

Reco Whitton, 19, was killed when his car spun out of control, struck another vehicle and crashed into a tree during a hardtop race at the Fairgrounds in 1955.

Charles "Doc" Strub, 73, Santa Clara University baseball player and part-owner of the San Francisco Seals baseball team with SCU classmate Charley Graham, died from the effects of a stroke in 1958.

Yeiji Toyota's "Black Marauder" dragster flipped 10 times while traveling 150 miles an hour at Fremont in 1959, fatally injuring the 21-year-old Campbell mechanic.

1950

Using only five players, SCU defeats defending NIT champ USF, 51-43. Bob McKillop's 14 leads Broncos . . . Officials disallow Gilroy High basket at horn after 15-minute debate. Mustangs fall to Mountain View, 49-48, despite Delaine Luft's 28 . . . SJS skier Herb Blatt grabs first place tie in collegiate slalom . . . Fremont High tops SCVAL wrestling meet behind champs Paul Lara, Frank Lara . . . SJS (21-7) ranks 17th in AP final hoops poll. Spartans' first All-American, Stu Inman, hits 416 points to end career with school record 1,504 . . . Lincoln High clips Bellarmine nine's 16-game win string, 13-10 . . . SJS boxer Mac Martinez wins Pacific Coast, NCAA titles . . . Lincoln High's Gordy Williams overwhelms Bob Wagner of Los Gatos 13 and 12 in biggest win in Nor Cal junior golf title history . . . San Mateo High snaps Lincoln's string of 31 straight dual track meet wins when coach Lee Cox holds out 440, 880, mile performers for relay meet next day . . . Live Oak High's Jack Robasciotti no-hits San Jose Tech, 3-2 . . . George Mattos of SJS soars 14-5 for Spartans' pole vault record . . . Johnny Mesa of Fremont High zips 100 in 9.8, 220 in 21.9 against Washington . . . San Jose High's Vern Wilson breaks NCS high jump record with 6-5 1/4 leap, ties for state crown at 6-2 . . . Stanford iron man Gay Bryan wins 100, 220, 120 high hurdles, long jump, high jump against

Campbell High pitcher John Oldham played at San Jose State, then coached baseball at San Jose City College and Santa Clara University. His teams won more than 800 games.

UCLA . . . Campbell High's John Oldham pitches one-hit, 9-1 victory over Santa Clara, fans 15, belts 360-foot homer . . . Golfers Ken Venturi of SJS, Gene Littler of San Diego State tie for CCAA crown. Spartans cop seventh straight team title . . . SCU defeats SJS, 6-5, despite two homers by Spartan third sacker Wil Concklin . . . Stanford's Bud Held throws javelin 216-8 5/8 for third straight NCAA title . . . Larry Headrick of San Jose captures 20-mile U. S. motorcycle title . . . Mino Yamate of Campbell High downs Don Straub of Los Gatos in featured singles as Bucs win SCVAL tennis . . . Lincoln High golfers tops in PAL as Lions' Stan Gum shoots 75 . . . Ralph Romero of SJS gives up only bloop single to Stanford's Dave Melton in five innings, wins top player award as CIBA stars top independent collegians, 7-3 . . . North state amateur golf crown won on 37th green by Bob Rosburg (Stanford) over Ken Venturi of SJS . . . SJS freshman Butch Krikorian wins city tennis . . . John Oldham of Campbell High top player in North-South prep all-star game, pitching four no-hit innings with 10 Ks . . . Bill Spadafore singles in deciding run as San Jose Post 89 wins American Legion title over San Mateo, 5-4 . . . Louis Rondini, stepson Richard O'Brien first local cyclists to win one-hour race at new 2,500-seat, one-tenth mile velodrome near Speedway . . . San Joseans Dick Austin (expert), Bill Bohlin (novice) capture Pacific Coast motorcycle hill climbs . . . Bud Bosque runs consecutive inning scoreless string to 59 as Western Gravel blanks Leon Terry's in district softball tourney, 7-0 . . . Winless since 1946, Gilroy High drops Pacific Grove, 18-0, to snap streak at 37 games . . . SJS fullback Harry Beck rushes for school record 209 yards, two TDs in 14-10 win over Santa Clara . . . San Jose's Mike Batinich wins California Stock Car Racing Association points crown . . . Paul Portera is Mercury-Herald bowling champ . . . Don Ewbank throws three passes, all for TDs, as SCVAL champ Santa Clara High (9-0-0) clips Bellarmine, 26-12 . . . SCU stops Loyola's 12-game grid win streak with 28-26 win . . . Ernie Pieper nips Gordy Williams in city golf, 1 up . . . Palo Alto High breezes past 10 grid opponents by average margin of 30 points . . . Linemen top high school all-stars: Santa Clara tackle Richard Mendence (SCVAL), Palo Alto end Merle Flattley (PAL) . . . Semi-pro San Jose Packers average 40-plus points, rack up 11 straight victories until 25-7 loss to league champ Petaluma Leghorns. Packers top Seattle Ramblers in Spartan Stadium postseason meeting, 20-0 . . . Palo Alto High's Jim Farrell rushes 139 yards, catches passes for 128, has five TDs in 42-6 victory over San Mateo . . . LaBrucheries lead Live Oak High to win against Salinas, 63-51. Armand hits 22, Ray 25.

■ 1951 ■

Three-minute stall gives SJS 55-50 victory over Santa Clara. Chuck Crampton tops Spartans with 16 . . . Lincoln High's Carroll Williams hits 15 in 43-35 win over Jefferson . . . Herb Boesch of San Jose wins 190-mile Tin Hat Derby motorcycle race through Santa Cruz mountains . . . Live Oak wallops Half Moon Bay, 73-44, behind Burt Millard's 26 . . . Lick High opens new gym with 48-28 win over Gilroy. Billy Hudson leads Comets with 14 . . . Sal Taormina leads Winter League batters at .412 . . . Palo Alto's Bob Pederson, Clyde Connor of South San Francisco pace PAL with 150 points . . . Stanford's Gay Bryan wins Pan-American Games broad jump at 23-5 . . . Buster Burgos hits 27 for Santa Clara High in 59-46 win over Campbell . . . SJS boxer Mac Martinez loses first bout to Neil Ofstun of Minnesota . . . Los Gatos High wears SCVAL hoops crown. Fremont's Shelly Beebe leads league with record 177 points . . . Dick Caldwell of Santa Clara High wins Nor Cal junior golf . . . Ken Venturi of SJS sweeps Northern California college, amateur, state amateur golf titles . . . Los Gatos High's Ken Wilson steals six bases in 4-1 win over Lick . . . Richard Gatto of Santa Clara High takes 26-mile bicycle race at Lake Merced . . . Lincoln High miler Carroll Williams finishes undefeated with victory in PAL league meet . . . Larry Lindsay of Los Gatos High runs 440 in 50.8 . . . Pair of triple plays aid Bellarmine in 11-3 win over Santa Clara . . . Campbell High's Howard Kaeding posts records in both hurdles as Santa Clara takes SCVAL track . . . Prep catchers are bat kings: Palo Alto's Frank Mills, .448 (PAL), San Jose Tech's John Picone, .577 (SCVAL) . . . San Jose High's Boyd Faulk wins city, county junior tennis titles . . . All-SJS final as Butch Krikorian tops Chet Bulwa in county singles. Palo Alto's Ben Holmes, Sandy McKay win doubles . . . Army private Eli Bariteau Jr. retains county golf title . . . San Jose JoSox pitcher Jack Heinen no-hits Stockton, loses no-hit bid to ninth inning single in next start against Fresno . . . Ann Myren captures second straight county women's golf title . . . San Jose motorcyclist Kenny Eggers takes U. S. 20-mile title. Palo Alto's Joe Leonard tops field in amateur 10-miler . . . Locals cyclists Richard O'Brien (senior), Hal Scammon (junior) win Northern California, take second at nationals . . . Jerry Brusachetti's single, grand slam in inning leads Foresters over Royal Arcanum, 15-6, in first San Jose Little League title contest . . . Bud Bosque's one-hitter gives Western Gravel state softball title over Sonoma . . . Don Titcomb of Los Gatos tops state horseshoe pitchers . . . Top SCVAL player Art Hernandez scores two TDs as Lick High defeats San Jose Tech, 27-0, for Comets' first grid win. Tech drops football after losing first four games by aggregate of six points to 140 . . . Driving last 84 miles without brakes, Tony Bettenhausen takes 100-miler at Fairgrounds for AAA national dirt track crown . . . SCU's Del Rasmussen runs 73 yards to touchdown on first play in 21-12 upset of No. 19th Arkansas . . . Ken Wilson tallies twice as Los Gatos High wins league, beating Campbell, 14-7 . . . Dick Jones of Willow Glen High tops county passers with 63 of 125, 1,204 yards . . . 49ers nearly ignore Billy Wilson (Campbell, SJS), drafting him in NFL's 22nd round.

■ 1952 ■

Before Spartan Gym standing room crowd, SJS upsets Oregon in last five seconds, 51-49. George Clark has 19 . . . SCU boxers top Stanford, 5-3. Broncos' Marv Gregory scores first round TKO over heavyweight Marv Tennefoss . . . Gonzaga ends SJS boxing dual meet win streak at 26 . . . All-PAL John Stewart leads Palo Alto High to hoops title . . . SCVAL scoring leader Jerry Tutman (17.8 average), teammate John Escano hit 24 apiece in Mountain View High's 71-39 rout of Lick. League MVP Dick Christensen leads Live Oak to title tie with Washington . . . SJS captures Pacific Coast boxing title behind individual winners Don Camp, Jerry Stern, Chuck Adkins. Adkins wins NCAA, Olympic crowns, is honored at downtown parade on return . . . Stanford's one-two punch of Ed Tucker (184 points), Jim Ramstead (177) top Southern Division's basketball scorers . . . Andy Miller drives in Joe Bonfiglio with winner as SJS ends SCU winning streak at nine, 5-4 . . . Jack Scheberies, Mac Martinez (both SJS) win national AAU boxing titles . . . Palo Alto High's John Radford sets U. S. prep record of 2:00.6 in 200 freestyle . . . Lick High's Ernie George takes Nor Cal junior golf . . . John Oldham fans 16 USF batters in 3-2 SJS win . . .

Stanford's Bob Murphy was a pitcher for Oakland in the Pacific Coast League.

Ron Tomsic of Stanford set a PCC division scoring mark, hitting 40 points against USC.

Orv McElrath of Mountain View High no-hits Santa Clara, 2-1 . . . PAL record setters: Frank Hermann of Willow Glen, 23-2 broad jump, Don Malinoff of Palo Alto, 147-4 discus . . . George Mikan hits 22, Jim Pollard 14 for NBA champ Minneapolis Lakers in 91-74 Civic Auditorium win over California Pro All-Stars . . . Bob McMullen sets SJS mile record in 4:15.7, wins 3,000-meter steeplechase NCAA, AAU titles, twists ankle to finish fourth in Olympic trials . . . Bill Priddy of SJS ties for NCAA pole vault title at 13-9 . . . Lick High takes first league baseball crown with 3-0 win over Campbell . . . Bob Wagner leads Los Gatos High to SCVAL golf trophy . . . Fremont High's Chuck Reynolds is league bat champ at .619. Lick pitcher Louis Aldama is MVP . . . Ernie Pieper wins county golf . . . San Jose's Joe Hostetler captures 10-mile U. S. amateur motorcycle race . . . Jiro Nakamura's two-hitter gives San Jose Zebras title win over Los Angeles Nisei in state tourney . . . Butch Krikorian of SJS takes NAIB tennis . . . Behind pitcher Bud Bosque, Western Gravel wins fourth straight district softball crown . . . East All-Stars (with Toughie Braushun) beat Panthers (Annis "Red" Jensen), 27-25, in Roller Derby's first Civic Auditorium appearance . . . San Francisco 49ers clobber San Jose Packers at Spartan Stadium, 76-0 . . . San Jose High's new gridiron at 24th Street campus dedicated with 20-7 win over Campbell . . . Watsonville ends Palo Alto High's 18-game win streak, 18-0 . . . Roy Hiram's late 38-yard TD run gives SJS win over COP, 26-21 . . . Bob Ball wins 100-mile AAA title race at Fairgrounds . . . SCU tops San Jose State, 15-7, in Broncos' last major football game . . . Bellarmine's Dick Pfaff is All-America lineman, back Lou Valli is No. 1 All-City player. Campbell tackle Dick Gleed tops on SCVAL list . . . Bellarmine marks fall in 79-43 win over San Jose Tech. Don McNeil hits record 29, Dick Venezia adds 24 points.

■ 1953 ■

Richard Andree, Joe Burchfiel of San Jose High undefeated as Bulldogs take PAL wrestling . . . Mits Fukumura, Larry Brady each score 21 in San Jose High win over Menlo-Atherton . . . Ron Tomsic's 38 for Stanford against USC ties PCC Southern Division mark. He breaks mark with 40 a year later . . . Willow Glen High's league scoring king Eric Anderson hits school record 27 in 57-45 upset of Lincoln, leaving Lions, Palo Alto tied for SPAL at 6-4. Lincoln wins playoff, falls to Jefferson in finals . . . SCVAL champ Campbell High tops Fremont, 49-40, with Tom Hansen hitting 13 for Bucs. John Lozano (Mountain View), Jim Choate (Fremont) league co-players of the year . . . Dick Venezia establishes Bellarmine marks with 33 points against Washington of Fremont, 441 for season. Don McNeil also tops old record with 355 points for 21-4 Bells . . . Big payday washed out at Muni Stadium when storm prevents New York Giants from playing Cleveland Indians . . . Los Gatos High's Jimmy Johnson fans 14 in no-hit win over Live Oak . . . SJS sophomore Mike Guerrero wins NCAA boxing title . . . Competing for Santa Clara Youth Village, Herm Wyatt (SJS) soars over high jump bar at 6-9 7/8 . . . SJS heavyweight Lyle Hunt takes first AAU judo tournament title . . . Willow Glen High nine clinches SPAL championship with 27-1 win over Menlo-Atherton, gathering 13 hits, 17 walks. George Wilson scores six runs after double, five walks. Rams' pitcher Dick James is SPAL's best player . . . Big day for Stanford pitcher Bob Murphy: three hits, three-hit win over SCU . . . Lots of support for Mountain View High's Orv McElrath, who no-hits Fremont, 21-0 . . . Lick High wins SCVAL track crown as Ned Warriner runs best 440 time, 52.9 . . . SJS ends season on high note when Ron Kauffman throws no-hitter against San Jose Zebras. Dick Brady leads Spartans with batting average of .323, pitcher John Oldham fans 166 for school record . . . Johnny Baldwin wins inaugural 500-lap "Little Indy" midget car race at Speedway . . . Wayne Belardi (Bellarmine, SCU) pinch hits twice in same inning for Brooklyn, walks, hits grand slam against St. Louis . . . Bellarmine's Dick Venezia (.400 average, 33 RBIs) tops All-City . . . Jack Lovegren shoots last round 68 for county golf title . . . Campbell High's Dick Gordon leads field as Bucs take SCVAL golf . . . San Jose High's Chuck Hightower sets junior AAU pole vault mark at 13-0 3/4 . . . Lang Stanley of SJS wins NCAA 880 in 1:52.4. George Mattos (SJS), Don Laz tie for AAU pole vault at 14-1 . . . Ray Raineri wins record fourth straight Speedway hardtop race . . . Jim Small (Bellarmine) hits three triples in Memory Post 399's 14-4 win over Monterey for American Legion regional title . . . Ernie George takes county junior golf . . . Cyclist Richard Gatto wins Northern California title . . . Gene Menges drives in three, Pete Sanders pitches no-hit win as California Supply cops city softball tourney . . . Joe Leonard wins U. S. five-mile motorcycle title . . . Driving Kurtis sports car, Bill Stroppe wins first Moffett Field Handicap, traveling 55 laps (192 miles) before 40,000 spectators . . . With pitcher Dutch Johnson unavailable because of his wedding, Leon Terry drops 7-3 decision to Air Base Market Liquors for district softball title . . . Jim Small gets three hits for USA All-Stars in 5-1 win over New York All-Stars at Yankee Stadium . . . Ken Venturi chalks up record 9 and 8 victory over Scotland's James Wilson as U. S. wins Walker Cup, 9-3 . . . Ronnie Rhoads of San Jose takes U. S. amateur cycling title. Jack Hartman of Los Gatos is junior champ . . . Palo Alto High tops Willow Glen, 14-13, on Harlow Rothert Jr.'s 15-yard scoring pass to Del Boccinone with 10 seconds to go. Leigh Lynn adds PAT . . . Bellarmine's Lou Valli scores on runs of nine, 80, 49, 45 yards in 32-7 win over Washington. Valli's 18 TDs is school season mark . . . Al "Fritz" Andrade wins city golf over Ernie Pieper, 7 and 6 . . . Don Davis crosses goal twice as Campbell High beats Los Gatos, 20-7, to grab title tie with Fremont . . . Record 92,000-plus are shoe horned into Stanford Stadium to see Paul Larson rally Cal to thrilling 21-21 Big Game tie . . . McCune Citrus, local five loaded with ex-SJS stars, tops San Jose Junior College, 85-43, in Jaguars' first athletic contest . . . Oregon defeats SJS, 74-70, despite 27 from Carroll Williams . . . Center Al Francis of Bellarmine voted Nor Cal's top lineman, Scholastic Magazine All-American . . . Larry Brady scores 28, but SJJC falls to Willow Glen High . . . Players of the year: Lincoln High back John Stewart (SPAL) Fremont back Jerry Hitchman (SCVAL) . . . 2,000 spectators turned away as SCU tops Hawaii, 68-49, at Watsonville High, star Ken Sears' high school alma mater.

■ 1954 ■

Chet Bulwa wins city tennis singles . . . Jack Scheberies (SJS) turns pro, KOs first two opponents in opening round . . . Jack Searfoss goes for Lincoln High record 36 as Lions defeat San Jose Tech, 60-51 . . . Campbell High wins Nor Cal wrestling with champs Rich Calloway, Ron Webb, Russ Camilleri . . . Bellarmine (17-8) finishes season with 66-55 win over Serra as soph Ralph Brandt scores 20 . . . Gilroy High ties Pacific Grove for CCAL-B hoops title. Mustangs' Tony Vigna circuit's top scorer, only unanimous all-league . . . Lincoln High upsets Willow Glen in final, 50-49, giving Palo Alto SPAL title. Rams' Eric Anderson is player of the year, first to average 20 points (20.6) in league. Palo Alto captures PAL playoff, loses to St. Ignatius, Albany in TOC . . . Roger Stienstra bowls record 2,009 in Palo Alto city tourney . . . Stanford's Russ Lawler, George Selleck top PCC Southern Division hoops scorers . . . Undefeated in nine pro bouts, Chuck Adkins (SJS) is knocked out by Ernie Green at Civic Auditorium . . . SJS boxers Vic Harris, Dick Bender, Tom Stern win PCI titles . . . Consecutive no-hit games by Bellarmine's Dick Polhamus (against Santa Clara), Frank Cornell (against San Leandro) . . . SJS swimmers capture state college title. Dick Threlfall gains three victories . . . Bob Laubacher of SCU throws first CIBA no-hitter in 21 years to defeat USC, 3-0 . . . Palo Alto High wins 21st league swim title, taking first in all but one event . . . San Jose High bats around in inning for sixth time in seven games, tops Menlo-Atherton for SPAL title, 13-3 . . . Doug Boehner's 3-0 three-hitter over USF closes books on SJS's first winning year (12-10) in five . . . Unbeaten league champ Fremont High hits .370 as team, 110 points above second place Los Gatos . . . San Jose brothers Dale, Matt Miholovich take U. S. trapshooting doubles. Matt wins

Carroll Williams, a high scoring guard at San Jose State, was head basketball coach at Santa Clara University for 22 years and then became the Broncos' athletic director.

Class D singles . . . Player of the year Ben Gonzales of San Jose High pitches, leads SPAL batters with .483 . . . Discus dropped from state meet, but exhibition toss by Palo Alto High's Rink Babka travels 148-2 3/4 , three feet farther than old mark . . . Bellarmine's Jim Small (.435, 33 RBIs) tops All-City team . . . Memory Post 399 wins fifth straight American Legion district baseball title, loses to El Cerrito in regionals . . . SJS's first soccer squad in dozen years winless in six games under coach Julie Menendez . . . Don Ouelette's homer gives Willie Oiler district softball title over California Supply, 1-0 . . . Jack Bariteau captures Northern California golf . . . SJJC opens first grid campaign, losing to Vallejo, 27-13 . . . Ray Raineri takes season record 14 wins at Speedway, loses point title when he, Palo Alto's George Rogge are suspended in purse money dispute . . . Al Coppel of Los Altos wins California Sports Car Club under 1500cc title . . . Gilroy dumps Hollister, 26-0, for first win over 'Balers in 33 years . . . SJS picks off five passes in upset 19-14 win over Stanford, Spartans' first in series dating back to 1900 . . . Lou Faler takes city golf with 6 and 5 win over Glenn Dooley . . . Russ Cahill, Jim Ryley each score two TDs in Campbell's 44-12 romp over Los Gatos for SCVAL title . . . Denny Dudley tallies twice, throws 14th TD pass to Wayne Thush in Lincoln's 33-13 win over San Jose. Dudley sets county passing record with 1,259 yards . . . Joe Leonard takes U. S. motorcycle title with wins in eight of 18 races . . . Jim Fuller has Los Gatos High hoops record 39 against Watsonville . . . Eighty-six men enter San Jose holiday bowling event, but Jane Johnson wins it . . . Failing to force taller opponents out of zone with stall, Willow Glen High falls to Lincoln, 17-16, in SPAL record low scoring game.

■ 1955 ■

Ron Tomsic's 25-foot buzzer beater gives Stanford 59-57 win

over Cal . . . Willow Glen High whips San Jose, 63-53. Wayne Marion has 32 . . . Herm Wyatt (SJS) sets world indoor high jump mark of 6-10 at Boston . . . League co-champ Gilroy High beats Carmel, 67-42, as Chris Costello makes school record 37 . . . SJJC's Hank Nose hits 18 of 19 free throws in 61-56 win over Hartnell . . . Santa Clara High downs Washington, 9-6, as Huskies hold basketball most of game. Panthers, who start freshmen Larry Guilford, Bob Lister, win SCVAL. Los Gatos High's Jim Fuller is scoring champ . . . Willow Glen High's Wayne Marion sets SPAL mark averaging 21.4, named All-City co-player of year with Lincoln's Jim Brazda . . . Hook-shooting Ralph Brandt (18.0) leads Bellarmine (19-2) to 18 straight victories against prep competition . . . Bill Wiswall first SCU boxer to win Pacific Coast title since 1938. SJS champs are Dick Bender, Max Voshall, who takes NCAA crown . . . Jerry Clifford of SJS hits two homers in 5-2 win against Oregon, finishes year with club-leading three . . . Jim Walsh's (Stanford) 45-footer gives Phillips 66 Oilers victory against Colorado in national AAU hoops final . . . Cal pitcher Doug Weiss (Lincoln) one-hits SCU . . . Eddie Brewer takes both hurdles races as SJJC wins Coast Conference track title . . . Walt Garrett of Stanford runs 47.7 440 in victory over SJS . . . Lincoln High's Hank Olquin is PAL meet's top point-maker with wins in 100, 220, fourth place in broad jump . . . Barbara Wilson's 267 at Santa Clara Bowl ties county women's record . . . Pete Castellanos' hit scores Ron Citta, gives Campbell 7-6 victory over Washington, share of league title with Fremont (17-1). Lick outfielder Steve Corbett league's MVP . . . SPAL repeat player of the year Ben Gonzales fans 16 as league champ San Jose High pins 7-2 loss on Bellarmine (25-9). Gonzales shares all-city's top honor with Bells' Jim Small, who signs $35,000 Detroit Tigers' bonus contract . . . Dave Stokes of San Jose High sets county broad jump record with 23-2 leap . . . Larry Helms wins three events as Stanford takes sixth straight PCC Southern Division swim crown . . . SJS judo team captures Pacific AAU junior, senior titles . . . Mike Roach's 100-yard backstroke, record 150-yard individual medley wins lead Santa Clara High to one-point win over Palo Alto for NCS swim title . . . SJS nine (16-14) loses to Fresno State in NCAA regionals, 5-1 . . . Palo Alto's Scotty McBeath scores 208 to lead field in county 54-hole golf tourney . . . Don Gale, Shirley Krikorian win county singles. Chet Bulwa, Dave Parnay tops in doubles . . . San Jose's Larry Lujan wins open gas roadster class at U. S. hot rod championships . . . Pat Cavataio leads Burbank Little League with numerous no-hitters, averages 16 Ks per game, has 11 home runs while no other player has more than one . . . Stacy Hennel of Palo Alto Post pitches no-hit game against Memory Post 399 in American Legion district final, loses 2-1 on errors . . . Palo Alto's Don Harper of Ohio State wins NCAA 3-meter diving . . . Pat Cavataio hits homer, pitches one-hitter, but Burbank makes six errors in 3-2 loss to Visalia in state Little League playoffs . . . Golden Hornets, county's first Pop Warner football squad, opens with 27-0 victory over San Rafael . . . Many drivers abandon NASCAR to compete at Western Auto Racing's new Alviso Speedway . . . SJS runs 70 plays to Arizona State's 21 as Stan Beasley, Joe Ulm each rush for 100-plus yards in 27-20 win . . . Fremont High's Frank Aquinaga breaks league cross-country mark as Lick wins title. Palo Alto takes SPAL, NCS crowns behind Ron Larrieu . . . City golf is won by Jack Lovegren over Fred Seymour, 2 and 1 . . . Don Hubbard leads SJS to Northern California cross-country title with record 22:03.8 over Stanford course . . . Live Oak High's first football team (1-7-0), gains lone win over Camden JVs . . . Lincoln High's Dick Brown rushes for 140 yards, two TDs in Lion's title-clinching 27-14 win against San Jose. Lincoln (8-1-0) ranks 7th in north state poll, end Wayne Thush is All-Nor Cal . . . SJS ties Washington State, 13-13, in blizzard at Pullman before "crowd" of one paid customer . . . Ron Larrieu of Palo Alto High wins title in first Nor Cal cross-country race . . . Gilroy ties for CCAL-B grid crown second year in a row . . . Stanford fans taunt California coach Lynn "Pappy" Waldorf with "Goodbye Pappy" as Indians win only Big Game during his decade at Berkeley, 19-0 . . . Lick High's Larry Helmhout voted best SCVAL back, Campbell's Roger Lukehardt is top lineman . . . Larry Guilford scores 13 as Santa Clara High five tops Lincoln, 39-31, for title of first Lick High basketball tournament -- Northern California's oldest.

■ 1956 ■

Ralph Brandt racks up Bellarmine record 35 points in 59-41 victory over Lick, elevates it to 41 against Serra. Brandt averages 23.9, makes All-American as Bells go 20-2 . . . Eddie Diaz hits 30-footer at buzzer for 54-52 SJS win over Santa Clara . . . Alan Wright's 20 leads Lincoln High to 56-35 title clincher over Palo Alto . . . Roger Lukehardt pins Nick Zoria to give Campbell High fourth straight SCVAL wrestling title, later gains most outstanding honors at Nor Cals . . . Center Marv Branstrom grabs SJS record 28 rebounds as Spartans top Arizona State, 82-71 . . . Fremont, Mountain View, Sunnyvale tie for SCVAL hoops title. Santa Clara's Bob Lister is scoring champ (17.6), Fremont's Curtis Schwartz top player . . . San Mateo dumps Lincoln, 57-55, in playoff for TOC berth . . . Stanford edges SJS, 72-70, with Barry Brown hitting 33 . . . Lincoln High's Dick Brown runs 100 in 9.6, 220 in 21.0 . . . Loaded with former, present SJS players including Carroll Williams, Green Frog Supermarkets is first county team to reach national AAU basketball tournament, but loses opener to Chicago team, 79-62 . . . Al Suarez sets college pistol record leading SJS to West Coast title . . . Ron Larrieu of Palo Alto High runs two-mile in state record 9:39.0, later tops milers at state meet with 4:20.1 . . . Larry Peterson fans 13 as league champion SJJC defeats East Contra Costa, 10-5 . . . Cisco Andrade wins 10-round decision over Jorge Macias at Civic Auditorium . . . Lang Stanley of SJS runs 1:48.7 in 880 against Olympic Club . . . Kay Hansen's 1,734 pins takes all events title at California Women's Bowling Association tourney . . . Mike Birmingham has five hits with double, homer, eight RBIs, John Russo has double, home run, knocks in seven runs as SCU trounces Cal, 30-12 . . . Campbell High nine wins first undisputed title on Bob Sutton's one-hit win over Mountain View, 3-1. Player of the year Sutton goes 11-0 for season . . . Bellarmine joins Catholic League . . . Leading Masters, amateur Ken Venturi (SJS) shoots final round 80, allowing Jackie Burke to make up eight stokes to defeat him for coveted green jacket . . . Records topple as Campbell High wins league track crown: Russ Ray (Lick), 1:59.1 in 880, Max Kinsey (Campbell), 12-3 3/4 pole vault, Mike Profit (Campbell), 57-7 3/4 shot put . . . Robin Moore of Stanford sets world record of 48.9 in 100 freestyle . . . Jerry Clifford first SJS player to hit .400 . . . Willow Glen falls to Jefferson in baseball playoffs . . . Campbell High's Mike Profit sets north state shot put record of 59-4 1/8 . . . Tommy Morrow of Sunnyvale wins "Little Indy" 500-lap midget auto race at Speedway . . . Bellarmine pitcher Steve Schott (26-9 for career) makes Bay Area All-Catholic squad . . . Ernie George

The San Francisco 49ers were stocked with many players and coaches who had ties to Santa Clara County, including Stanford quarterback John Brodie (center), San Jose State end Billy Wilson (right) and Santa Clara coach Buck Shaw, shown with the 'Niners Y. A. Tittle.

of SJS wins county golf with record-tying 205 over 54 holes . . . Butch Krikorian, Eunice Bowman win county singles tennis . . . Deena Vickey captures Speedway's first Powder Puff Derby women's stock car race . . . Flash Elorde takes 10-rounder from Davey Gallardo . . . Charlie Leider tops Chris Sgambati, 7 and 5, in first tournament at new Palo Alto muni course . . . Joe Leonard wins U. S. 20-mile motorcycle title for third time in four years . . . Olympic gold medals go to Stanford crew men Jim Fifer, Duvall Hecht (pairs), Dan Ayrault, Conn Findley, Armin Kurt Sieffert (pairs with coxswain) . . . San Jose's Dave Rhoads falls, catches pack to take last spot on USA Olympic cycling team in 125-mile qualifying race at San Francisco . . . Stanford's Ron Tomsic, Jim Walsh on USA Olympic gold medal basketball squad . . . Jerry Volpe to Steve Flynn passes of 26, 35, 74 yards hit pay dirt as Mountain View wallops St. Mary's of Stockton, 70-12 . . . SJJC breaks 20-game Menlo College win streak, 16-14, when end John Ventry nails Oaks' QB for late safety. Jaguars (7-1-1) win conference . . . Little Bonneville drag strip opens on King Road . . . Gerald Sota takes city golf title . . . In closest win, Palo Alto (9-0-0) trails by 19 in first quarter, rallies to nip Willow Glen, 27-25 . . . Jim Josephson leads Bellarmine (9-0-0) over SCVAL co-champ Lick, 34-20, rushing for 189 yards, three TDs. He ends season with 1,058 yards, 8.3 average, makes All-Catholic with end George Honore, guard Bill Del Baggio . . . Lou Valli has 23 carries for Stanford record 209 yards, but Cal upsets Indians, 20-18, giving retiring coach "Pappy" Waldorf happy send off . . . Mike Filice hits 25 as Bellarmine tops St. Ignatius, 59-40, for 40th straight hoops win . . . SJS soph Art Powell tops U. S. receivers with 40 catches . . . Seattle's Elgin Baylor nets 27, but Jerry Bachich (22) paces SCU win, 85-76 . . . John Brodie (Stanford) named MVP in West's 7-6 Shrine Game win.

■ 1957 ■

Art Powell scores 23 points with 20 rebounds in 79-75 OT win over Fresno State, quits SJS to sign with pro football Toronto Argonauts . . . Lincoln High's Bruce Cassell buckets 35 against St. Ignatius for Palo Alto tournament mark . . . Despite Rich Hosley's 22, Lincoln High bows to Burlingame, 42-39, for TOC berth . . . Phil Kelly, Bub Bowling lead Fremont High (25-0) to postseason Carmel tourney title, extend winning string to 30, finish No. 2 in north state . . . Bellarmine's Mike Filice tops county hoops scorers (19.0 average), gains all-area honors . . . Prep no-hit hurlers include Willow Glen's Ed Cypert over Gilroy with 18 Ks; Joe Sandoval of Lincoln over Willow Glen, Campbell's Jack Keech against Sunnyvale . . . Lick High's Kin Mune fans 15 Bellarmine batters . . . Ray Norton posts SJS records in 100 (9.4), 220 (20.3), but both marks are wind-aided . . . SJJC's Ed Citti tosses no-hit, 11-0, win over East Contra Costa . . . Art Lambert leads SJS swimmers to state college title with three wins . . . San Jose's Bill Dial chalks up California League record 40 straight shutout innings . . . Mike Profit of Campbell High puts shot 60-7 1/2 . . . Bellarmine's Jerry Brusachetti gets three home runs, eight RBIs against Marin Catholic . . . Tommy Heinsohn pours in 29 as touring Boston Celtics trim Pro All-Stars at Civic Auditorium, 121-110 . . . Ernie George champion medalist as SJS beats Stanford in Northern California college golf tourney . . . USC falls to Stanford, 4-0, on Bob Leopold's no-hitter . . . Santa Clara High's Larry Guilford wins both hurdles, sets broad jump mark at 23-1, but Fremont takes league meet . . . Campbell High edges Bellarmine, 34-32, for NCS swim crown . . . Grand slam by Ron Cataldo gives Lick 6-3 win over Washington for league title . . . Stanford swimmers win eighth straight PCC crown . . . Russ Ray of Lick High takes NCS 880 in 1:55.7 . . . San Jose High's Marv Mecklenberg (10-2, .345) is first non-Bellarmine competitor named All-City baseball player of the year . . . County golf winners: Mrs. Aubrey Babson, Jack Lovegren . . . SCVAL's top player is Los Gatos High catcher Lou Leonard (.560) . . . Doug Weiss (Lincoln) pitches 9-1 win over Iowa State to put California into finals of NCAA College World Series, where Bears down Penn State. Weiss (14-4) signs with New York Yankees . . . Joe Leonard wins three U. S. motorcycle titles including 25-miler at Bay Meadows . . . Lou Tamone's three-run homer gives Serio Painting 4-1 win over

Welding Service, trip to state softball tourney . . . Don Titcomb of Los Gatos takes third straight state horseshoe pitching title, but for second year loses nationals in playoff . . . Motorcyclist Sam Arena wins 220-yard Madrone hill climb title in 8.2 seconds . . . Campbell Swim Club's 16-year-old Steve Skold sets four national AAU age group marks . . . Tyrone Fabro of Mountain View High completes only four passes, but three hit pay dirt in 21-13 win over Campbell . . . Jim Josephson of Bellarmine has 92-, 94-yard kickoff returns in 52-21 rout of Riordan, wins Nor Cal back of the year, All-America awards, leads state in scoring with 145 points . . . Jack Bariteau tops Gerald Sota, 4 and 2, in city golf final . . . Palo Alto High's John Northway tops both fields as Palo Alto wins league, NCS cross-country . . . Mike DeVita scores twice as unbeaten San Jose Hornets win Northern California Pop Warner grid title over Livermore, 27-6 . . . SJS takes seventh consecutive state college water polo crown. Peter Ueberroth leads all scorers . . . Lick High QB Chon Gallegos sets county records in completions (101), yards (1,297) . . . SJJC's Nick Clock scores 24 points, snares 20 rebounds in win over CCSF, 64-57 . . . In first home basketball loss to SJS in nearly three decades, Stanford falls, 66-59. Marv Branstrom has 14 points for Spartans . . . Lineman Don Manoukian of Stanford named most outstanding East-West Shrine Game defender.

■ 1958 ■

Mike Sharp wins Pacific Coast heavyweight wrestling title at Civic Auditorium when Ramon Torres is disqualified . . . Frank Sobrero scores 28 in SCU's 60-59 victory over Pepperdine . . . SJS breaks team scoring mark with 92-61 win over Pepperdine. Eddie Diaz has 19 . . . Motorcycle champ Joe Leonard adds 100-mile Pacific Coast trophy to collection . . . San Jose High's Frank Regalado is top SPAL wrestler . . . Bruce Cassell hits 21, Lincoln High defeats Palo Alto, 57-40, to clinch third straight league crown . . . SJJC takes Coast Conference hoops, 85-58, over East Contra Costa with Ron Wyrsch scoring 19. Jags fall to Long Beach in state tourney . . . San Joseans Gene Enright, Angel Ledesma win regional Golden Gloves titles . . . MVP Bob Lister of Santa Clara High hits 16 against Sunnyvale to lead SCVAL in scoring with 16.5 average . . . All-Nor Cal hoops honors accorded Rich Hosley of Lincoln High (25-4) . . . Gilroy High's Dick Smith tops vote count on All-CCAL-B . . . Marv Mecklenberg sets SJCC strikeout record with 15 in 6-2 victory over Santa Rosa . . . Roger Crist of Stanford wins downhill race in Badger Pass college ski meet . . . Stanford's Kirk Reed hits two penalty kicks in Big Scrum rugby loss to Cal, 23-6 . . . Hungarian expatriate Laszlo Tabori runs 9:15.1 two-mile for Santa Clara Valley Youth Village . . . Averaging nearly 100 mph, Joe Leonard grabs U. S. 200-mile motorcycle crown . . . Russ Camilleri of SJS wins PCI wrestling title . . . Ray Norton timed at 9.4 in 100, 21.2 in 220 in win over Cal . . . SJS wins Pacific Coast, NCAA boxing crowns. Individual champs in both: T. C. Chung, Welvin Stroud, Archie Milton. Bob Tafoya wins NCAA title, Nick Akana is PCI champ . . . Only two balls leave infield as Willow Glen High's Dennis Daly pitches no-hit win over Palo Alto, 5-1 . . . USC's Rink Babka (Palo Alto) sets NCAA discus mark at 190-7 1/2 . . . MVP Yosh Kumagai's jumper gives San Jose Zebras 70-68 win over Los Angeles in national Japanese-American Citizens League title game . . . Ex-SJS tennis star Don Gale defeats Gil Rodrigues of SJS for county championship, then teams with him for doubles win . . . Campbell High's Bob Whitewing gives up no hits in 6-0 win over Fremont . . . Nine-year-old Steven Papp of Palo Alto wins first runabout boat race at Calero Reservoir . . . Steve Skold of Campbell High swims NCS 100 freestyle in record 51.5 . . . Joe Palma's homer gives SJJC 5-3 win over Monterey for league title . . . Joe Blum pitches no-hit ball for Bellarmine to win CAL playoff final against Riordan, 4-0 . . . NCS titles go to Denny Boyle (Bellarmine), 880 in 1:56.4; John Northway (Palo Alto), mile in 4:24.6; Larry Guilford (Santa Clara) low hurdles in 14.5 . . . Willie Morton of San Jose takes 10-round decision over Mexican lightweight champ Baby Vasquez at Civic Auditorium . . . Bob Overmire produces five hits, four RBIs in Los Altos High's pennant-winning 15-4 win over Sunnyvale . . . Mrs. Aubrey Babson repeats as county women's golf winner . . . Birdie on 18th gives Cliff Davis of Palo Alto county junior golf crown . . . American All-Stars couple Ray Henningsen's one-hit pitching, John Aronson's homer to nip Burbank for area Little League title . . . In district softball final, Vern Grafton leads Freeman Paving at bat, on mound to 6-1 win over Congdon-Crome . . . Recovered from injury, motorcycle pro Joe Leonard tops field in 50-mile national championship race . . . Jim Curtis of San Jose wins Madrone motorcycle hill climb in record 7.68 seconds . . . Chon Gallegos (Lick) handles ball only 11 times, passes for two TDs, runs for another as West Bay All-Stars down East Bay at Kezar Stadium, 36-0 . . . Four down with 10 holes to play, Eli Bariteau Jr. takes state golf on 36th hole . . . Sam Arena Sr. wins two national motorcycle hill climbs at Modesto. Sam Jr. takes novice title . . . Camden High's Mel Profit runs for 184 yards, three TDs in 20-6 win over Mountain View . . . Jay Cheatham of Sunnyvale sets one-quarter mile dragster record of 9.4 at Half Moon Bay . . . SJS scores more points than in previous three games in 21-20 upset over Arizona State in first contest at new Sun Devil Stadium . . . Joel Spinola beats Gerald Sota for city golf title . . . Santa Clara Valley Hornets' 17-game Pop Warner football winning streak stopped by Millbrae Lions, 19-0 . . . Bellarmine generates three TDs in seven minutes to dump St. Mary's for CAL title, 19-7 . . . Ed Tarbell's four goals lead way to Los Altos' 11-5 water polo win over Lick for second straight league title . . . Los Gatos High capitalizes on six Campbell turnovers, scores on runs by Hugh Campbell, Phil Monk to beat Bucs for

Bellarmine touchdown leader Jim Josephson.

league title, 14-0 . . . Led by George Linn, Palo Alto High sweeps NCS cross-country . . . Tied at 212, Bob Duden beats Bob Rosburg in sudden death at Almaden Open. LPGA's Jackie Pung, with special permission to play in former all-male tourney, shoots 234 . . . Frank Sobrero hits 33 as SCU whips UCLA, 56-42 . . . Bellarmine linemen John LoCurto, Mike Brennan make All-CAL. Tops in SCVAL: QB Bob Berry (Willow Glen) in east, lineman Otis Gresham (Santa Clara), back Ken Buran (Campbell) in west . . . SJCC's Al McKinney is conference hoops tourney MVP as Jags win crown over Diablo Valley, 61-54.

■ 1959 ■

Ken Venturi (SJS) fires 63 to come from eight strokes back to win Los Angeles Open golf tournament . . . Henry Rapp contributes 26 as San Jose High dumps Lincoln, 42-30 . . . Hollister High wins Gilroy wrestling tournament, first team other than host to take it in seven years. Willow Glen's Bob Jackson is 154-pound champ . . . In first visit to San Jose in 19 years, Cal coach Pete Newell starts second string against SCU. Broncos' coach Bob Feerick is insulted, starts reserves, who play first 10 minutes of game won by Bears, 66-55 . . . Ring debut of SCU's 6-foot-5, 201-pound Max Baer Jr. fails when Stanford's Trev Grimm puts him away with first round TKO . . . Karl Laucher grabs loose ball, fires 40-foot field goal at buzzer to give Los Gatos High 42-40 win over Los Altos . . . Whitney Reed of SJS wins Northern California college tennis singles, joins Bob Hill for doubles crown . . . SJJC's Gerry McDowell hits 19 in 84-69 playoff win over Monterey for league title . . . Dick Holden's one-hitter gives SJS 1-0 win over Stanford . . . Camden High (27-0) captures inaugural Peninsula Basketball Tournament over Willow Glen, 49-35 . . . Ramon Torres stops The Mask to end dispute over Pacific Coast wrestling title . . . Ayer High survives seven errors to win first Lions Easter baseball tourney, 5-3, over Campbell . . . Palo Alto High four-mile relay team of George Linn, Ric Bradi, Mike Lehner, Mike Chilton sets national record of 17:51.8 . . . Steve Schott pitches 10 strikeout, 3-2 win over UCLA for SCU's 12th in a row . . . SJS nips Idaho, 24-22, for NCAA boxing crown. Nick Akana, Ron Nichols champs . . . Jim Pusateri gets three hits, Larry Williams fans 12 as SJS hands SCU first loss, 7-2 . . . NCS champs are Doug Schoenwetter (Fremont), 173-2 3/4 discus, George Linn (Palo Alto), 4:24.8 mile . . . Camden, Los Gatos nines tie for WSCVAL title . . . Despite Jim O'Rourke's double, triple, seven RBIs in first game, SCU (23-13) falls to Fresno State in NCAA playoffs . . . Nat Martinez of champion Willow Glen is ESCVAL player of the year, tossing two no-hitters in 12-2 season with 0.31 ERA . . . Ernie Pieper fires 208 over 54 holes to win 12th county golf title . . . Palo Alto High's George Linn lowers state two-mile mark to 9:31.4 . . . Ray Norton of SJS is disqualified for false starts in NCAA 100, but wins 220. Errol Williams of SJS ties for high jump at 6-9 3/4 . . . Walt Christiana pitches no-hit, 1-0, win for Santa Clara Post over Sunnyvale in American Legion league opener . . . San Jose golf pro Willie Goggin wins Northern California Senior tourney; takes $2,000 in U. S. National Senior Open at Palm Springs in playoff with Smiley Quick, Olin Dutra, snares PGA Senior crown, takes world pro senior title in Scotland with 5 and 3 win against Arthur Lees . . . Jack Lucenti of San Jose State bows to Dick Crawford in NCAA golf final on same

San Jose State linemen (from left) Jim Cadile, Oscar Donohue, Clair Appledorn and Dan Colchico await the 1959 opening game. Cadile played 11 years with the Chicago Bears and Colchico was a San Francisco 49er for five seasons.

day brother Ron tops Bob Pearson for Palo Alto title . . . Bowler Lorraine Anderson leaves one pin standing on last ball for women's county high 299 . . . Whitney Reed of SJS wins NCAA tennis singles, place on U. S. Davis Cup team . . . John Brodie's (Stanford) course record 65 wins Northern California Pro-Am golf Sweepstakes at Almaden . . . Ray Cardoni of Cupertino wins 48 cubic inch hydroplane race at Lake Yosemite . . . Santa Clara defeats Memory Post 399 in American Legion district playoff finale, loses in regionals . . . Pitchers John Oldham, Doug Boehner (both SJS) all-tourney as Nesbit Masonry tops San Mateo Blues, 6-5, for state semi-pro title . . . Tom Macedo (SJS) breaks American 200-yard backstroke mark . . . Joe Leonard takes Vacaville 42-mile, Dodge City 100-mile grand prix motorcycle races . . . St. Francis High golf captain Pat Lewis grabs county junior golf trophy . . . Cass Jackson scores twice on ground, once on pass from Terry Maruyama in San Jose High's 28-6 win over Gilroy . . . County tennis titles go to Conway Catton (singles), Butch Krikorian, Don Gale (doubles), Don Kliss (junior singles) . . . In its first football game, Foothill College tops Shasta, 27-20 . . . Steve Moreno's 317 yards passing, five TDs lead Palo Alto High over Woodside, 46-0 . . . SJCC dedicates new stadium with 13-6 win over Hartnell. Ken Buran rushes for 227 yards with TDs on 60-, 55-yard runs . . . League MVP Tyce Fitzmorris scores five TDs on way to 17 for year in Fremont High's 34-14 victory over Buchser . . . Tom Gallagher scores 16th TD as Bellarmine clinches CAL title with 27-14 win over St. Mary's. Bells' guard John LoCurto is league, Central Coast MVP . . . Pop Warner champion Hornets defeat Salt Lake City Indians, 13-0, on Rod Ebertowski's two TD runs . . . Trying to equal Bellarmine's area record of 43 straight basketball victories against high school competition, Camden High's streak ended at 42 by Willow Glen, 44-31.

The 1960s

Stanford football had its "Vow Boys" and Santa Clara basketball its "Magicians of the Maplewood."

But, the most descriptive nickname of them all may have belonged to San Jose State in the 1960s, when the Spartans' track team was truly, "Speed City."

Many great runners performed for the Spartans from the mid-1950s into the 1970s, but the top track standouts were world record-holding sprinters Ray Norton, Tommie Smith, Lee Evans and John Carlos.

The slender Norton burst onto the track scene in 1958 when he ran a 9.3 in the 100-yard dash to match the world mark and later equaled the world 220-yard record in a wind-aided 20 seconds flat.

A year later, Norton won both sprints at the national AAU and USA-USSR meets and equaled the world record for 220 around a turn at the Pan-American Games. In one race at San Jose, he tied the world 100-meter mark at 10.1.

His performances in early 1960 were remarkable. In fewer than four months between March and July he ran at record pace three times in the 200-meters, a 20.6 at Berkeley on March 19, another 20.6 at Philadelphia on April 30 and a 20.5 at Stanford on July 2. He also was timed in 9.3 at 100 yards and 20.0 for 220 in early April.

Unfortunately, Norton peaked before the Rome Olympics in September. He made the finals in both of his events, but ran last behind Germany's Armand Hary in the 100 and Italy's Livio Berruti in the 200.

Norton's final chance for a gold medal was thwarted when the USA 4x100-meter relay team won its race, but was disqualified because Frank Budd and Norton exchanged the baton outside the passing zone. The 6-foot-2, 185-pound Norton played football for the Spartans and was drafted in the NFL's fourth round in 1960 by the San Francisco 49ers and played two seasons of professional football.

Smith was the Spartans' next world champion speedster. Brilliant at every sprint distance whether it was 100, 200 or 400 meters, Smith held 11 world records at one time, including the indoor 440 mark.

He broke the world 200-meter record at Sacramento in 1966 at 20.0 and lowered the mark to 19.83 two years later at the Olympics in Mexico City. He also was an accomplished long jumper, setting the SJS record at 25-11.

Smith's record performance in Mexico City has been largely overshadowed by his demonstration on the victory stand, where he and SJS teammate John Carlos -- who took the bronze medal -- stood with their heads bowed and one gloved fist raised above their heads in a Black Power salute.

San Jose State's 1967 "Speed City" mile relay team was composed of (from left) Bob Griffin, Ken Shackleford, Lee Evans and Tommie Smith.

Deeply influenced by the civil rights movement in the United States in the 1960s, Smith rejected the idea, as he put it, that he was, "the fastest nigger on campus."

Smith told broadcaster Howard Cosell, "my raised right hand stood for the power in black America. Carlos' raised left hand stood for the unity in black America. Together, they formed an arch of unity and power." At his induction into the San Jose Sports Hall of Fame in 1997, Smith remarked that the protest was, "for human rights. It wasn't saying, 'kill some honky.' "

Smith and SJS teammate Lee Evans contemplated joining a boycott of the Olympics by the team's black athletes, but they ran instead, producing world class performances. Following their demonstration, Smith and Carlos were suspended from the games and ordered to leave the Olympic village. The 6-foot-3, 190-pound Smith later played in two games at wide receiver with the Cincinnati Bengals in the American Football League.

Evans was another of the Spartans' speed burners. Evans, who attended Overfelt High and San Jose City College, dominated the 400-meter field while in college.

Evans suffered a rare 400-meter defeat to Smith in 1967. Smith allowed Evans to take the lead in the first half to the race, but swept past Evans to edge him by one-half second and set a new mark of 44.5 in the process. Smith never ran the 400 again.

At the high altitude of Mexico City, Evans became the first man to break 44 seconds over 400 meters, running 43.86 for a mark that stood for two decades and won another gold with the record-setting 4x400-meter relay team.

Evans made no overt protest during the ceremonies and was scorned by some Black Power radicals. Unlike Smith, Evans continued to compete, winning the 400-meter race in the 1972 AAU competition.

Evans failed to make the 1972 Olympics in his event, but was a member of the 4x400-meter relay team, which didn't compete because of another protest.

Two members of the United States team, Vincent Matthews and Wayne Collett, were suspended for showing contempt during the playing of the Star Spangled Banner during the 400-meter medal ceremonies. Without them, the USA couldn't field a relay team.

Evans coached track in Africa for many years and was among the first five athletes inducted into San Jose's Sports Hall of Fame in 1994.

The year after the Mexico City protest, Carlos tied world records at 60 yards (5.9) and 100 yards (9.1). He led San Jose State to the NCAA team title in 1968 with victories in the 100 and 220 and anchored the winning 440-yard relay team.

■ GOING FOR GOLD AND GLORY

Coach George Haines' Santa Clara Swim Club owned the world's swimming pools in the 1960s.

Members of the club set scores of American, world and Olympic records and won 46 medals in three Olympics with nine coming in 1960, 16 in 1964 and 21 in 1968.

Club swimmers would have finished fifth among the countries represented in all sports at the Tokyo Olympic Games in 1964 and its 13 Olympic gold medals would have placed fourth in the world behind the Soviet Union, the United States and Japan. They would have finished sixth among 113 nations at the 1968 Mexico City games.

In this country, the club chalked up win after win in AAU competition. It was the first organization to take both the men's and women's AAU outdoor championships in the same year and did it four straight times. In 1967, it won an unprecedented AAU double, taking the men's and women's titles in both the indoor and outdoor competitions.

The Olympics' roll call began in 1960, when Chris von Saltza and Los Gatos High School classmate Lynn Burke became the first Santa Clara County female athletes to win gold medals. The 17-year-old von Saltza picked up three golds and a silver while Burke won two golds. There were no women's collegiate swimming programs at the time and Burke retired the following year, saying, "the thrill is gone." Von Saltza continued to compete in 1961, then quit the pool to enter Stanford.

As Haines' reputation as a teacher grew, parents outside the county began sending children to live with swim club families so they could train with him all year around. Santa Clara High's swimming team grew in stature as new students arrived. The Panthers broke Los Altos High's 83-dual meet win streak in 1962, won 215 straight, took many North Coast Section titles and every boy's crown in the new Central Coast Section from 1966 to 1977. Haines produced more than 300 high school All-Americans, who held every national record in the late 1960s and early 1970s. Among the newcomers from elsewhere were Donna de Varona and

Santa Clara Swim Club dominated competition in the 1960s and 1970s with the help of such stars as (from left) Mark Spitz, Donna de Varona and Don Schollander.

Don Schollander, two of the club's brightest stars in the 1964 Olympics.

The record-setting de Varona won many races before retiring in 1965 to become a TV commentator. Schollander became the first swimmer to win four gold medals in a single Olympics, was voted Associated Press male athlete of the year and won the Sullivan Award. When his career was over, he had set 22 world and 37 American records.

In addition to Schollander's 1964 gold medals, Steve Clark won three, de Varona and Gary Ilman took two each, Lillian "Pokey" Watson and Dick Roth, one apiece. Club members Sharon Finneran and Claudia Kolb each took home a silver and Terri Stickles collected a bronze.

By 1965, Mark Spitz was shaving seconds off American age group freestyle records and catching up with Schollander, who had joined Clark at Yale. Greg Buckingham was added to the mix as Santa Clara swimmers stocked USA teams in foreign meets as well as on American soil.

The 1967 club was loaded with so much talent that it won the AAU Far Western competition while most of its stars were at the Pan American Games.

Schollander won his final Olympic gold medal in the 800-meter relay in 1968, but earned only a silver in his last race in the 200-meter freestyle. Kolb took two individual golds in the medley events.

Prior to the Mexico City games, Haines predicted Spitz would win five or six gold medals. The quote was attributed to the swimmer, who was ridiculed for bragging when he won only two gold medals in relay events. The two had a falling out in 1969 and Haines dropped the 19-year-old Indiana University superstar from the club's roster. Spitz had competed in the Maccabian Games in Israel and told Haines he wouldn't swim with the club in the national AAU meet.

Spitz continued competing elsewhere, led Indiana to three NCAA championships and won seven gold medals at Munich in 1972, a record for a single Olympics.

■ RECORD-SETTING RAMS

Nobody knew it at the time, of course, but a midseason football loss in 1959 took on greater significance at Willow Glen High as the years rolled by.

The Rams dropped a 25-13 decision to Washington of Fremont, coached by Bill Walsh (SJS), but won their final six games to finish 8-1-0. They would not lose again until 1963, a state record 42 consecutive games.

San Jose's fourth public high school had been open almost a decade when the streak began. San Jose State graduate Bob Berry was Willow Glen's only coach, moving over from San Jose High where an unbeaten 1949 team had boosted his four-season record to 18-14-4.

The Rams had only one winning season in his first eight before the juggernaut began to develop in 1958. Led by the coach's quarterback son, Bob, Willow Glen took all nine games in 1959, ripping Walsh's depleted Washington Huskies squad in the season finale, 51-0.

League MVP Bucky Rosen ran 78 yards to score in Willow Glen's 6-0 win over San Jose to close out 1960 with the streak intact at 24 games. With no county playoffs, fans

Mike Gervasoni (left) and Eric Paulson were Santa Clara's high-scoring 1965-66 back court.

argued whether Willow Glen's potent defense could contain unbeaten Campbell High's 33 point-a-game offense led by star quarterback Craig Morton.

The Rams continued to roll through 1961 unbeaten with another of the coach's sons, Ken, at quarterback and all-everything Jack Longinotti at one tackle. In 1962, Willow Glen dealt Lincoln its only defeat, 13-12, when Bob Walters picked off Bob Toledo's pass at the two-yard line on the last play and reeled off another 9-0-0 season.

The streak came to an end in the 1963 opener when Andrew Hill High twins Jim and Joe Zito hooked up on a 16-yard TD pass with 13 seconds left for an 18-13 victory.

■ BRONCOS IN THE NCAA

The 1960s opened with Santa Clara going to the NCAA basketball tournament again and closed with three of the most powerful Bronco teams of all-time.

SCU's first team of the decade was Bob Feerick's last championship quintet. He left after the 1961-62 season to coach the San Francisco Warriors, an NBA team recently arrived in the Bay Area from Philadelphia, and was succeeded by former Bronco star Dick Garibaldi.

Catholic All-American Frank Sobrero, Jim Russi and Joe Sheaff paced the team to 21 wins and its fourth WCAC championship with a 59-53 playoff victory over Loyola. In the NCAAs, the Broncos lost to eventual national champion California, 69-49, and to Utah in a consolation game.

Santa Clara led the NCAA in defense in 1960-61 and 1961-62, producing the last sub-50 point average (48.7) in the former year when they went 18-9 and averaging 52.1 in the latter season while posting a 19-6 record.

Santa Clara was out of the championship picture until

Santa Clara coach Dick Garibaldi talked with the 1967-68 Broncos' starting lineup (from left) Joe Diffley, Ralph Ogden, Bud Ogden, Dennis Awtrey and Bob Heaney.

1967-68, when three talented sophomores, Dennis Awtrey (Blackford), Ralph Ogden (Lincoln) and Kevin Eagleson joined senior Bob Heaney and junior Bud Ogden (Lincoln).

Bud Ogden, who had ignored the lingering effects of a broken nose in scoring a school record 55 points against Pepperdine a year earlier, led the team with an 18.9 average.

SCU took a 21-3 record into the NCAA regionals at Albuquerque. They went up by 20 points at halftime before handling New Mexico easily, 86-73, but lost the next night to eventual national champion UCLA, 87-66.

In 1968-69, Santa Clara won 21 in a row before being upset by San Jose State, 73-69. They were ranked No. 2 behind UCLA with a school best 26-1 record as the tourney approached. Since NCAA brackets were set up on a strictly regional basis at the time, the Broncos were matched against the powerful Bruins, who destroyed them with a great press on their home court at Westwood, 90-52.

It was a great year for Bud Ogden, who made the cover of Sports Illustrated, was a second team All-American, finished as SCU's second all-time scorer and went to the Philadelphia 76ers in the first round.

The Broncos returned to the regionals again in 1969-70, but lost in the first round to Utah State, 69-68. They were led to a 23-6 mark by Ralph Ogden (21.9) -- Bud's younger brother -- and the unselfish Awtrey (21.2), who closed out his career as SCU's all-time scoring leader by average (19.9) and in rebounds (1,135).

■ COUNTED OUT

When Wisconsin's Charlie Mohr died eight days after an NCAA championship match with a San Jose State fighter in 1960, NCAA boxing passed away with him.

Mohr walked to the locker room, but fell unconscious 15 minutes after losing to Stu Bartell. The Spartan had sent Mohr to the canvas for a mandatory nine count and forced his opponent into the ropes with a flurry of blows before the referee stopped the bout at 1:49 of the second round.

Doctors who operated on Mohr for a brain hemorrhage determined that it wasn't the blows the boxer received in the ring that killed him, but a brain aneurysm that had been present for some time.

Wisconsin had won eight team and 38 individual NCAA titles after boxing was sanctioned in 1937.

One of the Badgers' chief competitors was San Jose State, who produced national titles in 1958, 1959 and 1960 along with 11 individual champions, including two-time winners Archie Milton and Ron Nichols. In 1952, the Spartans' Chuck Adkins won the NCAA crown and the light welterweight gold medal in the Olympic Games.

The last Spartan championship team in 1960 had six NCAA title holders: Dave Nelson, Charlie Brown, Steve Kubas, Nichols, Milton and Bartell.

Wisconsin dropped boxing after Mohr died. San Jose State followed suit along with other schools, including Stanford, California, Penn State, Michigan State, Army and Navy. Limited competition resumed in the 1970s, but collegiate boxing never regained the press attention or public acclaim it had achieved before.

■ YOUNG CHAMPIONS

Four national youth baseball championship teams came out of Santa Clara County in the 1960s.

San Jose's Colt All-Stars won the first championship in 1960. Leo Ruth pitched his fourth win without a loss in the title game, downing Tampa, Fla. Lee Schmidt hit a grand slam and Bill Schmidt also homered as the team closed its playoff run with a 13-1 record.

In 1962, the Moreland All-Stars annexed the most prestigious youth title of them all, the Little League World Series, at Williamsport, Pa. The team's Mutt and Jeff pitchers were the keys to victory. Ted Campbell, at 6-foot-3 and 185 pounds the largest player to appear in the championship series, pitched a three-hit, 3-2, win over Rolling Hills in the regionals. Campbell's home run and the one-hit pitching of Vaughn Takaha (5-foot-6, 115 pounds) gave Moreland the title over Hawaii, 3-1, and a trip to the World Series.

In the Series opener, Moreland set records in a 22-2 win over Poitiers, France. Dave Schneider had four hits, including two homers, five RBIs. Other contributors were Mike Ucci (four hits, five RBIs), Mike Murata (two doubles, home run) and Takaha (three hits, home run).

Takaha stopped Monterrey, Mexico, with a one-hit shutout in the semifinal. Campbell struck out 11 and gave Kankakee, Ill., no hits in the final, won by Moreland, 3-0.

Many of the same players helped the Campbell-Moreland Pony team win the national title in 1964. Tom Sanford threw a perfect game to put the team in the regional finals and Campbell (10-0) beat Canoga Park, 4-1, to move on to the World Series.

Takaha hit a three-run homer to top Gadsden, Ala., 4-1, in 16 innings and coach Joe Gagliardi's youngsters whipped Padukah, Ky., 5-0, with Mark Taku fanning 15. In the final, the stars beat Gadsden again, 8-2, as Sanford hit a three-run homer and pitched shutout relief.

The 1966 West Valley All-Stars were national Colt champs. Ron Curnett's seventh inning homer beat Shawnee, Okla., 1-0, and Carl Troedson struck out 11 in a 5-4 victory over Hagerstown, Md. A win over El Paso put the stars in the final, where they beat Padukah Ky., 4-0, with a four-run inning topped by Lou Gaspar's two-run double.

In 1968, Santa Clara Colt All-Stars beat Beaumont, Tex., 8-0, on Randy Boyd's three-hitter and Honolulu, 4-3, when Steve Bartkowski tripled in the tying run and scored the winner on Greg Merritt's single. Boyd fanned 15 batters in a 9-2 win over Springfield, Ill., for the championship.

■ COMRADES ON THE FARM

Stanford had hosted the national trials for the USA Olympic Games' team in 1932 and 1960, but the most significant gathering of track and field athletes in county history took place in the big bowl in 1962.

More than 154,600 fans turned out for the fourth meeting between the USA and USSR, world track and field powerhouses who had run one-two in the medal counts at the previous three Olympics. It was the largest two-day crowd in the history of the sport in this country.

The fans got their money's worth. Local favorite Jim Beatty, who ran for Santa Clara Valley Youth Village, set an American record 1:46.4 in the 800-meter race, and world records were set by Hal Connolly in the hammer throw and Al Orter in the discus. The Russians' Tamara Press broke a women's meet mark in the shot put.

The weekend's highlight came late one afternoon. With all eyes focused on the high jump pit, the USSR's Valery Brumel soared over the bar at 7-5 to set a new world record. It was the second time in two years the Stanford high jump pit was the scene of a world mark. John Thomas of Boston University had cleared 7-3 1/2 in the 1960 Olympic trials.

For those who were keeping score, the Americans won the men's competition, 128-107, and the Soviet women were victorious, 66-41.

The meet closed with American and Russian athletes walking arm in arm around the huge oval in a show of good will and sportsmanship that was impressive in the days of the Cold War. It was a spectacle that brought tears to the eyes of many spectators.

Bob Garibaldi

■ WORLD SERIES TIME

Santa Clara had always stowed the bats and put away its baseball gloves when the regular season ended. But in June, 1962, the Broncos not only were still playing, they were competing for the College World Series title.

Santa Clara had been in the CIBA with St. Mary's and the Pacific Coast Conference southern division schools off and on since 1927 with only second place finishes in 1929, 1943 and 1949 to show for their efforts.

Coach John "Paddy" Cottrell's 1962 Broncos were different. Led by pitcher Bob Garibaldi and future big leaguers Tim Cullen, Ernie Fazio and John Boccabella, SCU posted the best record in school history, 39-8.

The powerful 6-foot-4 Garibaldi, who also was a Bronco basketball star, tossed a 10-0 no-hitter over USC, their closest pennant rival and defending national champion. Later, Fazio hit two home runs to beat the Trojans, 6-3, to knot the league race, which the Broncos won by one game.

Santa Clara downed Fresno in two of three NCAA regional games with Garibaldi striking out 12 in the opener. He fanned 16 more in the first game against PCC Northern Division champion Oregon State and picked up a save in the second to send the Broncos off to Omaha ranked first in the nation ahead of Michigan.

After losing the opener to Florida State, the Broncos swept four straight, beating Texas in the last one, 4-3, in 10 innings on outfielder Mickey McDermott's inside the park home run. Another extra inning struggle followed, but the Broncos lost the title to Michigan, 5-4, in 15 innings.

Garibaldi, who pitched in five of the six World Series games, was tournament MVP. He finished with a 10-3 record, a 1.86 ERA and 168 strikeouts in 125 2/3 innings pitched. Garibaldi signed with the San Francisco Giants for

Luis Molina

$150,000, but never succeeded in the majors.

Fazio hit .356, led the nation with 15 home runs and made first team All-American. Garibaldi and Boccabella, who batted .357, were on the second squad.

The next time Santa Clara made it to the postseason was 1968, when the No. 6 Broncos (31-12) won the first of four straight West Coast Conference crowns under coach Sal Taormina, but fell to Los Angeles State in the first round. All-American outfielder Vince Bigone hit a school record .401. SCU gained an at-large berth in the 1969 playoffs with a 40-10 record, but lost to UCLA.

Thwarted from its first outright baseball title since 1931 by two losses to SCU, Stanford finished in a tie with California for the CIBA crown in 1965. The Indians went to the NCAA because they had beaten the Bears in three of four games, but were eliminated by Washington State.

Stanford reached the College World Series for the first time in 14 years two seasons later, when present coach Mark Marquess, who batted .404 at first base, and future 10-year major league shortstop Frank Duffy were All-Americans. With pitcher Sandy Vance a perfect 11-0 with a 1.53 ERA, the team posted a 36-6-1 mark for its best winning percentage this century (.849).

The Pac-8 champions took two of three games from Fresno State to qualify for the trip, but lost twice to Arizona State in the series and were eliminated.

■ LUIS MOLINA

Boxer Luis Molina was the box office king of San Jose in the 1960s, surpassing popular Eddie Chavez for the title.

The fourth-ranked junior welterweight was, "strong as steel, but crude as iron ore," *San Francisco Chronicle* boxing reporter Jack Fiske wrote in 1964. "He punches like a mule, but appears a jackass when he misses."

The popular Puerto Rican polished his skills in the Santa Clara Valley Youth Village ring and made the 1956 USA Olympic team. After three years in the Marine Corps, where he won several service titles, and with an amateur record of only five losses in 138 bouts, Molina turned pro. He ran off 19 straight wins with 15 KOs, setting a Civic Auditorium box office record of $17,200 in his 19th bout.

The streak ended in 1962, when southpaw Kenny Lane danced away from Molina's brawling rushes and decisioned him at Civic Auditorium on national television.

Molina kept on fighting, scoring the 16th knockout of his career against Ben "The Bandit" Medina. Molina was Ring Magazine's boxer of the month after winning an upset 10-round decision over former lightweight champion Joe Brown in a match that drew 6,500 spectators and a record outdoor gate of $27,645 at Municipal Stadium.

Molina lost for the second and third times in his career in a pair of decisions to Doug Vaillant in 1963, but still ranked high among welterweights the following year when his appearances included a televised Madison Square Garden loss to Frankie Narvaez.

Molina never achieved more national glory, but kept on fighting in San Jose, where the fans loved him.

■ BASEBALL BEES A-BUZZING

The California League gave San Jose a new baseball franchise in 1962, granting Jack Quinn a team he nicknamed the Bees, an historic local moniker that recalled the popular semi-pro baseball team of the 1930s.

The Bees were real professionals, however, remaining competitive throughout the 1960s despite another ownership change. Quinn obtained a working agreement with the Los Angeles Angels, brought back Red Marion as manager and saw his Bees take the first half title and a playoff victory over Reno. Quinn was named Class A executive of the year by the Sporting News.

The Bees' top players were outfielder Dick Simpson, who bashed a team record 42 home runs, knocked in 113 runs and batted .315, and pitcher Fred Newman, who was 15-1 before his promotion to the Texas League.

In 1964, two former minor leaguers from San Jose, John "Bud" Urzi and Pete Filice, bought the team and hired Rocky Bridges as manager. The humorous Bridges was no joke on the field, taking the Bees to the playoffs the next year and beating Stockton in two straight for the title.

The Bees tied for the first half pennant in 1966, but lost a playoff to Modesto. That same year, unusual scheduling sent the Bees to Candlestick Park after a Giants-Phillies game, where they beat Fresno in 10 innings, 6-5.

San Jose made it to the playoffs the next two years, taking the 1967 title over Modesto, but losing to Fresno in 1968. The Bees were down in the standings in the decade's last year, but Monte McMillan made it into the league record book by beating Bakersfield, 1-0, with a seven inning no-hitter and Dayle Campbell tied a league record against Bakersfield by becoming the first San Jose player to belt three home runs in a game.

■ FOR THE RECORD

Golf pro Dean Cummings set a world record in 1962 by playing 678 holes of golf over 91 1/2 hours at Ironwood

Hugh Campbell shows teammates his prolific pass receiving prowess. Campbell set NCAA pass reception records during his three seasons at Washington State.

Golf Club in San Jose. The 22-year-old Cummings had 10 hours of sleep during his marathon.

In 1962, Bob Stoecker of Los Altos High broke his own state discus mark with a national record toss of 195-4.

Jeff Chase of Santa Clara Valley Youth Village broke an American record in 1963 in the rarely contested pole vault for distance. He went 28-8, six inches beyond the old mark set in 1910 in New York.

Charlie Harraway scored on San Jose State's longest run from scrimmage, 94 yards against Pacific in 1965.

Keith Swagerty (Camden), one of the NCAA's top five rebounders during each of his three years at Pacific, grabbed a school record 39 against UCSB in 1965. He had 20 or more rebounds in a game 33 times between 1965 and 1967.

San Francisco State quarterback Bob Toledo (Lincoln, SJCC) completed 33 of 50 passes for 501 yards and eight TDs in a 68-34 win over Humboldt State in 1967. Toledo ended the year with season college division records for pass attempts (396), completions (211), yards (3,513), TDs (45).

■ HUGH CAMPBELL

When his three-year career at Washington State ended in 1962, receiver Hugh Campbell was the NCAA leader in passes caught (176), receiving yards (2,453) and touchdown receptions (22).

The 6-foot-1, 190-pounder from Saratoga was largely overlooked by college recruiters, although he had a fine prep career at Los Gatos High, primarily as a quarterback.

College freshmen weren't eligible for the varsity, but when Campbell was a sophomore at WSC in 1960, he led the nation with 66 receptions, a record 881 yards and 10 touchdowns. He ranked first in catches the next year with 53 and was third as a senior with 57 receptions.

Campbell was the MVP in both the East-West and College All-Star games. He ran precise pass routes and was sure-handed, but the San Francisco 49ers cut Campbell, saying he was too slow to be a professional receiver.

Campbell played in the Canadian Football League, where he was the top scorer in 1966, an all-league flanker several years and set receiving records for the Saskatchewan Roughriders. He coached Edmonton to six Grey Cup finals and won five straight league titles (1978-1982) and was head coach of the Houston Oilers in 1984 and 1985.

■ BROBDINGNAGIAN (*) BELLS

There have been few major California high school football teams that compiled a single season record as impressive as the 1965 Bellarmine Bells.

The football team at Bellarmine Prep, the private Jesuit school in San Jose, was coached by John Hanna. It played nine games that fall and won them all. The Bells not only won, they dominated their opponents, shutting out eight of nine while averaging 34.4 points per game.

The narrowest margin of victory was a 17-0 win over a San Leandro team that entered the game with 18 straight wins. Their biggest win was 60-0 over Catholic rival Serra.

St. Mary's of Berkeley was the only team to score against the Bells in a 36-6 loss. But Bellarmine's defense was perfect throughout the season, because the Panthers' touchdown came on a 51-yard pass interception return.

Some of Bellarmine's best players in the fantastic season were QB Dan Pastorini, All-American John Albanese and Phil Burton, who had 118 points, with five field goals.

This was the fourth in a line of great Bellarmine clubs that won 36 of 37 games, including 31 in a row dating back to a 21-16 loss to Serra in 1962.

The string ended in the 1966 opener when Pittsburg High, led by QB Horace "Butch" Cattolico, beat the Bells, 33-14. Cattolico is well known locally as the century closes as the successful football coach at Los Gatos High.

(*) Brobdingnag was a land inhabited by giants 60 feet tall in Swift's *Gulliver's Travels.*

■ HARDWOOD PIONEERS

Women's basketball wasn't recognized as an official collegiate sport until 1974-75, but Santa Clara University honors the pioneer female hoopsters who played in the decade before that season by including their records in the school's media guide.

Santa Clara was unbeaten during its first two seasons of women's basketball, defeating California, Stanford and San Jose State in the inaugural year (1963-64) and downing all six opponents the following season.

The Lady Broncos extended their winning streak to 11 with wins over San Jose City College and Stanford in the

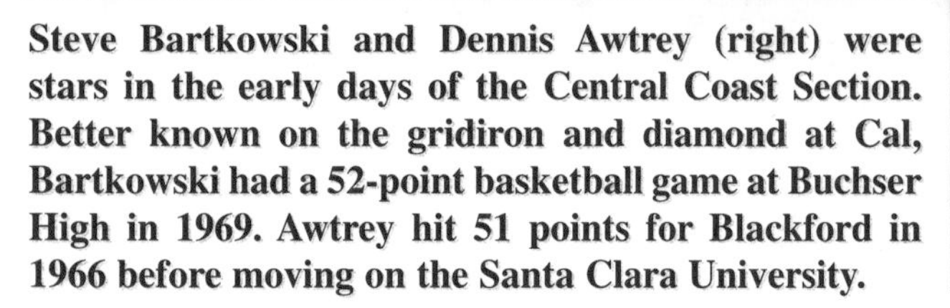

Steve Bartkowski and Dennis Awtrey (right) were stars in the early days of the Central Coast Section. Better known on the gridiron and diamond at Cal, Bartkowski had a 52-point basketball game at Buchser High in 1969. Awtrey hit 51 points for Blackford in 1966 before moving on the Santa Clara University.

first two games of 1965-66 before falling for the first time in the program's history, 27-22, to Cal State Hayward.

■ A SECTION OF THEIR OWN

High schools in Santa Clara County and nearby counties got their own athletic organization when the Central Coast Section was formed in 1965. The CCS is one of 10 divisions of the California Interscholastic Federation, which has administered high school athletic programs since 1914.

The sections provide students attending 1,200 member schools a chance to participate in 26 boy's and girl's sports. The CIF offers statewide competition in basketball, golf and track and field as well as girl's volleyball and boy's wrestling.

By the end of the century, more than 100 schools joined the Central Coast Section, which has jurisdiction over Santa Clara, San Mateo, Santa Cruz, Monterey and San Benito counties, a region stretching from Daly City to King City. Several San Francisco Catholic schools and some Christian schools in Alameda County also compete in CCS leagues.

Many CCS schools belonged to the North Coast Section until 1965, when its sprawling territory was divided to create the new section. CCS competition began with wrestling in 1966.

The following spring, male swimming and track and field competition began. Baseball playoffs came in 1967 and basketball opened the next winter. Cross-country started in 1969 and soccer a year later, followed by tennis, golf and football (1972). In 1974, water polo became a championship sport. Division 3 soccer began in 1988.

The first girl's competition was track and field in spring of 1974. Swimming was added that fall, followed by tennis, badminton and volleyball in 1975. Field hockey, gymnastics and softball came a year later and soccer, basketball and cross-country in 1977. Since then, golf and water polo have been added.

Volleyball became the first new boy's program in more than two decades in 1997, balancing the CCS program at 13 sports each for boys and girls.

■ HONORS

SJS quarterback Chon Gallegos led the NCAA in pass completions with 117 for 1,480 yards and 14 TDs and was named 1961 winner of the Palo Club's Glenn "Pop" Warner Award as the top senior football player on the West Coast.

Three-sport star Eric Paulson of Sunnyvale High was Northern California athlete of the year in 1961.

In 1963, QB Ron Calcagno became the first Santa Clara

University player to gain Little All-American honors.

Jim Lonborg (Stanford) of the Boston Red Sox won 22 games and the 1967 American League's Cy Young Award.

Tim Rossovich (St. Francis) was the first football player from a county high school to be named a consensus All-American. The USC defensive lineman achieved the honor in 1967, then played six seasons in the NFL.

San Jose State outside left Mani Hernandez was winner of the Hermann Award as 1968's best college soccer player and teammate Fred Nourzad made the All-America team.

Hall of Fame inductees in the 1960s were Stanford's Ernie Nevers (pro football); 1930s Stanford basketball coach John Bunn (college basketball); Don Schollander, Chris von Saltza, Donna de Varona (swimming); Ken Venturi, Ernie Pieper, Lawson Little (California golf) and Marge Higley of San Jose (women's bowling).

■ UNDEFEATED HOOPS

Undefeated basketball teams are a rarity, but San Jose high schools produced two of them three years apart.

The first was the 29-0 Lincoln High team of 1965-66, ranked No. 1 in the state along with undefeated Los Angeles Jordan (18-0).

The other was Willow Glen's 1968-69 team, a quintet that took 27 straight games, won the Central Coast Section's second basketball championship and was ranked second in California behind Compton (30-0).

Lincoln was led by 6-foot-5 center Ralph Ogden, who averaged 23.7 points per game and made the Scholastic Magazine prep All-America squad along with Dennis Awtrey, 6-foot-9 Blackford High center, who led all Northern California scorers with a 28.4 average.

Defense was Lincoln's strong suit and the Lions had no trouble winning the Mount Hamilton Athletic League title, averaging 62 points while holding opponents to only 36. They moved into the Peninsula Basketball Tournament for the fourth straight year.

The PBT began at Stanford's Men's Gym in 1958-59 to provide postseason competition for Santa Clara County and Peninsula league champions that had been gradually squeezed out of the Northern California Tournament of Champions played annually at Cal's Harmon Gym.

Lincoln closed its season with a 59-53 win over San Carlos for the PBT title. Ogden hit 27 to lead the tournament with 93 points in three games.

Three seasons later, fans were comparing the Lions with Willow Glen. The Rams breezed through the Santa Teresa Athletic League, outscoring opponents 77 to 45.

The offense was led by 6-foot-5 All-Northern California center Phil White; Bob Titchenal Jr., son of the former San Jose State football coach, and guard Mark Skillicorn.

The Rams were seeded first in the CCS playoffs, and easily disposed of Del Mar and Archbishop Riordan before winning the championship from Santa Cruz, 64-53, to end its perfect season.

■ APACHES ON THE WARPATH

The San Jose Apaches put the city on the minor league football map of America in 1967.

The Apaches joined the Continental Football League's Western Division and hired Oakland Raiders' assistant Bill Walsh as their head coach and general manager. Walsh later said he was thinking about leaving coaching and took the job because he could work part-time while teaching and doing graduate work at his alma mater, San Jose State.

Walsh promised to field a first class product without any "football bums." Just before league play opened, Walsh cut 25 of 35 players and filled the roster from NFL taxi squads. Players were paid $125 to $150-a-game.

There was talk of calling the team the Lobos, but that name was already taken by a Los Angeles soccer team and Apaches was a familiar name in San Jose.

Another San Jose semi-pro eleven called the Apaches had competed in the Pacific Football League for several years. In 1965, a Chon Gallegos to Mike Roach scoring pass with 40 seconds left gave the 12-1-1 Apaches a 7-6 playoff win over four-time champ Redwood City. The next season, they lost to the Seattle Ramblers, 48-13, on Dick Berg's (Stanford) five scoring passes. The Apaches finished 13-1-0 after a 100-7 win over Paso Robles and Roach set a U. S. semi-pro season record with 24 TDs.

Walsh's new Apaches, wearing discarded black and silver Oakland Raiders' uniforms, opened the 1967 season in Oregon with a 40-20 win over Eugene. A week later, 2,400 fans turned out at San Jose City College to watch tight end Bill Peterson (SJS) snare two touchdown passes in a 29-2 win over the Victoria (B.C.) Steelers. Peterson went on to the NFL, playing until 1975.

The division champion Orange County Ramblers beat San Jose early in October and then came to San Jose for a crucial return game. The year's largest home crowd of 4,391 was disappointed when the Apaches lost. San Jose finished the season second with eight wins and two losses.

Walsh said the team lost $60,000. In June, after failing to gain permission to move into Spartan Stadium -- where there was a chance to draw larger crowds -- the team folded. As a final insult, the IRS ordered the Apaches' equipment sold to settle a $14,887 tax debt.

■ RACIAL PROTESTS

The racial storm that swept across America in the 1960s came to San Jose State several times, including twice on the football field and once on the basketball court.

The Spartans were scheduled to meet the University of Texas-El Paso in the 1967 football opener, but the game was canceled after black students at San Jose State complained about racial inequity in housing and discrimination against African-American athletes and threatened demonstrations at Spartan Stadium.

UTEP was known as Texas Western a year earlier when it had started the first all black lineup in NCAA basketball tournament history and defeated Kentucky, 72-65, for the championship.

In 1968, seven black SJS players refused to participate in a football game against Brigham Young University at Spartan Stadium on grounds that the Mormon Church supported racist policies.

Several hundred police ringed the field every few feet because of threats and only 2,500 spectators attended the game. There were no incidents from the protest, but fans got their money's worth of thrills from action on the field.

A 67-8 loser to BYU the previous season, San Jose State scored 22 unanswered points in a five-minute period in the third quarter and held off the Cougars to win, 25-21.

Two days after the football game, black basketball players Darnell Hillman, C. J. Howard, Ron Tribble and Bernie Veasey refused to play in the Spartans' opening game against St. Mary's.

In 1969, SJS football players voted to play BYU, but wore black arm bands to protest the church's racial policies. The Cougars won, 21-3.

■ TRIVIAL PURSUITS

With only one opponent available at a 1960 meet, Al Jongewaard of Santa Clara Valley Youth Village entered his four-year-old son in the hammer throw. Dad was second while Eric Jongewaard took third place with a toss of 3-6.

When rain apparently wiped out Stanford's track meet against USC in 1963, the Indians' Sheridan Downey left for home in Santa Rosa. The CHP failed to intercept him when the meet was moved to Foothill College's all-weather track. Without the points Downey was expected to produce in the long jump and triple jump, the Indians lost, 73-72.

Two of Buck Shaw Stadium's biggest baseball crowds showed up 1965. A record regular season gathering of 5,250 saw Santa Clara and USC split a twin bill on April 11 and two days later 11,255 turned out when the San Francisco Giants downed the Broncos, 8-4, in an exhibition game.

British freshman sprinter Pat Morrison was benched by Stanford coach Payton Jordan in 1966, because his hair was longer than allowed by the school's athletic department policy. "The length of one's hair is irrelevant to track," said Morrison, who balked at Jordan's request for, "a little trim, so it won't hang over his ears and down his neck."

The Roller Derby champion Bay Bombers, who brought their banked track show to Civic Auditorium and Municipal Stadium in the 1960s, reportedly drew more than one million fans throughout Northern California in 1968.

Leigh High football fans really needed a game program in 1968 when seven sets of brothers, including two sets of twins, were on the team: Greg and Mike Franz, Gary and Ron Graham, Barry and Brian Hinman, Jim and Steve Knell, Doug and Steve Oliver, Tim and Tom Reedy, Warren and Willis Stone.

Ron Wyden, Palo Alto High basketball star who graduated in 1968, later was elected to Congress from Oregon.

■ STATE CHAMPION KNIGHTS

Los Altos High dominated the local prep track scene in the late 1960s, taking three of the first five Central Coast Section titles and winning a state championship in 1970.

The Knights were CCS champions in 1967, 1969 and 1970 and second in 1968. Brad Lyman won the 100 twice (including a meet record 9.7 in 1967) and the 220 once early in the period. Middle distance star Rick Brown and weight man Chris Adams sparked the team to its last two section titles and the state championship.

Brown ran six races in 1970's two-day state meet, becoming the first runner to record a double victory in the

San Francisco Bay Bombers female favorite Joan Weston (38) blocks an opponent on the Roller Derby's banked track.

440 (47.8) and 880 (1:50.6) and ran a blistering 47.0 anchor leg to lead the CCS champs to a win in the mile relay.

Defending CIF champion Adams thrilled 13,000 spectators at the Berkeley final, sailing the platter 201 feet 3 inches to break the state record and his own pending national mark of 201 feet even.

■ VALLEY HALL OF FAME

Eight football players and coaches were among the first 12 athletes voted into the Santa Clara Valley Hall of Fame by writers and broadcasters in 1968. The first class included five players from Stanford, basketball immortal Hank Luisetti and gridders Ernie Nevers, Monk Moscrip, Frankie Albert and Bob Mathias, also a world decathlon champion.

From Santa Clara University came baseball player Marv Owen, basketball player and coach Bob Feerick and football coach Buck Shaw, quarterback Nello Falaschi and Len Casanova, who played and coached with the Broncos.

San Jose State tailback Leroy Zimmerman and football coach Dud DeGroot also were honored.

■ IN PASSING

Lynn Dunaway, 21, top golfer on the San Jose State squad, died at his Napa home in 1961 after an illness.

Jack McDonald, 55, "The Old Walnut Farmer" who was play-by-play broadcaster for the San Francisco Seals in the 1930s and 1940s and the San Jose Red Sox in the early 1950s, died at his Scotts Valley home in 1962.

Robert "Buzz" McGee, 51, former 49ers publicist, died at his Burlingame home in 1963. He was a tackle with Santa Clara University's 1937 Sugar Bowl champions.

Tom Brogan, 21-year-old Santa Clara University first baseman, drowned in the surf near Honolulu in 1965 despite efforts of teammate Bob Gilbert to rescue him. The team was in Hawaii to play in a postseason tournament.

Racing driver Cliff Rogalsky of San Jose died at the

Craig Morton (left) and Jack Schraub were teammates at Campbell High School and Cal.

Speedway in 1967 when his car hit an oil slick and crashed.

Vietnam War casualties in 1968 included Cpl. Thomas Diefenderfer, 23, champion swimmer at Santa Clara High and Foothill College, and Marine Lt. Gatlin "Jerry" Howell, 31, San Jose State half-miler. In 1969, former St. Francis High golfer Jim Hannibal died in a helicopter crash.

■ 1960 ■

Ken Venturi wins Crosby Pro-Am golf with 286 . . . Harlem Globetrotters draw 2,984 fans who pay top Civic Auditorium hoops gate, $8,218 . . . Pat Cavataio hits 38 for Lincoln High in 60-57 win over Logan . . . SCVYV's Jim Beatty upsets Dyrol Burleson at Madison Square Garden mile in 4:05.4. Later, he sets American marks in mile (3:58.0), 5,000 meters (13:51.7) . . . Doug Smith of San Jose breaks 99 of 100 targets for U. S. trapshooting title . . . Walt Threadgill's hoops record 32 helps Lick High destroy Ayer, 62-28 . . . Conference player of the year Jack Searfoss scores 52, snares 30 rebounds in SJCC's 100-63 win over Menlo . . . Del Mar High's Rich Gugat leads county hoops scorers with 21.3 average, joins Palo Alto's Rich Hunt on All-Central Coast . . . Charley Clark of SJS sets NCAA 3,000-meter steeplechase record . . . Hill High's Fred Hood, who closed 1959 with no-hitter, stops Buchser with another to open 1960. Later, he no-hits San Jose . . . Bob Lister nets 20, Gerry Gilbert 19 as SJCC takes state JC hoops crown over Fullerton, 77-67 . . . On same day Peter Cortez of Ayer High no-hits Logan, San Jose's Leon Coronado does it to Washington . . . Stanford's Tom Peterson captures NCAA 100 breast stroke . . . Vance Barnes high jumps 6-10 for SJS . . . Mickey McWhorter hits 11 as state champ San Jose falls to Puerto Rico, 44-37, in Biddy Basketball tournament play . . . Robin Ruble of Los Altos High runs Nor Cal 880 in 1:53.1 . . . Record 19 Buchser High batters go down on strikes as Walt Christiana of Campbell wins, 8-1 . . . Doug Schoenwetter of Fremont High flips discus 175-5 . . . Laszlo Tabori's 3:59.6 mile helps SCVYV set American distance medley relay mark of 9:34.9 . . . Mrs. Frank Cavier wins county women's golf . . . Ernie Cunliffe sets Stanford marks in 440, 660, 880, mile . . . WCAC baseball champ SJS (27-14) in 6-5 NCAA playoff loss to Pepperdine . . . Willow Glen High's Roger Olsen leaps 6-6 1/4 to tie for state high jump title . . . Prep MVPs star in finals: Nat Martinez Ks 16 as Willow Glen High rips Washington for ESCVAL crown, 10-0; Campbell takes WSCVAL over Del Mar, 4-3, as Bucs' Craig Morton, Central Coast MVP, goes four for four . . . Del Mar High's Pete Danna extends county triple jump record to 45-7 . . . Randy Cowherd of San Jose drives Lotus XI to two wins at Laguna Seca . . . Jack Bariteau's 207 good for fifth county golf title . . . Ron Lucenti takes Palo Alto city golf for fourth straight year . . . Hank Lucenti falls, 3 and 2, to Ron Ginn of SJS for city title . . . Olympic trials draw 125,000 to Stanford where Don Bragg breaks world pole vault mark at 15-9 1/4 . . . San Jose Friction Material's team -- Hank Bernardi, Al Cunha, Bill Santos, Manuel Rodrigues, Frank Silvia -- capture California Men's Bowling Association tournament . . . Don Titcomb of Los Gatos tosses record 156 ringers to win world horseshoe pitching title . . . Boxer Henry Campbell (SJS) turns pro after loss in Olympics . . . San Jose's Marshall Sargent grabs Speedway record 16th main event for season, captures NASCAR points title . . . Cubberley High slips past Tennyson, 25-19, on Don Castle's 71-yard kickoff return with 90 seconds left . . . Washington State's Hugh Campbell (Los Gatos) comes home, catches seven passes in 29-6 win over SJS before record Spartan Stadium turnout of 19,500 . . . Central Coast player of the year Craig Morton completes 12 for 18 for 227 yards, six TDs in 51-32 Campbell High romp over Del Mar. End Jack Schraub catches four TDs . . . SJS beats Idaho, 22-20, when Vandals' end intercepts pass near goal, is tackled in end zone for safety with three seconds left . . . Eugene "Red" Elkins of San Jose wins Milton Berle's Jackpot Bowling over Dick Weber, Bill Pace to become first in TV series with back-to-back wins . . . Cigar-smoking Charlie Sifford wins $2,000 first place prize in Almaden Open with birdie on first extra hole . . . Cal Poly football players Ted Tollner (Palo Alto), James Farley (Gilroy) are injured, but survive Toledo plane crash that kills 22, including 16 teammates . . . Billy Wilson (Campbell, SJS) retires after decade with 49ers,

Jim St. John of San Jose is enshrined in the National Bowling Hall of Fame.

5,902 receiving yards, 49 TDs, six Pro Bowl appearances . . . Joe Leonard wins 41 national motorcycle races during year.

1961

Ernie Cunliffe of Stanford records world 1,000-yard marks indoors at Boston, outdoors on The Farm . . . Jim St. John of San Jose throws 12th frame strike to defeat Therm Gibson in sudden death on TV's Jackpot Bowling . . . Down by 18 early in second half, Stanford rallies for 53-52 hoops win over Cal. John Hendry hits 18 for Indians . . . Gary Chiotti's school record 26 for Foothill helps defeat Cabrillo, 70-51 . . . Gilroy's Rick Wentworth pours in all-time area record 43 against San Lorenzo Valley. Eric Paulson of Sunnyvale equals mark against Camden . . . Carol Zeigler becomes first woman to officiate basketball in county, handling Bellarmine-SCU Frosh contest with San Jose's Harley Dow . . . SJS and SCU carry ball control antics to extreme as Broncos win, 30-29, on Gene Shields' hook shot with five ticks left . . . League MVP Kent Hinckley hits 21 as Palo Alto High downs Sequoia, 49-47, for second straight SPAL basketball title . . . Bill Connolly scores 18 as Bellarmine tips O'Dowd, 48-41, in Catholic playoffs for spot in PBT . . . Egg-throwing SCU fans delay Civic Auditorium game for five minutes, nearly cost Broncos 60-53 victory over St. Mary's . . . Jamaican sprinter Dennis Johnson of SJS runs 9.3 in 100 at Stanford, duplicates feat three more times before season ends. A 9.2 clocking at Mount San Antonio College relays is disallowed because of wind . . . Buoyed by mid-season return of Eddie Sims, SJCC (25-8) wins Coast Conference, loses state hoops final to Fullerton, 94-85. Jaguars later forfeit crown on discovery one player lied about where he lived . . . Fred Salisbury of Los Altos sets U. S. mark for standing quarter mile in Modified A sports car . . . Prep swim titans draw 700 to rain-soaked meet at Los Altos High, where Knights down Santa Clara, 58-37. National freestyle records fall to Steve Clark of Los Altos in 100, Jerry Macedo of Santa Clara in 400 . . . John Boccabella drives in two, scores winner on wild pitch in ninth as SCU slips past Notre Dame at Muni Stadium, 9-8 . . . John Jurivich sets SJS bat record with .437 average . . . Cubberley High's Don Washer pole vaults 13-5 for area mark . . . Charley Clark of SJS sets U. S. record in two-mile . . . Bob Benson, Steve Clark lead Los Altos High to NCS swim title . . . Batting champ Dave Gonzales (.478) of Bellarmine makes All-CAL . . . Prep league MVPs shine: Bob Barthle scatters seven hits as Los Altos beats Campbell, 5-1, for WSCVAL crown, shortstop Bucky Rosen blasts fifth homer as Willow Glen takes third straight ESCVAL title over Pioneer, 6-0 . . . Ten-foot birdie putt on 36th green gives John Lotz of SJS Northern California amateur title over Stanford's Kent Winton. Lotz wins county golf crown one week later . . . New state marks: Cubberley High's Don Castle in shot put (65-7 3/4), Bob Stoecker of Los Altos in discus (188-6 1/2) . . . Red Elkins rolls 300 game to start San Jose Open in first local pro bowling tournament of note at Saratoga Lanes . . . Dick Gear of SJS ties for first in NCAA pole vault with 15-4 . . . Primo Carnera refs one bout, teams with Lord Blears in tag team victory over Clyde Steeves, Ed Miller at Municipal Stadium . . . Craig Morton's (Campbell) 88-yard TD pass wins North-South prep game in Los Angeles, 7-2 . . . Muni Stadium crowd of 3,000 sees Ray Stevens retain U. S. heavyweight wrestling title against Ray Stern . . . Bruce Bellandi's four-hitter tops Oakland's Bill Erwin Post, sends Palo Alto to American Legion's state playoffs . . . Ernie Pieper wins state amateur golf . . . Dennis Destefano's double, grand slam leads San Jose Colt all-stars to 10-3 win over Hawaii for sectional title. In West Coast finals, locals down Tri-Cities, 10-0, on Bruce Pfeffer's 13 strikeouts, take Provo, Utah, 3-0, on Roger Ruth's two-hitter before losing to Rancho . . . Bob Jones of San Jose wins Sports Car Olympics at Squaw Valley in 1600 Porsche . . . American Basketball League introduces the three-point basket to San Jose as San Francisco Saints defeat Los Angeles Jets, 109-85. Ken Sears nets 13 for Saints . . . After dropping all 10 games in 1960, Stanford breaks grid loss streak with 9-7 win over Tulane . . . Los Altos High blanks Cupertino, 21-0, at Foothill College, where game starts with half new lights working, ends with 10 minutes left when rest go dark . . . Chris Sgambati beats Ron Ginn in city golf final, 4 and 3 . . . Al Kogura's 80-yard punt return, Terry Maruyama to Ray Hilliard PAT pass gives SJCC upset 14-13 win over Diablo Valley . . . Clyde Palmer of San Jose wins Speedway points title . . . Chon Gallegos tosses four TD passes, Rey Pena kicks 21-yard field goal as SJS beats Pacific, 29-26 . . . Santa Clara Valley Hornets down Fresno on Dave Rodarte's three TDs, 24-6 . . . SJS suffers year's first loss to Oregon in NCAA cross-country . . . San Mateo JC spills Allan Hancock in Prune Bowl at Spartan Stadium in rain, 6-0 . . . Delos Brown of champ Los Altos High (8-1-0) is top WSCVAL lineman, Fremont's John Travis top back . . . Joe Fillipelli's 27 leads Gilroy High in win against Watsonville, 60-34 . . . Whitney Reed (SJS) top ranked amateur on U. S. Lawn Tennis Association list . . . SJCC drops Foothill in league hoops tourney final. MVP Henry Rapp hits 26 . . . Oregon's Mike

Lehner (Palo Alto) wins national junior AAU 25K run at Stanford.

■ 1962 ■

SJS (2-22) forfeits 11 basketball games after Bill Robertson, Joe Braun ruled ineligible . . . Rich Levitt tallies Bellarmine record 43 in 80-60 win over Riordan . . . Campbell High blows out Del Mar in hoops with 24-6 fourth quarter to win league title. Bucs' Jeff Goodere has 21, Mike Smith 20 . . . Eddie Sims hits 19 as SJCC nips Foothill for league crown, 61-57. Jags lose to Citrus in state playoffs . . . PBT championship goes to Ravenswood High after memorable five-overtime, 60-58, win over St. Elizabeth . . . SJS Judo team wins ninth Northern California title, follows with first NCAA crown. Lee Parr tops 160-pound field . . . Sunnyvale High's Eric Paulson averages 18.5 points, wins All-Northern California spot second straight season . . . Jon Douglas of Stanford, Whitney Reed of SJS on American Davis Cup team . . . Sunnyvale High reserve Eddie Evens no-hits Logan in opener of Lions Easter tourney. Jets reach final, but lose to Bellarmine's Ted Litchfield, 1-0 . . . National TV audience sees bowler J. B. Solomon win San Jose Open . . . Franklin Mieuli, Bay Area radio-TV executive from San Jose, buys share of San Francisco Warriors . . . Harry Edwards sets SJS discus mark at 178-3 . . . Homers by Gary Roberts, Herk Evans, Don Geiger pace Sunnyvale High's 18-hit attack against Awalt . . . San Jose bowler Dick Agee wins Las Vegas Open . . . Lick High's Gary Ilman wins 400 freestyle, 100 butterfly as Comets take ESCVAL title . . . Foothill becomes first Northern California team to win state JC swim title. Owls' Bob Benson sets national 400 freestyle mark . . . Lincoln High's Eddie Escobar twirls 1-0 no-hitter over Willow Glen . . . George Beardsley of Palo Alto High cracks SPAL pole vault record at 13-7 3/4 . . . Hurdler Bruce McCullough only SJS winner, but Spartans end USC's 16-year reign in West Coast Relays at Fresno by one-half point . . . State tennis title goes to Whitney Reed of SJS . . . Dave Gigliotti's 10th inning three-bagger scores last run in SJCC's 11-10 pennant winner over Foothill . . . Eric Paulson belts grand slam, drives in six runs as Sunnyvale High wallops Fremont, 10-4 . . . Ron True wins first main event in home town, taking 100-lap Gold Cup Century at Speedway . . . Prep league MVPs: pitchers Lon Raymond (Campbell), Rod Bruck (Lick), infielder Pete Middlekauff (Los Altos) in tie with Eric Paulson (Sunnyvale) . . . John Lotz of SJS wins county, Northern California amateur golf titles . . . Jerry Siebert of SCVYV does 880 in 1:47.0 to edge Ben Tucker of SJS, who runs school record 1:47.8 . . . Bees get no hits off Stockton's Darrell Knowles, beat him anyway on walks, errors, 3-0 . . . Los Altos High's Steve Coy triple jumps 46-8 . . . Jane Albert wins state girl's singles tennis at San Jose Swim and Racquet Club . . . San Jose husband-wife team of Sam, Rosie Borges take Pacific Coast men's, women's water ski titles . . . Jim Wiechers tops Jim Sullivan in all-Bellarmine final in U. S. junior golf championship, 4 and 3 . . . UC Davis drops SCU, 27-6, in first grid game at Buck Shaw Stadium . . . Bob Haines of Santa Clara drives M&R Special to 189.86 mph world record at Fremont Drag Strip . . . Guard Jim Cadile (San Jose, SJS) begins 11-year career with Chicago Bears . . . Ron Calcagno goes 12 for 18 with four TD passes in 47-0 SCU romp over UOP . . . KGO-TV viewers see St. Francis High down Burlingame, 20-6 . . . Camden's Dean Bowman throws 39-yard pass to end Keith Swagerty for deciding score against Los Gatos. Cougars' 18-12 win gives them share of WSCVAL title with Wildcats . . . Ron Davis, Jeff Fishback, Danny Murphy, Ben Tucker of SJS finish in dead heat for Northern California cross-country title, then win NCAA . . . Stanford (8-2-0) makes NCAA soccer quarterfinals, falls to eventual champion St. Louis . . . Lincoln High's Dennis Mason rushes for 178 yards, two TDs as Lions regain Big Bone from San Jose, 26-14. Mason has 1,098 yards for season, ties league MVP Bob Martin of Willow Glen for scoring title with 73 points . . . Led by all-league back John Travis, Foothill smashes Santa Rosa in Prune Bowl, 41-6 . . . Fremont wins league, but Sunnyvale end Van Peterson, QB Tom Lundy are MVPs . . . Hornets stop Buena Park's 27-game Pop Warner win skein, 26-0. Randy Pelache, Jim Molinari each score twice . . . SJS wrestlers win Nor Cal crown behind Warren King, Don Anderson, Paul Hodgins . . . Mountain View's Clyde Palmer is NASCAR champ . . . Harry Edwards of SJS scores 12 in 55-51 win over St. Mary's for WCAC tourney title.

■ 1963 ■

San Jose's Ray Perez retains North American flyweight crown when ref stops bout against Ray Pacheco in eighth . . . Crowd at packed Civic Auditorium sees SCU stop SJS, 67-55. Joe Weiss has 19 for Broncos, Dennis Bates 21 for Spartans . . . San Jose's first NBA result: Warriors, 109; Chicago Zephyrs, 107 . . . Keith Swagerty of Camden High sets CCS record with 44 in 66-43 win over Los Gatos . . . Gilroy High's Bob Stuckey drops in 40 against King City . . . SJS soph Danny Murphy pushes former Spartan Charley Clark to American two-mile record before 13,721 track fans at Cow Palace. Hill High's Bill Fosdick sets national prep pole vault mark of 13-7 1/2 . . . Jack Gleason has school record 31 for Foothill against Chabot . . . World featherweight champ Davey Moore KOs Gil Cadilli in five at Civic Auditorium in non-title fight . . . Rod Welch of Cupertino High is top wrestler in Nor Cal Invitational . . . SCU beats USF, 66-65, when Dons' Duey Thomas misses two free throws after time expires. In next meeting, Dons win WCAC title on Dave Lee's free throw with two seconds left, 62-61 . . . Larry Keller sets Ayer High record with 32 in 75-36 win over Overfelt . . . SCU's Charlie Marcenaro beats Fresno State on no-hitter, 4-0 . . . Gilroy High, with Bob Stuckey averaging 20.9 points, wins 25 straight, falls to St. Elizabeth of Oakland in PBT final . . . UCLA defeats Stanford in Big Six title playoff, 51-45. Indians' Tom Dose scores 19. Tribe (16-9) makes first basketball poll appearance as UPI's No. 10 . . . Bellarmine's Ray Henningsen gets single, triple, two homers, eight RBIs in 12-5 win over Los Gatos . . . L. A. Angels down Houston, 5-1, in first major league exhibition at Muni Stadium . . . Don Gale of Mountain View takes county tennis singles, Horst Ritter, Rodney Kop win doubles . . . SJS wins Western college golf title. Spartans' John Lotz is medalist . . . Pan-American Games gold medals won by Ben Campbell of San Jose (judo), Jeff Fishback of SJS (3,000-meter steeplechase) . . . Leigh High's Jim Beauchamp no-hits Los Gatos . . . Larry Questad gets top Stanford marks in 100-yard dash (9.3), 220 (20.6) . . . Whitney Reed, Jane Albert take state tennis singles . . . John Lotz of SJS wins third straight state amateur golf tourney . . . Roger Ruth's three-hitter gives Bellarmine playoff victory over St. Elizabeth for Catholic title, 8-1 . . . Muni Stadium record 7,145 spectators see Salinas defeat San Jose Bees, 4-0 . . . Santa Clara County opens $18,500 Hellyer Park Velodrome, one-fifth mile asphalt track with 23 degree banked turns at Coyote Creek near Sylvandale Avenue . . . Overfelt High loses all six practice games, wins MHAL with

10-1 mark as Jack Wool pitches no-hitter over Pioneer for title. Royals' pitcher Dan Romero is league MVP . . . Mrs. Jay Hopkins of Los Altos retains her county women's golf title . . . Prep state champs: Bill Fosdick of Hill in pole vault at 14-8 3/4, Bruce Wilhelm of Fremont in shot put at 63-4 3/4 . . . Dick Lotz shoots San Jose Country Club record 59 in county golf tourney's first round, beats brother, John, in sudden death . . . Jim Wiechers of SCU wins county junior golf with record 207 . . . San Jose's Bob Brandon tops north state junior cyclists . . . Judy Wejek of Willow Glen High performs with San Francisco Merionettes, U. S. outdoor synchronized swim team champs . . . San Jose (14-3) falls to Charlotte, NC, in Colt World Series final, 5-3 . . . San Jose's Ron Stroke wins Sports Car Olympics . . . Joe Leonard quits motorcycles for hardtop autos, takes first big race at Clovis . . . Bowler George Howard takes San Jose Open by three pins . . . Marty Brill, Tim Barnes each pound out 100-plus yards in Palo Alto High's 33-7 romp over Blackford . . . Soph Bob Miranda chalks up 178 yards, four TDs in 28 carries as SCU stops Chico State, 48-28 . . . Craig Morton completes 10 passes for Cal record five touchdowns in 34-13 thrashing of SJS . . . Les Fleming in 1 up win over Fritz Andrade for city golf crown . . . Bellarmine whips Riordan, 16-7. Rich Ravizza returns opening kickoff 87 yards for score . . . Al Geiberger takes second straight Almaden Open golf . . . Larry Agrella throws two TD passes as Pop Warner champ Santa Clara Hornets top Syracuse, 19-13 . . . QB Ron Calcagno finishes SCU career owning school passing record 4,309 yards. His three-year total, 3,325, also tops John Pasco's mark, set in 1949-51 . . . MVP Dennis Mason of Lincoln High tops MHAL with 1,534 yards, 17 TDs . . . Saratoga High's Mike Hitchman throws two scoring strikes to Jim Priest, runs for third as Falcons down Camden, 27-13, in WVAL title contest . . . Rick Barry buries 34 for Miami, but SCU wins at Civic Auditorium, 86-77, behind Bruce Asch's 28 . . . Foothill's John Travis (Fremont), makes JC All-America as defensive back . . . UCLA end Mel Profit (Camden) all-PCC . . . Bellarmine's Terry Shea, future SCU Little All-American Ray Calcagno of St. Ignatius High tie for state prep lead with 18 TD passes . . . Bellarmine's Chris Dempsey pours in 40 in 69-44 win against Woodside . . . Tim Barnes has 1,039 rushing yards, 106 points for SPAL champ Palo Alto High (9-0-0) . . . Harry Edwards leads SJS to third straight WCAC tournament title, downing SCU, 58-55.

■ 1964 ■

Camden Wall (Los Gatos) hits 23 including layup for Cal's deciding basket in 65-64 win over USC . . . Camden High falls to Del Mar, 59-53, despite 30 from Joe Ferguson . . . SJCC in record 127-88 win over Oakland City College. Jags' Donnie Hicks hits 40 . . . Al Holguin of San Jose takes Golden Gloves title . . . Wilcox High wrestlers capture Nor Cal crown. Bob Hicks, Mickey Abbott take titles . . . Bud Ogden scores 24 as Lincoln High trips Lick, 50-31, in MHAL playoff for PBT spot . . . Mission Trails champ Gilroy wins 54th straight league game, 87-40, over Pacific Grove. Steve Voorhies tops Mustang scoring with 29 . . . Undefeated Stanford pins first rugby loss on Cal, 15-11, as Gordon Waddell converts five penalty kicks beyond 30 yards . . . Tom Dose cracks Ron Tomsic's career scoring record with 42 against Washington State for 1,428 . . . Russ Vrankovich hits 44 including 16 straight free throws as SCU tops Pepperdine, 98-78 . . . SJS (14-10) leads NCAA in basketball defense, surrendering only 54.5 points per game . . . Otto Sarlo of San Jose wins giant slalom race at Dodge Ridge . . . Yale swimmer Steve Clark (Los Altos) breaks three marks at NCAA finals . . . Ross Randall of SJS wins Far Western college, county junior golf crowns . . . SJS soph John Garrison runs 880 in 1:49.6 . . . John Figueroa of Sunnyvale High clocks 9.5 in 100, 20.5 in 220 . . . Prep no-hitters by Jim Beauchamp (Leigh) over Los Gatos, Scott Sonne (Cubberley) versus Ravenswood with 15 Ks, Roger Harrington (Fremont) over Buchser, whiffs 15, Guy Martin (Del Mar) against Los Gatos . . . Jim Visher of SJS throws seven-inning no-hitter at St. Mary's . . . Forward Al Korbus becomes first SJS soccer All-American . . . Santa Clara High's Don Schollander sets NCS 400 freestyle mark . . . Stanford women win AAWU tennis with Jane Albert singles champ. Marianne Pietschmann, Carole Lepter snare doubles . . . Dual for MHAL titles decided when Lincoln High catcher Jim Fisher hits homer off Bob Walters' first pitch, gets another hit in Lions' 5-4 win over Willow Glen for league crown. Fisher edges Walters .486 to .483 in batting race. Fischer, teammate pitcher Eddie Escobar are league co-MVPs . . . Murray Hall Ks 12 in champ Campbell High's 6-0 win over Camden in WVAL final . . . League MVP hurler Jeff Finley (7-2) figures in all Fremont High's decisions as Indians win SCVAL . . . Led by outfielders Pat Cavataio, Jim Gama, pitcher Wayne Harper, SJCC wins conference, bows to Fresno in state JC playoffs . . . SCU finishes 16-4 in CIBA, game behind USC. Pete Magrini has six league wins, is 11-1 overall . . . State high jump record goes to Max Lowe of Awalt High at 6-10 1/2 . . . Wilcox High's Mike Ryan lowers own state two-mile record to 8:57.8, sets six-mile, 10,000-meter marks . . . Los Gatos High's Bob Brannan puts shot 62-7 1/4, Mike Ryan of Wilcox runs 4:11.2 mile for state meet crowns . . . Ron Cerrudo nips Ernie Pieper by stroke for county golf crown . . . Bothered by oppressive heat, PGA player of the year Ken Venturi rallies for U. S. Open golf title . . . Russ Camilleri is national AAU meet's top wrestler . . . Sally Griffith (SJS) sets U. S. women's record for 200-meter hurdles . . . Bud Ogden drives in three runs with three hits as Memory Post 399 wins American Legion district title over Santa Clara, 6-5. Concord dumps Memory in regionals . . . Roberta Armstrong of Santa Clara wins national outdoor synchronized swim solo title . . . Ken Baker of Los Altos sets record 101.05 miles an hour in hydroplane with outboard motor . . . Fans admitted free as San Francisco Warriors open first annual training camp at San Jose City College . . . SCU's Jim Wiechers wins two golf tourneys in two days: Western Junior title at Air Force Academy, Palo Alto city title at Stanford . . . West Valley College tops Vallejo in first football game, 18-12 . . . Ray Calcagno breaks brother Ron's records, passing for 263 yards, four TDs in SCU's 45-6 win over Chico State . . . Phil Burton's 24-yard field goal for Bellarmine nips St. Francis, 3-0, before Buck Shaw Stadium full house. Burton registers four TDs, seven PATs, field goal for school record 34 points in 64-0 win over St. Mary's . . . Lincoln High's Mike Goodman intercepts Jim Plunkett pass, goes 65 yards for deciding TD with five seconds left as Lions top Lick, 20-14 . . . Billy Caspar drops six-foot putt on third extra hole to win $3,300 at Almaden Open . . . Gilroy's George Archer retains Northern California Open golf title . . . Jim Plunkett throws five TDs as Lick High dumps San Jose, 45-12 . . . John Shores' seven goals give Awalt High Nor Cal water polo title over Los Altos, 16-8 . . . Santa Clara Hornets defeat Pittsburg in Pop Warner Bowl, 21-7 . . . Wilt Chamberlain's 31 points pace San Francisco Warriors to 120-114 victory over Baltimore at Civic Auditorium . . . Future West

The San Francisco Warriors downed Baltimore, 120-114, in 1964 at San Jose Civic Auditorium. Nate Thurmond (42) attempted to block Gus Johnson's shot while the Warriors' McCoy McLemore (71) and Wilt Chamberlain and Bullet Bailey Howell (15) watched the action.

Valley College coach Bob Burton (Campbell) hits 21, Dave Galos (Santa Clara) adds 25 more as WVC debuts with 92-81 victory over Gavilan . . . Joe Leonard is USAC's top stock car rookie . . . Foothill repeats as state JC water polo champs. Mike Garibaldi collects record 80 goals.

■ 1965 ■

Craig Morton hooks up with Cal, Campbell High teammate Jack Schraub on TD pass giving West 11-7 win over East in Shrine game . . . MVP Eric Paulson hits 20 as SCU downs USF in WCAC tourney final at Civic Auditorium, 73-71 . . . S. T. Saffold's 28 leads SJS over Loyola, 72-63 . . . San Jose boxer Willie Richardson suspended for going berserk before Oakland fight, kicking, slugging state heavyweight champ Roger Risher . . . SJCC whips Chabot, 90-74. Jags' Jack Matulich hits 29, Clyde Dawson adds 23 plus 24 boards . . . SJCC leads Foothill, 66-60, when bomb scare ends year's final game with 8:28 to go. Paz Rocha has 18 for Jags, Dick Treglown 27 for Owls, leaving him nine short of school record 516 . . . WVC's Bob Burton paces league with 25.4 average, high of 41 against Monterey . . . SCU racks up school scoring record in 104-94 win over Pepperdine. Mike Gervasoni has 35 . . . National Skating Derby moves into Roller Derby's territory at Civic Auditorium as Bay Shamrocks tangle with Texas Outlaws . . . Les Bond breaks SJS triple jump record with 52-0 3/4 leap . . . Dick Ragsdale has eight points as Stanford ruggers defend Monterey tourney title with 14-0 win over Peninsula Ramblers . . . Willow Glen High's John Souza sets down Irvington with no-hit, 14K shutout . . . Wilcox High's Mike Ryan adds state three-mile, 5,000-meter records to collection . . . Fremont High's Terry Parks fans 16 in blanking Saratoga . . . Max Lowe of Foothill College high jumps 7-0 . . . Hill High's Steve Wright throws 4-0 no-hitter against Mountain View to win Lions Club Easter tourney . . . Foothill's Ed Ortegon (two-mile), Max Lowe (high jump) take state JC titles . . . Russ Camilleri tops AAU freestyle wrestlers . . . Stanford 440 relay team races to 39.9 world record at Fresno. SJS captures 880 relay with Tommie Smith clocked in 19.9 anchor leg . . . Giants' Willie Mays hits two homers, cuts down runner at plate with rifle throw in 9-3 win over SCU . . . Tim Harper's two homers power SJCC to 5-2 win over Santa Rosa, berth in state JC tourney, where Jaguars (31-6) bow to Fresno . . . Palo Alto High wins NCS swim title as Santa Clara's Mitch Ivey sets 100 backstroke record . . . Joe Leonard qualifies for Indianapolis 500 . . . MVP Ron McGregor of Ayer High scatters four hits to stop Pioneer for MHAL title, trip to Redwood Invitational, where Trojans lose to St. Elizabeth . . . Former county preps capture NCAA titles: Bill Fosdick of USC (pole vault), Bob Stoecker of Stanford (discus) . . . Lick High's Forrest Fezler wins State Junior Chamber of Commerce golf title . . . Barry Weitzenberg's last second goal for Foothill Aquatic Club dunks Inland Nu-Pike for AAU water polo championship . . . Ron Cerrudo wins Northern California Golf Association amateur crown . . . Lew Fraser of SJS named soccer All-American . . . Los Altos High stays on ground, whips Fremont, 26-19, with K. C. Jackson rushing for 132 yards, Terry Pennell 130, Larry Warren 111 . . . Neither rain nor SJCC can stop CCSF's O. J. Simpson, who scores six TDs on runs between 14 and 89 yards in 48-6 victory . . . One-eyed SCU student Roger Uyeda, wins California Archery Association title . . . Sonny Brasile to Ed Kensill pass ices Santa Clara Hornets' 12-6 win over Santa Clara Lions for Pop Warner title . . . Rich Woolworth's two TDs gives Westmont 14-0 win over Leigh, perfect 9-0-0 season . . . Palo Alto blanks Sequoia, 20-0, for SPAL title share as Tom Hamilton runs for 118 yards . . . Foothill College falls to Monterey, 30-20, in Salinas Lettuce Bowl . . .

O. J. Simpson scores three times as CCSF defeats Long Beach City College in Prune Bowl, 40-20 . . . Stanford's Dave Lewis leads nation's punters with 44.9 average . . . Central Coast co-MVPs: Lick High's Jim Plunkett, (1,200 passing yards, 17 TD tosses), Bellarmine's Phil Burton (118 points).

■ 1966 ■

Paz Rocha hits 28 as SJCC dumps Chabot, 97-89 . . . SJS water polo goalie Bruce Hobbs is All-American . . . Leigh High's Wayne Watkins pours in 38, but Del Mar triumphs, 80-67, behind Bill Drozdiak's 28 . . . Stanford ends UCLA's 36-game league win string, 74-69, as Art Harris pumps in 24 . . . In battle of mighty mites, Gary Anderson of Buchser High scores 21 in 77-73 win over Wilcox, led by Bobby Medrano's 27 . . . Ken Venturi on comeback trail with win in Lucky International Open golf . . . With S. T. Saffold hitting 27, Pete Newell Jr., 25, SJS blasts Pepperdine in record 101-79 win . . . San Jose's Wayne Melton, Stephanie Gruber win national roller skating pairs title . . . Del Mar High's stall fails to block Blackford's bid for 40th straight league hoops victory. Braves win, 25-13 . . . Central Coast prep scoring mark falls often: Blackford's Dennis Awtrey hits 46 against Saratoga, Lincoln's Ralph Ogden raises it to 47 against Piedmont Hills, Live Oak's Paul Scheidegger pumps in 51 versus Gonzales. Awtrey averages 28.1 for season, ties mark with 51 against South San Francisco in PBT . . . Fremont High wrestlers win first CCS crown. Lick's Jim Plunkett takes 194-pound title . . . Julie Heldman of Stanford wins Northern California college tennis . . . S. T. Saffold of SJS tallies 30 points in 78-67 win over St. Mary's to become second all-time scorer . . . Bill Fosdick (Hill) of USC wins NCAA indoor pole vault at 16-0 1/4 . . . 191-pound Stan Hackett of Foothill takes state JC wrestling crown . . . Awalt High pitchers Al Withol, Dave Gibson throw consecutive no-hitters at Buchser, Sunnyvale . . . Tommie Smith wins 100, 220, long jump, anchors relay in SJS victory over Cal . . . Homeless Piedmont Hills High baseball players attend class at Ayer while their school is built, take Lions tournament. Harley House drives in winning run to beat Del Mar, 3-2 . . . Nine-time AAU champ Russ Camilleri takes Greco-Roman wrestling title . . . Featherweight Alex Benitez of San Jose cops state title from Danny Valdez in Civic Auditorium 12-rounder . . . Russ Hodge of Foothill College wins record seven events -- 100, high hurdles, intermediate hurdles, long jump, shot put, discus, relay leg -- against San Mateo . . . Lincoln High's Ken Escobar throws 2-0 perfect game against Hill . . . Lick High takes 10 of 11 events over Pioneer for 59th win in last 60 dual swim meets . . . Dave Gibson (Awalt), Roger Hibler (St. Francis) each pitch second no-hitter of season . . . Paul Haber of San Jose is national handball champ . . . Foothill wins state JC swim title . . . Burlingame High defeats Fremont, 17-16, for first CCS track and field title . . . Lee Evans of SJCC wins state JC 440 in 46.9, Foothill's Russ Hodge takes shot put . . . Piedmont Hills High nine's 15-game win streak ends in 9-5 loss to San Jose . . . John Reardon (high hurdles, long jump), Jim Dediego (sprints) double winners as Bellarmine captures fourth straight CAL track title . . . Jim Wiechers of SCU wins three-hole playoff from Ross Randall of SJS for Northern California Golf Association title . . . Paz Rocha of SJCC is league bat champ with .420 average . . . Alan Cockerill fans 13 in five innings as Lincoln High downs Willow Glen, 8-4, in playoff to advance to Redwood Invitational, where Lions beat Skyline, fall to Marin Catholic . . . Santa Clara "A" Team wins AAU women's water polo title . . . Ron Cerrudo is county golf champ . . . Unbeaten Lee Evans runs 45.7 in 440 at Berkeley . . . Seventeen drivers, pit men injured at Speedway when hardtop race car spins out of control after collision . . . Mike Garibaldi's late goal gives Foothill Aquatic Club 8-7 double OT win over Inland Nu-Pike for AAU water polo crown . . . Bob Tetzlaff of Campbell rides through rainstorm to win 125-mile U. S. road race title . . . Third ranked featherweight Raul Rojas decisions San Jose's Pete Gonzales at Civic Auditorium . . . Sunnyvale High runners cover 5,000 miles in world record 24 days, 22 hours. Frank Mateos leads team with 350 miles . . . Saratoga's Brad Lozares takes Palo Alto golf title . . . SCU's Bob Spence, Rocky Daly, Rod Austin hit homers as Boulder (Colo.) Collegians beat West Point, Miss., 5-3, in National Baseball Congress finale . . . Stanford defeats Tulane, 33-14, on Bill Shoemaker's record four field goals . . . Danny Holman's 20 for 37 passing with two TDs, gives SJS first ever win over Cal, 24-0 . . . Rick Barry hits 43 as San Francisco Warriors beat Chicago Bulls at Civic Auditorium, 121-111 . . . Terry Adams rushes for six TDs as Cupertino High rips Santa Clara, 39-19 . . . Los Altos stops Homestead in battle of unbeatens, 28-14, for SCVAL crown when injured QB Brad Lyman comes off bench to lead Knights . . . O. J. Simpson's five TD runs give CCSF 46-34 win over SJCC . . . Bill Gobin's PAT for Gunn High upsets Palo Alto, 13-12 . . . Jim Ferguson is MVP as Awalt High wins regional water polo title . . . Kip Jackson, Los Altos High running back, scores record 140 points for state's No. 2 Knights (9-0-0) . . . La Mirada beats previously unscored upon Santa Clara Stingers for state midget football title, 19-0 . . . Long Beach terminates Foothill's 66-match win string in state JC water polo playoffs . . . Laney College holds O. J. Simpson to 26 yards in 11 carries, beats CCSF in Prune Bowl, 35-13 . . . SJS in record 114-85 win over Idaho State. Steve Schlink has 24 . . . Buchser High guard Gary Anderson hits 26 of 41 field goal tries on way to CCS record 55 points in 85-50 win over Blackford . . . Mike Gervasoni cans 42 as SCU helps dedicate Oakland Coliseum Arena with 99-91 double OT win over Missouri.

■ 1967 ■

Bill Drozdiak bangs in 38 for Del Mar High in 96-51 victory over Mountain View . . . Wilcox High misses 10 chances to crack 100 in 99-67 victory over Logan. Bobby Medrano scores 30 . . . Bowler Jim St. John takes $5,000 top prize in Western Open at Saratoga Lanes . . . Foothill defeats SJCC, 77-75, despite 32 by Jags' Steve Blaser . . . Paul Scheidegger of Live Oak High sets county career hoops record with 1,677 points . . . SJS downs St. Mary's, 92-74, as Jim Meyer pops in 24, Steve Schlink, Gary Cunningham 22 apiece . . . Awalt High's Jim Ferguson named nation's best water polo player . . . Jim White hits 32 in WVC's 114-86 win over Gavilan . . . Bill Vukovich takes 100-lap midget main event at Speedway . . . Fremont High wrestlers win north state title. Mountain View's Bernie Olmos takes third straight crown . . . Mitty High's 41-game hoops schedule helps Steve Gera become state's first prep to surpass 1,000 points (1,066) in year . . . Chris Papanicolaou sets SJS pole vault record at 16-5 . . . Greg Buckingham leads way with three gold medals as Stanford wins first NCAA swim crown . . . Art Strane, Rod Austin hit homers off San Francisco pitcher Juan Marichal, but Giants beat SCU, 7-3 . . . John McMullin of San Jose retains PGA Northern California medal play crown . . . Yuji Moriya grand champion as SJS takes sixth straight NCAA judo title . . . Piedmont Hills High gets two no-hit wins in a week from Duane

Joe Leonard is one of only two men inducted into the Motorsports Hall of Fame in two sports. He was a champion motorcycle rider for years before switching to auto racing. Leonard finished third in the 1967 Indianapolis 500 race.

Larson (against Overfelt), Harley House (Lick) . . . Foothill beats CCSF, 4-3, on Ken Wagner's 10th inning, two-run homer to clinch league title . . . Gretchen Siegfried is Pacific Women's Golf Association champ . . . Homers by Mark Marquess, Ron Shotts give Stanford 5-1 win over Cal, trip to NCAA regionals . . . Jan Dukes of SCU no-hits Pepperdine, 4-0 . . . Willow Glen High nine tops Camden, 8-5, for first CCS title . . . Mrs. Charles Brooke retains county women's golf title . . . Ernie Pieper birdies three of last four holes to take county golf title by stroke over Ross Randall of SJS, who captures Northern California amateur title . . . Foothill swim team takes sixth straight state JC crown, sets 13 national records . . . Tommie Smith of SJS wins first NCAA title with 20.2 in 220 . . . San Jose High's Dominic Cusimano, Fremont's Brent Noon champs in national prep wrestling meet at Overfelt . . . San Jose's Mike Yarn wins first race on Fairground's new indoor motorcycle track . . . Forrest Fezler repeats as county junior golf champ with record low 201 strokes . . . USA wins Pan-American Games water polo. Gary Sheerer of Los Altos leads scorers with 12 goals . . . Bellarmine QB Dan Pastorini is MVP in North-South grid contest, won by North, 24-22 . . . Campbell-Moreland Pony All-Stars reach World Series, lose to Hawaii . . . Denise Carter, Tina Lyman of Los Altos win state junior tennis doubles . . . Don Titcomb takes state horseshoe pitching title. Kevin Turner of Los Gatos is junior winner . . . Don Gale captures California men's over-35 tennis singles . . . George Roeder wins U. S. seven-mile motorcycle title . . . De Anza stuns Foothill in grid debut, 13-0. Dons' first score is by Terry Adams (Cupertino) . . . Ex-SCU ace Nelson Briles pitches St. Louis to 4-1 World Series win over Boston . . . In Civic Auditorium hoops action, Nate Thurmond nabs 24 rebounds as Warriors top St. Louis Hawks in exhibition, 108-102; Oakland Oaks of American Basketball Association get 28 from Laverne Tart in win over Denver, 112-102 . . . Bill Scott becomes first San Josean since Marshall Sargent in 1960 to win Speedway points crown . . . WVC crushes Menlo, 48-7, on Tom Rundell's five TD tosses . . . Dave Jones returns two interceptions for TDs as Lincoln ends Willow Glen's unbeaten streak at 22 with 26-6 win . . . Campbell High's Chuck Hawthorne scores record seven TDs in 66-6 win over Branham, chalks up 25 for season to lead state scorers with 156 points . . . Ron Gregory's PAT after Dave Stewart to Steve Orbansky TD pass gives Pioneer High (9-0-0) 7-6 win over Willow Glen, STAL championship . . . SJS tips Long Beach State, 7-6, for state college water polo crown . . . SJS All-America forward Henry Camacho hits three goals in 4-3 soccer playoff loss to eventual NCAA co-champ St. Louis . . . Japanese Olympic boxers down American team at Civic Auditorium, 7-3 . . . Despite Mike Harrison's TD returns on kickoff (92 yards), punt (68 yards), Palo Alto High loses traditional to Sequoia, 48-27, before 26,000 at Stanford . . . Jerry Strangis scores on 60-, 15-yard runs in Santa Clara Hornets' 53-20 win over Salt Lake City Leopards in Toys for Tots Bowl . . . San Jose Cindergals win national AAU under-13 cross-country . . . Orb Greenwald ends Foothill career with record 129 goals as Owls take state JC water polo . . . SJCC tops Fresno, 87-78 behind Everett Breaux's 38 points.

■ 1968 ■

Piedmont Hill High defeats Mount Pleasant, 65-43, but Terry Dorsey of Cardinals leads scorers with 39 . . . STAL standings revised when San Jose, Willow Glen forfeit wins because of ineligible players . . . SCU gains eighth straight win, taking St. Mary's, 107-78, behind Bud Ogden's 26, Dennis Awtrey's 25 . . . Mike Yarn of San Jose wins winter indoor motorcycle title at Fairgrounds over Bruce Anderson, who doubles as WVC hoops star . . . USA's Billy Gaines of San Jose High runs world record 5.4 in 50-meter race at Moscow . . . Coby Dietrick hits 24 as SJS upsets Loyola, 86-80 . . . John Carlos, sitting out first year at SJS after transfer from East Texas, runs 9.3 in 100, 20.6 in 220 for SCVYV on Spartan Field's new Tartan track . . . De Anza jumps from fourth to first in league basketball when WVC, Gavilan, Laney forfeit wins for ineligible players. No Cinderella finish as Dons (20-8) lose state JC tourney opener to Pasadena, 78-55 . . . Future sportscaster Gary Radunich of Branham High scores 47 against Camden to lead county with 26.4 average, grab CCS MVP award . . . Gary Houston pitches 12 strikeout no-hitter for SJCC over Contra Costa . . . Former Stanford oarsmen Larry

Hough, Tony Johnson capture Pan-American Games pairs without coxswain . . . San Mateo's 22-year home course golf win streak ends with loss to SJCC . . . Down 14-0 after three innings, WVC wins, 16-15, on pair of RBIs by Gary Handley, who goes 7 for 7 . . . Santa Clara Valley Youth Village ends 16-year run as track and field powerhouse, dropping sport to concentrate on gymnastics . . . SJS adds seventh NCAA judo trophy to collection. Luis Gonzales, John Kimura, Gary Martin take titles . . . Canadian Ralph Hutton leads Foothill to seventh straight JC swim title, wins Olympic silver medal in 400 freestyle . . . San Jose High's Billy Gaines equals state mark, clocking 9.4 in 100 . . . Leigh High's 10 errors give Homestead 8-0 victory in Lions baseball tourney final . . . Defending champion Ernie Pieper shoots 210 for 54 holes, wins 14th county golf title . . . Mountain View's John Millage captures Formula II sports car race at Vacaville . . . Lori Pippin rolls 300 at Cambrian Bowl, first woman to bowl perfect game in county sanctioned league . . . Joe Leonard drives turbine Lotus record 171.559 mph to gain pole position at Indianapolis 500. Leads until car problems knock him out of race with nine laps to go . . . Sam Caruthers of SJCC pole vaults 16-0 for state JC crown . . . Homestead High nine takes CCS title over Santa Cruz . . . San Jose Municipal Golf Course opens with fees of $2.50 daily, $4 on weekends, holidays . . . Ronnie Ray Smith of SJS, Jim Hines, Charlie Green all run 100-meter world record 9.9 in heats at national AAU meet. Lee Evans wins 400-meter title with 45.0 . . . Forrest Fezler takes third straight county junior golf crown . . . Sam Lima wins Northern California senior table tennis title . . . SJCC's Ed Morris is Pacific Coast amateur golf champ . . . Maren Seidler of Palo Alto establishes American girl's record with 51-5 1/4 shot put . . . Palo Alto's Jim Rice wins U. S. seven-mile motorcycle title at Fairgrounds . . . Lee Evans runs 440 in 44.0 at Lake Tahoe Olympic training camp . . . Jim Plunkett debuts for Stanford in 68-20 win over SJS, completing 10 of 13 for 277 yards, four TDs . . . Dave Ellis completes 15 of 21 for three TDs in SJCC victory over CCSF, 39-25 . . . Mani Hernandez scores school record six soccer goals as SJS shellacs Stanford, 11-0. Spartans top USF, 2-1, for league title, lose to Maryland in NCAA playoffs in OT, 4-3 . . . De Anza beats WVC, 27-21, to tie for conference title. Dons fall in state playoffs to Citrus, 35-20 . . . Los Altos High clobbers Cupertino, 33-7, for SCVAL title as Jim Shepner races for 137 yards, three TDs . . . Bill Norbey runs 124 yards for SPAL season record 1,068 as Gunn High beats Cubberley, 13-6. He tops county scorers with 115 points . . . Campbell High dumps Los Gatos for WVAL crown, 53-14, on Gary Tomasso's five TD passes . . . STAL title goes to Lincoln High, 41-18 over San Jose in Big Bone clash. QBs Craig Cirello (Lincoln), Aaron Foster (San Jose) each toss three TD passes . . . SJCC linebacker Randy Ingraham is JC All-American . . . Everett Breaux hits 27 as SJCC defeats WVC, 86-85. Gary Anderson leads Vikes with 25 . . . Wide receiver Gene Washington (Stanford) tops East-West offensive players, is San Francisco 49ers' No. 1 draft pick.

■ 1969 ■

Tied at 48 after four quarters, Sunnyvale High beats Cupertino, 68-66, in record five OTs . . . Pioneer High hoops mark falls when Barry Keegan scores 51 against Leland . . . Stanford loses opener at $3.3 million Maples Pavilion -- named for principal donor Roscoe Maples (Class of '04) -- to Brigham Young, 95-89. Next night Indians get first win at Maples over BYU, 94-78, as Don Griffin nets 33 . . . Andy Jurian (Bellarmine) pumps in 37 for Menlo College in 75-62 loss to Cabrillo . . . Conference champ Gavilan tips Ohlone, 88-61, as A. J. Richardson hits 33 . . . San Jose native Peggy Fleming, 19, is Associated Press female athlete of the year . . . George Archer cleans up on golf tour, winning $25,000 in Bing Crosby Pro-Am, green jacket, more cash at Masters . . . Stanford swimmers snap 12-year, 108-meet USC win streak with Olympian John Farris taking 200 medley, 200 butterfly . . . San Jose's George Benson takes USAC 100-lap U. S. midget title at Speedway . . . Chabot nips SJCC, 94-92, despite 46 by Jags' Larry Carter (Ayer), who leads league's scorers, makes JC All-American . . . Len Borchers of Stanford wins Pac-8 outstanding wrestler award . . . Oakland Oaks defeat Minneapolis Pipers, 138-132, in American Basketball Association game at Civic Auditorium . . . Mount Pleasant High slips past Piedmont Hills for league title, 57-56, as refs disallow tip-in at buzzer by CCS player of the year John Coughran. Pirates' star has 29 to finish with 24.9 average . . . Stanford's Steve Dunning tosses 10-1 no-hitter over Cal Poly-Pomona . . . Mani Hernandez of SJS repeats as soccer All-American . . . Gary Houston fans 15 as SJCC clips Merritt, 6-4 . . . Mike Sigman throws 87 pitches as SCU defeats Oregon State for 14th straight win, 4-0. Oregon University ends streak in next game . . . Gunn High's Tom Birtwhistle ties state discus record at 195-4 . . . Roberto Amaya registers ninth round TKO over Hernando Villegas to remain unbeaten . . . SJS picks up eighth straight NCAA judo crown. Keith Pickard is grand champion . . . Foothill wins conference, Nor Cal, state JC swimming championships . . . Horacio Lopez scores twice as Mexico's Club America defeats California Clippers, 2-1, at Spartan Stadium in pro soccer's debut in county . . . Walt Kaczmarek of Santa Clara High Ks 16 in no-hit, 1-0, win over Mountain View . . . De Anza nine tops Yuba, 6-2, behind Tom Chagnon for league titlc . . . Felix Ponte wins singles, teams with Steve Stefanski in doubles as Foothill takes Northern California JC tennis . . . Bill Hiegel, Doug Plut get two hits each in St. Francis's High's win over Serra in WCAL playoff finale . . . Shortstop Tom Corder of SJS is league MVP . . . SJCC's Forrest Fezler wins county, state JC, state amateur golf titles . . . John Baggerly's two-run triple helps Los Gatos whip Branham for WVAL crown, 5-1 . . . Todd Breitlinger's 3-0 no-hit win against Sunnyvale High gives Los Altos league title . . . Phil Barry of St. Francis High takes county junior golf . . . SCU bowlers tops in Northern California college tourney. Broncos' Steve Thatcher averages 205 for 39 games . . . Eliza Pande of Palo Alto takes state junior girl's tennis singles in two age groups . . . John Ginere of Palo Alto wins pro Central California Bowlers tournament in Mountain View . . . De Anza Aquatic Foundation beats El Segundo, 15-6, for national AAU water polo title. Steve Barnett of Cupertino is named top player . . . Gail Hansen of Palo Alto falls to Sharon Walsh in U. S. Girl's Grass Court Tennis finals at Philadelphia . . . Briarwood-Santa Clara loses to China, 5-0, for Little League World Series title . . . Santa Clara Laurels defeat Valley Rockets, 3-2, on Diane Kalliam's 12th inning home run, advance to national women's softball tourney . . . SCU defeats St. Mary's, 43-7, before Kezar Stadium crowd of 11,300 in first Little Big Game since 1950 . . . Kent Raley scores four TDs in Saratoga High's 30-28 win over Willow Glen . . . San Jose's Bill Scott wins 12 super modified events, Speedway points crown . . . Leigh High's Mike Franz, Bob Hampton combine for 238 rushing yards, two TDs each in 35-6 romp against Pioneer . . . Overfelt High wallops Ayer, 36-14. Larry Lloyd carries ball 26 times for 145 yards, three TDs

San Jose State's Mani Hernandez won the 1968 Hermann Award as America's top collegiate soccer player.

. . . Mountain View's Don Gale tops Butch Krikorian for fifth straight Pacific Coast senior tennis title . . . NCAA slaps SJS track program with year probation after John Carlos, Sam Caruthers compete in unsanctioned meet . . . De Anza (8-1-0) beats WVC (state's No. 1), 54-41, on Jay Cruze to Paul Reynoso 13-yard pass, for title. Dons forfeit all wins because of ineligible player. WVC loses to Chabot in state JC playoffs . . . SJS downs USF, 3-1, for third straight conference soccer crown, but Dons turn tables with 3-1 NCAA victory . . . Ray Taroli scores one, throws for two TDs as Willow Glen High captures STAL with 33-0 win over Live Oak . . . Jim Plunkett completes 22 for 38 with 278 yards, two TDs, giving him school record 17 TDs as Stanford beats Air Force 47-34 . . . Francie Larrrieu's 11:26 two-mile leads Cindergals to women's state cross-country title . . . Overfelt High takes MHAL title with 32-29 win over Lick despite four TDs by Comets' Harold Fulton . . . Darrell Marcotte falls on blocked punt in end zone, Akira Tana sneaks for TD to give Gunn High (9-1-0) 14-6 win over Cubberley for first football crown . . . Fremont High whips Wilcox, 44-16, for league title. Chris Racanelli has four TDs . . . Cary Mitchell breaks De Anza hoops record with 35 against Menlo . . . De Anza defensive lineman Bob Busick makes JC All-American . . . Steve Bartkowski hits 24 of 34 on way to 52 points in Buchser High's 93-62 win over Sequoia . . . John Ralston coaches West to 15-0 win in first Shrine football game played at Stanford.

The 1970s

It took Santa Clara County nearly three-quarters of a century to gain membership in a national professional sports league and many people weren't impressed when it happened. After all, it wasn't a game traditionally thought of as American. It was soccer!

The sport that today is one of the area's best drawing cards looked like a real stepchild in 1974 when the San Jose Earthquakes joined the North American Soccer League. Some residents worried that the team's nickname sent a bad message and league officials preferred a team in prestigious San Francisco, not some sprawling suburb 50 miles away.

Owner Milan Mandaric had luck on his side and he won the right to make the first pick in the draft of players from two defunct teams. He chose Paul Child, a 20-year-old Englishman who had been an all-star for two seasons at Atlanta. Art Welch was the Earthquakes' second selection.

College players Mani Hernandez of San Jose State, Archie Roboostoff of USF and the Demling brothers, Buzz and Mark from St. Louis, were added along with veteran foreign players, including goalkeeper Mirko Stojanovic, Dieter Zajdel, Johnny Moore and bearded Laurie Calloway.

Ivan Toplak was hired as the 'Quakes coach, although he would miss the early part of the NASL season while serving on the staff of the Yugoslavian national team. During his absence, former Oakland and California Clippers' defender Gabbo Gavric filled in for the first 15 games.

San Jose played exciting soccer and led the NASL with 43 goals, including 15 by Child, the league's top scorer. But they also gave up 38, the second highest total in the league, and finished behind Los Angeles in the Western Division with a 9-8 record. The Earthquakes were eliminated in the opening playoff round by Dallas, 3-0.

The 'Quakes didn't disappoint at the Spartan Stadium box office, leading the NASL with an average attendance of 16,576. San Jose topped the league in attendance three of the first four seasons, peaking in 1976 at 19,282 and setting a record with eight sellouts the following year.

League officials no longer turned up their noses at San Jose, which had become a soccer hotbed. The 1975 Soccer Bowl championship game was awarded to the city and a capacity crowd saw Portland's 2-0 win over Tampa Bay.

San Jose rebounded from 1975's cellar finish (8-14) by going 14-10 to win the 1976 division title and setting a pre-expansion Spartan Stadium record when 25,048 saw a 2-1 win over the New York Cosmos and its star, Pele.

Mike Hewitt was exceptional in the net, defenders John Rowlands and Miro Pavlovic were added to the "No Goal Patrol" defense and Child and Ilija Mitic combined for 27 goals. San Jose won its first round playoff game over Dallas, but dropped a 3-1 verdict to Minnesota in the semis.

Paul Child

San Jose won the NASL's 1975 indoor championship by downing Tampa Bay, 8-5, at the Cow Palace behind three goals each from Roboostoff and Child, but bowed in the playoffs's first round each of the following two seasons.

The 'Quakes were third in the division in the 1977 outdoor season with a 14-12 mark and Mandaric sold the team and brought the Oakland Stompers into the league.

San Jose finished out the decade with two dismal last place teams, losing 13 straight games in 1978 for an 8-22 finish and dropping nine in a row the next season on the way to a 9-23 mark. The fans remained loyal, however, and the team averaged more than 15,000-a-game in 1979.

Fans were disappointed when the hard-working Child was sold to Memphis in December. The team's most popular player left with 61 goals and 156 points in 147 games.

■ BACK-TO-BACK BOWLS

The proliferation of football bowl games helped Stanford make it to the postseason four times in the 1970s and the Indians/Cardinal won every time.

A record Rose Bowl crowd of 103,839 sat in warm sunshine on Jan. 1, 1971, as heavily favored Ohio State was upset, 27-17, by two fourth quarter Stanford scores.

The Big Ten champion Buckeyes were undefeated in nine games and came into the game ranked No. 2 by United

Quarterback Jim Plunkett closed out his career at Stanford by winning the Heisman Trophy and leading the Indians to an upset victory over Ohio State in the Rose Bowl.

Press International and No. 5 by Associated Press. Coach John Ralston's 8-3-0 Indians were eighth and tenth in the polls and featured Jim Plunkett at quarterback and the vaunted "Thunderchickens" on defense.

Tired of living in the shadow of the Stanford offense, guard Steve Lazetich had named the defensive line the "Thunderchickens" after a motorcycle gang in his home town of Billings, Montana. "They're wild and reckless and run all over the place like we do," he explained.

Plunkett won the Rose Bowl MVP award, passing for 265 yards and a touchdown on 20 of 30 completions and kicker Steve Horowitz hit a record 48-yard field goal.

Stanford took an early 10-0 lead, but trailed 17-13 at the beginning of the last period. Jackie Brown scored his second touchdown to cap an 80-yard drive and the Indians intercepted a pass on Ohio State 25-yard line on the next series to set up a Plunkett to Randy Vataha scoring pass that iced the win.

The 8-3-0 Indians were an underdog again the following January, facing undefeated Big Ten champion Michigan.

Trailing 12-10 with 1:48 remaining, MVP quarterback Don Bunce hit five straight passes to move Stanford from its own 22 to the Wolverines' 31-yard line. With 12 seconds left, Rod Garcia kicked his second field goal to complete the comeback win, 13-12.

Fifteenth ranked Stanford appeared outside the Rose Bowl for the first time in December, 1977, meeting LSU in the Sun Bowl. Bill Walsh was in his first year as head coach of the Cardinal, which was led by quarterback Guy Benjamin, a consensus All-American and Pac-10 player of the year who topped the NCAA in passing.

Stanford had fashioned a 9-3-0 record and finished tied for second in the Pac-10 behind champion Washington. The Cardinal surrendered 307 yards on the ground to LSU, but allowed only two scores. Benjamin connected on three touchdown passes, with two to James Lofton, to rally Stanford from a 14-10 halftime deficit to a 24-14 victory.

The win moved Stanford's all-time postseason record above the .500 mark for the first time at 6-5-1.

Walsh's team gave Stanford its fourth straight postseason win the following year with a come-from-behind 25-22 victory in the Bluebonnet Bowl over highly regarded Georgia (9-1-1). The Cardinal had finished tied for fourth in the Pac-10 with a 4-3-0 conference mark and was 7-4-0 overall.

Stanford didn't get untracked until the second half. Aided by three Bulldog fumbles, the Cardinal wiped out a 22-0 deficit with 25 unanswered points in six-and-one-half minutes for the victory.

Quarterback Steve Dils sparkled, completing 17 of 28 passes for 210 yards with two scoring passes to All-American receiver Ken Margerum and another to running back Darrin Nelson, who rushed for 100 yards in 16 carries.

With the score knotted at 22, kicker Ken Naber booted a 24-yard field goal to decide it. Stanford's defense, led by Gordy Ceresino's 20 tackles, held on for the win.

■ BIG LITTLE MEN AND WOMEN

Santa Clara County teams continued doing well in youth baseball in the 1970s. Campbell appeared in three Little League World Series, finishing second to New Jersey in 1970 and bowing to Far East teams in 1976 and 1979.

Several area Bobby Sox all-star teams also made it to their national tournaments during the decade.

A Cupertino team won the Big League World Series in 1971 behind pitcher Steve Kelley and Tim Kenworthy's 11 for 16 series batting performance. West Valley Colts lost in the nationals.

The 1973 Santa Clara Mission team took the Pony national championship with a 4-3 win over Fort Worth as Jeff Fricke won his third game of the series.

Campbell Post 158 won the state American Legion baseball crown in 1974, beating Hawaii, 19-9, with three-run homers from Ted Bertron and Jim Guardino.

The county had two champs in 1975. Gagliardi Brothers of San Jose captured the Thorobred World Series when Jeff Mason hit a three-run triple in a 6-3 win over Wilmette, Ill. A week later, Rob Ferguson pitched two-hit ball against Joliet, Ill., as Santa Clara won the Colt title.

Gagliardi Bros. won the Thorobred title again in 1976 and the Central Coast All-Stars reached the Big League World Series with a 4-0, one-hit win by Rusty McDonald over Puget Sound, but lost two straight in the nationals.

In 1978, Rich Alvarez pitched Campbell-Moreland to the Pony World Series title with a 13-strikeout no-hitter over Joliet, Ill. It was his seventh postseason win and fourth shutout. The league's all-stars repeated as champions in 1979 with a 10-3 win over Houston on the pitching and hitting of Tom Gricius and battery mate Randy Nishijima.

■ GOLFING GIANT

Any number of fine golfers have connections to Santa Clara County. Stanford turned out such top notch stars as Tiger Woods, Tom Watson and Lawson Little, while San Jose State produced Ken Venturi, Patty Sheehan and Juli Inkster, to name just a few.

If you've been paying attention, you've noticed the name Ernie Pieper frequently in this book. He's certainly the most astonishing amateur golfer with local roots.

A member of the California Golf Hall of Fame, Pieper won his first tournament in 1929 as a 16-year-old and his last in 1970, a remarkable span of six decades.

He performed in almost all of the top state and county amateur tournaments and several times reached the U. S. amateur championship's quarterfinals.

Pieper started his trophy collection by winning the 1929 county amateur crown. He took his 14th county title in 1968 and started the 1970s two years later with a victory in the California senior tournament. The county golf tournament has been named in his honor.

Pieper won scores of club championships and took the San Jose city title several times. Among his most productive years were 1941, when he won both the state amateur and San Jose tournaments, and 1944, when he set a scoring record of 209 winning the 54-hole county title and defeated Bobby Rosburg of Stanford for the state crown.

Ernie Pieper, the area's greatest amateur golfer, is shown holding his 12th county tournament trophy and his son, Ricky, in 1959.

■ STADIUMS AND ARENAS

No fewer than four proposals to build major sports facilities surfaced in the county in the 1970s, continuing a trend that had begun a decade earlier.

As early as 1960, a study of an idea by San Jose councilman Bob Doerr concluded that a $1.8 million major league baseball stadium could be built north of Hillsdale Avenue and west of Monterey Highway.

Three years later there was a proposal to build a $5.7 million stadium in San Jose. It grew into a plan for a city-county $30 million complex combining a 12,000-seat arena and 60,000-seat stadium near Montague Road and Guadalupe River. The plan eventually was shot down by county supervisors. In 1966, San Jose voters failed to give $7.7 million in arena bonds the necessary two-thirds majority.

A $22 million, 15,000-seat arena package won approval on a 1973 ballot, but a tax plan to pay for it failed.

Private developers suggested they could build a 16,000-seat arena for $30 million, but the plan died in 1975 for lack of funds. A year later, a proposal to move the California Seals hockey team from Oakland to a 17,000-seat North San Jose arena failed when the team relocated to Cleveland.

In 1977, Santa Clara began studying a voter-backed proposal to construct an arena of up to 25,000 seats near Great America amusement park, later the proposed site for a baseball stadium.

None of the projects became reality. The situation did not change until the late 1980s, when voters backed a plan that resulted in the opening of the San Jose Arena in 1993.

■ TRIVIAL PURSUITS

Future Green Bay Packers' coach and motorcycle devotee Mike Holmgren performed as "Manifold Mike" with Big Bop and the Choppers, a rock 'n' roll band of Oak Grove High faculty who raised money for after school sports.

With Santa Clara well on its way to a 56-10 blowout over San Francisco State in 1971, coach Pat Malley let end Steve Cippi drop kick a PAT after the Broncos' seventh TD. Cippi's successful kick was the first by that method since Bronco Orval "Bud" McKee used it regularly in 1923.

Mimi Sherman was the first female coxswain in Intercollegiate Rowing Association history, appearing in the 1973 regatta with SCU's four-oared freshman crew.

Santa Clara Swim Club star Keena Rothhammer sued the AAU in 1974 to allow female swimmers to wear suits without a "modesty panel" across the lower front and modeled after those worn by the East Germans. The suits were allowed later in the year at the AAU national meet.

Which Santa Clara County player or coach owns the most Super Bowl rings? If you said Bill Walsh, who won three as the San Francisco 49ers' head coach, think again. The answer is linebacker Loren Toews (Del Mar), who collected four with the Pittsburgh Steelers championship teams in the 1975, 1976, 1979 and 1980 Super Bowls.

Pro cheer leader Krazy George Henderson (SJS) offered to lead a Bicentennial Cheer in 1975. He'd stand at the Mississippi River at noon on July 4th before television cameras and radio microphones. At his signal, everyone east

Mac Wilkins (left) and John Powell (center) were Olympic medal winners and world record holders in the discus from the county. San Jose State linebacker Dave Chaney put on an All-American performance in a stunning 13-12 upset victory over a Rose Bowl-bound Stanford team in 1971.

of the river would shout, "United," followed by everyone west of the river responding with "States." George predicted, "We'll blow out every window in the country."

When NFL referee Fred Silva (SJS) blew his whistle in the 1977 Baltimore-New England game, Miami fans said he blew the call, too. The ex-SJCC football coach ruled a play dead when Colts' QB Bert Jones was tackled and before a fumble that would have given the Pats the ball. The Colts won, eliminating Miami from the playoffs. Silva was well regarded by NFL executives and worked Super Bowl XIV.

■ WEIGHT MEN SUPREME

San Jose police officer John Powell and bearded Mac Wilkins, an athlete best known for his unconventional views and scathing criticism of U. S. Olympic officials, were two of America's best discus men in the 1970s and continued their winning ways late into the next decade.

Each held the world record for a time and Powell won seven AAU titles while Wilkins captured eight.

Powell took several discus events in Europe for the USA touring team in 1973 and the following year picked up the AAU discus title with a 214-11 toss. Powell got his world record in Long Beach in 1975 when he added two feet to the existing mark with a 226-8 throw. In the Olympics, Powell won a silver medal in 1976 and a bronze in 1984.

In 1976, Wilkins broke the world record three times in one day at San Jose State's Bud Winter Field with a best toss of 232-6 and won the gold medal at the Montreal Olympics. He took a silver in the event eight years later.

■ IN PASSING

Bartender and ex-heavyweight boxer Al Rovey was shot and killed by an irate patron in 1970 at the Tower Bar in downtown San Jose.

John "Red" Marion, who compiled a 385-338 record as manager of five San Jose teams in the California League in the 1950s and 1960s, died in San Jose in 1975, one day before his 61st birthday. Marion's teams made the playoffs four times and were champions in 1953 and 1962.

Bob Hagen (SJS), whose Gilroy High School basketball teams won 457 games and lost 209 during his 27-year career, died in 1977. He was state coach of the year twice and national coach of the year in 1973.

Sal Taormina, 57, Santa Clara University baseball coach for 15 years, died of a heart attack while driving home from a 1979 workout. An outstanding minor league player, his Bronco teams (511-249) never had a losing season.

■ SPARTANS 13, STANFORD 12

In a football game that ranks among the most satisfying of the century for San Jose State fans, the Spartans upset Rose Bowl-bound Stanford in 1971, 13-12.

Stanford had steamrolled the Spartans 68-20, 63-21 and 34-3 in their previous three meetings. Going into the game, Pac-8 champion Stanford was 7-2-0 and SJS was 3-4-1.

Dave Chaney, San Jose State's 5-foot-11, 210-pound linebacker, nailed down an Associated Press selection as the Spartans' first modern major All-American by making 12 unassisted and five assisted tackles, recovering two fumbles and intercepting a pass.

The Indians could have won on their last play. But, with the ball at the SJS 10-yard line and 17 seconds left, Rod Garcia missed his fifth field goal try of the game.

■ A TREE BY ANY OTHER NAME

Stanford officials changed the university's athletic nickname from Indians to Cardinal in 1972 after deciding the former was an insult to Native Americans.

In a 1975 campus student referendum, a move to restore Indians as the nickname was rejected, 2-1, but politically incorrect students narrowly voted in favor of Robber Barons over Sequoias as a replacement. The chosen name was an historic reference to a group of wealthy 19th Century industrialists which included university founder Leland Stanford.

That choice even offended H. D. Timm Williams, a Yurok Indian born on a Northern California reservation who was well known to football fans as Prince Lightfoot.

USF graduate Williams first danced in Native

Dan Pastorini starred at Bellarmine and Santa Clara and in the National Football League.

American costume at the 1951 Big Game rally and continued performing at games after Stanford touchdowns and during pregame and halftime shows. He quit after the name change, arguing that the Indian nickname, "was chosen to show strength and courage." He didn't support Robber Barons because it was "derogatory to students and alumni."

School officials agreed. The result is as visible today as Prince Lightfoot was for 20 years. It's The Tree, Stanford's entry in the goofiest college mascot contest.

■ QUARTERBACK COUNTRY

It defied all the odds. In 1972, four of the NFL's 26 starting quarterbacks came from Santa Clara County high schools and a fifth's roots were at Stanford. In order of graduation, the local preps were:

• Bob Berry (Willow Glen, Class of '60), Atlanta.

• Craig Morton (Campbell, Class of '61), Dallas.

• Jim Plunkett (Lick, Class of '65), New England.

• Dan Pastorini (Bellarmine, Class of '67), Houston.

Each played in all 14 games that season, while John Brodie (Stanford '56) was the San Francisco 49ers' starter, but missed 10 weeks with a severe ankle injury.

All were first round draft choices except Berry, who had set passing records at Oregon before being taken in the 11th round of the 1964 draft by Philadelphia. He played in the league 11 seasons.

Bad knees and bad teams failed to keep Morton from starring at California before moving on to an outstanding NFL career. The 6-foot-4, 215-pound Morton was the Golden Bears' first pro-style quarterback. After riding the bench for five games as a soph, Morton debuted against Penn State, completing 20 of 28 passes for 274 yards and three TDs in a 23-21 loss. When he left Cal, Morton owned most of the school's passing records.

Morton led Dallas into Super Bowl V where the Cowboys lost to Baltimore, 16-13. He lost the starting job to Roger Staubach and early in 1974 his plea for a trade was answered when he was sent to the New York Giants.

Morton moved to Denver in 1977 and guided the Broncos to Super Bowl XII, only to lose to Dallas and Staubach, 27-10. Morton finished his 18-year career in 1982.

Plunkett stands out as the greatest in Stanford's long line of outstanding quarterbacks. The Indians were 22-8-2 in his three seasons. Plunkett led the Indians to a Rose Bowl win over Ohio State in his senior year, was a consensus All-American and won the Heisman Trophy, the Walter Camp and Maxwell awards and was UPI's player of the year. He was the first player chosen in the 1971 NFL draft.

After being rookie of the year with New England, he was beset with injuries, traded to San Francisco and eventually released. The 33-year-old Plunkett was Pastorini's backup with the Oakland Raiders in 1980 until Dan broke a leg. Picked to finish last, Oakland (11-5-0) made the playoffs as a wild card team and beat Philadelphia, 27-10, in Super Bowl XV with Plunkett throwing three TD passes.

Two years later, he led the 12-4-0 Los Angeles Raiders to a 38-9 win over Washington in Super Bowl XVIII. Plunkett played through 1986.

Pastorini came into the NFL from SCU and was the Houston starter through 1979. He went to Oakland the following year and played only 10 more games with the Los Angeles Rams and Philadelphia after his injury.

Brodie was with the 49ers from 1957 through 1973, leading them into the playoffs three times.

■ BEES AND MISSIONS

There never had been a year quite like 1973 in San Jose's nearly quarter century in the California League. It was a season marked by:

• Two San Jose no-hitters, including a perfect game.

• A team attendance record.

• A double-header in two states that decided the team's pennant hopes.

• A book covering San Jose's season, *A Year in the Minors*, by Richard Lyttle, published by Doubleday.

San Jose was in the third year of its affiliation with Kansas City, a relationship that blossomed after the California Angels severed their ties with the team after 1969.

Serving as a farm club for the progressive Royals brought scores of outstanding prospects into Municipal Stadium. Among those who would succeed in the majors were Manager Steve Boros and players George Brett, Al Cowans, Steve Busby, Frank White, and Dennis Leonard.

It was Leonard who made the first mark in the league record book in 1973, pitching an April 26 no-hit shutout against Visalia for one of his league-leading 15 wins. He missed a perfect game only because he walked the first batter of the game before retiring the next 27 in order.

Four months later, reliever Ray Brown got one of his rare starts and became the first California Leaguer to throw a perfect game in a seven-inning, 3-0 win over Modesto.

As a team, San Jose was well down on the team batting

1972 San Jose players who often were in the lineup included (from left) Rex Goodson, George Brett, Steve Staggs, Jimmy Smith, Roger Schmuck, John Wathan, Bob Servoss, Frank White and Rocky Craig.

list despite the presence of league batting champion Dave Cripe (.310) and Kenzie Davis, who hit .299 and led the circuit with 82 stolen bases.

San Jose finished the first half in fourth place at 36-34, but rose to within a game of the second half title in an exciting race that helped draw a record 125,047 fans, more than one-quarter of the league's entire attendance.

On the last day, the Bees were nosed out for the title and played what is believed to be baseball's first two-state twin bill. They flew to Reno where they won an afternoon makeup game and returned to San Jose to play Modesto that night. San Jose could have tied Bakersfield for the second half title, but fell one game short by losing to Modesto in a game that started at 10:45 p.m. and ended at 1:30 a.m.

It was their best finish so far in the decade. San Jose had been out of the money in 1970 and 1971, when the distant fences at Municipal Stadium didn't stop Frank Ortenzio from topping the league with 32 homers. They were in the middle of the pack in 1972, when future American League batting champion Brett made his appearance in San Jose's outfield, hitting .274 in 117 games.

In 1974, emulating the San Jose State "Speed City" track team operating across Alma Street from the Bees' ballpark, San Jose stole bases in amazing numbers. They had thefts in a minor league record 47 straight games and established a league mark by swiping 372 topped by Sheldon Mallory's 72 in only 83 games. San Jose won the second half, but fell to Fresno in three of five playoff games.

For two more seasons, the franchise was saddled with an unproductive working agreement with Cleveland that placed them at or near the bottom of the standings. In 1977, owner Joe Gagliardi gambled that San Jose was ready to take a step up from Class A baseball to Class AAA.

He acquired the rights to the Sacramento franchise in the Pacific Coast League, moved the ball club to San Jose and renamed it the Missions. The team was an Oakland A's farm club, but failed both on the field and at the gate. It finished in the Western Division's cellar with a 64-80 record and was a distant last in attendance, drawing only 88,200 through the Municipal Stadium turnstiles.

The club was affiliated with Seattle in 1978, but the results were even less rewarding. The light-hitting Missions went 53-87 and attendance plunged to 67,000, which was the lowest for San Jose in a decade and only half of what the team drew five years earlier in a lower minor league.

When the season was over, Gagliardi dropped the PCL affiliation and brought the Missions back into the California League, where he also operated Stockton and a new franchise in Santa Clara nicknamed the Padres.

San Jose won the second half Southern Division crown, defeated first half champion Visalia and knocked off Stockton in the championship playoff. The Missions drew 71,320, second best in the league, while their neighbors in Santa Clara struggled afield and at the box office.

The Padres had moved from Rohnert Park and split their home games between Santa Clara's Washington Park and Municipal Stadium. The team set a California League futility record, dropping its first 10 games and 21 of 22.

Finishing last in both halves of the season, the Padres produced a 47-93 record and drew a paltry 19,952 customers at home. The team was managed by Joe Volpi, Blackford High School's baseball coach, who took a leave of absence to try his hand at professional baseball.

Gagliardi may have set a baseball record in 1979 as the only owner who umpired a game involving his own team. He was pressed into emergency service in a twin bill between Santa Clara and Reno when the regular umps failed to show up. When his attempts to find several amateur umpires for the game failed, he bought an umpire's cap and worked his first game in years. Santa Clara won a pair, but Reno players congratulated Gagliardi for his impartiality.

■ A DECATHLON OF SORTS

San Francisco Warriors' forward Rick Barry proved the most versatile Bay Area athlete in a 1973 charity decathlon at Stanford and Foothill College.

The 6-foot-7 Barry scored 813.5 points to win the competition easily over Warriors' teammate Jim Barnett, 710. Barnett got a measure of revenge by edging Barry at his specialty, taking the free throw shooting contest with 29 out of

Golden State's Rick Barry

30. Barry dropped in 28 with his famous underhand toss.

Barry took the three-game bowling series, 50-meter swim and hit the longest softball drive. Barry's prize was a two-week Mediterranean sea cruise for two.

Other athletes (with winning events in parenthesis) in order of finish: Cazzie Russell, Warriors (880-yard run); Fred Biletnikoff, Oakland Raiders (football throw); Jim Wiechers, pro golfer (nine holes of golf); John Brodie, San Francisco 49ers; Bruce Gossett, 49ers; Barry MacKay, tennis pro (tennis round robin); Charley Smith, Raiders (100-yard dash, 12-pound shot put); Tom Haller, ex-San Francisco Giants; Cedric Hardman, 49ers.

■ DOWN THE DRAIN

The Santa Clara Swim Club, which had dominated the amateur sport through the 1960s, began to decline in 1974, when coach George Haines left to head UCLA's program.

In the early 1970s, the club added several more AAU men's and women's championships to the list of titles that totaled 43 at the time Haines departed.

New champion swimmers carried the club's colors, including Jenny Bartz, Lynn Vidali, Tracey Finneran, Keena Rothhammer, Karen Moe, John Hencken, Brian Job, Steve Doyle, Joe Bottom and Mike Finneran.

Former club star Mitch Ivey succeeded Haines as coach and helped develop more champions, including world record holder and 1976 Olympic silver medalist Linda Jezek and gold medal winner Mike Bruner.

But by 1979, these and other swimmers had quit the Santa Clara club, often because of disagreements with Ivey, who became the target of parent criticism and attempts to have him replaced as head man.

The club failed to qualify a single swimmer for the Pan American Games and for the first time in a decade did not produce any winners in the 1979 national AAU meet.

As the decade drew to a close, other clubs including De Anza and San Jose Aquatics were drawing away many of the swimmers who formerly flocked to the powerful and prestigious Santa Clara team.

Haines returned to the county in 1981 to run the De Anza club and there were discussions of a merger with Santa Clara. Nothing came of the talks immediately and Haines became women's swim coach at Stanford. Ivey quit in July, 1981, and the clubs merged two months later.

Coinciding with the swim club's decline was a similar drop off in the quality of the Santa Clara International Swim Meet which began in the late 1960s at the city's swimming center. Once the nation's best meet and magnate for some of the greatest international swimmers, it suffered from a loss of television coverage in 1974.

Loss of local big name swimmers who once dominated the meet also hurt its box office appeal.

■ THE LONGEST DAY

Live Oak High's Tim Almeida and Pioneer's Ken Flores took the mound on May 10, 1974, hoping to pitch a complete seven inning game. When darkness finally forced the umpire to call the 0-0 game after 18 innings, Almeida and Flores were still out there throwing.

Coaches were asked why the teens were allowed to go the route in the county's longest double shutout. They said that careful counting of the pitches convinced them the young men's arms weren't in jeopardy of injury.

Flores threw 180 pitches (averaging 10 per inning), while Almeida was even more frugal, tossing only 160.

The next time the teams met, Flores beat Live Oak for the STAL title, 7-2. Almeida pitched in relief after the game was lost.

■ BRUCE JENNER

Bruce Jenner captured the hearts of America and earned his way onto the front of a Wheaties cereal box when he won the decathlon at Montreal in the 1976 Olympic Games that was decidedly short on USA medals.

The fact that Jenner raised the world record to 8,634 points didn't damage the drama created by his televised gold medal performance.

Jenner had trained for his event for several years in San Jose, although he wasn't from this area originally. After high school, he entered Graceland College in Iowa on a football scholarship. A schoolboy high jump and pole vault champ, Jenner turned to the decathlon after injuring a knee.

He made the USA Olympic team as its third decathlete in 1972 and finished 10th at Munich. In 1975, Jenner won decathlons in New Zealand and at the Pan American Games and set a world record of 8,529 points with six lifetime bests in the USA-Poland meet.

Jenner had been aiming for a score of 8,600 points for several years and the Olympics provided his last chance to achieve that mark. He was third at the end of the first day, but was looking forward to the last five events, where he was stronger than the leaders.

Coming into the final 1,500-meter event, Jenner needed

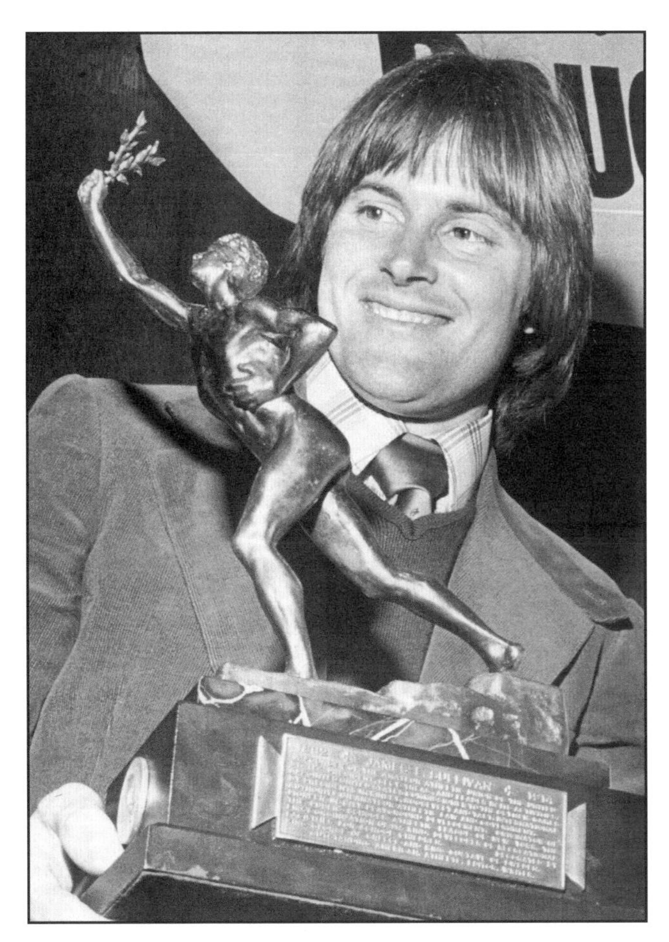

Bruce Jenner holds the Sullivan Award trophy.

Becky Dyroen-Lancer (left) with Jill Sudduth.

to run the fastest race of his life to crack the record. When he pounded across the finish line and looked at the clock, he knew he had made it, setting the new record.

In addition to his Wheaties glory, Jenner was the Associated Press male athlete of the year and won the coveted Sullivan Award as the nation's best amateur athlete. He appeared in several movies and later worked in television.

■ AQUAMAIDS

Kay Vilen left behind a remarkable coaching record in 1976 when she died of a stroke at age 66.

Her Santa Clara Aquamaids, founded in 1964, won 15 indoor and outdoor AAU synchronized swimming titles, several international crowns and scores of individual medals.

The young women who performed for her combined the strength of a water polo player with artistic ballet moves. The sport was frequently derided, even being lampooned by a skit on television's Saturday Night Live. But by the 1990s, it won recognition and became an Olympic sport.

Kim Welshons was the first big star for the Aquamaids, taking more than a dozen AAU titles through the end of the 1960s as well as international triumphs in Japan, Denmark and Canada. Welshons was the solo competition star and Nancy Hines frequently was her duet partner.

The names changed, but the results were the same in the 1970s. Terry Anderson and Gail Johnson were the stars early in the decade, winning AAU titles and grabbing more gold as the Aquamaids took the first world's championship in Yugoslavia in 1973. Later married, Gail Johnson Buzanos became the team's head coach after Vilen died.

In the mid and late 1970s, Sue Baross, Robin Curren McKinley, Linda Shelley, Pam Tyron and Michelle Barone led the team to wins in this country and abroad. They owned the AAU competition throughout the decade.

Club fortunes ebbed in the 1980s, but surged again in the '90s when it took numerous national titles and put key performers on the 1996 USA gold medal Olympic team.

Becky Dyroen (later Dyroen-Lancer) won numerous national, Pan-American and world competitions. The former Valley Christian High and De Anza College student was regarded as the most powerful and technically accomplished performer, scoring the first perfect 10s ever awarded in synchronized swimming during an Olympic qualifying meet in 1996. Paired with Jill Sudduth, she won numerous duet competitions.

■ SUNBIRDS AND RAINBOWS

San Jose stepped up to the plate with its first female professional franchise in any sport in 1976 when the Sunbirds were formed and joined the International Women's Professional Softball Association.

Many players were ex-members of the highly successful amateur Santa Clara Laurels, including national all-star southpaw shortstop Diane Kalliam, who batted .425 in 15 seasons, and manager Laura Malesh. Top pitchers were former Laurels Charlotte Graham and Bonnie Johnson.

The Sunbirds shared Municipal Stadium with the California League's Bees, whose management was unhappy when the stadium's lush grass infield was replaced with

The Santa Clara Laurels amateur softball team provided the nucleus for the San Jose Sunbirds pro squad. From left, (back) Carolyn Spady, Barbara Tabler, Marcia Watts, Alle Henderson, Charlotte Graham, Barbara Courtney; (middle) Laura Malesh, Marva Eichelberger, Gloria Barron, Frankie DeRossiet; (front) Eileen Lum, Bonnie Bryant, Diane Kalliam, Bennie Carroll.

$30,000 worth of artificial turf to accommodate both the baseball diamond and the shorter softball dimensions.

Playing 30 double headers both at home and on the road, the Sunbirds proved to be a strong aggregation. They opened at home with a twin bill sweep over the Southern California Gems before a crowd of 4,216 and won the league's Western Division with a 77-43 record. The powerful Connecticut Falcons swept the Sunbirds in the league World Series.

Malesh resigned after the season and was succeeded by former Del Mar High School baseball coach Gary Cunningham. Graham took her pitching wizardry to Santa Ana, leaving mound chores to Johnson and Rhonda Ebersole.

The team opened 1977 with a double-header win over St. Louis before 1,332 at Municipal Stadium, less than a third of the attendance on opening night a year earlier. By year's end, the light-hitting Sunbirds had lost a reported $132,000, nearly double the final deficit the previous year. San Jose finished third and was knocked out in the first round of the 1977 playoffs by Santa Ana.

Kalliam, Johnson and several others boycotted the team in 1978 in a dispute over salary and other issues. By July, the last place Sunbirds were averaging about 350 fans per game and completed the season as a road team. At their last home game, the crowd was so small that three boys sitting in the top row had to be told to turn down their radio because the noise distracted the players on the field.

The Sunbirds (12-58) folded, but a new franchise, the San Jose Rainbow, joined the association in 1979. Its core was the 1977 pre-strike Sunbirds' team, with Kalliam as player-manager and Johnson on the mound.

As the season progressed, expense money and regular salaries shrank even before four of the league's ten teams dropped out. Kalliam led the league in hitting with a .360 average and Johnson won 16 regular season games as the Rainbow made the four-team playoffs, but was eliminated by Buffalo, three games to two, in the first playoff round. The team did not return to action in 1980.

■ SPECIAL SPARTANS

The one-two punch provided by All-Americans Karen Mason and Elinor Banks led the San Jose State women's basketball team to its three greatest seasons from 1977-78 through 1979-80.

The team went 17-10, 24-4 and 22-9 during the period, but lost in the first round of AIAW playoffs each season.

The best team was the 1978-79 aggregation, whose record stood at 2-3 when it won a school record 22 straight games to capture the league championship.

Mason and Banks comprise the Lady Spartans' greatest scoring tandem. Mason averaged 15.9 points over her career, with Banks right behind at 15.1. Banks was perhaps the school's greatest all-around female player, holding career records of 9.7 rebounds and 1.4 blocked shots per game.

■ HONORS

Umberto Abronzino of San Jose was a founder of the Peninsula Soccer League with four teams in 1957 and saw it grow to more than 80 junior and senior teams by 1971, when he was elected to the National Soccer Hall of Fame.

SCU football center Jim Leonard made several college division All-America teams in 1979. The 6-foot-3, 260-pounder played in the NFL and USFL for seven seasons.

Hall of Fame honorees of the 1970s: Back Nello Falaschi, end Tom Fears (one year) and coaches Buck Shaw and Len Casanova of Santa Clara, plus Stanford end Bill McColl (college football); county native Harry Hooper (baseball); Live Oak High sprinter Hal Davis, Palo Alto High high jumper Les Steers and San Jose State sprinter Tommie Smith (track and field); Dorothy Wise of Sunnyvale (women's pocket billiards); Mark Spitz of Santa Clara High and Olympic and Santa Clara Swim Club coach

Marshall Sargent and Howard Kaeding (right) were two of San Jose Speedway's top drivers. Kaeding won a record 112 feature races while Sargent took 88 events.

George Haines (swimming).

■ RACING FAN'S FAVORITE

San Jose Speedway, an Eastside landmark for three decades, was closed in September 1977 and demolished to make way for a housing development, leaving thousands of racing fans looking for something to do on Saturday night.

The Speedway first came to 28 acres at Tully Road and Swift Lane near the Reid-Hillview Airport in 1946 from another site near Alum Rock Avenue and King Road. It began as a flat quarter-mile dirt track and had several configurations until it became a sunken oval with banked curves.

The track survived driver boycotts in 1954 and 1976 as well as scores of injuries and at least six deaths including one in the only motorcycle race ever held there.

It provided racing fans with an opportunity to see many great racing performers, including local favorites Joe Leonard, Marshall Sargent, Bill Scott and Howard Kaeding, along with such national big name drivers as A. J. Foyt, Bobby Unser, Billy Vukovich and Parnelli Jones.

Earl Kelley won the last race at the venerable track in 1977, the Coors 100-lap, and Mike Sargent nailed down the title as the Speedway's final points champion.

The dirt track originally was designed for midget car racing, but in the 1950s and 1960s under the management of Bob Barkhimer, the emphasis shifted to stock cars and the track joined NASCAR.

As hundreds of homes began encroaching on the track, residents petitioned the city to move the Speedway to end the noise. Track owners realized it had outlived its usefulness and found a buyer who wanted to develop the land.

A dirt track at the County Fairgrounds became the new Speedway home for automobile and motorcycle racing.

■ NO DAY AT THE BEACH

San Jose became the home of professional volleyball in 1979 when the San Jose Diablos joined the International Volleyball Association.

It was a coed league, allowing no more than four players of the same sex among the six on the floor at any time and prohibiting rotation of players, except to serve the ball. The winner of three 12-point games took the match.

It was unclear why a city named after Saint Joseph had a team named for the devil when the Diablos opened in spring of 1979. Opposing teams came from such volleyball hot beds (?) as Seattle, Denver and Albuquerque.

Under coach Carlos Feitosa, the Diablos concluded the season 13-27 and ahead of only last place Albuquerque. Average attendance at Civic Auditorium fell short of 1,000.

If there was a season highlight, it was the East-West All-Star Game, won by the West in five games, before 2,219 at the Auditorium. San Jose players Larry Beneke, Martin Castillo and Mary Jane Smith made the West squad.

Early in 1980, Jim Blair announced the team would disband. It was losing more often than not and before smaller crowds than before. Other owners kept the Diablos alive and offered "free" games, where fans were asked to pay on their way out if they stayed until the end of the game.

Eventually, Diablo players took over the team, which kept losing while producing paydays of up to $3,300 under the unique "pay if you stay" plan. Other clubs were in financial trouble, too, and the league closed down for good in mid-July. The Diablos had a 7-13 record.

■ FOR THE RECORD

A Jim Plunkett to Randy Vataha pass that covered a school record 96 yards in Stanford's 63-16 victory over Washington State in 1970 also gave Plunkett the NCAA mark for career total offense.

Jay Miller (Lynbrook), caught an NCAA record 22 passes for BYU against New Mexico in 1973 and led the nation in receptions (100) and receiving yards (1,181).

QB Steve Bartkowski (Buchser) passed for a school record 2,580 yards, leading Cal to a 7-3-1 mark and selection as a 1974 consensus All-American. He was the National Football League's first draft choice by Atlanta, played 12 years and passed for 156 touchdowns.

The New York Mets' Mike Vail (Mitty, De Anza), had a bad day in 1975, setting a National League record by striking out seven times in a double header.

Al Feuerbach of San Jose set a world shot put record at 71-8 in 1973 and Terry Albritton of Stanford increased it in 1976 with a 71-8 1/2 heave.

Penny Dean, a former Foothill Aquatics Club star from Santa Clara, swam across the English Channel in 1978, cut-

Ex-San Jose State quarterback Steve DeBerg set NFL passing records for the 49ers in 1979 and was still playing two decades later.

ting one hour, five minutes off the old record.

In 1979, San Jose State defensive back Ken Thomas returned three interceptions for touchdowns, an NCAA record. He added two more scores before his career ended in 1982 for a career NCAA mark of five TD returns.

Gunn High's state record 11-year, 200-match tennis winning streak ended in 1979 with a 5-2 loss to Carmel.

San Jose State and Utah State set an NCAA football record for the highest scoring tie, 48-48, in 1979.

Coach Bill Walsh turned quarterback Steve DeBerg (SJS) loose for the hapless San Francisco 49ers (2-14) in 1979. DeBerg set NFL records with 578 pass attempts and 347 completions.

In the 1970s, Maren Seidler of San Jose won seven straight AAU women's shot put titles and elevated the American record by more than six inches to 62-7 3/4.

■ 1970 ■

SJCC's Wayne Watkins hits 47 versus Ohlone, 45 against Chabot . . . SCU scores record 121-84 win against UNLV . . . Dennis O'Neill's (Bellarmine) two free throws in final second gives Stanford 73-71 win over Cal . . . Gilroy High snaps Willow Glen's 20-game basketball win streak, 56-38, behind Pat Kawaguchi's 29 . . . Standing room Encina Pool crowd sees Yale topple Stanford swimmers, 58-55 . . . Del Mar High's Bruce Posey posts school hoops mark 41 against Campbell . . . Boxer Frankie Crawford decisions San Jose's Ray Echavarria at Civic Auditorium . . . Coby Dietrick's 36 sets SJS record in San Diego State loss . . . Willow Glen High's Ray Taroli, STAL's top football player, repeats as basketball MVP . . . Steve Dunning's homer off Rich Troedson (Camden) gives Stanford 1-0 win over SCU. Dunning wins 13 games with 144 Ks in 108 innings, 1.70 ERA, is NCAA player of the year, Cleveland's second draft pick . . . Wayne Watkins scores 36, sets SJCC mark of 608 points in 109-107 win over Chabot. MVP Jack Pierce ends career with 571 rebounds . . . Greg Brock sets Stanford two-mile record with 8:45.2 against SJS . . . Los Gatos High repeats as CCS wrestling champ. Lick's Albert Nanez (39-0) is top heavyweight . . . Otto Sarlo hot on Dodge Ridge slopes, wins veterans giant slalom. Beverly Brockway of Los Altos tops women . . . Section player of the year Randy Johnson hits 22, Steve Bartkowski adds 25 as Buchser (26-2) topples Alisal in CCS basketball final, 83-62 . . . Stanford's Phil Keller no-hits Arizona State, 1-0 . . . Mitty High bows to Sequoia in first CCS boy's soccer final, 1-0 in eight OTs . . . Stanford's Brian Job wins NCAA 100, 200-yard breaststroke . . . Aladin Rodrigues is SJS soccer All-American . . . Wilcox High's Randy Boyd whiffs 23 in 11-inning, 8-5 win against Sunnyvale . . . SCU tops Long Beach State, 12-4, in NCAA playoffs. Bruce Bochte goes three for four with grand slam, five RBIs. Broncos (42-16) lose to USC . . . Peninsula Ramblers lose to Great Britain's Penguin Rugby Club at Buck Shaw Stadium, 14-6 . . . State senior golf title goes to Ernie Pieper . . . Homestead High's Mike Fenton, Randy Zylker combine for 3-1 victory over Willow Glen in section baseball final . . . Cindergal Francie Larrieu breaks girl's 880, mile marks . . . Jim Rice of Palo Alto in third straight Grand National motorcycle win at Fairgrounds . . . Harold Solomon whips Jimmy Connors for state junior tennis title at San Jose . . . San Jose Kings cop Northern California Soccer League playoffs, lose to Vancouver, Western Canada champs, 2-1 . . . New baseball coach Gene Menges guides SJS to first winning season in 10 years . . . Los Altos High's Chris Adams sets state meet discus record at 201-3 . . . Steve Bohn of SJS wins Northern California amateur golf . . . Ralph Castellanos of San Jose retains state heavyweight karate title . . . In Hawaiian preps first loss to mainland team, St. Francis edges Kaimuki, 6-0, on Don Nava's 25-yard TD toss to Bob Reilly . . . No. 2 junior welterweight Enrique Jana decisions Felipe Torres at Civic Auditorium . . . Whitney Reed downs Davis Cup teammate Tom Brown for county tennis title . . . Steve Flynn rushes for 161 yards, scores four TDs in 42-29 Leland High win over Wilcox . . . Bill Scott is NASCAR super modified Speedway champ . . . Alex Romanowski of Blackford High bowls pair of 300 games . . . Chris Papanicolaou (SJS) first to clear 18 feet in pole vault . . . Two Tony Suffle goals lead SJS to 3-0 soccer victory over Cal for conference title. Spartans fall to Denver in NCAA . . . SJCC's Jack Bush (Piedmont Hills) wins state JC cross-country . . . JC grid champs: WVC, Gavilan . . . SCU tops Humboldt State, 61-41, as Carl Brayboy runs for 175 yards, Dan Pastorini throws four TDs . . . Gilroy's Dick Soutar wins third pro bowling title in month . . . QB Jim Chasey (Leigh) leads unbeaten Dartmouth to 28-0 win over Penn . . . Ray Townsend throws two TD passes to Keith Van Amburg as San Jose Hornets top Venice, 28-6 . . . Los Altos High ends Leigh's unbeaten string at 18 with 30-23 win in first county postseason grid final . . . Mike McGillis (Los Altos), Mike Franz (Leigh), CCS lineman, back of year. Franz also tops Nor Cal backs . . . All-pros John Brodie, Gene Washington (both Stanford) lead San Francisco 49ers to first division title, 17-14, over Minnesota . . . Doug Oliver of WVC scores 30 in 98-89 win over Sacramento . . . Mike Stewart's 28 paces SCU, but Broncos fall to Notre Dame, 85-83.

■ 1971 ■

De Anza inflicts first home hoops loss in history on Contra Costa, 73-66. Mike Tarabonovic snares 21 rebounds, Dave Blasquez scores 18 . . . Three penalty kicks by Rod Sears, two by

Sal Taormina never had a loser in 15 years as Santa Clara University's baseball coach. One of his future big leaguers was Bruce Bochte (right).

Ken Berry give Peninsula Ramblers 18-8 rugby triumph over Stanford . . . Five of eight St. Mary's players foul out as SCU wins, 114-111, in double OT at Oakland Coliseum Arena . . . Art Romswinckel (SJS) scores twice as San Jose Grenadiers drop Portuguese AC, 2-1, for Northern California amateur soccer title . . . Barry Keegan hits 31 in SJCC's 88-81 win over Diablo Valley . . . Claude Terry tallies 41 points in Stanford's 97-85 win over Oregon State for Maples Pavilion mark. Terry breaks school season record with 544 points . . . SJS (2-24) ends year with 21st straight loss, 92-86, to Los Angeles State. Johnny Skinner hits 29 points for 466, Spartans' second best season total . . . Randy White sets Stanford 440 hurdles record at 51.3 . . . Overfelt High wrestlers Carlos Rodriguez, Richard Calderon win state titles . . . De Anza loses state JC playoff to Ventura, 75-71 . . . Wayne Glusker of SJS travels seven miles, 468 yards to win AAU junior one-hour race walk . . . Rich Troedson whiffs 15 St. Mary's batters in 7-3 SCU win . . . State JC wrestling crowns worn by Bruce Blanchard of Foothill, Bruno Bicocca of WVC . . . Stanford beats Peninsula Ramblers for Monterey rugby title, 9-3. Kip Oxman scores two penalty kicks . . . Army draftee Darnell Hillman (SJS) leads Armed Forces All-Stars over Marathon Oil for national AAU title, 90-77. Warriors select Hillman in NBA draft's first round . . . Lynbrook High's Jay Miller hits two home runs in second straight game, but Los Altos wins, 6-5 . . . Mike Rusk of SJS strikes out 17 in 11-inning, 2-1, win over San Diego State . . . Dave Sloan of Santa Clara High tops Fremont, 8-2, with 15 K, no-hit effort . . . Fastest mile ever in San Jose run by Arne Kvalheim of Norway at 3:58.1 . . . Bellarmine wins second WCAL title, 7-6, over St. Francis when Ron Morey bats in Sean Hennessey in eighth . . . Branham High's Jeff Gingrich, with one loss in two seasons, blanks Cupertino in CCS final, 2-0 . . . Santa Clara Laurels (62-22) fourth in women's national fast pitch softball tourney . . . De Anza's Jim Petraglia takes state JC 440 hurdles title, SJCC's Harry Freeman wins triple jump . . . Duane Larson of SCU repeats as WCAC player of the year. Broncos win league title, dump PCAA co-champ SJS in NCAA regionals, lose to USC . . . De Anza Aquatic Foundation takes sixth national AAU water polo title . . . Francie Larrieu sets U. S. mile mark at 4:41.5 . . . Mrs. James Roessler repeats as winner of county women's golf title . . . Stanford's Shelley Hamlin wins U. S. women's college golf . . . Jay Gingrich pitches Campbell-Moreland Colt League's first perfect game . . . Brothers Antonio, Leroy Gatto of San Jose capture state cycling titles . . . Palo Alto's Kate Latham takes Oregon's state women's tennis singles . . . Robert Kemper of San Jose wins weight lifting gold medals at Pan-American Games. Bill Gerdts (SJS) scores three goals as USA wins water polo championship over Cuba, 6-4 . . . Undefeated San Jose Kings take Northern California Soccer League, lose playoff to San Francisco . . . Joe Leonard takes California 500 race at Ontario Motor Speedway, wins USAC title . . . QB Jay Cruze (Cupertino, De Anza) leads Cal to 20-10 victory over West Virginia . . . Jorge Ramos comes back from early knockdown to decision Ray Echavarria at Civic Auditorium . . . Gil Torres wins first city golf tourney held since 1965 . . . Roger Cantrell's 272 yards rushing, five TDs give Branham High 41-14 win over Westmont. Cantrell tops CCS with 132 points . . . Nelson Briles (SCU) throws two-hit shutout for Pittsburgh over Baltimore in World Series Game 5 . . . Free safety Chuck Hawthorne (Campbell) intercepts two Don Bunce passes as Washington State nips Stanford, 24-23, on last play field goal . . .

Mountain View High's Gordy Olmos rambles 274 yards to four TDs in 35-26 win over Los Altos . . . In pre-expansion days, Arizona State draws Spartan Stadium's largest crowd of 23,500 . . . Led by conference MVP QB Sonny Brasile, WVC ties Santa Rosa for championship . . . Saratoga High wins WVAL title, crushing Blackford, 72-26, as Cliff Johnson throws for 283 yards, Dave Slade scores five TDs . . . Nov. 27 bad day for Spartans when UCLA dunks SJS (20-1) in water polo, USF bumps SJS (12-3-1) in NCAA soccer playoffs . . . Mitty High's Pat Kohlman, WCAL lineman of the year as end in 1970, takes top back award at quarterback . . . CCS most valuables: guard-linebacker Dan Lloyd (Lick), back Steve Davis (Campbell) . . . Howard Kaeding of Campbell takes second NASCAR state super modified title with 33 race victories . . . Stanford captures fourth straight Monterey National Rugby Tournament . . . In first postseason game since 1949, PCAA champion SJS (5-6-1) falls to Memphis State in Pasadena Bowl, 28-9 . . . Dan Pastorini (SCU) is top offensive player in West's 17-13 victory over East in Shrine contest.

■ 1972 ■

After 32 years, Peninsula Ramblers grab first rugby tourney with Jack Schultz of Stanford scoring five times in 36-3 win against Mission Beach AC at San Diego . . . George Archer wins Los Angeles Open with playoff round of 66 . . . Leigh High record falls when Jody Desin hits 40 points in 75-66 loss to Campbell . . . K. C. Jackson (Los Altos) has Foothill record 37 in 99-75 win over San Mateo . . . SJS beats California in basketball for first time ever, 86-83 . . . Sunnyvale's Steve Hernandez wins 20-lap Yamaha Silver Cup motorcycle race at Madison Square Garden . . . Cal's John Coughran (Piedmont Hills) pumps in school record 47 points in 96-87 loss to Utah State . . . SCU whips St. Mary's at Civic Auditorium, 107-65, after six black Gaels, including three starters walk out at halftime to protest dismissal of school dean Odell Johnson . . . Overfelt High wins CCS, Nor Cal wrestling. Unbeaten Dan Lloyd of Lick High takes state 194-pound title . . . Stanford first round NFL picks: linebacker Jeff Siemon (Minnesota) defensive tackle Greg Sampson (Houston) . . . Goalie Greg Higgins gives Mitty High third straight shutout, 2-0 win over Silver Creek in CCS soccer final . . . Gavilan College's Tom Powell averages 22.4, wins conference hoops MVP award . . . Claude Terry ends career with 1,566 points, moves past Tom Dose (1,441) as Stanford leader . . . Hill High's Frank Cyr loses one-hitter, 1-0, when Oak Grove's Don Imel tosses perfect game . . . Work on Leland High field leaves fences 275 feet from plate. Chargers hit four homers, Willow Glen six in 10-9 Leland win . . . John McBride has SCU record five hits with two homers in 15-12 win over UC-Irvine . . . Paced by league MVP pitcher Rich Troedson (13-2), SCU wins league, falls to UCSB in NCAA . . . Scott Overton of Los Altos High third Knight in a decade to top state discus field, spinning platter 185-10 . . . Jackie Dixon of Westmont High wins inaugural women's six-mile Crazylegs Marathon at New York . . . Kelly Davis of Campbell High nine (26-5) one-hits Gunn for CCS title . . . San Jose Cindergals set marks: Valerie Eberly has U. S. record 9:31.2 in 3,000 meters, Francie Larrieu runs world record two-mile in 9:55.9, U. S. record 1,500 meters in 4:14.2 . . . Sandra Woodruff wins county women's golf . . . 1968 Olympic water polo champ Yugoslavia falls to USA at De Anza, 9-3 . . . Alex "Sandy" Mayer, Roscoe Tanner of Stanford take NCAA tennis doubles . . . Charlotte Graham of Santa Clara Laurels throws 16th no-hitter, first career perfect softball game against San Jose Dusters . . . Leland High's Ken McMaster wins county junior golf . . . Semi-pro San Jose Kings upset USA Olympic soccer team, 3-1 . . . Armando Claudio of Ayer High captures Nor Cal junior golf . . . In series renewal, SJS edges Santa Clara, 33-28, on Craig Kimball's two-yard TD pass to Jimmie Lassiter with nine seconds left . . . Campbell's John Van Hooser wins first NASCAR early model stock car race . . . Cupertino's Bob Potthast retains county men's tennis singles title. Marcie O'Keefe of Mountain View is women's champ . . . Howard Kaeding wins state NASCAR super modified title . . . Hector Flores rushes 178 yards in 16 carries for four TDs, Ralph Corral totes ball for 168 more as Gilroy whips San Jose, 41-13 . . . Police Olympics gold medalist Reno de Caro of San Jose lifts record 1,520 pounds . . . Chon Gallegos beats Guy Gordon in sudden death for city golf title . . . Cubberley High QB Danny English passes 14 for 14 for three scores in 20-18 win over Palo Alto . . . Joe Leonard takes second straight USAC title . . . 59 percent of voters back Measure A, advising county supervisors to build sports and entertainment center . . . St. Francis High (3-7-0) has last losing football season of century . . . Mike Franz scores three TDs as WVC defeats De Anza for league title, 28-22. Vikes lose to Chabot in playoffs . . . Southern University cancels football game against SCU when two Southern students are slain by police in campus protests . . . Mike Loughlin, David Post chosen co-MVPs as Buchser High (24-0-1) wins Nor Cal water polo . . . Francie Larrieu tops five-time champ Doris Brown in AAU national cross-country . . . Leland High's Jim Miller hits 13 of 22 for three TDs in 41-16 CCS final over Riordan. All-American Miller leads state with 28 TD passes . . . Defensive linemen Bob Olson (SJCC), Matt Thatcher (De Anza) on JC All-America squad.

■ 1973 ■

Johnny Skinner's 17 points help SJS upset Long Beach State, 68-61 . . . Pepperdine's Bird Averitt hits 41, but SCU drowns Waves 86-77 behind Mike Stewart's 25 . . . Mike Benton of Mitty is soccer All-American . . . Del Mar High's Scott Russell sets mark with 43 in 79-53 win over Campbell . . . San Jose's Al Feuerbach records world indoor shot put mark of 69-5 3/4 . . . Lick High basketball mentor Dan Fukushima is U. S. coach of the year . . . Everett Breaux, SJCC star in 1968, celebrates return to school with 24 points in 65-63 victory over Merritt . . . Soviet Union's 1972 Olympic water polo champs top SJS, 10-6, lose to USA at De Anza, 5-4 . . . Francie Larrieu eclipses women's world indoor mile mark at 4:35.6 . . . Bert Gonzales, Richard Calderon of SJCC capture Nor Cal JC wrestling titles . . . Cupertino hands St. Ignatius first loss, 1-0, in CCS soccer final . . . SJS football lineman Donnell Jackson wrestles to rehabilitate injury, captures PCAA crown . . . Oak Grove High's Fred DeLeon is 178-pound champion in first state wrestling tourney . . . Eric Bauer of Prospect High pitches 12-strikeout perfect game against Westmont . . . SJS heavyweight Dan Kikuchi grand champion as Spartans take 12th straight NCAA judo title . . . League MVP Gene Little fans 17 in WVC's 5-2 victory over Santa Rosa . . . Australian Olympic swimming champion Shane Gould competes for Foothill Aquatic Club, wins three events at AAU indoor swim meet . . . Oak Grove High's 6-foot-10 hoops star Korky Nelson throws second no-hit game, downs Silver Creek, 4-0 . . . Joe Charboneau triples to drive in run, scores winner on Tom Stephens' sacrifice fly in 4-1 Buchser High win

Millard Hampton (left), who won both CCS sprints three straight years at Silver Creek High, later led San Jose City College to the state title and won a gold medal at the 1976 Olympics. Jack Pierce, ex-San Jose High and SJCC star, hit 395 home runs in the minors.

over Pioneer for Lions Easter tourney championship . . . Palo Alto High's Carl Florant ties state 110 hurdles mark at 13.6 . . . Steve Bartkowski (Buchser), breaks Cal home run record with 12 . . . 268-pound ironworker Bill Harrison of San Jose is world heavyweight wrist wrestling champion . . . State JC triple jump title won by Foothill's Jim Krebs . . . Jeff Gingrich (Branham), strikes out 21 for SJS in 20-inning, 1-1 tie with Long Beach . . . Campbell High nine takes second straight CCS title with 7-2 win over Mitty . . . Sandy Mayer takes singles, joins Jim Delaney for doubles title as Stanford wins first NCAA tennis championship . . . San Jose Grenadiers lose to Philadelphia, 3-0, in soccer's U. S. Amateur Cup . . . Santa Clara Coralettes capture junior synchronized swimming championships in Holland, Germany . . . Campbell-Moreland Bobby Sox minor division team loses to Fullerton in World Series final, 12-0 . . . Santa Clara High's Kurt de Varona wins Junior Olympics all-around gymnast title . . . Veteran driver Howard Kaeding wins state NASCAR title . . . Mountain View's Walt Maas takes regional Sports Car Club of America crown . . . Santa Clara High opens with 7-0 gridiron victory over Hollister, snapping 33-game winless string dating back to 1969 . . . Pip Livesey smashes SCU mark, rushing 197 yards in 10 carries as Broncos topple Cal State Hayward, 28-13 . . . Cubberley High stomps Sequoia, 73-6. QB Larry Beyer throws eight completions for 213 yards, six TDs . . . SCU defeats SJS for first time in soccer, 3-2 . . . Gary Lynn sits out second half after rushing 251 yards, scoring five TDs as Los Gatos High tramples Camden, 43-18 . . . QB shootout decided when Lick High linebacker Tony Sacolo kills late drive with interception in 38-27 win over Oak Grove. Lick's Dave Calderon passes 238 yards, three TDs, Eagles' Bill Christopher counters with 233 yards, three TDs . . . Rod Garcia, who leads NCAA by hitting 62 percent of field goals, boots record 59-yarder, adds three more at 42, 52, 25 yards, but Stanford bows to USC, 27-26 . . . Craig Kimball of SJS passes for 326 yards on 26 of 43, but Spartans drop 28-21 decision to Utah State . . . Leigh High's Jeff Beeson sets county mark with 46.8-yard punting average, including 82-yarder against Camden . . . Cindergals' Cindy Poor wins state AAU women's cross-country . . . SJCC loses 17-7 to San Mateo for league title, but Jaguars' All-American back Marv Stewart gains 78 yards to break state JC rushing record with 1,624 . . . Gavilan College wins state small JC football crown over Mira Costa, 16-0, forfeits title for transfer rule violations . . . Saratoga's Dan Herick scores 38 in 73-68 hoops win over Gonzales . . . Saratoga defeats St. Francis, 32-30, in CCS grid final . . . Stanford rebound king Rich Kelley retrieves school record 27 in 78-77 loss to Kentucky.

■ 1974 ■

Willow Glen High records fall when Mike Rudder hits 37 in 103-64 trouncing of Live Oak . . . Eastridge Mites hockey team takes Montreal by storm, winning six of seven . . . In just two weeks, Francie Larrieu sets world indoor marks in mile, two-mile, 1,500 meters, U. S. outdoor 1,500-meter record . . . Ken Spalding's jumper puts Leigh High over century mark for first time in 105-80 win against Blackford . . . Camden High takes league title with 67-49 victory over Del Mar as Ray Townsend sinks 35 . . . De Anza College (25-5) whips WVC, 93-69, for league crown with Mitch Platt hitting 24, K. C. Jackson, Russ Carlson adding 22 each . . . Donnell Jackson is heavyweight champ as SJS takes second straight PCAA wrestling . . . Vicki Hayes, Stanford's one-woman team, sets 50-yard breaststroke mark in national collegiate swim meet . . . Ray Lunny III remains undefeated with unpopular 10 round draw against Miguel Mayon . . . Ray Townsend (Camden), Korky Nelson (Oak Grove) on all-Northern California prep hoops squad . . . Phil Convertino's two homers lead SCU to 12-3 win over San Francisco Giants . . . Dan Kikuchi repeats as grand champion in SJS's 13th straight win in NCAA judo tourney . . . Steve Hug of Stanford takes third straight NCAA gymnastics all-around title . . . Dennis Smith of SJS rips six hits with two home runs in 15-5 win over UCSB . . . Ayer nips Milpitas, 1-0, with Louis Rodriguez throwing no-hitter with 11 Ks, including nine in a row . . . Foothill steals 11 bases in win over WVC for league title . . . Jim Visher posts nine-inning strikeout mark for SJS with 20 against USC . . . Jay Pushkin of

Foothill tops JC state discus field . . . Foothill captures state JC swim title, sets seven national records . . . Gene Delyon leads SCU (38-17) with school record .420 average, NCAA record 19 home runs . . . Cubberley High's Pam Blackburn wins state high jump, Silver Creek's Millard Hampton -- only winner of three section 100, 220 races -- speeds 21.1 in state 220 . . . SJS sophomore Mark Schilling runs 4:04 mile . . . Jerry Machado, Gus Albers of SCU capture national college pairs without coxswain race . . . Rick Foley pitches, bats Leigh High to 16th straight win, beating Sunnyvale for CCS title, 5-1 . . . Gary Vandewegh is county golf champ . . . Don Gale wins over-45 state tennis singles over Butch Krikorian . . . In all-Stanford final, John Whitlinger beats fraternity brother Chico Hagey for NCAA tennis singles title. Cardinal takes team crown, Whitlinger, Jim Delaney win doubles . . . Gary Lynn of Los Gatos High scores four TDs as South tops North, 48-36, in Almaden Rotary's first all-star game. Another star is North's tight end Doug Cosbie (St. Francis), who plays at SCU, later is NFL all-pro with Dallas . . . Barry Nathan of Palo Alto defeats Yit Louie of Sunnyvale for state men's over-35 tennis title . . . Sunnyvale's Roger Hedlund sets four world records for land speed by electric car in his "Battery Box" on Utah's salt flats . . . Forrest Fezler has first win on pro golf tour, taking $20,000 in Southern Open . . . Branham High clips Saratoga's 21-game win streak, 20-12, takes first league grid title. Bruins' Mike Terronez gains 135 yards behind blocking of Howard Meyer, moved from tackle to fullback for game . . . CCS player of the year Paul Jones plows 367 yards in 43 carries for Mitty High in 46-7 romp over Serra. Jones sets county records with 2,221 yards rushing, 32 TDs . . . Paul Frederickson of De Anza leads field as Dons win Northern California JC cross-country . . . Los Gatos defeats Campbell, 35-19, on Steve Hosmer's five TD passes . . . SJCC beats Laney, 34-12, for first grid title. Future Cal, New York Jets' running back Tom Newton (Overfelt) sets Jags' single game mark with 287 yards. Jags fall to East Los Angeles, 33-14, in state final . . . Stanford trips California, 22-20, on Mike Langford's last second 50-yard field goal . . . Despite nine road games, SJS (8-3-1) has best year in two decades as QB Craig Kimball rewrites passing records with 175 for 355 attempts, 2,401 yards, 23 TDs . . . SJS (13-3-3) knocked out of NCAA soccer playoffs by UCLA in three OTs, 3-2 . . . Awalt High's Terry Martin passes for 296 yards as Spartans topple Leland, 21-14 for CCS crown before 12,500 . . . SJCC guard Manny Fernandez, linebacker Jim Reed make JC All-America team . . . Andy Pecota hits 28 as Peterson High rips Branham, 79-68.

■ 1975 ■

Russ Carlson's 25 leads De Anza to record 108-71 win over San Mateo . . . In first win over UCLA since 1966, Stanford stops No. 2-ranked Bruins' 12-win streak with Rich Kelley, Ed Schweitzer each canning 22. Two nights later, Kelley tallies 30 as Cardinal handles No. 5 USC, 63-62 . . . Dan Ripley of SJS sets world indoor pole vault mark at 18-1 . . . UCLA's Francie Larrieu erases women's world indoor 1,000-meter record, later smashes outdoor mile mark with 4:28.5 against USSR . . . Vester Robinson has 25 as SCU scores 26 of 42 field goals on layups in 92-77 win over Loyola . . . Foothill College record falls in 113-60 win over Diablo Valley. Steve Maehl has 23 . . . De Anza beats WVC for conference title, 76-71. Warren Jackson hits 35 for Dons, who lose to L. A. Harbor in state playoffs . . . Tip-in by top CCS player Kurt Rambis gives Cupertino High 61-60 section final victory over St. Ignatius . . . Los Altos High breaks school mark, recording 64th straight track dual meet victory against Peterson . . . Valley Christian High sophomore Kevin Flanagan bowls consecutive 300 games at Alma Bowl . . . Sunnyvale High tops Homestead, 13-3, on Joe Santiago's grand slam, three-run triple . . . Diane Kalliam racks up record .641 batting average as Santa Clara Laurels finish second in U. S. women's fast pitch softball tourney . . . Dan Kikuchi wins third NCAA heavyweight judo title as SJS takes 14th team crown . . . Tri-Valley defeats San Jose Winchesters for Western Basketball Association semi-pro title, 108-106 . . . SJS takes PCAA tennis, golf, track titles. Ron Livers high jumps 7-2 in league meet, wins NCAA triple jump . . . Mitty High's Fred Long strikes out 18 in win over Riordan, 6-0 . . . Don Gale takes state over-45 tennis singles from Butch Krikorian . . . Deformed arm doesn't stop Awalt High's Ken Stott from being selected all-league as pitcher, football defensive back . . . Don Thomas of SJS defeats Rick Gordon in sudden death playoff for county golf crown . . . Pioneer High pitcher Gary Kleinfeldt, Mitty outfielder Mike Codiroli make All-Nor Cal team. Carney Lansford leads Wilcox into CCS baseball finals, but El Camino takes title, 9-3 . . . Leigh High's Conrad Suhr wins state 880 in 1:51.0 . . . SJCC ties Glendale for state JC track title as Cal Overstreet (100), Don Livers (220) speed to victory . . . Jeff Robinson of Los Gatos captures state junior tennis singles . . . Fred Samara of San Jose takes AAU decathlon . . . Golfer Roger Maltbie (Lick) wins first pro title in Quad City (Ill.) Open . . . Mike Bruner of De Anza Swim Club wins AAU 800-meter freestyle . . . Infielder Randy Duarte (Branham) steals 31 bases, hits .435 at Iowa State to set four Big Eight records, win All-America acclaim . . . Cirildo Rodriguez first Police Athletic League boxer to capture national Junior Olympics title . . . Ron Livers of SJS tops 7-4 1/4 in high jump in USA-Africa meet . . . Harry Goularte of Morgan Hill leads all the way to win first 100-lap Silver Cup stock car race at Speedway . . . Mike Bauer of Leland High repeats as county junior golf champ . . . Stanford's Mike Langford kicks 33-yard field goal with nine seconds left to tie No. 3 Michigan, 19-19, boots 37-yard field goal on last play to give Cardinal win over USC, 13-10 . . . Westmont High beats Blackford, 50-32, as Ben Skarmas throws three TDs to Rocky Pena, who catches eight passes for 172 yards . . . Santa Teresa High (630), Piedmont Hills (458) combine for record 1,088 yards total offense in 45-43 shootout won by Saints with nine seconds to go on Mike Profit's 36-yard field goal . . . Rick Kane has fifth straight 100-plus yards rushing game in 31-7 SJS win over San Diego State for PCAA title . . . Kaipo Spencer throws NCAA Div. 2 record 72 times against Portland State, owns many SCU passing marks at season's end . . . Undefeated Los Gatos High (10-0-0) produces 371 points as QB Mike Couchee throws 28 TD passes, Holden Smith averages 30.1 yards per catch. Wildcats miss playoffs when WVAL declines invitation so league teams can play Thanksgiving Day traditionals . . . Santa Teresa High, 0-9-0 in 1974 inaugural season, wins 10 straight before playoff loss to St. Francis . . . Playing hoops on campus for first time since 1951 under world's largest air supported roof, SCU tops Stanford, 70-60, at $4.6 million Toso Pavilion . . . SJS corner back Louis Wright goes to Denver in NFL draft . . . De Anza whips SJCC 76-62. Jaguars' Roy Joshua scores 30, Vance Walberg has 24 for Dons . . . Stanford's Pat Cornett wins state women's amateur golf . . . Giant-killer Mountain View High (9-3-0) upsets Monta Vista (10-1-0) in CCS grid final, 29-16 . . . University of Mexico

Saratoga High football coach Benny Pierce.

women's hoops team defeats De Anza, 49-47. Mary Renneke has 15 for Dons . . . Mark McNamara of Del Mar High scores 17, helps hold Cupertino's Kurt Rambis to 10 as Dons capture Sunnyvale tourney, 60-55 . . . WVC linebacker Steve Bauer is JC all-state . . . All-American back Glenn Cannon of Mount Pleasant High ends career with 4,400 yards, 44 TDs.

■ 1976 ■

After Dick Vermiel's UCLA Bruins upset Ohio State in Rose Bowl, ex-SJS quarterback becomes Philadelphia Eagles' head coach . . .Trailing 18-17 at half, tiny Gilroy High hoops squad stalls against towering Leland, still loses 21-17 . . . With only seven on roster, SJS plays six iron men in 82-80 upset over Cal. Ron Fair has 22 . . . Jack Ledesma's 36 leads Lincoln High over Willow Glen, 60-42 . . . Stanford takes third straight NCAA indoor tennis crown over USC . . . Dan Ripley (SJS) has indoor record 18-3 3/4 pole vault . . . Mike Sargent wins first feature super modified race at Speedway . . . Judo champion J. B. Thompson subs as wrestler to give SJS win over Fullerton State for PCAA title . . . Kurt Rambis scores Cupertino High record 50 against Ravenswood . . . SJS (17-10) falls to San Diego State in first round of PCAA tourney, 67-64 . . . De Anza upsets league hoops co-champs Laney, CCSF in playoffs, loses to Santa Ana in state JC tourney, 64-62 . . . After 102 scoreless minutes, Riordan bests Cupertino for CCS soccer title, 1-0 . . . Section MVP Kurt Rambis hits 17, holds Del Mar's Mark McNamara to four as Cupertino High wins section semifinal, 71-54. Rambis adds 27 in final over St. Ignatius, leads 30-2 Pioneers to TOC consolation crown . . . Lick High wrestler Ryan Kawaoka unbeaten as state 127-pound champ . . . Randy Sumida, Bob Baggott lead SJS to 15th straight NCAA judo crown . . . . SJS women fencers win second national college title behind Stacey Johnson . . . Florida's Houston McTear sets U. S. prep 100-meter record of 10.1 at San Jose Relays . . . San Jose Winchesters win Western Basketball Association playoff crown over Stockton, 121-105. Mike Quick scores 40 . . . Female pro boxers Princess Red Star, Dianne Syverson battle to four-round draw at Civic Auditorium . . . Larry Stefanski of Foothill matches brothers Steve, Rich by winning state JC tennis title . . . SJS women bowlers capture national college title in roll off over Wichita State. Spartans' Dianne Stoops tops with 195 average . . . Leland High gymnast Chris Klipfer wins every event in first CCS championship . . . Roger Maltbie is PGA rookie of the year . . . Marquita Belk of Silver Creek captures 440 at state meet in 55.2 . . . Millard Hampton leads SJCC to state JC title with wins in sprints, 440 relay, takes silver medal in 200, gold in relay at Olympics . . . Camden wins first CCS softball crown, 9-1, over Santa Clara . . . Stanford's Mike Bruner, John Hencken, Kim Peyton take Olympic gold medals. Benny Brown (Sunnyvale, UCLA) runs with winning USA relay team . . . Bruce Wilhelm (Fremont) retains AAU super heavyweight lifting title . . . County junior golf title goes to Phil Shannon (Leland) . . . Stanford ties Concord Aquatics in AAU water polo final, loses title on results against other teams . . . Stanford downs SJS in aerial circus, 28-23, with Cardinal's Guy Benjamin 25 for 41, 277 yards, Spartans' Steve DeBerg 21 for 34, 235 yards . . . Mervyn Fernandez scores decider on 45-yard end around in last quarter of Hill High's 32-20 win over Santa Teresa . . . Stu Pederson rips off 179 yards in record 39 carries as Palo Alto High tops Awalt, 26-6 . . . Casey Wingard crosses goal line four times in fourth quarter as SJCC whips WVC, 35-18 . . . Charlie Pasarell defeats Andrew Pattison for Tennis Classic of San Jose singles title at Civic Auditorium . . . Los Altos High wins, 16-3, but fourth quarter, 25-yard field goal by Mountain View's David Azcueta ends Knights' county record-tying shutout string at seven . . . Steve Swadley's two goals leads SJS to 4-1 soccer win over Washington in NCAA, but Spartans fall to national champion USF, 5-0 . . . Willow Glen High first CCS field hockey champ over Lynbrook, 2-1 . . . SCU downs Fresno State, 20-17, on Lou Marengo's 43-yard field goal with nine seconds to go . . . Tim O'Hare's goal gives Foothill 1-0 win over Santa Ana for state JC soccer title . . . SJCC defeats Contra Costa in Bay Bowl for regional crown, 24-19 . . . Goalie Chris Dorst is MVP as Stanford whips UCLA to capture NCAA water polo, 13-12 . . . Saratoga is state's No. 3 after winning CCS grid title, 17-3, over Leland . . . All-time assist leader Ken Mickey sets SJS mark with 17 against Illinois State . . . Mark McNamara has 33 points, 23 rebounds in Del Mar High's 79-70 win over Wilson of San Francisco . . . All-State: Kyle Stevens of Yerba Buena High, who rushes county record 2,004 yards, Leland tackle Pat Graham. Saratoga's Benny Pierce, who will end career in 1990s with 270-84-4 record, is coach of the year . . . Miami's No. 1 pick Kim Bokamper (SJS) is East-West Shrine's best defender.

■ 1977 ■

Wayne Whitworth's 26 leads Overfelt High to record 106-38 win over Hill . . . Tom Watson (Stanford) captures Crosby Pro-Am golf tourney with four-round record low of 273 . . . Roscoe Tanner (Stanford) takes Australian tennis open . . . SJS downs Long Beach State, 75-76, at Independence High before 4,000 fans, largest hoops crowd to watch Spartans in San Jose . . . Russ Dyer hits 20, hauls down 20 rebounds as Branham High snaps Del Mar's 22-game win streak, 54-50 . . . Jiri Hrebek defeats Sandy Mayer in San Jose Grand Prix tennis singles finale . . . Goal by Leigh's Perry Jones in OT gives Longhorns 3-2 win over Saratoga for CCS soccer title. Los Altos bows to Woodside for first girl's crown, 1-0 . . . WVC's Steve Oravetz (Campbell) sets national JC pole vault record at 17-1 . . . SJCC's Roy Joshua makes JC All-State . . . Mary Hile's 13 points, 17 rebounds lead Peterson High to first CCS girl's basketball title over Camden,

Stanford players celebrate their 27-24 Big Game win over California to regain The Axe in 1976.

39-32 . . . All-Nor Cal Mark McNamara leads Del Mar (30-3) to second straight third place finish in TOC . . . Dave Schultz of Palo Alto High wins state 168-pound wrestling title . . . Rick Foley twirls SCU's first no-hit game since 1968, blanking St. Mary's, 4-0 . . . Del Mar High baseball players don shorts in some games . . . State champs: Lynbrook's Kris Costello, low hurdles; Camden's Ann Regan, 880; Independence's Roxanne Bier, two-mile; Silver Creek's Andre Phillips, low hurdles; Willow Glen's Mark Stillman, mile . . . Mark Schilling victor in 880, 1,500 as SJS wins PCAA track crown . . . Gary Scott captures U. S. 25-mile motorcycle title before 15,000 at Fairgrounds . . . Leland takes third consecutive CCS golf crown. Vince Baxter of Los Gatos shoots 70 for medal honors . . . Stanford beats Trinity, 5-4, for NCAA tennis title. Stanford's Matt Mitchell (Gunn) wins NCAA singles . . . Sandra Woodruff retains county women's golf title . . . Barbara May of Live Oak High wins section all-around gymnastics championship . . . Buchser High battery of pitcher Rob Ferguson, catcher Dave Hodgins, is All-Nor Cal . . . Miguel Avila, Cam Ackerman score as Santa Clara Soccer Club wins McGuire Cup under-19 soccer crown over Dallas, 2-1 . . . Golfer Tom Watson wins British Open . . . Marc Brant of San Jose wins junior men's eight-mile race at U. S. cycling championships in Seattle . . . Marisela Maurcio of San Jose pitches 57 percent ringers to capture state women's horseshoe title . . . Bellarmine opens with 48-12 whipping of Silver Creek behind QB Mike Jones' five TD passes. Bells score 40 or more points in record seven straight games before losing two of last three . . . Steve Dils to James Lofton scoring strike with 32 seconds left gives Stanford 32-28 win over UCLA . . . Kent Gerber of Los Gatos High throws record seven TD passes as Wildcats crush Blackford, 60-30 . . . Lincoln High's Robbie Rocha snares 11 passes, intercepts three more in 27-0 win over Gilroy . . . After playing home basketball games off campus for years, Bellarmine opens $1.2 million Wayne Valley Gym . . . NFL first round draft pick is SJS defensive linemen Wilson Faumuina by Atlanta . . . State JC cross-country crowns go to SJCC (men), De Anza (women). Ann Wotherspoon of WVC takes individual title . . . Mel Holland paces Silver Creek High with 34 in 66-64 win over Leigh, led by John Russo's 27 . . . SJS field hockey team (18-2) first from West to reach winner's bracket at U. S. tourney, finishes third . . . Greg Lambert of Awalt High is MVP as Spartans win section water polo title . . . De Anza takes state JC water polo with Ray Wylie's five goals in 8-5 win over Modesto . . . Willie T. Ribbs of San Jose wins Dunlop Formula Ford auto race in England, named Motor Sports Press Association future star . . . St. Francis takes CCS grid final over North Salinas, 6-3. Lancer linebacker Frank Morze is top CCS defender . . . De Anza's Rich Hersey runs for 1,468 yards in 10 games, named All-State.

■ 1978 ■

Stan Hill rips nets for SJS record 37 points in 76-69 win over Sacramento State . . . Tom Watson wins rain-soaked Crosby Pro-Am . . . Roxanne Bier of Independence High captures national junior women's 10,000 meters . . . Randy Arrillaga hits 49 as Saratoga High drops Fremont, 78-74, in two OTs . . . Terry Visgar takes top driver award from Sports Car Club of America . . . Silver Creek High wins section hoops title over Monta Vista, 45-43, when Mike Baldwin blocks Haakon Austefjord's shot with four seconds left. Raiders lose to McClymonds of Oakland in TOC. Raiders' Mel Holland is All-Nor Cal . . . Lincoln High quintet, averaging 6 feet tall, runs, presses way to 25-5 record, fourth place in CCS basketball tournament . . . Hill High captures state wrestling crown on heavyweight George Achica's pin. Palo Alto's Mark Schultz tops 154-pounders . . . First round NFL draft picks: Stanford tackle Gordon King (New York Giants), wideout James Lofton (Green Bay) . . . Ted Rafalovich has 28 goals, 23 assists for Stanford soccer team . . . SJCC (21-7) whips Canada, 67-61, to enter state JC hoops play, loses to Bakersfield . . . UCLA guard Ray Townsend (Camden) is Golden State Warriors' No. 1 choice. Younger brother Kurt (Camden) leads Menlo College to conference title, makes JC All-State . . . Lansford brothers give Wilcox High 7-6 victory over Campbell as Phil blasts three-run homer, Jody smacks grand slam . . . Duncan McDonald (Stanford) wins inaugural San Jose Mercury-News 6.6-mile race. Roxanne Bier tops women . . . Largest track and field crowd in city's history (8,000) at SJCC for San Jose Relays. UCLA's Greg Foster blazes over high hurdles in 13.3 . . . SJS grabs fourth straight U. S. collegiate women's fencing title against Penn, 90-88. Spartans' Stacey Johnson takes second crown in three years . . . Monta Vista High's Mark Cipres strikes out 17 Lynbrook batters . . . SJS judo team wins 17th straight NCAA title. Spartan women take their first. Champs: Mike Vincent, Keith Nakasone, Colleen Fitzpatrick, Dolores Brod . . . SJS women take fourth straight Western college bowling title. Men win first . . . SCU's Rick Foley no-hits SJS, 3-0 . . . San Jose Portuguese top San Francisco Glens for Far West amateur title, 4-2 . . . Bill Bender belts Giants' pitching for five hits, but SCU loses, 8-3, before 7,220 . . . Arthur Ashe defeats Bernie Mitton, wins $8,500 in Smythe Grand Prix tennis singles at Toso Pavilion. Gene, Sandy Mayer (Stanford) down Hank Pfister, Brad Rowe (SJS) in doubles . . . Lincoln High boxer Al Romero wins national AAU light-heavyweight crown . . . Pepe Hinojosa gets three walks for Stanford in 7-5 win over St. Mary's, sets NCAA

Stanford hoops great Jeanne Ruark Hoff averaged 17.6 points from 1978 to 1983.

career record of 203, finishes with 221 . . . SJCC's Thurlis Gibbs sets national JC high jump mark at 7-3 1/4 . . . Lynbrook High dethrones 12-time section swim champion Santa Clara as Vikings Todd Trowbridge, Chris Cavanaugh each take two events . . . San Jose's Ross Packard ties pro record with three 300 games in Alma Bowl tournament . . . Frank Johnson has two homers, five RBIs, but SJS (40-24) falls to SCU in NCAA playoff, 10-9. Fullerton eliminates Broncos . . . Ron Livers of SJS wins third straight NCAA triple jump, Stanford's James Lofton takes long jump . . . Independence High scores 10 runs in CCS title game's last inning, takes Soquel, 10-3. Lincoln High pitcher Ron McGee (13-0) is section player of the year . . . Wayne Gray of WVC wins state JC decathlon . . . Andrew Hill High wins state girl's track title with Kelia Bolton first in 100, 220. Camden's Ann Regan (880), Lynbrook's Kris Costello (hurdles) also champs . . . Dave Righetti (Pioneer) registers 9-3, 2.32 ERA record at SJCC. In start for Texas Rangers' farm club in Tulsa, strikes out Texas League record 21 batters . . . San Jose's Robin White captures state girl's 16-under tennis . . . SJCC's Andre Phillips takes 400 hurdles, anchors winning mile relay team in state JC meet . . . Fontanetti's Sporting Goods ends 16-year Humboldt hold on state semi-pro baseball, beating Crabs twice in Eureka. Shortstop Ruben Zarate is tournament MVP . . . Unbeaten Stanford whips UCLA for second straight NCAA tennis title. Freshman John McEnroe wins singles, turns pro . . . San Jose's Ben Rogers wins bow hunter division in U. S. field archery title . . . Foothill pitcher Henry Torres (10-4) is JC All-State . . . All-America outfielder Dave Stieb (Oak Grove) bats .394 with 12 home runs at Southern Illinois . . . San Jose's Larry Lundin grabs NASCAR stock car title at Speedway . . . Peterson High crushes Mountain View, 57-14, with Ben Bennett throwing for 274 yards, five TDs . . . Ex-Lincoln High combo of QB Rick Rebozzi to receiver Robbie Rocha accounts for three TDs in Gavilan's 24-22 win over Hartnell . . . Steve Dils cranks up arm for 32 completions, 430 yards, five scores as Stanford whips Washington State, 43-27 . . . SJS teammates Lisa Goedecke, Juli Simpson tie for county women's golf title. Goedecke wins playoff . . . Lee Leeson of Sunnyvale wins 45-mile American Road Race of Champions at Atlanta . . . Rich Hersey has two last quarter TDs as No. 3 De Anza downs No. 2 San Mateo, 19-17 . . . SCU upsets UC-Davis, 26-20, with Dave Alfaro passing for 208 yards, two TDs . . . SJS defeats Pacific, 33-31, on last second five-yard TD pass from Ed Luther to Rick Parma . . . Gavilan's All-State Clay Richards leads with 10 interceptions . . . NCAA bans SJS soccer team (19-3-0) from playoffs because of ineligible player . . . De Anza's Pat Yates scores eight goals as Dons take north state water polo over College of Sequoias, 20-12 . . . Kathy Perkins leads WVC to state JC cross-country title . . . Randy Arrillaga hits 31, Marty Abate 30 in Saratoga High's 106-67 win over Mountain View . . . Peterson High gains revenge for earlier 47-0 loss to Los Altos, beating Knights, 17-14, on Jacques DeBra's 23-yard field goal as time expires . . . De Anza falls to Santa Ana in state soccer final, 2-1 . . . Rhonda Clark's 27 paces Los Gatos High girls to 77-17 hoops win over Leigh . . . Oak Grove High embarrasses St. Francis in CCS grid final, 52-7 . . . Stanford tops No. 3 UCLA 75-72, with Wolfe Perry hitting 34 . . . Ayer High's Gary Hopkins pours in 48, but Randy Arrillaga's 17-footer gives Saratoga 79-77 win in St. Francis tourney final. They're CCS co-MVPs.

■ 1979 ■

Foothill defeats De Anza, 71-63, behind Tony Hentley's 37 points . . . Kathlene Koudela of Monta Vista High tops women in Paul Masson Marathon . . . Luanne Ferguson sinks 29 points as Homestead downs Monta Vista . . . Saratoga establishes CCS playoff mark with 113-103 win over Menlo-Atherton. Falcon's Randy Arrillaga tops section with 27.8 average, is Nor Cal player of the year . . . St. Francis High teams set combined boy-girl basketball mark with 59-3 record as boys (32-2) take CCS, 48-46, over Fremont, but girls lose for first time to Terra Nova, 60-44 . . . CCS girl's soccer title goes to Monta Vista High, 2-1, over Saratoga on Allison McCargo's goal in fifth OT . . . Future USC All-America and Baltimore Colts tackle George Achica of Hill High closes wrestling career with 130-6 record, one state, three CCS titles . . . Pat Rodgers scores 20 as St. Francis falls to Castlemont of Oakland, 71-53, in TOC final . . . Tracy Ambler (Santa Teresa) hits 21 as Cabrillo tops Butte, 68-64, for state JC women's crown . . . Mary Hile (Peterson) has USF record 39 points, 23 rebounds against Pepperdine . . . Buchser High's Roy Sanfillipo whiffs 14 Cubberley batters in 3-1 win . . . Neal Pyke of Palo Alto sets U. S. 5,000-meter mark at Stanford Relays . . . Keith Nakasone, Geraldo Padilla, Mike Stubblefield take individual honors as SJS captures NCAA judo crown. Lady Spartans win second consecutive women's title . . . Led by Joy Ellingson, Diane Knoblach, SJS wins fifth straight national college fencing title . . . Renaldo Nehemiah speeds to world record 13.16 clocking in 110 hurdles at Bruce Jenner Classic . . . John McEnroe (Stanford) downs Peter Fleming in two-hour, 40 minute final of Smythe Grand Prix tennis tournament at Civic Auditorium . . . After hour rain delay, 41 lead changes, San Jose's Steve Eklund wins San Jose Mile motorcycle race at Fairgrounds . . . Ron Earl (SJS), Marty Goffstein take U. S. handball master's doubles . . . Fresno State's Dan Gladden (Monta Vista, Westmont, De Anza) hits two-run home run in 4-0 victory over SJS in NCAA. Gene Menges of SJS (39-20) is region's coach of the year for second time . . . Mark Ackernecht steals 33rd, 34th bases for Oak Grove High in playoff victory over Independence . . . John Sevely of Foothill is state JC tennis singles champion . . . League MVP Rick Dominguez of SJCC has three hits, four RBIs

Anchored by Bill Green, who set a national prep record of 45.51 at 400 meters earlier in the year, the Cubberley High relay team won the CCS title in 1979. From left, Jess Moss, Chris Cooke, Terry Smith and Green.

in 13-2 state JC playoff opener over Oxnard. Jaguars fall to Cerritos . . . State prep track winners: Camden's Ann Regan (880), Cubberley's Bill Green (100) . . . Bowlers Mark Roth, Marshall Holman take $16,000 in Columbia Doubles Classic at Saratoga Lanes . . . Jody Lansford of Wilcox High is top CCS baseball player . . . Stanford's Kathy Jordan captures AIAW tennis singles, doubles with Alycia Moulton . . . WVC wins state JC track as Ann Wotherspoon captures 3,000. SJCC's mile relay team (Eloise Mallory, Della Hampton, Tina Gibbs, Jocelyn West) breaks U. S. mark, Jags' Willie Jackson (100, 200), Andre Phillips (110, 400 hurdles) win . . . Cubberley High's Bill Green produces U. S. high school record 45.51 in 400 meters . . . Cindergals capture third straight AAU national age group cross-country title . . . With only 20 players on hand, Lincoln High drops football for year . . . SCU's Dave Alfaro, who leads NCAA Div. II passers, completes 20 of 23 for 298 yards, four TDs in 35-6 win over Simon Fraser . . . Ken Naber's 56-yard field goal with no time left gives Stanford 27-24 win over UCLA . . . Steve Eklund is first non-factory rider in 25 years to capture U. S. pro dirt track motorcycle championship . . . Brian Oldfield of Sunnyvale tosses 18-pound stone for record 63-1 at Scottish Games in Campbell . . . In last home football game before Campbell High closes, Bucs trample Branham, 48-7, behind John Simpson's 274 rushing yards, four TDs . . . Ben Bennett's 21 for 35 passes, 374 yards, five TDs too much for Santa Clara High as Peterson wins, 36-20 . . . After trailing 21-0, SJS beats UOP, 32-21. Ed Luther hits 34 passes for 421 yards . . . Terry Davis pours in 40 points in Lincoln High's 97-94 victory over Harbor . . . 46-yard Jack Overstreet to Mervyn Fernandez pass sets up Scott Hertler's winning 32-yard field goal as De Anza downs Contra Costa in Bay Bowl, 15-14, for first undefeated (11-0) season. Center Mike Farley makes All-State . . . Debbi Vanni's goal gives De Anza 1-0 win over Golden West in state JC field hockey final . . . Saratoga High whips Leigh, 77-61, behind Marty Abate's 38 . . . CCS volleyball champ Fremont loses state title match to Palisades . . . Sally Voss (Stanford) wins state women's amateur golf crown . . . Salinas High ends Oak Grove's 23-game victory streak in section playoffs, 32-29, but loses CCS grid title to St. Francis, 23-22, with eight seconds remaining on Mike Naki's TD pass to Jim Friedl plus PAT by Bill Leonard . . . Nor Cal player of the year Marty Mornhinweg of Oak Grove High ends career with state record 62 TD tosses . . . Santa Clara High's Linda Walsh tops Wilcox, 59-32, with 37 points, 21 rebounds. Her freshman sister, Margaret, adds another 18.

The 1980s

Neither San Jose, the California League, nor Organized Baseball had ever seen a team quite like the 1987 Bad News Bees, an aggregation of major league castoffs and under-skilled hopefuls who set records for futility.

During the decade's first eight years, only the 1980 San Jose team finished above .500. The 1987 team, operating as an independent club without firm ties to a big league club, was unbelievably bad, setting league records for fewest wins (33), most losses (109) and worst percentage (.232).

The road to the mother of all cellar finishes could be traced back to 1981, when Joe Gagliardi sold the franchise to Woody Kern and became the California League's president. The team affiliated with the Montreal Expos for a year with Harry Steve taking over as general manager.

The renamed San Jose Bees went independent in 1983, getting help from several major league teams and gaining nationwide publicity through an arrangement that brought players from the Seibu Lions of Japan's pro league.

The Bees were near the bottom of the standings annually and attendance, which had been a shade below 100,000 in 1981, fell to nearly half that over the next four seasons. Clearly something had to be done to save the financially distressed franchise.

The era of the Bad News Bees began in 1986, when Steve abandoned the successful program that had sent nearly 90 players to the majors over the years. Instead of loading his roster with young prospects, Steve began signing former big league players whose names he believed might attract more fans to Municipal Stadium.

Among the available veteran players with troubled pasts involving abuse of drugs or alcohol were pitchers Mike Norris and Steve Howe and infielder Ken Reitz.

Norris, who had won 22 games for the Oakland Athletics in 1980, still was unreliable, was dropped after repeated tardiness, then returned briefly to post a 4-3 record.

Howe, a former Dodger fire balling southpaw reliever, won the home opener before a crowd of 4,911, but became ineligible after testing positive for drugs. Reitz hit .233 in 111 games while Japanese second baseman Norio Tanabe led the team with a .306 batting average.

Steve managed the team himself until mid-June when he was succeeded by Mike Verdi with the Bees standing last in the Western Division at 27-40. The team rose to 37-34 in the second half and had its best box office showing in five years at 87,235.

Former big league first baseman Daryl Sconiers was the only bright spot in 1987, batting .313 on a team that hit an abysmal .207 to finish last in both halves and 61 games behind Stockton.

San Jose fans were given a reprieve the following year, when a group headed by Palo Alto residents Tony Cox and Richard Beahrs bought the team for an estimated $400,000. They signed an agreement with the San Francisco Giants, who had dropped their farm club in Fresno, and the San Jose Giants were born. Steve stayed on as general manager.

Success was immediate. Under the guidance of manager Duane Espy, the Giants had the league's second best record (.636) and took the second half division title, only to lose to Stockton in the playoffs. Attendance soared beyond 100,000 for the first time in 15 years.

San Jose was led at the plate by Mark Leonard (.345), an outfielder from St. Francis High School and De Anza College who topped the circuit with 118 RBIs and a team record 50 doubles, and Rich Aldrete, who hit .301. Pitcher Eric Gunderson had a 12-5 mark and led the team with 151 strikeouts in 149 innings.

The Giants closed out the decade in 1989 with another trip to the playoffs and another loss to Stockton as attendance rose slightly to 108,458. Pitching was strong with Mark Dewey picking up a league record 30 saves, Steve Lienhard (12-3) tops in ERA at 1.79 and Bryan Hickerson (11-6) and Rod Beck (11-2) as major contributors.

■ NICE ON THE ICE

Until the 1980s, Santa Clara County had never been thought of as an incubator for international ice skating stars, with one notable exception.

Even that exception came with an asterisk. Although Peggy Fleming was born in San Jose and now resides in Los Gatos, she lived and honed her skills elsewhere while winning five consecutive U. S. women's figure skating titles and three straight world championships in the 1960s.

Her crowning achievement was at the 1968 Winter Olympics in Grenoble, France. Skating effortlessly and elegantly, Fleming wowed the audience with her agility and poise and took the USA's only gold medal.

The first truly local champion was Brian Boitano of Sunnyvale, who appeared on the scene in the late 1970s. As a 13-year-old, Boitano won the freestyle competition in the 1977 men's national novice figure skating championships. A year later, he took the U. S. junior men's title.

Debi Thomas, a 13-year-old San Jose girl, captured the U. S. novice championship in 1980, performing on a pair of third-hand used skates. By 1982, she was doing well in senior skating events.

That same year, San Jose's 12-year-old Rudy Galindo

Ice skating champions (from left) Brian Boitano, Rudy Galindo and Debi Thomas.

competed at the national championships and Boitano won a gold medal in the National Sports Federation competition.

At the 1985 U. S. figure skating championships, Boitano took gold in men's singles and Thomas was third in the women's event. The medals kept on coming as Boitano took bronze at the world's championships and both he and Thomas won gold at the National Sports Federation.

Thomas and Boitano captured national titles the next season and Thomas, by now a Stanford premed student, skated off with the world title and ABC's Wide World of Sports' athlete of the year award.

Galindo was back in the news, partnering with Fremont's Kristie Yamaguchi in doubles competitions. They won the world junior pairs title in Australia in 1987, the same year Boitano missed what would have been an historic quadruple jump in the 1987 nationals, when he captured the men's title. Thomas failed to repeat as U. S. champion but continued training for the coming Olympics.

Boitano and Thomas won at the 1988 nationals and Boitano proved he was the best male skater in the world by taking Olympic gold with eight perfect triple jumps. Thomas took the bronze medal and she and Boitano turned pro. Thomas retired four years later to enter medical school.

Yamaguchi and Galindo showed there were more medals in their futures as they won the U. S. pairs in 1989 and Kristie took an individual silver. They won again in 1990, but split up to skate as singles. Yamaguchi won two world titles and was U. S. and Olympic champion in 1992.

Galindo's greatest moment came in 1996. Skating on home ice at San Jose Arena, the 26-year-old upset three-time United States champion Todd Eldridge to become the oldest person to win the national title. Two months later Eldridge captured the Olympic title with Galindo taking the bronze medal.

■ POSTSEASON HOOPS

The 1970s hadn't provided much excitement for college basketball fans, with only Santa Clara's men and Stanford's women breaking out of the doldrums and into the NCAA playoffs. But that began to change early in the new decade.

San Jose State, missing from the NCAA lineup since 1951 and coming off a 7-20 season, showed early signs of life in 1979-80 under new head coach Bill Berry.

With a 3-3 record that included two overtime losses, the Spartans pulled off the Cable Car Classic's biggest shocker, dumping unbeaten and highly regarded Virginia, 83-79, and holding 7-foot-4 Ralph Sampson to 12 points.

The Spartans were led through their 17-12 campaign by senior Wally Rank, who hit 16.3 points a game, scored a team record 40 points against Sacramento State and finished the year as the school's third all-time points producer with 1,432. San Jose closed the season with a 61-51 loss to Missouri in the NCAA's first round.

The next season, Sid Williams averaged 15.1 to end his career as the ninth best scorer in history as the 21-9 Spartans went to the NIT and lost to Texas-El Paso, 57-53.

Santa Clara was the next school to step into the post-season parade, gaining four NIT invitations and another to the NCAA tournament.

The best of the lot may have been the first NIT team, a 22-10 aggregation headed in 1983-84 by juniors Howard Keeling (18.3), Nick Vanos (17.0) and Fremont High's Scott Lamson (9.0), with strong rebounding help from Mike Norman of St. Francis High. They took two tournament games on the road against Oregon and Lamar, then were blown out, 97-76, at Southwest Louisiana in the quarterfinals. They were back the next year with a 20-9 mark, but lost a heartbreaking NIT opener at Fresno State, 79-76.

Coach Carroll Williams' 1986-87 team (18-14) went to the NCAA as WCC tourney champs with Dan Weiss (Independence) and Jens Gordon leading the way to the title over Pepperdine. The Broncos fell to Iowa in the NCAA opener. Gordon led the 1988-89 five back to the NIT, but a loss to New Mexico left SCU with a 20-10 record.

Stanford quintets also came on strong at the end of the decade. In 1987-88, the men produced an 88-70 NIT win over Long Beach State as Todd Lichti tossed in 34, but

Arkansas State defeated the Cardinal in the next round.

After suffering four straight postseason losses dating to 1978, Katy Steding led the Cardinal women to an NCAA playoff victory over Montana in OT, 74-72, to make the Elite Eight, where they lost to Texas, 79-58. Rated No. 13 by AP, the Cardinal finished the season with a 27-5 record.

Both Stanford teams were ranked in 1988-89 and Tara VanDerveer was named women's coach of the year. The AP rated the 28-3 women in the top 10 for first time at No. 4 as they ran off 22 straight wins including a 98-74 NCAA win over Iowa before being eliminated by Louisiana Tech.

The Stanford men (26-7) were rated 12th in the UPI poll, 13th by AP and made their first NCAA appearance since 1942, losing to lowly Siena in an embarrassing 80-78 upset. Four-time All-Pac-10 Lichti led the team with a 20.1 average and finished his career owning 22 conference and school records, including 2,336 career points.

Todd Lichti

■ TIGERS AND BANDITS

Semi-pro football was a staple on the city's sports menu from the late 1970s through the 1980s in a team known first as the Tigers and later as the Bandits.

San Mateo meat broker Lou Cherry was the Tigers' principal owner when the team was organized in 1977. He hired former SCU quarterback Jesse Freitas as head coach.

The Tigers (14-0) drew crowds of up to 3,000 at Police Activities League Stadium where QB Craig Kimball (SJS) and running back Pat Kohlman (SJS) led a high-scoring offense. They won the California Football League playoff against San Gabriel and met the undefeated Pierce County (Wash.) Bengals in a bowl game. The Bengals won, 28-27, on a fumble recovery that was returned 65 yards for a touchdown in the last minute.

Kimball starred again for new coach Billy Wilson's Tigers in 1978, throwing 35 touchdown passes, with 15 going to Eric Dahl (SJS). The team was ranked No. 1 among the nation's semi-pros by Pro Football Weekly.

In two postseason games, the Tigers walloped the Shreveport Steamers, 32-6, in the King Kong Bowl at Louisville for the American Football Association crown and toppled Pierce County, 43-13, before 8,431 spectators in the Holiday Bowl at Spartan Stadium.

The team was ranked first again in 1979, winning its third title in a row as Kimball threw at least one touchdown pass in every game.

The 1980 team finished 12-1, but lost the final league playoff game, 31-0, to the national champion Twin Cities (Yuba City-Marysville) Cougars. In 1981, the club moved its games to Campbell High and was dubbed the Campbell-San Jose Tigers. Another successful season closed with an 18-10 playoff loss to Twin Cities.

After being absent for a year, Kimball returned in 1982 to direct the team, which tied Twin Cities with a 9-1 record. They met in the league playoff at Municipal Stadium, but the Tigers lost again, 31-9, and the league folded.

A new semi-pro outfit known as the Bandits organized in 1985 and played an independent schedule before joining the American Football Association for several seasons. The Bandits met teams in California and other states. Newspaper coverage was spotty to non-existent and efforts to develop an accurate record of the team have been unsuccessful.

■ TRIVIAL PURSUITS

In the "my how times have changed" department, Bellarmine football coach Walt Arnold remarked at the start of the 1980 season that the Bells had "never won a CCS championship in anything but speech and debate."

In 1981, 12 cities in the county provided softball competition for 17,500 players on nearly 1,100 teams.

In hopes of evening the odds against highly ranked Catholic rivals Riordan and St. Ignatius in the 1981 CCS basketball playoffs, Gunn High players joked they played for "St. Gunn." The Titans handed Riordan a 47-43 OT loss in the semis, but fell to SI in the final, 56-54. Kent Lockhart scored 26 for Gunn to end his career with 1,484, ninth highest points total in CCS history at the time.

In 1984, Stanford's John Paye became the second NCAA freshman to start on both the varsity football and basketball teams. Indiana's Quinn Buckner was the first in the 1972-73 season.

Cupertino High's two-man team of Pete Thompson (discus) and Roger Creedon (shot put), took first and third in their events in the 1984 Northern California meet to give the Pioneers fourth place, the highest among CCS teams.

Branham High's high scoring Gary Radunich was the quintessential high school hoops hot dog. In one 1985 game, he shot one free throw right-handed and a second southpaw. Another time, Radunich made a jump shot and trotted to the water fountain for a celebratory drink. Radunich dropped the "u" from his last name and went on to a career as one of the Bay Area's most popular radio and television sports broadcasters.

San Jose Mercury-News columnist Charles Bricker reported in 1987 that Bill Walsh's master's thesis, "Flank Formation Football," was missing and presumed stolen from the San Jose State library files. Not about offense, Walsh's work described defending against the pro attack.

■ BOWLING WITH THE SPARTANS

The most successful period in modern San Jose State football history saw the Spartans go to four postseason bowl games between 1981 and 1990 while compiling an overall record of 70-43-2.

Jack Elway was in his third season as head coach in 1981 when the Spartans (9-3-0) beat both Stanford and Cal in football in the same year for the first time.

Wide receiver Mervyn Fernandez (Hill, De Anza) scored all three Spartan touchdowns in the California Bowl at Fresno, but Toledo upset SJS, 27-25. Steve Clarkson went 43 for 62 for 467 yards and Gerald Willhite, whose Number 47 later was retired, caught 18 passes for 124 yards.

With QB Mike Perez leading the country in total offense in 1986, San Jose State (10-2-0) returned to the California Bowl. The Spartans came out on top this time against Miami of Ohio, 37-7, in the school's first postseason win in 37 years. Head coach Claude Gilbert's defense intercepted five passes and MVP Perez threw for three touchdowns.

Perez was the most valuable player again the following season, but the Spartans (10-2-0) fell to Eastern Michigan in the California Bowl, 30-27. Perez also won the 1987 Glenn "Pop" Warner Award, given by the Palo Club to the Pacific Coast's top senior football player.

Coach Terry Shea's first team compiled a 9-2-1 mark in 1990, winning the California Raisin Bowl against Central Michigan, 48-24. SJS tailback Sheldon Canley ran for 164 yards and scored five touchdowns.

■ THE PLAY

Stanford fans would rather forget Nov. 20, 1982, but California fans gleefully dedicated a T-shirt to the winning touchdown in the Golden Bears' 25-20 victory at Berkeley.

Whatever your interest in the Big Game, the Bears' multi-lateral extravaganza that sent Kevin Moen into the end zone to score the winner and level a Stanford trombone player will always be known as The Play.

The underdog Cal eleven had taken a 19-17 lead late in the 86th meeting between the Bay Area's biggest college rivals. But, Stanford quarterback John Elway put together one of his best last-minute drives and a field goal moved Stanford back on top, 20-19.

San Jose State coach Jack Elway (left) consoles his son, Stanford quarterback John Elway, after the Spartans beat the Cardinal, 28-6, in 1981.

A look at the Memorial Stadium clock showed just six seconds remaining. It appeared The Axe would return to The Farm, so Stanford band members were on their feet and headed for the end zone to begin serenading Cardinal fans.

Stanford's short hop kickoff went to Moen who tossed the first of five laterals as the Bears moved up the field toward the end zone. He gathered in the last of the rugby style passes and crashed into the musician with the final score in football's most improbable winning play.

■ GOODBYE EARTHQUAKES

The Earthquakes produced one more great season and two truly exciting players to thrill the Spartan Stadium faithful before the North American Soccer League collapsed in financial ruin in 1985.

George Best, a former world class striker from Northern Ireland who had difficulty staying away from the booze, arrived in 1980. The 5-foot-8 Best had been in the league four years with Los Angeles and Fort Lauderdale, producing 26 goals and 25 assists in his first two seasons

San Jose State bowl stars included back Gerald Willhite (left), who delighted fans by doing a back flip to celebrate scoring a touchdown, and QB Mike Perez.

only to see his production fall off badly in the next two.

San Jose's record improved little during his two years in midfield, but Best put on many marvelous shows despite the fact his skills had eroded badly from when he was one of the world's most exciting players with Manchester United.

The 'Quakes were only 9-23 in 1980 and last in the Western Division, but Best gained the team's MVP award with eight goals and 11 assists. Goalkeeper Mike Hewitt continued to be the fans' favorite, playing behind a porous defense that gave him little help. The 1981 season was only slightly better. San Jose finished in the division cellar again with a slightly improved 11-21 mark.

Best provided the highlight play of the Earthquake's 11-year run, dribbling through most of the Fort Lauderdale team with a remarkable series of fakes to score the NASL's "Goal of the Year." Film of the memorable play at Spartan Stadium appeared from then on in the team's television ads.

By 1982, the NASL was in deep trouble, down to only 14 teams from a high of 24 two years earlier and with attendance off 50 percent in the same period. San Jose averaged 11,011 topped by 15,546 against Tulsa, a crowd boosted by fans waiting to attend a Tubes' post game rock concert.

After failing to report in 1982, Best was suspended and then cut loose. The team, under the new ownership of a group headed by Carl Berg, managed only an 8-8 home record, finishing at 13-19 and next to last in the division.

Renamed the Golden Bay Earthquakes because it played indoor games at the Oakland Coliseum Arena, the team hired Don Popovic as its new coach in 1983. Popovic improved San Jose's chances to be competitive with the signing of forward Steve Zungul and several other key players, including Jan Goosens, Fernando Clavijo and Bill Irwin, who went into goal after Hewitt was sold.

The Yugoslavian Zungul had played exclusively indoors for five season, leading the New York Arrows to four titles while setting league scoring records. Although he missed eight games with a hamstring injury, Zungul still led the team with 16 goals and 15 assists. He and teammate Stan Terlecki both made all-NASL as the Earthquakes won 20 of 30 games to finish second in the division.

The Earthuakes were unbeatable at Spartan Stadium, taking all 15 games. The last home game against Seattle looked like a draw until Leo Cuellar sent 14,271 fans home happy when he scored a goal with just over a minute to go. The 'Quakes clobbered Chicago, 6-1, in the playoff opener and split a pair at Chicago to move into the semifinals. Their season ended when they lost twice to Toronto.

Zungul's presence helped the team during the indoor season. He was the league MVP with 63 goals, 56 assists, eight game winners and 11 hat tricks as the team ended the year 19-13 and lost in the playoffs to San Diego.

The 'Quakes had opened their first year with Paul Child winning the league scoring title in 1974. They did the same in the league's final season in 1984 when Zungul won the crown and was named league MVP.

The team wasn't nearly as successful, closing the season with an 8-16 record and last in the West again. Zungul, Clavijo and Branko Segota were sold to San Diego after the season for $300,000 as 'Quakes owners cut their losses.

Scoring leader Steve Zungul was a soccer MVP both indoors and outdoors for the Earthquakes.

After the NASL folded, Bay Area soccer fans were entertained by the Bay Blackhawks, a Western Soccer League team that played games all over the region, including some in San Jose. Former Earthquakes' owner Peter Bridgewater founded the league and when the new national professional circuit, Major League Soccer, began in 1996, he became president of the San Jose Clash.

■ WINNING ONE FOR THE COACH

Countless athletic events in this century have been decided by a play late in the game. None was more dramatic -- nor inspirational -- than the one that ended the Central Coast Section's high school football championship game between Los Gatos and St. Francis in 1985.

Wildcats' linebacker Mike Scialabba had knocked down a PAT pass that would have given the Lancers a tie earlier, so Los Gatos led, 14-12, with 42 seconds left. More than 7,000 fans watched from the Spartan Stadium stands and thousands more stared at their television screens at home.

Wildcats' head coach Charlie Wedemeyer, stricken with Lou Gehrig's disease in 1977 and coaching his last varsity football game, sat in his golf cart as the Lancer's place kicker, Luca Adriani, lined up for a 29-yard attempt that would put undefeated St. Francis in front.

The ball was snapped, set up by the holder and Adriani's kick sent it toward the uprights. But, Jeff Borgese, who had scored both touchdowns for the Wildcats, tore across the field, leaped and blocked the kick to preserve Wedemeyer's 78th career win, give him a 12-1-0 season and end a string of three consecutive CCS crowns for St. Francis (12-1-0).

Aided by his wife, Lucy, who read his lips and passed

Charlie Wedemeyer, shown with his wife, Lucy, continued to coach football at Los Gatos High after he contracted Lou Gehrig's disease. The Wildcats won the CCS title in his last year as varsity mentor.

his instructions along to other coaches, the amazing Wedemeyer continued to coach Los Gatos High football at the frosh-soph level through the 1990s.

■ DIAMOND CHAMPS REPEAT

The powerful Stanford baseball program, which had sent scores of players into professional baseball, produced back-to-back College World Series championships in 1987 and 1988, only the third time any school had achieved consecutive NCAA titles.

Cardinal diamond fans saw their team advance to NCAA postseason competition for the seventh straight season in 1987 with a record of 48-16. The team tacked on five more victories against only a single loss in the competition at Omaha and closed the books on a record 53-17 season.

After winning two games and losing one, Stanford was on the verge of elimination from the tournament, trailing LSU, 5-2, in the last of the 10th inning. In one of the most dramatic moments in Stanford athletic history, freshman outfielder Paul Carey hit a grand slam for a 6-5 win.

The Cardinal's first national baseball title was realized two games later in a 9-5 victory over Oklahoma State, giving All-American pitcher Jack McDowell his 13th win.

Carey hit .381 and knocked in seven runs to win the World Series Most Outstanding Player award. Joining him on the all-series team were designated hitter Mark Machtolf, who led the club with a .429 series average, and shortstop David Esquer, who batted .350 with six RBIs. Coach Mark Marquess was named NCAA coach of the year.

Stanford returned to Omaha in 1988 and won the title the hard way. The Cardinal had failed to take the Six-Pac title, finishing 18-12 in conference play, and entered postseason play with a record of 37-21.

Stanford captured the Northeast regional with wins over Fordham, Rutgers and Kentucky twice to earn another trip to the College World Series as the seventh seeded team.

In the final, Stanford met Arizona State, six-time victor over the Cardinal in conference play. Stanford got an early start to the title with a five-run outburst in the first inning topped by Ed Sprague's 22nd homer and Brian Johnson's two-run double and coasted to a 9-5 victory. Pitcher Lee Plemel, who registered his 11th and 12th wins at Omaha, was voted the series' top player.

Stanford peaked at the right time since the Cardinal's .667 win-loss percentage (46-23) was the lowest by a champion in NCAA history.

Coach Marquess capped another great year by guiding the USA Olympic baseball team to a gold medal. Sprague and catcher Doug Robbins were members of the squad.

Stanford made five other NCAA appearances from 1981 to 1986 and Santa Clara University (43-18-1) qualified in 1988, topping Minnesota before being eliminated by two losses to Washington State.

The Cardinal equaled a school record with 43 wins in 1981, but failed to advance past the regional. The following year, a school record 14-game winning streak was ended by Texas in the College World Series and Stanford was eliminated in the next game by Maine to finish 49-18-1.

Stanford hosted its first NCAA Western regional in 1983, whipping UC Santa Barbara, 11-5, before a Sunken Diamond record crowd of 4,212 to advance to the World Series and a fifth place finish.

The Cardinal was eliminated in the regionals in 1984 and 1986. The 1985 conference champions finished fifth in the World Series.

■ THE COMEBACK KID

Pablo Morales disproves the thought, which may or may not have been expressed by Brooklyn Dodgers manager Leo Durocher, that "nice guys finish last."

The popular Bellarmine Prep and Stanford swimmer who became the San Jose State women's swimming coach in 1998, overcame a disappointing failure in the 1988 Olympic trials and came out of retirement at age 27 to finish first in a stunning comeback four years later.

Morales retired from the pool for three years after failing to qualify for the 1988 games and attended the Columbia University law school. Later, he resumed training

Mark Marquess

and beat the odds by winning gold medals in the 100-meter butterfly and the 400-meter medley relay at Barcelona in 1992.

Morales was a skinny, 6-foot-2, 155-pounder when he got his first chance at Olympic fame in 1984.

A product of the Santa Clara Swim Club, Morales had proved his worth in amateur meets and at Bellarmine Prep, where he led the Bells to their first two Central Coast Section swimming titles in 1982 and 1983.

Morales had won the CCS 100-yard butterfly in 1981, but gained notoriety the following season when he swam the event in 49.16, breaking the oldest section meet record held by Santa Clara High's Mark Spitz. Morales broke his own national record in the event in the 1983 CCS meet and began training for the Olympics.

Morales picked up a gold and two silver medals at the 1984 Games in Los Angeles. At Stanford the following year, he won three events and helped the relay team to victory as the Cardinal took its first NCAA men's swimming title. Stanford won the next two NCAA championships and when Morales -- a three time Academic All-American -- left school he had won a national collegiate record 11 events.

Pablo Morales won three Olympic gold and two silver medals in swimming in 1984 and 1992.

■ KILLER BEES STUNG

A potent offense crafted by coach Bill Walsh brought the San Francisco 49ers into the Super Bowl at Stanford in 1985, but a defensive decision shut down Miami QB Dan Marino and produced a 38-16 rout for the Prospectors.

The 49ers were almost perfect, building a 15-1-0 record with Walsh's multi-faceted West Coast offense leading the NFC with 475 points and the defense pacing the division by surrendering only 227. Wendell Tyler ran for more than 1,200 yards and quarterback Joe Montana's precision passing accounted for 28 scores.

Miami relied more on Marino's potent arm, which produced 48 TDs, so the 49ers decided to minimize this weapon by deploying five defensive backs. Marino threw 50 passes, hitting 29 for 318 yards, but only one touchdown. The 49ers picked off two of his tosses, held the Dolphins' running game to 25 yards and kept Miami's defense on the field for more than 37 of the game's 60 minutes.

Game MVP Montana completed 24 of 35 passes for a record 331 yards and three TDs as Miami's vaunted Killer Bees defense couldn't contain the 'Niners before a crowd of 84,059 at Stanford Stadium.

■ FOR THE RECORD

Kurt Rambis ended his four-season basketball career at Santa Clara University in 1980 as the Broncos all-time scoring champion with 1,735 points. He ranks second in career rebounds with 1,037.

In 1980, American speed skater Eric Heiden of Stanford became the first competitor to win five individual gold medals in the Olympic Winter Games.

Cal quarterback Rich Campbell (Santa Teresa) broke an NCAA standard in 1980 with 43 pass completions in 53 attempts for 421 yards in a 41-31 loss at Florida.

Santa Clara University's Brian Sullivan punted a school record 77 yards against Chico State in 1980.

Rainey Meszaros (Fremont, De Anza) caught a record 68 passes for University of the Pacific in 1980.

Jim McMahon, who attended Hill High School as a freshman and sophomore, set numerous NCAA season marks at Brigham Young University in 1980, including touchdown passes (47), yards gained (4,571) and passing efficiency (176.9). In 1983, Ben Bennett (Peterson) broke McMahon's career record of 9,536 passing yards, finishing four years at Duke University with 9,614.

In a 1982 Metro Santa Clara women's fast pitch game, the Coasters beat the Wallabies, 3-2, in 39 innings, a U. S. amateur softball record. Reliever Cheryl Stewart pitched the last 31 innings for the win.

Leigh High's Dana Jacobson kicked a county record 61-yard field goal in 1985 in a 37-20 loss to Los Gatos.

Dorinda Lindstrom of Santa Clara University set the women's single game basketball record in 1986, pouring in 39 points against Fresno State.

San Jose State lost at UNLV, 37-21, in the last baseball game of 1986. The Spartans had 21 hits and six home runs. UNLV had 28 hits with nine homers, including three by future big league star Matt Williams.

Stanford's Steve Smith set a Pac-10 record, passing 68 times against Notre Dame in 1989. Smith completed 39, but the Irish won, 27-17.

The Amateur Athletic Foundation paid $205,000 in 1989 for a San Jose sports library collected by Fred Imhof and once listed by the Guiness Book as the world's largest.

■ HONORS

Cleveland outfielder Joe Charboneau (Buchser) won the American League Rookie of the Year Award in 1980 and New York Yankees pitcher Dave Righetti (Pioneer, SJCC) took the same award a year later. George Brett of Kansas City, who once played third base for San Jose in the California League, was the American League's MVP in 1980 after topping the circuit with a .390 average.

All-America second team honors went to San Jose State pitcher Mark Langston (Buchser) in 1981 and Spartan

Local high schools produced two major league pitchers who were outstanding in the 1980s, Dave Righetti (left) of Pioneer and Mark Langston of Buchser.

outfielder Ken Caminiti (Leigh, SJCC) in 1984.

In 1981, John McEnroe (Stanford) became the first tennis player since Don Budge in 1938 to win the Associated Press Male Athlete of the Year award.

Linda Pereira (SJS), versatile front office staffer with San Jose's California League teams for more than a decade, won the Rawlings Woman of the Year Award in 1982.

The UOP Football Hall of Fame inducted coach C. E. "Swede" Righter (Campbell, Stanford) and end-back Cecil "Moose" Disbrow (San Jose) in 1982. End Willis Boyarsky (San Jose) was admitted in 1983.

Other 1980s Hall of Fame inductees were Olympic decathlon winners Bob Mathias and Bruce Jenner, Stanford javelin thrower Bud Held, San Jose State sprinter Lee Evans and coach Bud Winter (track and field); San Jose's Jim St. John (bowling) and Stanford quarterbacks Jim Plunkett and John Brodie (college football).

New York Cosmos forward Rick Davis (SCU) was North American Soccer League player of the year in 1983.

Time Magazine's 1984 Man of the Year was Peter Ueberroth. Honored as head of the Los Angeles Olympics Organizing Committee, the former SJS water polo star went on to become the sixth Commissioner of Baseball.

British Columbia wide receiver Mervyn Fernandez (Hill, De Anza, SJS) was the CFL's outstanding player in 1985 after catching 95 passes for 1,727 yards and 15 TDs.

Washington University tailback Jacque Robinson (San Jose) was the MVP in two postseason bowl games for the Huskies, the 1982 Rose Bowl and the 1985 Orange Bowl.

In 1987, golfer Patty Sheehan (SJS) was one of Sports Illustrated's eight Sportsmen of the Year.

■ DIGGING FOR GOLD

Major league coed volleyball had folded a decade earlier, but in 1987 a new women's six-team pro league called Major League Volleyball found its way to San Jose.

Although all its games were played at San Jose Civic Auditorium, the team was dubbed the San Francisco/San Jose Golddiggers in the inaugural season.

The nine-member squad, which included former San Jose State stars Lisa Ice and Teri DeBusk, played 11 home games on weekends. A crowd of 1,649 saw the team lose its home opener to the New York Liberties.

After a 14-7 regular season finish, the Golddiggers beat New York in the first playoff round, but lost to Los Angeles in five sets in the televised championship game.

The 1988 team was renamed the San Jose Golddiggers and had an 13-11 record after losing in the semifinal playoff round to Minnesota. Each player collected $750 third place money to supplement their base pay of up to $5,000.

The Golddiggers were favored to take the title in 1989. They lost the opener at Minnesota, but drew 2,209 for the home opener two days later, collecting a five-set victory over Los Angeles.

The team's record stood at 6-3 after road wins at Chicago and Portland, but when players got off the plane, owner Gary Schwing of Los Altos told them the league had suspended operations because of financial problems.

San Jose was among the circuit's strongest franchises with a season ticket base of 500 and average home crowds of 2,000. Neither the owner nor the players agreed with the decision to fold, but volleyball did not return in 1990.

■ BASKETBALL BOYCOTT

Ten San Jose State basketball players walked out of practice in mid-January, 1989, saying they would no longer play for coach Bill Berry. They complained about Berry's "verbal abuse and mental cruelty."

Berry had guided the Spartans to appearances in the NCAA and NIT in his first two years and owned a 137-121 record in nine seasons. Now, he was on a one-year contract and had been asked before the season by Athletic Director Randy Hoffman to improve his relations with players and be more restrained during games.

After the walkout, four football players including star running back Johnny Johnson joined the roster, which consisted of holdover freshman walk-on Kevin Logan, juniors Dwain Daniels and Tom Desiano and senior Jan Svoboda.

The Spartans played hard and were competitive near the end, but lost all 12 games through the rest of the season to finish 5-23. They led Cal State Fullerton, 69-67, only to lose on a three-pointer with one second left in overtime.

At State's final home game -- the last ever played in Civic Auditorium -- Number 34 worn by Berry's son, Ricky,

Kurt Rambis (left) starred at Cupertino High and at Santa Clara University and Ricky Berry of Live Oak High went on to San Jose State. Both are career basketball scoring leaders at their universities.

was retired. Ricky had left SJS in 1988 after setting career basketball records with 1,767 points and a 21.0 average and was the Sacramento Kings' first round draft choice.

The Spartans finished with a 70-62 loss to Utah State while the SJS women ended a 46-game league losing streak with a 63-61 win over UCSB. Bill Berry's contract wasn't renewed and five months later his 24-year-old son shot and killed himself after an argument with his wife.

■ THE BIG ONE

A powerful earthquake measuring 7.1 on the Richter Scale rocked Northern California on Oct. 17, 1989.

The temblor, which was centered in the mountains about 15 miles south of San Jose, shook the region for 15 to 20 seconds just after 5 p.m. It killed scores of people, collapsed sections of the Bay Bridge and Oakland's elevated Cypress Freeway and caused extensive damage throughout the region and locally at Los Gatos and Stanford University.

The San Francisco Giants and Oakland Athletics were preparing to play Game 3 of baseball's World Series when the earthquake hit. Damage to Candlestick Park delayed resumption of the Fall Classic for 10 days.

It also caused the San Francisco 49ers to move a regular season NFL game into Stanford Stadium for the first time. The 49ers defeated New England, 37-20, on Oct. 22 before a crowd estimated at 70,000. Joe Montana injured a knee late in the first half and Steve Young came on to throw three touchdown passes after the intermission.

Several other sporting events in the county were affected by the disaster. Damage at Los Gatos High forced Saratoga to relocate its game against Lynbrook. The game was moved to Saratoga and was first football contest played there in the school's 29 years of varsity play.

The Mount Pleasant-Silver Creek prep football game was shifted to the latter's campus because of damage to the Police Activities League Stadium in East San Jose.

■ IN PASSING

Charles "Bud" Finger, 62, ex-Stanford golfer and coach (261-72-6) died of a stroke in 1981 at Los Altos Hills.

Ex-Stanford fullback Kevin McMillan and pole vaulter Michael Becker were killed in 1981 when a sports car driven by another student crashed into a tree on campus.

Saratoga High line coach Dan Barry died in 1983 when a car hit his bicycle as he rode home from practice.

Tony Teresa, 50, former SJS and Oakland Raiders QB, died in a Salinas hospital in 1984 after a long illness.

Santa Clara University linebacker David Cichoke, 21, died of a brain hemorrhage 36 hours after being injured in a game at Cal State Northridge in 1985.

John Tuggle, 25, (Independence, Cal), 335th and last NFL pick who played on New York Giants special teams in 1983, died of cancer in a Tijuana hospital in 1986.

Wilson Faumuina, 32, San Jose State and NFL defensive lineman, died of congestive heart failure in 1986.

Nick Vanos, Santa Clara University's third all-time rebounder and ninth leading scorer, was killed in 1987 when an airliner crashed on takeoff at Detroit Metropolitan Airport. The third year Phoenix Suns player was 24.

Zeb Terry of Stanford, a major league infielder for seven seasons, died at age 96 in Los Angeles in 1988.

■ 1980 ■

Kurt Rambis has 31, Londale Theus 25 in SCU's 103-101 win over Pepperdine . . . Los Altos High ends Peterson's 29-game league winning streak, 41-39 . . . Santa Clara High girls wallop Awalt, 66-38. CCS player of the year Linda Walsh pours in 52 on way to 34.0 season average . . . Ron Livers (SJS) sets indoor record with 55-9 1/4 triple jump . . . Offense rules as SJCC tops Foothill, 135-107 . . . Rob Moreland of Independence High hits goal to top Branham, 2-1, in four-hour, 12 OT playoff . . . Heavyweight Casey Gulliford pins all opponents as SJS wins PCAA wrestling . . . Kim Belton of Stanford scores 41 in final game, 93-91 win over USC . . . Gilroy High takes first CCS wrestling title when Pete Kampa beats Matt Blevin, Mountain View heavyweight . . . Rick Palomino (Independence), Dan Chaid (Gunderson), Ruben Castillo (Overfelt) state wrestling champs. Chaid wins U. S. junior Greco-Roman title . . . San Jose's Harry Sims takes U. S. billiards crown . . . Santa Clara High, dominant in prep swimming for more than a decade, drops sport along with gymnastics, tennis, softball, citing lack of student interest . . . Palo Alto High (19-0) topples Woodside in CCS girl's soccer final, 3-0 . . . Fremont girls (41-4-1) win state Div. 1 volleyball . . . SJCC's Mickey Cutler captures javelin (221-7), shot put (55-0 1/2), discus (176-3) against Foothill . . . Robin Campbell (Stanford) wins 400, 800-meter races at Martin Luther King Games . . . Albert Candelaria beats Piedmont Hills High with Yerba Buena's first no-hitter . . . Rebecca Daughton of Los Gatos leads women in 40-mile Cat's Hill Criterium bike race . . . Buchser High's Kathy Nino shoots 77, wins state prep golf in playoff . . . Paul Bishop (discus), Craig Roberts (triple jump), Felix Bohni (pole vault) lead SJS to PCAA track title . . . Stanford rallies to down Cal, 5-3, for NCAA team tennis crown . . . John Fryhoff, Troy Carlson toss no-hitters as Gunderson High fashions 22-game winning streak ended by Hillsdale in CCS playoffs, 1-0 . . . SJS fails to win NCAA judo for first time since competition began in 1962 . . . WVC's barefoot runner Diane Figliomeni (1,500), Ann Regan (880) lead Vikings to women's state JC track title. Foothill's Malcolm Dixon wins men's 110 hurdles . . . Joe Tamburino of Willow Glen High takes Nor Cal prep, county junior golf titles . . . Saratoga High's Lindsey Meggs (.449, 35 RBIs) tops CCS softball . . . Curt Ransford of SJS wins NCAA javelin at 269-3 . . . SCU's 6-foot-11 center Mark McNamara transfers to Cal . . . 18-year-old Nathaniel Crosby, Bing's son, shoots 209 to take 54-hole county golf title . . . Lynbrook High swimmer Chris Cavanaugh, holder of world 50-meter freestyle record, is state's top prep athlete . . . Patty Sheehan's two-under par 72 wins NCAA women's golf . . . Linda Shelley, Suzanne Cameron of SJS lead USA to win in first American Cup synchronized swim . . . Brian Snyder's no-hitter gives San Jose Missions 4-0 win against Modesto . . . Tom Watson captures British Open by four strokes over Lee Trevino . . . John Munro of De Anza wins north state public links golf title . . . Santa Clara's Randy Mamola takes British Motorcycle Grand Prix 500cc race . . . Sterling McBride of Palo Alto wins U. S. Cycling Federation 70-mile junior title . . . Juli Inkster of SJS tops Patti Rizzo for U. S. women's amateur golf title, 2 up . . . Bob Melton has double, homer, five RBIs as Palo Alto defeats Hialeah, Fla., in American Legion national tourney opener . . . John McEnroe destroys Bjorn Borg's tennis Grand Slam hopes, beating him in U. S. Open . . . Several MHAL coaches cancel football games to support San Jose district teachers strike . . . Trailing Washington State, 20-3, QB Steve Clarkson rallies SJS with 295 passing yards, four TDs in 31-26 televised win . . . Foothill's Paul Franklin tallies four goals in record-setting 16-0 soccer win over Merritt . . . Perry Parmellee catches only two Dave Alfaro passes, but chalks up 121 yards in SCU's 33-6 victory over Cal State Hayward . . . QB John Elway's three TD passes help Stanford snap Oklahoma's 20-game win streak . . . Jim Meeks of San Jose takes Fremont Raceway's mini-stock car title, winning 13 of 20 main events . . . San Jose High's Jacque Robinson scores on 78-, 94-yard runs in 13-7 win over Willow Glen . . . LPGA tour back in San Jose for first time since 1966 with Amy Alcott taking Inamori Open . . . In final season, Buchser High stops Los Altos inside 10-yard line four times in 7-3 win for Bruins' first victory in 21-year series . . . Dave Alfaro's goes 25 for 35 with three TDs as SCU slips past Northern Michigan, 27-26, in NCAA Div. 2 playoff. Broncos lose to Cal Poly in semis . . . SJS women's field hockey team best in West, third in AIAW tourney . . . Oak Grove High QB Jeff Walsh leads state with 30 TD passes . . . John Webster's goal in OT gives Foothill 2-1 state JC title win over Chabot . . . Chris Kelsey has three goals as Stanford tops Cal in NCAA water polo final, 8-6 . . . State's top player Linda Vaughn leads Fremont High to state volleyball title . . . Saratoga High's Jeff Arrillaga (receiver, safety, kicker) is top CCS, Nor Cal player . . . Jacque Robinson scores 40 as San Jose High tops Gorman at Reno hoops tourney, 84-79 . . . Kent Lockhart's 41 leads Gunn High to Sunnyvale tournament title over Riordan, 74-61.

Gunn High great Kent Lockhart had 1,484 points in his career.

1981

Brian Sullivan (SCU) kicks 52-yard field goal, longest in Shrine game history, but East wins, 21-3 . . . Margaret Walsh has 31 for Santa Clara High in 60-48 win over Palo Alto . . . James Booker's 34 leads De Anza to 108-68 victory over San Mateo . . . SCU converts its first 21 free throws, 23 of 25, in 75-61 win over Gonzaga . . . Seven-game SJS hoops win streak (best since 1962) snapped by UC-Irvine, 90-78 . . . Mary Hile (Peterson) ends career as USF's all-time leader in points (2,324), average (20.2), rebounds (1,602). Coach Walt Bugler calls her, "the best USF athlete since Ollie Matson and that includes Bill Russell" . . . Paul Grame of Stanford no-hits Cal State Hayward, 8-0 . . . Francie Larrieu sets world indoor 2,000-meter mark . . . Keith Jones scores 23 as Stanford upsets UCLA, 74-72 . . . State high school wrestling champions: Dan Chaid of Gunderson, Matt Olejnik of Cupertino . . . Independence High's Frank vanden Brand Horninge first county soccer player on Parade Magazine All-America . . . After scoreless draw in CCS soccer final, unbeaten San Jose High beats Saratoga in 1-0 replay on goal by Primo Jauregui . . . Gymnast Sue Stednitz (Camden) captures gold medal in vault at Grand Prix de Paris . . . Five homers, including one by John Elway, lead Stanford over Arizona, 14-12 . . . Locke High beats Lynbrook (28-2), 73-61, in TOC final despite Jeannie James' 20 points . . . SJS regains NCAA judo crown with six winners. SJS women finish third as Christine Penick wins open division . . . Willie Banks' U. S. record 56-9 1/2 triple jump headlines Jenner Classic . . . Tom Watson tops Jack Nicklaus, Johnny Miller by two strokes for Masters title . . . Leland High takes CCS swim crown without winning single race . . . Joe Tamburino of SJS is medalist as Spartans win PCAA golf, later tops USC's Brian Lindley for state amateur title, 4 and 2 . . . Albert Candelaria whiffs 15 as Yerba Buena (19-2) captures MHAL crown with win over Oak Grove . . . Rich Campbell

Tom Watson of Stanford won a U. S. Open, two Masters and five British Open titles.

(Santa Teresa), who broke many of Craig Morton's Cal passing records, is Green Bay's first round pick, No. 1 QB drafted. Other NFL firsts: SJS wide receiver Mike Nichols (Detroit), Stanford tackle Brian Holloway (New England) . . . NCAA tennis singles title goes to Stanford's Tim Mayotte . . . St. Francis High nine blanks Capuchino for CCS crown, 4-0. Section co-MVPs: Lancers' catcher Mike Dotzler (.433), Monta Vista's Larry Dick (.434, 10-1 in league) . . . John McEnroe wins first Wimbledon crown, snapping Bjorn Borg's five-title run in epic match . . . Small crowds see World Games at Santa Clara where 16 events include tug-o-war, roller hockey, trampoline tumbling . . . Stanford's Neil Robinson wins Nor Cal amateur golf title . . . Boston's Carney Lansford (Wilcox) leads American League with .336 average . . . John Elway riddles Purdue defense with 33 completions, 418 yards, but Stanford bows, 27-19 . . . Hat tricks by Jorge Titinger, Fred Ueland lead Stanford to record 16-0 soccer win over Sonoma State . . . Dave Bearden's five TDs lead Los Gatos to 50-28 romp over Pioneer. Five weeks later, Bearden rushes for 381 yards, five scores in 55-36 win over Del Mar . . . SJS wins three straight national TV games over Cal, Fresno State, Fullerton. Steve Clarkson passes for six TDs in 65-33 win against Fresno . . . Kurt Cummings' 24-yard field goal with 10 seconds left propels Santa Clara High to 24-22 win over Palo Alto. On same night, Rich Alvarez splits uprights with 18-yard field goal with 15 seconds on clock as Blackford downs Pioneer, 19-18 . . . Hollis Stacy's six-foot birdie putt ends four-way playoff for Inamori Golf Classic title at Almaden . . . Three last period TDs capped by Steve Koch's 65-yard interception return give Santa Teresa 21-14 victory over Hill . . . Stanford amasses 693 yards, including 581 in air, still loses, 62-36, when Arizona State QB Mike Pagel tosses Pac-10 record seven TD passes . . . Stanford tops Cal, 2-1, in soccer when goalkeeper Henry Foulk scores twice on penalty kicks, last in second OT . . . LPGA rookie of the year Patty Sheehan (SJS) wins first pro golf title in Japan Classic . . . Bert Lee of San Jose awarded ninth round TKO win over Raphael Corona before 1,027 at Civic Auditorium, city's largest boxing crowd in a decade . . . Jim Bergeson collects six goals as Stanford (31-0) topples Long Beach State 17-6, for record 33rd straight water polo win, second in a row NCAA title . . . Maureen Formico's 30 points, 19 boards lead Mitty High to 50-20 win over Mount Pleasant . . . Live Oak High QB Mike Loera runs for one, passes for three TDs in CCS title win over Blackford, 26-20. Bellarmine, state's No. 1 at 12-0-0, beats Monta Vista, 7-3, for other CCS crown. Bell's guard/linebacker George Ebertin is top CCS player . . . Juli Inkster defeats SJS teammate Juli Ordonez for state women's amateur golf crown, 3 and 2 . . . Fremont High (40-2) loses to Santa Monica in state volleyball final . . . Michael Jordan hits 21 in North Carolina's 76-57 Cable Car victory over SCU . . . St. Francis High takes tourney title over Gilroy despite Mustang Steve Ledesma's 37.

■ 1982 ■

Jane Morgan collects 37 points, 25 rebounds, eight assists as Westmont High dominates Leigh, 77-24 . . . Overfelt High trounces Lick, 86-37, behind Tina Lei's 49 points . . . Nine minutes of stall ball gives UCLA 42-34 hoops triumph over Stanford . . . Bellarmine, St. Ignatius soccer teams scoreless after two regular, 14 sudden death OTs. Bells drop 1-0 replay in WCAL playoffs . . . Foothill (21-10) loses to Long Beach in state JC playoffs, 67-61. Owls' Ron Bush has 19 . . . CCS player of the year Suzy Meckenstock tops Los Gatos with 31 in 65-59 section title game triumph over Lynbrook. Orange Crush (31-1) wins Nor Cal crown, falls to Riverside Poly, Cheryl Miller's 41 points in state final . . . SJS students vote to finance $13 million campus Events Center . . . SJCC's Ken Caminiti (Leigh) pounds two homers in 5-2 win over Chabot . . . Joy Ellingson, Peter Schifrin take NCAA fencing titles for SJS . . . Cal's Mark McNamara leads NCAA Div. 1 basketball in field goal percentage (70.2) . . . Dave Morgan (405-180), Del Mar basketball coach since school opened 23 years earlier, retires. Teams never had losing season in his first 21 years . . . Bobby Berland takes two titles as SJS wins 20th NCAA judo crown . . . Led by Parade All-Americans Todd, Tom Rafalovich, Saratoga High's beats Leland, 1-0, for section soccer crown. Saratoga (17-1-1), Palo Alto (18-0-2) girl's co-champs after four OT, scoreless draw . . . Utah's Sue Stednitz (Camden), wins balance beam, all-around at first NCAA women's gymnastics championships . . . Pioneer High's Michelle Berkeland pitches no-hit, 16-strikeout softball over Live Oak . . . Monta Vista High's Ndidi Opia tosses her third no-hitter in 13-0 win over Cupertino . . . San Jose's first outdoor boxing card in several decades draws 1,600 to Municipal Stadium. Jose Luis Ramirez decisions Jorge Morales in 10 . . . Foothill's Ralph Preiman raises own national JC pole vault mark to 17-5 as Owls take state title . . . Ken Thomas of SJS first PCAA runner to take 100-meter race three straight years . . . Unbeaten Stanford women (20-0) defeat UCLA for first NCAA team tennis title. Cardinals' Alycia Moulton takes NCAA singles . . . SJS back Gerald Willhite is Denver's first draft choice. Minnesota selects Stanford's Darrin Nelson . . . Santa Clara High's Miiko Kimura sweeps all events,

Coach Dave Morgan's Del Mar Dons played 21 straight seasons of winning basketball.

but Leland edges Branham for CCS gymnastics title . . . Prospect High (18-7) tops Westmont, 8-7, in first CCS baseball final between schools from same league (WVAL) . . . Stanford NCAA women's track champs: Kim Schnurpfeil 10,000 meters, Ceci Hopp 3,000 meters . . . Saratoga High's Mark Kibort tops 17 feet in pole vault . . . Tom Watson follows two stroke U. S. Open win over Jack Nicklaus with one stroke win over Nick Faldo, Peter Oosterhaus in British Open . . . Campbell's Steve Cook takes Kessler Open at Futurama Bowl . . . USA's Martina Navratilova, Chris Evert Lloyd win singles matches over West Germany in Federation Cup play at Santa Clara's Decathlon Club . . . Tim Baker (Campbell, De Anza) captures world karate crown . . . Mike Gambello retains county junior golf crown . . . Juli Inkster first woman in nearly 50 years to win three straight U. S. amateur golf titles . . . Outfielder John Elway, New York Yankees' No. 1 pick in 1981 draft, signs $140,000 contract, hits .318 for Oneonta in New York-Pennsylvania League . . . Jim Harbaugh, who threw for 2,093 yards at Palo Alto High, starts career at Michigan, becomes Chicago Bears 1987 first draft choice . . . Aerial battle between Stanford's John Elway (382 yards, two TDs), Steve Clarkson of SJS (285 yards, 3 TDs), ends with three-yard Clarkson TD run in 35-31 Spartan victory . . . Rich Martig, Doug McCann each pick off record three passes in SCU's 26-21 win over Cal State Northridge . . . Split end Mike Mennard catches seven passes, scores twice in St. Francis High's 17-3 win over Bellarmine before largest prep audience (13,000) at Buck Shaw Stadium in 17 years . . . Patty Sheehan shoots record 15 under par 277 to capture Inamori Classic at Almaden . . . Shellie Onstead (Willow Glen) is Cal's first field hockey All-American . . . St. Francis High girls win CCS swim crown, but Saratoga's Carrie Steinseifer stars with meet records in 50, 100-yard freestyle . . . Eric Hawkins sloshes to 235 yards, two TDs on muddy field as Wilcox High tops Westmont in CCS opener, 27-8 . . . Lynbrook High wins third straight CCS field hockey title when Stacey Hall, Jennifer Averill score in 2-1 triumph over Saratoga . . . Matt Verga makes two goals as Santa Clara High retains CCS water polo crown over Monta Vista, 13-9 . . . St. Francis tops Nor Cal girl's cross-country field. Del Mar's Cory Schubert takes girl's title. Willow Glen is boy's champ . . . Inaugurating 30-second shot clock, three-pointer at Civic Auditorium, SJS bows to Nevada-Reno, 92-81 . . . Fremont High girls retain Nor Cal volleyball title, lose to Mira Costa in state . . . Del Mar's Dennis Calvert pours in 37, but Dons lose to Oak Grove, 105-52 . . . LaNetra Phillips of Mount Pleasant High sets school record with 37 in 71-24 win over Leigh . . . Dan Sampson's 45 leads Homestead High over Menlo-Atherton, 76-67 . . . SJS tops LMU, 94-80. Chris McNealy hits 15 of 19 shots on way to 34 points.

■ 1983 ■

West loses, 26-25, but QB John Elway (Stanford) is Shrine game's top player. Elway goes to Baltimore as NFL draft's first pick, won't sign, Colts swap him to Denver . . . San Jose boxer Glen Corbus, 98-10 as amateur, decisions Frank Valdivia in pro debut at Civic Auditorium . . . Lora Alexander tallies 27, grabs 20 rebounds for SJS women against Sacramento State . . . Albert Tsarnas of SJS leads Spartans to fourth straight PCAA wrestling title . . . De Anza falls to Chabot in league playoffs, 51-48, despite 27 by Braxton Clark, state's top scorer with 35.4 average . . . Live Oak High's Ricky Berry leads county with 20.9 average . . . Santa Clara High wins CCS girl's hoops, 60-42, over Cupertino. Margaret Walsh paces Bruins with 23 . . . All-State Jane Morgan of Westmont High sets girl's county season basketball marks: 878 points, 33.8 average, high game of 56; career totals: 1,691 points, 885 rebounds . . . Jeanne Ruark Hoff, Stanford's first female hoops superstar, ends career with 2,038 points, 17.6 average . . . Marybeth Linzmeier, who wins eight individual crowns in career, leads Stanford to first NCAA women's swimming title . . . Top CCS boy's player Pat Giusti leads Fremont to TOC final, falling to Bishop O'Dowd, 57-39 . . . SJS defensive back Gill Byrd goes to San Diego Chargers in first round . . . Santa Teresa High, St. Francis CCS boy's soccer co-champs after 100-minute, four OT scoreless draw. Lancers' Thomas Silvas is area player of the year, Parade All-American. Saratoga girls (18-0, state record four goals allowed) down Lynbrook, 1-0, for title on Janet Taylor's goal . . . NCAA track champs: Felix Bohni (SJS), indoor, outdoor pole vault, PattiSue Plumer (Stanford), indoor two mile, Carol Cady (Stanford) outdoor shot put . . . Stanford's Keith Jones scores 30 for season mark 553 as Cardinal tips Oregon State, 88-75, in finale . . . Independence High's Anthony Palomino of Independence High wins third straight CCS wrestling title, joins Branham's Dan Dodds as state champ . . . Beau Hastings fans 19 batters as Santa Teresa High downs Mount Pleasant, 11-2 . . . In first world title bout in San Jose, 2,684 jam Civic Auditorium to see Roger Mayweather knock out Jorge Alvarado in eighth in World Boxing Association junior lightweight battle . . . San Jose Seahawks beat San Francisco Club, 20-9, for third Golden Gate rugby crown in four seasons . . . Russ Keating, David Doll lead WVC swimmers to second straight state title . . . Del Mar High's Cory Schubert takes 1,600, 3,200 at state track meet. . . St. Francis (27-2) defeats Serra, 6-5, for CCS baseball title . . . Mountain View High wins CCS Div. 1 softball over Pioneer, 4-2 . . . Stanford captures NCAA men's tennis over SMU, 5-4 . . . Andre Phillips returns to SJCC track in Jenner Classic, wins 400-meter hurdles . . . Billy Ham's two-run homer gives Mission College 5-3 win over Los Medanos for state Div. 2 JC championship . . . John

Mary Hile (left) of Peterson High and Margaret Walsh of Santa Clara High top the all-time list of women's basketball scoring leaders at the University of San Francisco.

McEnroe wins second Wimbledon . . . New York Yankees' Dave Righetti no-hits Boston . . . Lynbrook High swim star Chris Cavanaugh wins Olympia Award from U. S. Olympics Committee . . . Tom Watson takes third British Open in four years . . . San Jose's Steve Romero decisions Canadian lightweight champ Davey Armstrong at Municipal Stadium . . . Joe Ferguson (Camden) ends 14-year career as big league catcher . . . San Jose's Jimmy Filice sets record, averaging 96.254 miles an hour in 25-lap Fairgrounds race . . . Patty Sheehan (SJS) is LPGA player of the year . . . SJS beats Stanford, 23-10, before series' largest crowd, 68,201 . . . St. Francis High extends win streak to 23 with 9-7 win over Bellarmine . . . De Anza picks off five aerials in 28-14 upset of No. 7 CCSF . . . Brent Jones' (Leland) two TD catches include game winner as SCU nips Cal Poly, 27-20 . . . Fremont High wins sixth straight section volleyball title . . . Bellarmine sets state water polo record with 33-0 mark . . . San Jose High, winless since beating Lincoln in 1980, ends 27-game loss streak with 7-6 win over Lions . . . Barbara Higgins pumps in 35 as Santa Clara High tops Branham, 46-27 . . . SJCC (10-1) ends Hartnell's 16-game win skein in Lions Bowl at Cabrillo College, 25-21, on Dave Keiser's two second half field goals . . . Andre Riley of Independence High paces CCS with 28 TDs, 1,997 yards rushing . . . State's No. 1 St. Francis High (13-0-0) blanks Oak Grove, 16-0, in CCS grid final . . . Independence High tops Piedmont Hills with 27 from Dan Weiss . . . Dr. Bobby Brown (Stanford), ex-New York Yankee infielder, is elected American League president . . . Homestead High's Dan Sampson hits 41 in 66-53 win over Del Mar.

■ 1984 ■

David Byrd of Los Gatos is stock car driver of the year . . . Nick Vanos has 18 points, 11 rebounds, six blocks as SCU topples Stanford 73-69 . . . Heavyweight wrestler Eric Volta of Santa Clara High wins CCS title . . . Rhoda Chew pulls down record 21 rebounds as SJS women nip SCU, 73-72 . . . John Moffet, Dave Sims lead Stanford to third straight Pac-10 swim title . . . Michele Miller's basket with two seconds left gives Piedmont Hills High 42-41 win over Los Gatos in CCS final, ending Orange Crush's 26-game win streak. Led by Missy Dallas, CCS player of the year Cindy Meckenstock, Los Gatos (29-2) wins Nor Cal, loses to Buena of Ventura, in state final, 37-30 . . . Welterweight Glen Corbus decisions Victor Abraham for state boxing title . . . Four OT draw in CCS boy's soccer title game leaves San Jose , Monta Vista co-champs. Mitty nips Saratoga, 1-0 in second OT for girl's title, ends Falcons' unbeaten streak at 46-0-2 . . . Julie Inkster wins Dinah Shore tourney on first extra hole, takes LPGA's biggest purse, $55,000 . . . SCU's Pat Penick takes NCAA light-heavyweight boxing . . . Live Oak High's Carlos Carrasco hurls two-hitter to blank Willow Glen in CCS quarterfinals, handing Rams' pitcher Jeff Knopf first loss of career after county record 23 straight wins . . . Stanford women take NCAA team tennis over USC. Cardinal's Linda Gates, Elise Burgin snare doubles . . . Monta Vista High's Ndidi Opia (18-1, .416) beats Mountain View, 6-1, in CCS softball final . . . Brian Oldfield has U. S. shot put record 72-9 3/4 toss in Jenner Classic . . . Ivar Moen of Los Gatos High tops state meet pole vaulters at 16-2, Mountain View's Shannon Clark takes 1,600 in 4:47.52 . . . Joanne Ernst of Palo Alto is top woman finisher in $50,000 Las Vegas Triathlon . . . Randy Mamola wins World Grand Prix 500cc motorcycle race . . . Ranked No. 1 for first time, John McEnroe captures third Wimbledon, beating Jimmy Connors in straight sets . . . SJCC baseball coach John Oldham (390-246) takes over at SCU . . . Saratoga High's Carrie Steinseifer, John Moffet of Stanford win swimming gold medals at Olympics. Palo Alto brothers Dave, Mark Schultz capture wrestling gold medals, gymnasts Pam Bileck, Michelle Disserre of Pioneer High take silver with USA team . . . Rick Davis scores twice as USA soccer squad defeats Costa Rica at Stanford, 3-0 . . . Los Gatos Little Leaguers fall to Florida in opening round of World Series, 2-1 . . . Nick Rescino of Sunnyvale is Fairgrounds super modified points champion . . . Bob Frasco's 333 passing yards can't save SJS from 28-27 loss to Stanford . . . Golfer Amy Alcott wins $26,250 first prize in San Jose Classic . . . Jeannie Gilbert scores school record 69th field hockey goal of career as SJS ties Cal, 2-2 . . . WVC takes ninth straight Golden Gate Conference cross-county title . . . Independence High crushes Santa Teresa, 34-7, as Andre Riley racks up 257 yards on ground, three TDs. Riley is CCS player of the year with 1,709 yards rushing, 29 TDs . . . Regina Jacobs, Alison Wiley, Ceci Hopp run

1-2-3 as Stanford captures Pac-10 women's cross-country . . . Todd Mayo's 182 yards, three TDs leads Los Gatos to 29-12 win over Seaside in CCS playoff lid-lifter . . . SJCC whips Santa Rosa, 37-31, for north state JC title. Jags pick off six passes, three by Val James . . . Oak Grove High ends St. Francis' 27-game grid win streak, 17-0 . . . Gunn High receiver Andy Coan grabs county record 79 passes . . . Oak Grove High QB Shannon Mornhinweg throws 63rd career TD pass to break brother Marty's record by one, sets marks for completions (422), yards (5,654) . . . Kit Lathrop (Leigh, WVC) is best lineman in United States Football League for second straight year . . . Ward Farris scores 25 as SJS dumps SCU, 74-67 . . . Nick Vanos (27), Howard Keeling (21), Scott Lamson (20), lead SCU to Cable Car Classic win over Nebraska, 78-59.

■ 1985 ■

SJS tops Cal State Fullerton, 97-92, in four OTs. Matt Fleming has 25 for SJS . . . Stanford stops USC for NCAA indoor tennis title, 6-3 . . . Gilroy High's Derek Bruton tallies 28 against Live Oak to break school career scoring record of 1,251 set in 1982 by Steve Ledesma. Bruton closes career with 1,565 . . . Bill Wiskel hits six goals as Gunderson High blanks Lincoln, in soccer, 7-0. Kristen Spiegel duplicates feat for Gunn's girls against Milpitas . . . Nick Vanos bags 44 in SCU's 91-70 win over LMU . . . Leigh High trips Prospect, 79-61. Craig Neibaur has 35 points, 15 rebounds . . . Randy Gil's 32 points pace Milpitas High to 65-61 win over Palo Alto for first league hoops crown . . . Six-time U. S. judo champ Christine Penick (SJS) takes 66-kilo Pan-American crown . . . Oklahoma State's Dan Chaid (Gunderson) is NCAA wrestling champ . . . After 18 straight wins, SJCC men lose to El Camino in state JC hoops final, 37-35. De Anza women fall to Los Angeles Tech, 109-83 . . . Mitty High's Brandi Chastain is state soccer MVP . . . Mark Saucedo of SJS hits in 21 straight . . . Third badminton state title goes to Rodney Barton (Palo Alto, Arizona State) . . . 20,000 jam Spartan Stadium as Mexico City's UNAM tops Naples (with Argentine superstar Diego Maradona), 2-1 . . . Stanford beats Cal, 9-1, as Mark Davis, Rick Lundblade, Toi Cook rip three hits apiece before Sunken Diamond overflow crowd . . . Oak Grove High's Tami Neuman has four hits, nine RBIs, 32-0 softball no-hitter against Piedmont Hills . . . Frosh Anthony Telford (Silver Creek), pitches first SJS no-hitter since 1953 in 5-0, seven-inning win over Fresno State . . . Craig Armstrong of SJS takes 200, 400, sparks relay team to PCAA meet win. Jim Doehring retains shot put title . . . Bob Eastwood's (SJS) first playoff hole bogey good enough to beat Payne Stewart in Byron Nelson Classic . . . Bellarmine (28-5), state's No. 1 nine, wins CCS over WCAL playoff champ Serra, 10-9 . . . Francie Larrieu wins 3,000-meters at Jenner Classic . . . Overfelt High's Jeff Rogers, first county prep high jumper to top 7 feet, soars 7-3 in CCS meet . . . State meet champions: Rebecca Chamberlain of Leigh High (3,200), Shannon Clark of Mountain View (1,600), Kristen Dowell of Santa Teresa (800), Mark Webster of Homestead (high jump) . . . Rick Davis scores once as USA soccer squad tops Earthquakes, 2-0 . . . Darin Brassfield of Los Gatos drives Ford Thunderbird to victory in GT race for production-based cars at Watkins Glen, NY . . . Aquamaid Patti Lynn wins four gold medals in national AAU junior synchronized swimming . . . Steve Sear becomes first golfer since Forrest Fezler in '60s to take three straight county junior titles . . . Roger Maltbie wins $126,000 World Series of Golf, tops $1 million in

Francie Larrieu was a champion distance runner.

11th year as pro . . . Chipper Vargas returns kickoff 90 yards for score, tallies three more TDs while rushing 174 yards for Wilcox High in 31-14 win over North Salinas . . . Joanne Ernst top woman in Ironman Triathlon world championship . . . John Paye completes 40 passes, but Stanford falls to San Diego State, 41-22 . . . Luca Adriani's 17-yard field goal with four seconds left gives St. Francis 17-14 win over Bellarmine . . . Greg Calcagno throws for 429 yards, SCU record six TDs in 53-30 win over San Francisco State . . . Nor Cal cross-country champs: Bellarmine boys, Los Gatos girls. Laurie Chapman of Gunderson outruns girl's field . . . Mike Tingler's OT goal gives Stanford 12-11 win over UC Irvine for NCAA water polo crown . . . Lisa Ice has 14 kills as SJS downs Long Beach State in NCAA volleyball opener. Cal Poly defeats Lady Spartans (27-7) . . . Mountain View High's Iwalani McCalla stops bid of Tiffany Silveria of Los Gatos for third straight CCS girl's tennis singles title . . . Top East-West Shrine defender is Garin Veras (Stanford) . . . Rex Walters hits 29 for Piedmont Hills High in 80-76 victory over Gunderson. Grizzly Shawn Sykes has 36.

■ 1986 ■

Oak Grove High lineman Tim Ryan selected on 1985 Parade All-America football team. He is consensus All-American at USC in 1989 . . . Sue Phillips has seven assists against Aptos High to become Mitty High's career leader . . . San Jose's Mike Jameson is Mike Tyson's 17th straight KO victim at Atlantic City . . . Piedmont Hills High's Lori Finnerty makes record 19 basketball steals against Santa Teresa . . . Shawn Sykes scores Gunderson High record 37 in 73-67 loss to Pioneer . . . Patty Sheehan edges Juli Inkster, Pat Bradley by stroke to win LPGA Sarasota, Fla., tourney . . . Mexico falls to East Germany, 2-1, as 6,000 fans endure steady rain at Spartan Stadium. Improved weather brings out 20,000 when Mexico, Santos of Brazil, play scoreless draw . . . 5-foot-7 Blackford High guard Damon O'Bannon leads CCS with 25.8 average . . . Giant-killer Pioneer High beats three higher ranked teams before falling to No. 1

Riordan in CCS hoops final. Homestead girls (26-2) defeat Mitty (26-1), 49-43, to become first repeat CCS champs . . . Gunderson High's Troy Dalbey wins seven medals with four gold at U. S. short course swim championships . . . 37th straight soccer match without loss gives Mitty High girls OT win over Monta Vista in CCS final, 4-2. Leland captures boy's crown, topping Bellarmine, 1-0 . . . Prospect High's Steve Bosco drives in nine runs with double, homer in 11-10 loss to Del Mar . . . League champ Mission College nine (27-8-1) bows to Sacramento City College in state playoffs . . . Patrick McEnroe, John Letts defeat Pepperdine in doubles to clinch Stanford's sixth NCAA tennis title. Patty Fendick, Dan Goldie capture NCAA singles champships . . . Bellarmine (28-6) wins second straight section baseball title, 2-0, over North Salinas. Bells' catcher Troy Buckley (.452) is co-player of the year . . . Softball player of the year Tamie Batista (.481) leads Pioneer High (24-2) over Mountain View's Pam Zink (29-3) for section Div. 1 title, 1-0 . . . Independence High takes sixth straight CCS boy's track crown . . . Canada's Ben Johnson runs 10.01 100 meters at Jenner Classic to beat Carl Lewis, Harvey Glance . . . Howard Kaeding takes Beard Classic at Fairgrounds, only major super modified race he had not won before . . . Gunderson High's Laurie Chapman wins state 3,200 title . . . County golf title goes to Andre Walewski of San Jose . . . Franklin Mieuli sells Golden State Warriors, who move training camp from San Jose after 15 seasons at SJCC . . . Kay Cockerill (Los Gatos) takes U. S. women's amateur golf title, beating Kathleen McCarthy of Fresno, 9 and 7 . . . Mike Sargent retains super modified points title at Fairgrounds . . . Jack Pierce (San Jose, SJCC) sets Mexican League homer record with 54 on way to 395 lifetime in minors . . . Patty Sheehan holes 12-foot birdie putt on first extra hole to win San Jose Classic playoff. . . Kale Wedemeyer has 146 yards rushing, four TDs in 35-28 Los Gatos High win against Saratoga . . . Prospect High tops Homestead, 38-7, as Jeff Grillo tosses four TD passes for second straight week . . . After rushing for 168 yards, five TDs, Branham High's Steve Bonafede suffers season-ending knee injury in romp over Leland, 34-2 . . . New York Yankees pitcher Dave Righetti sets major league record with 46 saves . . . Down by 10 with 42 seconds left, SJS hits pay dirt on pair of Mike Perez TD passes to whip Fresno State 45-41. SJS chalks up NCAA record with 24 penalties for 199 yards . . . Leigh High roars back from 17-0 half-time deficit to clip 18-game Los Gatos win streak, 18-17 . . . San Jose High pass play from Tom Chavez to Maurice Blaylock goes for 99 yards as Bulldogs lose to Leland, 28-17 . . . Haakon Austefjord (Monta Vista) hits 18 points with 12 rebounds as Norwegian national team beats SJS, 76-69 . . . Valley Christian High's Ronnie Harris gets TDs on 97-, 53-yard pass receptions as Warriors beat Upper Lake for North Coast Section Class A title, 14-10 . . . Craig Klass tallies four goals in Stanford's 9-6 win over California for NCAA water polo crown, record 45th straight win . . . Shannon McGee (Willow Glen) equals Fresno State women's basketball record with 33 points . . . Bellarmine trips Live Oak, 23-22, in CCS Div. 4A final with Mike Walker throwing three TD passes. Bells' linebacker Pat McPherson, Acorn QB Dominic Bejarano county's top players . . . SJCC (11-0-0) ends first perfect year with postseason win over Merced, 20-16. Jaguars rank No. 1, No. 2 in U. S. polls . . . Jennifer Hau of Prospect High wins fourth straight CCS 100 breaststroke . . . Alonzo Washington runs 201 yards for national JC record 2,239 as Gavilan tops Shasta, 21-6 . . . Trailing 27-0 at half, Stanford (8-4-0) rallies behind three Brad Muster TDs, but falls to Clemson in Gator Bowl, 27-21.

■ 1987 ■

WVC's Joel Tyrus pours in 41, 49 points against Canada, Alameda. . . Doug Shoji has four free throws in last 22 seconds as Santa Teresa High tops Independence, 62-59, in OT to snap 60-game 'Sixers league winning streak . . . Bellarmine blasts St. Ignatius, 70-54. Area player of the year John Sayers scores 27, retrieves 21 rebounds for Bells . . . Tim Mayotte upsets John McEnroe in all-Stanford final for U. S. pro indoor tennis title . . . Pinewood School's Eileen Shea goes for 36 against Presentation to pass 2,000 career mark after hitting 51 versus Castilleja . . . Santa Teresa High's Doug Borgel makes Parade soccer All-America . . . Long Beach State's Cindy Brown scores NCAA women's record 60 points in 149-69 romp at SJS . . . Stanford's Lisa Bernhagen sets U. S. college indoor high jump mark at 6-5 1/2 . . . Stanford dedicates Hank Luisetti statue at Maples Pavilion. Todd Lichti leads way with 26 as Cardinal nearly blows 37-point lead, but holds off Cal, 88-80 . . . Stacy Ball's three goals lead Santa Teresa girls to 4-1 win over Gunn in Div. 1 final . . . Led by Walter Watts' 22, Independence High ends Riordan's 17-game winning streak, 62-57, in CCS. 'Sixers lose final to Monta Vista . . . UNLV blasts SJS in PCAA hoops tourney final, 94-69 . . . Medalist Dana Lofland leads SJS women to PCAA golf win. Team takes first NCAA title with Anne Jones tying for medalist honors, but losing one-hole playoff to New Mexico State's Caroline Keggi . . . USA soccer squad ties Club America of Mexico, 1-1, before 14,302 at Spartan Stadium . . . No more "wait until next year" as Palo Alto High, early century baseball power, wins first league title in 60 seasons . . . Stanford women capture second straight NCAA team tennis, 5-1, over Georgia. Patti Fendick first woman to retain singles title . . . Chiazo Opia (Monta Vista) is Big 10 freshman softball player of the year at Northwestern. Sister, Ndidi, won same award in 1986 . . . Monta Vista High scores 1-0 win over Del Mar for section softball title. Dons' pitcher Michelle Sorci (16-2) top county player . . . Bellarmine nine (26-7) takes CCS Div. 1 over Oak Grove, 19-10. Bells' infielder Ed Giovanola is top county player, Dan Ardissone is state coach of the year . . . Nearly 25,000 fill SJCC stadium for two-day track meet. Carl Lewis wins 200 meters, tops long jump field. Edwin Moses takes 400-meter hurdles over Danny Harris, who earlier ended Moses' 127-race win string . . . State meet winners: Piedmont Hills High's Luis Juico (high jump), Bellarmine's Scott Robinson (1,600), Presentation's Mary Mendoza (3,200), Karen Lawson of St. Francis (long jump), St. Francis 400 relay team . . . Dan Goldie (Stanford) takes first pro title at Tennis Hall of Fame tournament . . . Liz Chiarelli wins record fifth county women's golf crown . . . Mexican Pan-American Games team whips Argentina, 3-0, before 15,104 at Spartan Stadium . . . Brad Klaus of Los Altos Hills posts 217 to win 54-hole county junior golf title . . . Vanessa Bergman of Los Altos takes one-meter world junior diving title in Norway . . . Jorge Urbana-Diaz beats Howard Petty for seventh straight Civic Auditorium victory . . . Steve Ledesma (Gilroy) averages 17.5 points for Mexico's national basketball team . . . Michael Swain (SJS) captures world, Pan-American Games judo titles . . . Campbell-Moreland boys lose Colt World Series final to Marietta, Ga., 7-6 . . . Quito All-Star girls win Senior softball championship over Williamsport, Pa., when Chelsea Gricius walks with bases loaded to force in Stephanie Balc with game's winning run . . . Kay Cockerill wins second straight U. S.

women's amateur golf title . . . Billy Owens passes for 258 yards, three scores in Bellarmine's 28-7 win over Gilroy . . . After Cal takes 25-24 lead with 27 seconds left, Mike Perez, Johnny Johnson hook up on 36-yard pass to set up Sergio Olivarez's game-winning 20-yard field goal for SJS . . . Mark Langston (Buchser, SJS) leads American League in strikeouts for third time with career high 262 . . . Kale Wedemeyer runs for Los Gatos High record 277 yards with five TDs in 34-14 win over Mitty . . . Jan Stephenson shoots tourney record 205 to win San Jose Classic golf . . . Pat Sheehy's goal gives Stanford first-ever soccer win over UCLA, 1-0 . . . St. Francis High's Steve Ruffin ties WCAL record with five TDs in 38-18 victory against Sacred Heart . . . First county girl to wear state prep cross-country crown is Kathy McCandless of Castilleja . . . SCU loses to Cal Poly, 33-31, but Greg Calcagno throws for 274 yards, three scores to end career with record 7,001 yards, 43 TDs . . . Ernie Hernandez rushes for 119 yards as Live Oak High rips Santa Teresa, 38-15, for CCS Div. 4A football crown. Saratoga's Dave Stoll splits uprights with last second 24-yard field goal for 12-10 win over Monterey in Div. 3A . . . SJCC, winner of 24 of last 25 grid games, is beaten by De Anza (8-2-0) in San Jose Bowl on Joe Fragia's last minute TD, 28-21 . . . Stacey Mays has 39 in Wilcox High's 49-46 hoops OT win over Prospect . . . Mountain View High's two-way lineman Mark Johnson is county's top player . . . Soph Keith Davis scores 26 for Independence High in 65-58 victory against Santa Teresa . . . Stanford tops UCLA, 116-110, in double OT. Howard Wright leads Cardinal with 30 . . . Rex Walters hits 25 points as Piedmont Hills falls to Gorman in Las Vegas hoops tournament.

■ 1988 ■

Los Gatos High shot deflects off Blackford defender for goal in last 30 seconds as Wildcats end Braves' 28-match unbeaten soccer streak, 3-2 . . . Sue Roshanzamir wins most of her matches as 100-pound wrestler on Independence High boy's team . . . Santa Teresa tops Independence, 67-52, with Brian Killian going for 27 . . . SJS loses to Utah State, 114-85, as Ricky Berry hits 29 to become all-time Spartan scoring king . . . Ron Reis of Monta Vista High scores 32 in 75-53 win over Saratoga to surpass ex-Falcon Randy Arrillaga as county's all-time hoops scorer . . . Parade names Santa Teresa's Sam Singer, Rob Danner of Cupertino to prep All-America soccer squad . . . County player of the year Lucius Davis of Piedmont Hills High hits 27 in 68-66 win over Santa Teresa in MHAL title playoff . . . Mike Flohr pumps in 38 as Bellarmine defeats Live Oak, 76-63 . . . SJCC falls to Skyline in state JC playoffs, 77-76. Jags' Rick Witmer (Pioneer) gets 16 . . . Lance Roehl's two free throws give St. Francis 74-73 CCS final win over Riordan. Greg Paulson leads Lancers with 25 . . . Leland High's Natalie Rynn (21.5 average), Jill Sperry (16.1) of Div. 1 girl's champ Gunderson are area co-players of the year . . . Wrestler Marco Sanchez of Independence High wins state crown . . . Pepperdine retires Maureen Formico's (Mitty) number after she ends hoops career with all-time record total of 2,190 points . . . Chicago Bears draft Stanford back Brad Muster in first round . . . Goalie Tim Rudd's 17th shutout gives Leland High CCS soccer co-title when darkness ends 105-minute, scoreless Div. 1 final with Overfelt . . . Greg Gohn pitches SCU's first no-hitter since 1978 against San Diego University, 10-1 . . . Kelly Bongatti of Westmont High throws season's third no-hitter to blank Branham, 3-0 . . . Conference MVP Steve Bosco (Prospect) hits .380, has 11

Monta Vista High's Ryan Hancock threw for 41 touchdowns and was picked as California's prep football player of the year in 1989.

homers, 48 RBIs, leads SJCC to league title . . . Lisa Green's upset win over Florida's Halle Cioffi keys third straight NCAA tennis title for Stanford . . . Stacey Mays fans 18 in Wilcox High's 3-0 win over Willow Glen. She pitches five no-hit, two perfect games to gain area player of the year honors . . . David Wheaton, Jeff Tarango win doubles to clinch NCAA tennis crown for Stanford, 5-2, over LSU . . . Scott Mollahan (11-1) pitches Bellarmine to fourth straight CCS Div. 1 title over Soquel, 6-4 . . . Julie DeVita's one-hitter gives Monta Vista 1-0 softball victory over Westmont in section final . . . Leland High's John Wirtz tops state preps with 192-10 discus toss. Independence's John Montgomery wins 330 intermediate hurdles . . . Catcher Troy Buckley (Bellarmine) sets SCU marks with .442 batting average, 82 RBIs, is WCC's top player . . . Twenty-eight yard field goal by Mike Crisafulli (Mitty) leads North to 22-21 win over South in state prep grid classic . . . Vu Tran's two scores give Santa Clara United 4-2 soccer win over Austin in U. S. under-19, but team loses McGuire Cup final to New Jersey team . . . David Gonzales of San Jose KOs Rich Velasquez for state lightweight title at Civic Auditorium . . . Golfer Steve Sear of Los Gatos High takes Northern California amateur title . . . Seven-footer Ron Reis of Monta Vista High enters SCU after four-year prep career as all-time CCS scoring leader, first county star to top 2,000 points (2,082) . . . San Jose Giants' Greg Connor hits record two home runs in 13-run first inning of 22-8 win over Modesto . . . Steve Papin has school record 258 yards, four TDs as Piedmont Hills High tops Blackford, 26-14 . . . Santa Clara's Ed Sans wins NASCAR late model stock car crown . . . Swimmer Troy Dalbey wins Olympic gold medal . . . Mitty High frosh top Sacred Heart, 14-6, in last football game at San Francisco's old Kezar Stadium . . . San Jose Classic golf crown for Kathy Guadagnino . . . Goalkeeper Elise Edwards of Stanford blanks San Francisco State, 1-0, for Stanford record ninth shutout in soccer . . . Very busy day for Monta Vista's Ryan Hancock in 40-37 loss to Saratoga. He completes 24 passes for 319 yards, three TDs, runs for two scores, kicks 50-yard field goal, quick kicks 70 yards, executes two successful on side kicks . . . SJS yardage records fall to Johnny Johnson (228 rushing), Kevin Evans (216 receiving) in 36-31 win over Utah State . . . Live Oak High defeats St. Francis, 33-22, in section grid final to extend unbeaten string to 24 games . . . Football coach Al Cementina (222-91-9) retires after 35 years service at Lick, Independence . . . Chabot hands De Anza first loss, 45-14, in San Jose Bowl . . . Greg Siwek hits 49 points in Monta Vista High's 89-55 win over Hollister . . . Kristen Chiaramonte of Willow Glen High is field hockey All-American . . . Monta Vista High girls beat Moreau, 54-42, behind Ami Touli's 35 . . . Jens Gordon's career high 37 leads SCU to Cable Car championship over North Carolina-Charlotte, 84-68 . . . Kenny Jackson (SJS) wins East-West game's offensive player award.

■ 1989 ■

Todd Lichti tops Stanford with 35 in 83-78 win over Arizona . . . Silver Creek High's LaDonna Irving has triple double (34 points, 18 rebounds, 11 assists) in 74-38 victory over Overfelt . . . De Anza hoops coach Tony Nunes chalks up win number 400 in 73-61 win over Los Medanos . . . Ricky Berry (Live Oak, SJS) has 34 with seven treys as Sacramento Kings down Golden State, 142-117 . . . Ed Giovanola's (Bellarmine) home run for SCU snaps 18-game SJS winning streak dating to 1988. Spartans win first 15 this season on way to 40-19 . . . Jon Payne of Cupertino High named Parade soccer All-American . . . Erik Johnson hits 23, Brian Steinback 22, but Prospect High (24-1) loses only game of season to Aragon in CCS playoffs, 91-79 . . . St. Francis High's Cory Clemetson scores 31, Darrin Connolly of Milpitas hits 33, as Lancers win CCS semifinal, 64-60 . . . Gunderson High (25-0) takes Div. 1 girl's crown, 45-38, over Monta Vista. Victory streak ends in Nor Cals. Piedmont Hills wins CCS Div. 2 against North Salinas, 61-60. Pirates' Kim Conway has 36 points, 20 rebounds . . . Overfelt High's Javier Gonzalez is state wrestling champ . . . Stanford women win NCAA swimming . . . Adam Noto, Heath Keller home runs lead St. Francis High to 8-1 win over Sacred Heart as 11-0-1 Lancers become first unbeaten WCAL champion . . . Pitcher Dave Tellers beats UCSB, ties SJS record with 12th win . . . Bay Blackhawks top Portland, 3-2, in double OT soccer at Cupertino High . . . Stanford men win fourth straight NCAA team tennis. Sandra Birch of Stanford takes NCAA women's singles . . . St. Francis girls cop record fourth straight CCS track and field title . . . Del Mar's Jim Lawrence takes state pole vault at 15-6 . . . Scott Parker wins San Jose Mile race before 16,000 at Fairgrounds . . . Pat Hurst medalist as SJS captures NCAA women's golf title . . . Boasting county record batting average (.398), Leland High defeats Los Gatos in CCS Div. 1 final, 3-0. Branham tops Carmel, 4-2, in Div. 2 . . . Paul

Santa Clara University's Cameron Rast (left) and Robert Gallo hold the 1989 NCAA soccer trophy after the Broncos (20-0-3) and Virginia tied for the championship, 1-1, in overtime.

Child scores for Earthquake old-timers in 3-1 reunion loss to Portland . . . St. Francis upsets De La Salle of Concord, 18-16, ending 14-game win streak for nation's 4th ranked football team . . . Troy Lau's 35-yard interception return for TD after time expires gives Palo Alto High 20-14 win over Pioneer . . . Trailing 17-0 with nine minutes left, Stanford gains 18-17 win over Oregon on John Hopkins' 37-yard field goal on final play . . . SJS back Johnny Johnson has 11 catches for 208 yards, four TDs in Spartans' 41-34 win over UOP . . . Beth Daniel shoots 11-under par 205 for one stroke win in San Jose Classic . . . Homestead High ends Lick's school record 15-game unbeaten string, 42-7 . . . SCU squads reach NCAA soccer Final Four. Men co-champs with Virginia, after four OTs, 1-1, women fall to Colorado . . . Lynbrook High bows to nation's No. 1 Manhattan Beach for state volleyball championship . . . State player of year Ryan Hancock of Monta Vista High produces county football records, passing for 3,599 yards, 41 TDs. He runs, passes, kicks for regular season state record 276 points . . . Sheldon Canley sets SJS all-purpose yards record with 2,513 for season, finishes second in NCAA . . . Jorge Paez registers sixth round TKO over San Jose's Lupe Guiterrez in Reno featherweight championship bout.

The 1990s

Landing a Shark was the big event early in the '90s and before long a Tiger carrying a golf club captured the attention of sports fans in Santa Clara County.

But, the local news that excited the most fans came not from the pros, but from members of a college team playing America's home grown game near the end of the decade.

The Stanford Cardinal basketball team played and treyed its way to a school record 30-5 season in 1997-98, topping the season with an appearance in the NCAA Final Four in San Antonio that ended with a spine-tingling 86-85 overtime loss to frequent national power Kentucky.

In 1998-99, the Cardinal (26-7) ended the century with its first league championship in 36 seasons and another trip to the NCAA postseason party.

Mike Montgomery, who became Stanford's winningest coach when he racked up victory number 258 against Arizona State in late February, 1999, had truly turned the program around. When he arrived on The Farm in 1986, the Cardinal had only two winning seasons in the previous 19 and hadn't played in the postseason for 44 years.

Stanford, a stranger to the Final Four since it won the NCAA title in 1942, out muscled Purdue, 67-59, then made it to the 1998 semifinals with a remarkable, come-from-behind 79-77 victory over Rhode Island. But, the Cardinal ran out of miracles when Peter Sauer's last second 80-foot desperation throw went wide and short against Kentucky.

After trailing by 10 points in both halves, the Wildcats' press took its toll in the second stanza, forcing 11 turnovers. Stanford rallied from four points down with 15 seconds left to tie the game and force overtime.

Center Tim Young fouled out on the first play and the Cardinal soon was down by five. A chance for victory remained when Sauer hit a three-pointer with .09 left to create the final one-point deficit. After Kentucky missed two free throws, Sauer retrieved the ball, but had no time to get off a decent last shot.

Overlooked on the All-Pac-10 team, point guard Arthur Lee (better known to the Maples Pavilion public address announcer as Arrrrthurrrr Leeeeee) made the Final Four squad, converting an NCAA record 35 straight free throws.

Lee propelled Stanford into the Final Four by scoring 26 points, with 13 coming against Rhode Island in the last two minutes of the quarterfinal. Trailing by six points with 59 seconds left, Lee produced five points and an assist before tipping the ball away from Cuttino Mobley. Mark Madsen grabbed the loose ball and was fouled as he threw down a thunderous dunk to put the Cardinal ahead by one.

The exuberant "Mad Dog" celebrated by jumping with arms raised, fists clenched, shouting at the top of his voice in a scene that will long be remembered. Madsen's free throw stretched the margin to two with 27 seconds left. Rhode Island's Tyson Wheeler was fouled on a trey attempt, but missed all three tosses and Stanford survived.

Coach Montgomery said the tournament, "proved we belong at the level we've achieved." Players and fans immediately began looking forward to the 1998-99 season, when 11 players and all five starters would return.

Before the new year began, Stanford was rated No. 1 in the preseason polls by three major national magazines and no worse that sixth in four other rankings. Playing its toughest non-league schedule, the Cardinal struggled early, losing the NIT final to No. 9 North Carolina, 57-49, and falling to Connecticut's smothering press for the second consecutive year, 70-59, before a home sellout crowd.

Bay Area reporters figuratively wrung their hands over the Cardinal's inability to dominate every opponent, but the veteran team won its first Pac-10 title with losses to only Arizona, USC and Oregon State.

Seeded No. 2 in the NCAA Western regional, Stanford rallied to whip Alcorn State, 69-57, in the opener only to fall to Gonzaga, 82-74, under a shower of 11 three-point shots by the Zags.

The loss could not dim the achievements of the powerful men's and women's hoops programs on The Farm in the century's last decade.

Tara VanDerveer was NCAA coach of the year in 1990 after her team's first of six Final Four appearances in the decade produced an 88-81 title victory over Auburn. Jennifer Azzi added tourney MVP to her list of honors that included U. S. player of the year. She was Stanford's first three-time All-Pac-10 performer and its first two-time All-American.

The Cardinal lost to Tennessee in the 1991 semifinal, but won the NCAA title again in 1992 over Western Kentucky, 78-62, with Mollie Goodenbour named tourney MVP. The women reached the Final Four again in 1995, 1996 and 1997, bowing in the semifinals each season, first to Georgia, then to Connecticut and finally to Old Dominion in an 83-82 overtime thriller.

In 1998, Stanford was unable to overcome the loss of starters Kristin Folkl and Vanessa Nygaard (who had a combined 33.8 points and 15.4 rebounds per game), but Harvard created the NCAA's biggest upset, 71-67, becoming the first regional 16th seed to beat a No. 1 and ending the Cardinals' Maples Pavilion win streak at 59.

After opening with losses to Arkansas and Duke in the

Leading figures in Stanford's rise to national prominence in women's and men's basketball include (from left) coach Tara VanDerveer and All-Americans Jennifer Azzi and Brevin Knight.

Four in the Fall tournament at the Arena in November, 1998, the women were unranked by the AP poll for the first time since the beginning of the 1987-88 season. UCLA ended their 67-game Pac-10 home winning streak, 80-72, and the Cardinal finished the year 18-12 with a startling first round 60-58 loss to Maine in the NCAA playoffs.

The 1990-91 men's team had a 20-13 record and made a fourth straight postseason appearance with a National Invitational Tournament title win over Oklahoma, 78-72. Adam Keefe was picked as the tourney MVP.

All-American point guard Brevin Knight led Stanford into the NCAA tournament in 1996, when it lost to Massachusetts, and again in 1997, when Utah knocked the Cardinal out in an overtime game at San Jose Arena, 82-77.

■ SAN JOSE GIANTS

San Jose operated one of the California League's best franchises in the 1990s, reaching the postseason playoffs seven times, winning the league championship in 1998 and barely missing it a year later.

The first honor came in 1990, when Baseball America named the Giants the nation's best run minor league franchise and winner of the Bob Freitas Award -- which honors a veteran minor league executive who worked for San Jose from 1947 to 1955. League player of the year Dan Rambo (12-2) led the league with a 2.19 ERA. The Giants won the second half, but bowed to Stockton in the playoffs.

The 1991 Giants had a 92-44 record, the best in franchise history, and drew a near record 123,905 through the turnstiles. They won both halves and led the league by seven games in overall standings, but fell to Stockton in the opening playoff round. Ace of the league's top pitching staff was Richard Hulsman, who topped the circuit with a 16-4 record, 216 strikeouts and a 1.83 ERA.

After finishing out of the playoffs two seasons, the Giants were second in both halves in 1994 and lost to Modesto in the postseason. The 1995 Giants fell to San Bernardino in the final playoff round while surpassing 140,000 in attendance for the first time. Pitching carried the team again with a league best 3.05 ERA. Keith Foulke was the top starter with a 13-6 mark and a 3.50 ERA

San Jose had four hitters above the .300 mark the next season, winning the first half and tying Modesto for the second half title, but bowing to Lake Elsinore in the playoffs. Top batters were Derek Reid (.343), Craig Mayes (.328), Tim Garland (.311) and Jon Sbrocco (.310). Pitcher Darin Blood (17-6) won the ERA title at 3.54.

San Jose's fortunes suffered in 1997 when the parent San Francisco Giants added another Class A farm team in Bakersfield and split its players between the cities. San Jose finished last in both halves with a combined mark of 60-80, but still set a team attendance record of 146,151. It was the third consecutive year above 140,000 and the 10th straight higher than 100,000.

A 16 of 17-game victory run gave San Jose the first half Valley Division title in 1998. The Giants fell to fourth in the second half, but won their first title since 1979 by beating Rancho Cucamonga in the playoff's final round and drawing 141,180 fans for the season.

Leading players included outfielders Juan Dilone (.320, 18 HRs) and Benji Simonton (.320, 16 HRs) and pitcher Jim Stoops, who saved 31 games before leaving the team as part of trade engineered by San Francisco.

The 1999 Giants (75-65) came within one game of winning back-to-back pennants while drawing a team record 157,598 fans. They were second to Modesto in the first half and rode an 11-game win streak into the thick of the second half race before slipping to third with a 37-33 record.

Second baseman Will Otero led the Giants with a .333 average in 96 games, while first sacker Tim Flaherty (25 HRs, 88 RBIs) and outfielder Mike Glendenning (23 HRs, 80 RBIs) provided some power.

San Jose slipped past Visalia, then upset champion Modesto for the North Division playoff title, but lost to Southern Division winner San Bernardino in the fifth and final game of the postseason championship series.

■ LADY BRONCOS

With sophomore Melissa King leading the way, the Santa Clara University women's basketball team concluded its best-ever season with 71-68 victory over Indiana to take the 1990-91 National Women's Invitation Tournament.

King averaged 19.2 points for the season, second highest in school history, and was the tournament MVP. The Lady Broncos (29-3) won their first six games and later took another dozen straight on their way to becoming the West Coast Conference champion for the first time.

There were plenty of honors for the team. Caren Horstmeyer was WCC Coach of the Year and King took both player of the year and newcomer of the year honors. Three-point shooting star Julie Lienert buried 89 treys for the season and was named to the all-WCC team.

Six-foot-four center Amy Vanos blocked a team record 38 shots during the season and pulled in 200 rebounds, four shy of the season record set by teammate Laura Hughes.

The next year, the Lady Broncos took the conference title and postseason honors with a 67-62 win over USF as MVP King hit 30 points. In their first NCAA appearance, they beat Cal before losing in the next round to Texas Tech and completing the season with a 21-10 record.

Led by Lisa Sacco and 6-foot-6 Christine Rigby, regular season champion Santa Clara (23-8) made another trip to the NCAA in 1998 after beating St. Mary's for the WCC tournament crown. They lost to Arizona, 75-63.

The 1998-99 team rolled to a 7-0 start, including a win over Stanford, 81-65, and was ranked 25th for the first time in history. They tied Pepperdine for the league title, but lost to St. Mary's in the WCC tournament semifinals.

Their record won an at-large spot in the NCAA tournament. Santa Clara raced to a 13-0 lead against Iowa State, but lost, 74-61, to finish the year 22-7.

All-time Santa Clara University scoring leader Melissa King paced the Lady Broncos to the 1990-91 National Invitational Tournament title.

■ ONE BIG WIN, TWO LOSSES

The biggest jewel in Santa Clara County's sports crown finally was in place when the San Jose Arena opened a few blocks west of downtown in September, 1993. The first event in the 18,200-seat facility, built by the city with voter's approval at a 1988 referendum, was a circus.

Sports took center stage several weeks later when San Jose's Geraldo Martinez won a 12-round decision over Eddie "Prime Time" Croft for the WBC Continental Americas super-bantamweight boxing title.

The Bay Area's first major multi-use facility built since Oakland's Coliseum complex had opened more than a quarter century earlier was packed with hockey fans for the first time in October when the San Jose Sharks beat the New York Islanders, 4-3, in an exhibition before 17,310.

Earlier in the decade, it had appeared that other major sports facilities might be built in the county.

After lengthy negotiations, owner Bob Lurie agreed in August, 1990, to move his San Francisco Giants to Santa Clara if voters approved financing for a new ballpark. The $153 million facility would have been built on a 98-acre site in Santa Clara and operated by a joint powers authority formed by the county and cities in the region.

But, voters in a county-wide election in November, 1990, turned down a 1 percent utility tax that would have paid off the 30-year bond issue to fund the project.

The tax measure failed by a slender margin of fewer than 3,000 votes. Some Santa Clara City Council members opposed the tax and San Jose Mayor Tom McEnery backed the stadium, but opposed its funding by a utility tax.

San Jose voters rejected another plan for a new home for the Giants 18 months later. Measure G, calling for a 2 percent utility tax hike to bankroll a $265 million stadium at Zanker Road and Highway 237, lost by 15,657 votes.

■ STAYING FOCUSED

Sports Focus, the popular Friday night television show featuring Bay Area high school teams and athletes, began as a Santa Clara County football program in 1991.

Originally called Football Focus, the program produced, directed and narrated by Robert Braunstein of San Jose television station KICU (Channel 36), went on the air for the first time in September, 1992.

The first highlights telecast were from a St. Francis High-Live Oak football game, won by the Lancers, 34-24.

After several years of featuring local football game highlights, the program branched out to cover a variety of boys and girls prep sports throughout the school year in Santa Clara, San Mateo, San Francisco, Contra Costa and Alameda counties.

■ NUMBER ONE TIMES TWO

It would be hard to pick the best two-sport female athlete to come out of a Santa Clara County high school this century, but high on the list would be Keri Sanchez of Santa Teresa High School and Kerri Walsh of Mitty.

Sanchez won both hurdles and the triple jump in the CCS championship track meet in 1988, took the hurdles and

Two of the county's top female prep athletes were Keri Sanchez (left) and Kerri Walsh.

long jump in 1989, then won all four events to lead the Saints to the section title in 1990.

On the soccer field, Sanchez was the state's top female prep player in 1990 and 1991 and had two assists as Santa Teresa took the 1991 CCS title with a 2-1 win over Homestead. After high school she started for North Carolina every season as the Tar Heels won four straight NCAA titles.

The 6-foot-3 Walsh graduated from Mitty in 1996 and won a Stanford volleyball scholarship. She may have been the best girl's volleyball player who ever played at a county high school and was among the top basketball players.

During her four basketball seasons, Mitty won four CCS, three Northern California and the 1995 state title. In volleyball, Mitty took four CCS, three Nor Cal and three state titles. She was a volleyball All-American, CCS player of the year in both sports and state athlete of the year.

As a freshman, Walsh helped Stanford win its third NCAA volleyball title over Hawaii. She was Final Four MVP and All-America. Walsh underwent shoulder surgery as a sophomore, but returned to join teammate Kristin Folkl on the All-America team as the Cardinal won another title. Walsh picked up more All-American honors in 1998, when the Cardinal fell to Texas in the NCAA semifinals, and in 1999 when Penn State beat Stanford for the title.

■ INTO THE SHARK TANK

After eight years in the National Hockey League, the San Jose Sharks still hadn't achieved a .500 season as the century ended. They came close again at the end, finishing 1998-99 with a 31-33-18 record before falling to Colorado in six games in the playoffs. The series' start was delayed and the first two games were moved to San Jose following the massacre of 12 students and a teacher at Columbine High School in a Denver suburb.

After scoring only two goals in a pair of home losses, the Sharks blistered the net in 4-2 and 7-3 wins at Denver, before being eliminated by losses in the next two games, the last a 3-2 overtime heartbreaker.

Other top seasons for the usually mediocre team came at mid-decade. San Jose went 33-35-16 in 1993-94, stunned Detroit in the first playoff round and took Toronto to game seven before being eliminated from the Stanley Cup hunt.

The next year, the 19-25-4 Sharks upset Calgary in the opening playoff round's seventh game, 5-4 in double OT, on winger Ray Whitney's memorable goal with 1:54 left. But, they went home after four straight losses to Detroit.

While a trip to the Stanley Cup finals hasn't come yet, the Sharks have built a tremendous fan following, starting with their debut in temporary quarters at Daly City's Cow Palace in 1991-92.

Bringing hockey to San Jose grew out of a 1990 proposal to shift the Minnesota North Stars to Oakland. When NHL officials agreed to study the move, Minnesota owner George Gund expressed interest in San Jose, where former Hartford owner Howard Baldwin had an exclusive temporary agreement to operate a new hockey team in the still unbuilt San Jose Arena. Gund sold Minnesota to a group headed by Baldwin on condition he would receive an expansion franchise for San Jose, which was approved in mid-1991.

With the Arena under construction, the team prepared to open at the Cow Palace, where $12 to $55 ticket prices would be near the top of the NHL scale. Sharks was picked as the team's nickname after a contest which produced such nominees as Breakers, Breeze, Condors, Fog, Golden Skaters, Icebreakers, Knights, Sea Lions and Waves. Uniforms featuring Pacific teal, black, white and gray with a shark chomping on a hockey stick were unveiled in early 1991.

Craig Cox got the Sharks' first goal in a 4-3 road loss to Vancouver. They fell to the Canucks again in their home debut, but got into the win column with a 4-3 victory over Calgary as Kelly Kisio scored the winning goal.

The season was interrupted for 10 days when players struck over trading card royalties, but the Sharks (17-58-5) sold out every home game at the 10,888-seat Cow Palace despite winding up a distant last in their division.

San Jose fell to 11-71-2 the following year and tied a NHL record by losing 17 straight. Popular goal tender Arturs Irbe's first shutout over Los Angeles was one of the few highlights and the team failed to sell out seven games.

Despite making the greatest turnaround in NHL history in their first season at San Jose in 1992-93 and with a 19-13-10 record on home ice, sellouts eluded the Sharks again as attendance averaged 16,595 in the 17,483-seat Arena, better known to locals as The Shark Tank.

That changed in 1994-95. Although the home opener was delayed until Jan. 21 by the NHL players lockout, fans flocked to see the Sharks, who had a six-game win streak early in the year and made the playoffs for the second time. Each of the 24 games were played before capacity crowds.

San Jose got off to a terrible 1-14-4 start in 1995-96, missing the playoffs as they moved players in and out, including sending their original top draft pick, Pat Falloon, away in a trade and acquiring high-scoring Owen Nolan.

One of the best moments in 1996-97 came in January when Nolan scored a hat-trick with two goals coming in a record span of eight seconds. His feat didn't help last place San Jose (27-47-8) gain a win since it came in the league All-Star Game before 17,442 at the Arena. Despite Nolan's heroic effort, the East won, 11-7. San Jose missed the playoffs as the team's string of 118 full houses ended, but youngster Jeff Friesen produced a club MVP season.

The 1997-98 Sharks (34-38-10) mixed youth and veterans to finish fourth in the division. They filled a hole in goal with veteran Mike Vernon, signed for three years at $2.7 million. As MVP he produced a better record than the team (30-22-8). Friesen had 31 goals, 63 points and productive rookies were Patrick Marleau (13 goals and 32 points) and Marco Sturm (10 goals, 30 points).

New coach Darryl Sutter's team got off to a shaky start, but played above .500 after December and clinched a playoff spot with a 3-3 draw at Calgary as a large crowd watched a free closed-circuit broadcast at the Arena.

The Sharks played Dallas even up through the first four playoff games, but lost the fifth, 3-2, when the referee did not ask to review a play where a Stars' player was in the crease on the winning goal. Dallas eliminated San Jose in the next game in a sudden death overtime, 3-2.

Accompanied by more than 100 fans, San Jose opened 1998-99 in Tokyo with two games against Calgary. Sutter, who had started his pro hockey career as a player in Japan in 1978-79, was unhappy about the trip. He was muzzled by league officials after saying the Sharks and Flames should spend the time in Hawaii and just tell the league they split the two games. San Jose came home with a loss and tie and didn't achieve a win until its ninth game.

Holdouts Friesen and Nolan signed contracts just after the season began and the Sharks continued their history of getting off to a poor start. San Jose fell to 6-15-7 before winning four straight, their best streak in four seasons.

In the early going, they saw the crowd count fall below capacity. Sutter was furious when the toothless Sharks lost to expansion Nashville, saying Nolan, Friesen and Marleau were the only players playing hard.

San Jose rallied to boost its record to 13-18-10 at midyear and continued to improve despite season-ending injuries to Gary Suter and Tony Granato.

On a grueling 17-day, 10-game road trip in February -- the longest continuous jaunt in NHL history -- the Sharks lost their last three, but still fashioned a 4-5-1 record. They acquired center Vincent Damphousse from Montreal just before the March trading deadline and he helped the Sharks extend their unbeaten streak to eight (5-0-3) and close in on the elusive .500 mark again. Damphousse was signed to a four-year, $18 million deal after the season ended.

The only Sharks ranked in the top 15 in any category in the decade's last season were goaltenders and co-MVPs Vernon and Steve Shields. The latter had a 15-10-8 record, clinched a playoff spot with a 1-0 shutout win over Phoenix in the 77th game and extended his unbeaten streak to 9-0-2 with a 4-1 win over Anaheim in his next outing.

■ AWESOME TWOSOME

Palo Alto High compiled a unique record among county boy's basketball teams in 1993 when it dumped highly rated and defending state champion Morningside of Inglewood, 79-59, to capture the Division 3 state title and finish the season with an undefeated 31-0 record.

Coach John Barrette's Vikings were led by All-CCS players David Weaver, Grant Elliott and Mark Thompson.

The 6-foot-4 Weaver played a strong all-around game and led the team with a 19.0 average and Thompson's 68 treys ranked third in the county.

One of their toughest tests came in the CCS finals against an unbeaten Harbor of Santa Cruz squad led by future Stanford star Tim Young. The Vikes scored on the opening tip and never trailed in their 69-58 win. Thompson led the way with 25 and Young was held to 20.

No county boy's team had been unbeaten since Willow Glen won the 1969 CCS championship with a 27-0 record in the days before the state playoffs began.

A powerful Archbishop Mitty girl's team duplicated Palo Alto's feat in 1999, posting a 31-0 record and capturing the state championship with a victory over Pacific Palisades at Arco Arena in Sacramento.

The top ranked Monarchs took their seventh straight

David Weaver celebrated after unbeaten Palo Alto High won the state Div. 3 basketball title.

CCS crown under California coach of the year Sue Phillips-Chargin -- who won a section title as a Mitty senior player in 1985 -- with a 65-37 Div. 1 win over St. Ignatius.

They cruised through the first two rounds of the Nor Cals with easy wins and beat Berkeley, 61-53, in the final as Rometra Craig, a junior transfer from Menlo School, scored 21 points and grabbed 16 rebounds.

With CCS player of the year Craig hitting 19, Mitty took an exciting 49-48 state final victory over Pacific Palisades. The winning basket came with nine seconds left when Aimee Grzyb passed to Domeneca Curran for a layup.

Craig, who also starred in track, was named the 1999 state athlete of the year by Cal-Hi Sports. Mitty and Bellarmine Prep were selected as the top schools for girls and boys sports, respectively.

■ TWO DOWN, ONE RETURNS

Critics called indoor soccer and roller hockey "trash sports," but Grizzly and Rhino fans were true believers, even if they didn't strain the capacity of the San Jose Arena.

Both teams debuted in 1994, the Grizzlies in the Continental Indoor Soccer League and the Rhinos as members of Roller Hockey International. The former drew 3,854 for a home opener loss to Sacramento and 4,675 showed up two nights later as the Rhinos beat the Oakland Skates.

Led by Mark Wolff, the second place Rhinos (13-7-2) were ousted from the 1994 playoffs by Anaheim. They were fourth the next year, but won the playoffs and RHI title. The Rhinos had a 15-12 mark in 1996, but didn't make it to the postseason and in 1997 fell in the playoff's first round to Anaheim after drawing average crowds of 5,200.

The league did not play in 1998 while trying to pay off a $1.5 million debt, but the Rhinos returned in 1999 to finish with a 12-11-3 record and the fourth playoff spot. They dumped Las Vegas in the semifinals, 6-5, but lost to Anaheim in the division final. Wolfe, the league's all-time leading scorer, retired after the season.

On the soccer front, even the acquisition of one of the indoor game's most prolific scorers couldn't put the 12-16 Grizzlies into the 1994 playoffs. Predrag Radosavljevic, better known as Preki, was back again in 1995 when his 400th career goal came in a win over San Diego and he was league MVP. The team qualified for the playoffs, but disbanded after losing to Sacramento.

Minor league basketball also failed in San Jose, when the Jammers moved to Bakersfield after two seasons.

The Continental Basketball Association's high scoring hoops game never caught on in the 1989-90 and 1990-91 seasons at the Event Center, where the Jammers finished third in their division each year. The fans weren't very interested, partly because the news media wasn't either.

The Jammers had some skilled players with Bay Area roots, including David Boone, Richard Morton and Rick Barry's son, Scooter. The club lost a reported $400,000 the first season on average attendance of 2,299. After drawing only 2,400 a game in 1991, it hit the road out of town.

■ WORLD CUP SOCCER

No sporting event except the Olympic Games equals the international flavor of soccer's World Cup tournament.

Bay Area sports fans, including many who had never attended a soccer game before, turned out in record numbers in 1994 to watch five matches at Stanford Stadium.

With hundreds of Brazilian supporters celebrating to the beat of dozens of samba drums, 81,061 saw Brazil whitewash Russia in the opener, 2-0. Star Romario deflected Bebeto's corner kick into the net for the first goal as the Brazilians began their climb to the eventual championship.

Four days later, Brazil crushed Cameroon, 3-0, before an even larger crowd of 83,401. That number was exceeded by 368 when Columbia beat Switzerland, 2-0. In the first round final, 74,914 saw Oleg Salenko score a World Cup record five goals as Russia crushed Cameroon, 6-1.

The first of two final round matches brought Brazil and USA into the stadium. An estimated 32 million TV viewers also watched as the Brazilians won, 1-0. A week later, the World Cup closed its memorable series here with Sweden besting Romania on penalty kicks after the teams tied 2-2 in soccer's equivalent of triple overtime.

■ SAN JOSE HALL OF FAME

The San Jose Sports Hall of Fame honored its first class in 1995, inducting Donna de Varona, Olympic swimming champion; Lee Evans, Olympic track gold medalist; George Haines, Santa Clara Swim Club coach; Jim Plunkett, Stanford Heisman Trophy quarterback; Charlie and Lucy Wedemeyer, inspirational Los Gatos High football coach and wife, and Bud Winter, San Jose State track coach.

Bronze plaques showing portraits of the inductees are displayed at the San Jose Arena. The hall also honors male and female amateur and high school athletes of the year annually. Other major honorees this century were:

1996 - Peggy Fleming, Olympic figure skating champion; John Hanna, Bellarmine football coach; Julie Menendez, San Jose State boxing and soccer coach; Yosh Uchida, San Jose State judo coach.

1997 - Payton Jordan, Stanford track coach; Hank Luisetti, Stanford basketball star; Bob Mathias, Olympic decathlon gold medalist; Albert Ruffo, San Francisco 49ers former part-owner; Tommie Smith, Olympic track gold medalist; Chris von Saltza, Olympic swimming champion.

1998 - Hal Davis, national champion sprinter; Pablo Morales, Olympic swimming gold medal champion; L. T. "Buck" Shaw, Santa Clara and San Francisco 49ers football coach; Debi Thomas, champion figure skater; Bill Walsh, Stanford and 49ers football coach.

1999 - Millard Hampton, Olympic champion sprinter; Claudia Kolb, Olympic champion swimmer; Pat Malley, Santa Clara University football coach; Patty Sheehan, LPGA Hall of Fame golfer.

■ BATTLE BETWEEN THE BOARDS

Minor league football had been played in San Jose with modest success off and on since the 1940s, but never with quite the appeal of the frenetic version offered indoors by the SaberCats.

Huge crowds of fans were attracted to the Arena by the gaudiest full-page color sports ads that ever appeared in the San Jose Mercury News. They stayed to watch "The 50-Yard Indoor War" offered up by Arena Football.

The combination of big hits on the Arena's hockey-sized field, plus games where the LOSER often scored 30 to 60 points satisfied even the most action-oriented spectator.

The SaberCats came to San Jose as an expansion team in 1995 and had no problem filling its roster with former college players willing to work for $600 to $1,000-a-game plus win bonuses. The fifth largest crowd in league history, 15,105, saw the opening night 43-37 loss to Arizona. Quarterback Tony Kimbrough's arm took the 'Cats to the playoffs, where they were eliminated by Orlando, 55-37.

Kimbrough was injured part way through the 1996 campaign and QB Ben Bennett (Peterson) filled in briefly, throwing his 250th Arena League career touchdown pass in one game. The SaberCats (8-6) missed the playoffs.

Kimbrough was recovering from ankle surgery in 1997 and the team finished 8-6 again, falling to Iowa, 68-59, in the postseason. San Jose's attendance averaged 14,519, fourth in the league. Many came to see swift little running back Steve Papin (Piedmont Hills, WVC), who scored 16 TDs in only five games.

The following year, Papin extended his league record for scoring a touchdown at the start of a career to 19 games. He set another mark with 3,192 all-purpose yards and was given the league's Don't Blink Award as the player who best represented the game's fast-paced action and versatility.

After an 0-3 start, head coach Todd Shell installed Ron Lopez at quarterback. San Jose beat Houston, 65-55, on eight TD passes by Lopez in the final game to sneak into the playoffs with a 7-7 record, but lost for the third straight year, 65-46, to top seeded Tampa Bay.

San Jose recorded its first opening game win in 1999 under new head coach Darren Arbet when Carlos Huerta kicked a 36-yard field goal in the final second to lift the SabreCats to a 54-53 victory at Grand Rapids.

When starter Scott Wood missed the fourth game to attend his brother's wedding, backup QB Mike Grieb (Oak Grove) led the team to 54-50 win over Arizona with a late touchdown pass to Shalom Baker.

In the next game Papin kept his TD string alive at 24 when he ran a kickoff back with 9.3 seconds left to defeat Milwaukee, 52-45. The streak ended when Papin was shut out in a 34-30 home loss to Iowa five days later.

The 'Cats faltered after a 4-1 start and general manager Terry Malley, a former SCU head football coach, became offensive coordinator. The offense continued to slump and San Jose's fifth year became its worst as the SaberCats failed to qualify for the playoffs with a 6-8 record.

■ STANFORD BOWLS

Stanford blanked Michigan State, 38-0, in the 1996 Sun Bowl in a game that veteran Cardinal football broadcaster Bob Murphy called, "the greatest performance by any Stanford team in a bowl game."

The Cardinal had started the year 2-5, but rallied to close the books on a 7-5 season after the Dec. 31 contest.

Quarterback Chad Hutchinson went 22 for 28 for 226 yards with a touchdown to take the offensive MVP award and defensive end Kailee Wong registered 10 tackles and two sacks to win honors among the defenders.

It was Stanford's fourth bowl appearance of the decade.

Bill Walsh

QB Steve Stenstrom, who closed his career in 1994 with 11 school and seven Pac-10 passing records, led Stanford into the postseason at the end of both 1991 and 1992.

Stanford was ranked No. 17 with an 8-3-0 record entering the 1991 Aloha Bowl, but lost to George Tech, 18-17, on a two-point conversion with 14 seconds left in the game. Stanford had led, 17-10, but the offense stalled after Tommy Vardell, who had gained 104 yards and scored twice, broke his collarbone.

On Jan. 1, 1993, the Cardinal ended its first 10-win season since 1940, thrashing Penn State in the Blockbuster Bowl, 24-3. Stenstrom passed for a pair of scores during a 17-for-28 day as head coach Bill Walsh's first team after his return from the NFL gained a No. 9 national ranking.

The final Cardinal bowl appearance of the century came in 1995 when first-year head coach Tyrone Willingham's Cardinals lost to East Carolina in the Liberty Bowl, 19-13.

■ CINDERELLA SPARTANS

At 6-foot-9, San Jose State sophomore sub Rich Taylor was an unlikely Prince Charming.

Taylor didn't have a glass slipper in his hand, but he did deliver a three-pointer with five seconds left to gave the Spartans a 76-75 overtime win over Utah State in the 1996 Big West basketball tournament's championship game.

Coach Stan Morrison's Cinderella Spartans had to win six of their last seven regular season games just to get into the tournament with a 10-16 record.

As Big West tournament winners, they played No. 1 seed Kentucky in the NCAA's first round and Cinderella's carriage turned into a pumpkin. SJS (13-17) led early, but fell to the Wildcats' second half onslaught, 110-72.

It was a great year for Bay Area hoops, nevertheless, as three other teams made it to March Madness in the big collegiate tournament. Cal (17-11) fell in the first round to Iowa State, but Stanford (20-8) moved past Bradley only to lose to Massachusetts. Santa Clara (20-9) tipped first round opponent Maryland, but bowed to Kansas in the next game.

■ TIGERMANIA

Stanford's Eldrick "Tiger" Woods was the most talked about young golfer with a county connection in the 1990s. In fewer than four years on the PGA tour, he established an earnings record unsurpassed in the history of the pro game.

As a Stanford freshman in June, 1996, he took the NCAA golf title by four strokes and captured an unprecedented third straight U. S. amateur title before turning pro.

Woods won his first PGA title after a month on the tour, beating Davis Love III in a playoff at the Las Vegas Invitational. Two weeks later, he won again with a final round 66 in the Walt Disney World/Oldsmobile Classic.

Late in 1997, AP reported his presence was making non-players pay attention to golf to the tune of $653.5 million in new money pouring into the sport in his first year on the tour. Ticket sales increased, TV ratings jumped, interest in golf rose and product sales by his main sponsors -- Nike, Titleist, American Express and Rolex -- soared.

Woods won seven of his first 30 tournaments for $2.91 million, putting him in the top 90 money winners of all-time, plus another $1.2 million in appearance fees.

His record 12-stroke Masters victory led some observers to believe he would always be in the running. But, the youngest Masters champ struggled and failed to make the cut for the first time at the Canadian Open in September, 1997. Then Tiger won only one of his four Ryder Cup matches as America lost to Europe. Woods became the fifth golfer to win the AP Male Athlete of the Year Award in the award's 67-year history. He took five tournaments and topped the $2 million mark in winnings.

Woods started 1998 -- the Chinese Year of the Tiger -- by staging his greatest comeback in January, making up an eight-stroke deficit to beat Ernie Els at the Johnny Walker Classic in Thailand on the second playoff hole. Favored to repeat as Masters champ, he finished ninth.

At the U. S. Open, the San Francisco Olympic Club course did not suit his game. His main strength is long off the tee, but the Olympic Club's deep rough put a premium on accuracy and Tiger finished tied for 18th. His stunning final round charge produced three birdies on the last four holes of the British Open, but he finished third.

A nine-month victory drought ended in February, 1999, when Woods won the Buick Invitational. He took the Western Open in July to gain the world's No. 1 ranking and won his second major with a one-stroke win in the PGA Championship. He closed 1999 by becoming the first golfer to top $7.6 million in earnings and the first to win at least eight PGA titles in a year since 1974.

■ SAN JOSE CLASH

A storybook finish -- with first year star Eric Wynalda scoring the league's inaugural goal with three minutes remaining -- gave the San Jose Clash a 1-0 win over D. C. United in the 1996 opening game of Major League Soccer.

The new team in the new league proved a hit at the box office as a Spartan Stadium record 31,683 turned out. The Clash later broke the record when 31,728 saw a match against Los Angeles and averaged 17,232 for the season.

Success at the gate was not matched on the field, however, as the team finished fourth in the West (15-17).

Tiger Woods

John Doyle was the league's top defender and Wynalda was San Jose's leading scorer and sixth in the league with 10 goals and 33 points. He won U. S. soccer player of the year honors after becoming the most prolific scorer in history with 25 goals in 74 national team appearances.

Although he was the team's marquee player, Wynalda missed 34 of San Jose's 64 games over the next two seasons to injuries and national team appearances.

In 1997, Ron Cerritos was the Clash's only all-league player, setting a MLS record with an 11-game string of making a goal or an assist.

Brian Quinn replaced Laurie Calloway (20-27) midway through the season as the Clash struggled to a 12-20 record. San Jose was unable to hold leads, losing seven games by giving up goals in the last 20 minutes. The team blew a two-goal lead against Los Angeles to lose the finale, and miss the playoffs as average attendance dropped to 13,597.

El Nino storms delayed construction work to widen Spartan Stadium's field by six feet, forcing the Clash to play its first three 1998 home games at Stanford.

The Clash suffered its 13th tie breaker loss in 19 tries in the opener at Los Angeles. They fell to the Galaxy in another shootout in the home opener before 15,028 at Stanford and dropped a third straight extra time game to Dallas after Wynalda went down with a knee injury that kept him out of the lineup for weeks.

At mid-season, a group headed by MLS founder Alan Rothenberg proposed to buy the team, which has been operated by the league since the its inception. The deal fell through several months later and the Clash was sold to Kraft Sports Group, owner of the league's New England Revolution and the NFL's New England Patriots.

Team president Peter Bridgewater left for a job with the league, but Quinn was retained after the team closed the season 13-19 and fifth in the western division.

A youth movement which reduced the 1999 team's average age to 24.7 years brought mixed results. Rookie Jamie Clark (Stanford) was one of the season's early stars with game and shootout goals that helped the team to its best start (4-1) in history with four straight shootout wins.

Wynalda was traded and the Clash obtained Raul Diaz Arce, the league's all-time top scorer. Diaz Arce was a bust, producing four goals and two assists in 18 games before being sent to Tampa Bay, where he broke out of his slump with five goals and four assists in his next four games.

The low-scoring Clash had six shootout wins, but no three-point victories until the 12th game. That win came before the smallest home crowd in franchise history (6,824) when San Jose rallied for three goals in 7:37 to defeat Colorado, 4-3, on Mauricio Wright's 77th minute goal.

Quinn was sacked when San Jose missed the playoffs and was succeeded by former Los Angeles Galaxy coach Lothar Osiander. San Jose closed the books on 1999 with a 19-13 record, including a league record 10 shootout wins. Home attendance fell to 11,082 per game

As a marketing ploy following the close of the 1999 season, the Clash was renamed the Earthquakes after the popular 1974-84 San Jose pro soccer team.

■ COMEBACK OF THE CENTURY

If a contest were held to pick the county's "Comeback of the Century," St. Francis High School's 1996 football team would receive many votes. Although St. Francis had dominated the Central Coast Section playoffs with five straight titles in the '90s, there were question marks about the Lancers early, but none by the end of the season.

Head coach Ron Calcagno resigned in January, 1996, to join the Oakland A's front office, ending his 24-year run at St. Francis with a 233-59-3 record and 10 section titles.

Assistant Mike Mitchell took over and saw his team stumble to six straight losses, including four to teams that made the playoffs: Live Oak, Oak Grove, Hollister and Bellarmine. It was the school's worst start since the Lancers went 0-9-0 in 1966.

The Lancers didn't win a game until they thumped St. Ignatius, 37-14, after a narrow 20-13 loss to Bellarmine in the West Catholic League opener. For the rest of the season, St. Francis was unstoppable, tying the once beaten Bells for the WCAL title to clinch a playoff berth.

In section play, the Lancers gained revenge for earlier losses, whipping Live Oak, 35-14, Bellarmine, 29-14, and Oak Grove, 34-6, to sweep to the section championship with a 7-6-0 final record .

Running back Charles Tharp led the offense all season. He set school records with 2,005 rushing yards and 26 touchdowns and later was WAC Pacific Division freshman of the year at the University of Hawaii.

■ THE LASERS' LIGHT GOES OUT

The American Basketball League, a spirited Silicon Valley start-up that gave women a chance to compete at the professional level in San Jose and eight other cities, threw in the towel just before Christmas Day in 1998.

Among the victims of its demise were the San Jose Lasers, one of the top franchises in the circuit founded by Palo Alto public relations executives Gary Cavalli and Anne Warner Cribbs, and the ABL All-Star Game scheduled for the San Jose Arena the following January.

Ron Calcagno's St. Francis High teams won 10 Central Coast Section football titles in his 24 seasons as the Lancers' head coach.

The entertaining league, whose players actually were willing to set a pick or take a charge, began operating in 1996, but failed to gain solid national television exposure and couldn't compete with the better-financed Women's National Basketball Association, sponsored by the NBA.

The Lasers packed the 5,000-seat Event Center for the ABL's 1996-97 opener, a 78-70 win over Atlanta with Sheri Sam blistering the nets for 35 points.

The season went into the dumper after 11 games, when Number 1 draft choice Jennifer Azzi (Stanford) dislocated a shoulder and missed the rest of the year.

San Jose ended its first season 18-22 and second in the Western Division and was eliminated from the playoffs after the first round. Coach Jan Lowrey was fired following a low key revolt by her players and replaced by former Nebraska coach Angela Beck.

The Lasers moved four games into the Arena in an attempt to boost attendance in 1997-98 and the ABL gained some exposure through a TV contract with the Fox network. San Jose fell to third place (21-23), but made it to the second playoff round. The Lasers recorded their first ever post-season win, 80-78, at Hartford and moved on with another victory over the Blizzard before Columbus knocked San Jose out of the title hunt.

Azzi was hurt again as the 1998-99 season began, but hit 12 in a 78-73 win over Portland while wearing a small cast which protected the torn ligament in the thumb of her non-shooting hand. The opener attracted 8,025 to the Arena.

San Jose (9-6) was second to Portland in the West and averaging 4,447 per game when Cavalli announced the league would file for Chapter 11 bankruptcy. It was a disappointing loss for the fans, which included a large number of women and girls who had adopted the team as their own.

Loyal customers paid $25 to $1,500 to attend a fan-sponsored all-star tribute game the following January at De Anza College, where 14 players appeared for $5,000 each.

Azzi was picked fifth in the 1999 WNBA draft by Detroit. Other former Lasers drafted included Kendra Holland-Corn, taken 14th by Sacramento; Clarisse Machanguana, 16th by Los Angeles, and Sheri Sam, 20th by Orlando.

■ TRIVIAL PURSUITS

Santa Clara University's Omar Johnson returned a blocked Sacramento State point-after-touchdown kick 97 yards to score a safety in a 33-32 loss in 1991.

Salina Espinosa was a 6-foot-2, 205-pound female tackle on the Lincoln High varsity football team in 1992.

Starved for baseball during the 1994 major league strike, fans listened to San Jose Giants' games broadcast by Hank Greenwald and Ted Robinson on station KNBR.

Because of a physical problem, Stanford basketball star Brevin Knight wore a knee length surgical stocking on one leg, then the other in two seasons in the mid-1990s. Style conscious Bay Area high school players, believing it was a fashion statement by Knight, emulated his one sock attire.

By the mid-1990s, four members of Campbell's Kaeding family were racing at San Jose Speedway: Howard, a dirt track hall of famer who began in the 1950s; son Brent, a frequent sprint car champion, and grandsons Tim and Bud.

Until North Carolina coach Dean Smith retired in 1997, few knew that West Valley College's basketball success rested partly in the Tar Heels' system. "I probably study it as hard as anyone," said WVC coach Bob Burton. After adopting the style in 1990, Burton's teams won more than 85% of their games.

Just before he became the first French citizen to play in the NBA in 1997, Sacramento Kings rookie Olivier Saint-Jean (SJS) took the name Tariq Abdul-Wahad to reflect his conversion to Islam.

Darnell Hillman (SJS), who played for Indiana, was honored at the American Basketball Association's 1997 reunion as the player who wore the biggest Afro hairdo. "I will cherish it dearly," joked 6-foot-9 "Doctor Dunk".

Darnell Hillman

Tight end Brent Jones ended his 11-year NFL career after the 1997 season, leaving punter Bryan Barker as the last Santa Clara University player to appear in the league.

Independence High cousins Jacob and Ricky Palomino won state wrestling titles in 1998, giving the family five champions. Others were their uncle, 76ers' coach Anthony Palomino (1981-1983); Ricky's father, Rick (1980) and Jacob's brother, Jason (1997). Jacob was the first wrestler to win a state title as a freshman in 1998 and the first to repeat as a sophomore the following year.

In 1999, Sports Illustrated ran retrospectives honoring Bud Ogden, a Valley Christian High teacher and basketball coach who starred on Santa Clara University's 1969 basketball team and was featured on SI's front cover that season, and Dan Gladden (Monta Vista, Westmont), an outfielder on Minnesota's 1987 and 1991 World Series champs.

■ SOCKO IN SOCCER

Santa Clara University's outstanding men's and women's soccer programs gained warranted recognition in the 1990s as two of the best in America.

Coach Jerry Smith took over in 1987 and guided the women to 10 straight trips to the NCAA tournament, but lost in the semifinals six times through 1998, when one of his top squads finished 21-1-1. The program sent Tamie Batista, Linda Hoffman, Jennifer Lalor and Smith's wife, Brandi Chastain, on to play with the national team.

Despite a disappointing finish, SCU's greatest season came in 1999. The No. 1 Broncos entertained a record Buck Shaw Stadium crowd of 4,051 as Aly Wagner scored two goals in a 4-0 win over No. 3 Notre Dame. Led by 20-goal scorers Jacqui Little and Mandy Clemens -- winner of the national Hermann Trophy as college soccer's top player -- SCU was 23-0-0 going into the NCAA finals at Spartan Stadium. But the Broncos were eliminated, falling to Notre Dame, 1-0, in the only game in which they trailed all year.

SCU's men tied Virginia for the 1989 NCAA crown, and lost the 1991 final to the same school on penalty kicks.

They capped a successful decade in 1999 with a 16-4-3 team that toppled Connecticut, 2-1, on Shawn Percell's game-winning goal in the four overtime NCAA semifinal, then were defeated by Indiana, 1-0, for the title.

■ WAC ATTACK

San Jose State officials were stunned in May, 1998, by news that eight schools intended to drop out of the Western Athletic Conference a year later to form a new league.

Bolting the 36-year-old conference were Air Force, BYU, Colorado State, New Mexico, Utah, Wyoming, San Diego State and UNLV. Loyalists were SJS, Fresno State, Hawaii, Tulsa, Texas-El Paso, TCU, SMU and Rice, who retained the WAC name and vowed to stay in business.

Forming a new league dubbed the Mountain West, the Breakaway Eight cited geographical problems created by teams spread across four time zones and nearly 4,000 miles. The WAC accepted SJS in a six-team expansion in 1996.

There was some discussion of taking in other Western

schools who had applied for WAC admission in 1996 to form a manageable east-west division of schools. Nevada, Boise State and Louisiana Tech were approved for future membership, but TCU left to join Conference USA.

The NCAA had ruled the remaining eight schools had rights to the WAC name and $2.7 million in basketball tournament revenue. Another result of the split was the loss of an affiliation with the Holiday Bowl football game.

University and community officials turned the bowl loss into a $25 million plan to gradually expand Spartan Stadium to 50,000 seats. The larger facility will host an annual postseason Silicon Valley Bowl game, pitting a top WAC team against another from outside the conference.

■ SUPER BOWL SUPERSTARS

Quarterback John Elway of the Denver Broncos, the third NFL field general with Santa Clara County roots to lead his team into the Super Bowl, became the second one to win it twice with victories in 1998 and 1999.

In 1998, the Broncos produced a memorable 31-24 win over the defending champion Green Bay Packers.

"This is three times better than anything you can imagine," said Elway after the Super Bowl XXXII victory.

It got even better as the Broncos polished off Atlanta, 34-19, the following season and Elway, 38, was named the game's MVP after throwing for 336 yards and a touchdown. It was Elway's last game and the victory became a stepping stone to his retirement.

The ex-Stanford star first joined Craig Morton and Jim Plunkett as former county residents who guided Super Bowl teams in 1987, when the Broncos lost to the New York Giants, 39-20. Denver fell again the following year to Washington, 42-10, and to the 49ers in 1990 in an embarrassing 55-10 rout.

Morton, a Campbell High product, played on losing Super Bowls teams at Dallas and Denver and Plunkett, a graduate of Lick High and Stanford, led the Oakland-Los Angeles Raiders to two victories in the NFL title game.

Although he didn't play in Super Bowl XXXIII, ex-San Jose State QB Steve DeBerg, 45, became the oldest man to make the postseason roster, serving as a backup for Atlanta.

■ WORLD SERIES REGULARS

In the last decade of the 20th Century, Stanford's baseball team competed in the NCAA playoffs every year except 1993 and made it to the College World Series four times.

Big changes came to college baseball in the century's final year. The Six-Pac added Oregon State, Washington and Washington State and the NCAA playoff field was expanded to 64 teams. Stanford (48-13) captured the conference title with a 19-5 record to win an automatic NCAA berth.

The Cardinal won the super-regional and defeated USC in two straight playoff games at Sunken Diamond to move to the College World Series. Jason Young fanned 10 Trojans in the 1-0 opening victory to pass Chad Hutchinson's KO record with 161 and Justin Wayne set down 12 to complete the sweep with a win, Stanford's 21st in 22 games.

The light-hitting Cardinal, the tournament's sixth seed, downed Cal State Fullerton in the opener as Young won his 12th game. A 10-6 win over Florida State gave Stanford another game against the Seminoles. They blew an early four-run lead and lost, forcing a third meeting between the teams with the winner to meet Miami for the title.

Despite a grand slam by John Gall (St. Francis), who hit .611 in the series, and a two-run shot by Edmund Muth, which put his team up 9-7 in the seventh, Stanford (50-15) lost in the 13th inning, 14-11, and finished third.

There were other outstanding years. In 1990, outfielder Jeffrey Hammonds had a 37-game hitting streak as the team won a school record 59 games on the way to a third place World Series finish. In 1992, Hammonds signed a $1 million bonus contract with the Baltimore Orioles.

Stanford first sacker David McCarty (.420, 24 homers, 66 RBIs), was NCAA player of the year the following season, but Stanford fell to Fresno State in regional postseason play. Stanford was eliminated in the regionals again in 1992 and 1994. In the latter season, catcher A. J. Hinch (.381, 11 HR) was a consensus All-American.

Hinch and pitcher Kyle Peterson (14-1) led the Cardinal to a 40-25 record and a fifth place finish in the 1995 College World Series. Stanford had an even better record in 1996 (41-19), but was thwarted in its effort to reach Omaha again with a loss to Cal State Northridge in the regionals.

Stanford lost the 1997 Pac-10 crown when Washington topped the Cardinal for first time since 1920. Stanford rallied to win the West and take third in the College World Series. Hutchinson fanned a school record 156 batters, but rejected a $1.5 million offer from the Atlanta Braves to stay in school and play football. The following year, Hutchinson signed with the St. Louis Cardinals for $3.4 million.

What started out as the best year for Coach Mark Marquess' 1998 Cardinal squad turned into Stanford's most disappointing season in some respects. Stanford topped the polls all year until it dropped six of its last seven games to end its bid for the NCAA title with a 42-14-1 record.

The Cardinal won 16 straight before pitcher Brent Hoard (Bellarmine) was beaten by Arizona State. Jeff Austin's nine-game unbeaten sting was clipped not long afterward when last place Cal ended its own nine-game losing streak against Stanford, 4-3.

Stanford wrapped up the Six-Pac before 2,818 at home on Austin's five-hit, 10 K win over USC, but lost the last two regular season games to the Trojans, then fell twice more to Washington for the Pac-10 championship.

The Cardinal still was the top seed in the Sunken Diamond regional. Austin (12-4) lost to LMU in the opener, bumping the Cardinal into the losers bracket, where it broke the five-game losing streak by shelling Minnesota, 19-1, in the greatest offensive showing in school playoff history. They were led by Joe Borchard's two doubles and two home runs and two doubles and a homer by Gall. Stanford's season ended with a 5-1 loss to Long Beach State.

■ GOLFING GREATS

Golfer Juli Inkster of Los Altos saved the best for last, going eagle-birdie-birdie on the final three holes to take the LPGA title and a career modern Grand Slam in 1999.

Inkster shot a record-breaking 16-under-par 272 to win

Julie Inkster (above) and Patty Sheehan are two former San Jose State golfers who rank among the all-time leading LPGA money-winners.

the women's U. S. Open in early June and followed it with another 16-under-par 268 victory in the LPGA championship three weeks later. A September win in the Safeway tournament gave her the last point needed for an automatic place in the LPGA Hall of Fame.

Inkster won $645,000 in the tournaments, boosting her winnings for 1999 to more than $1.2 million. She joined Pat Bradley as the only players to win all four major events on the women's tour -- the LPGA, Open, Dinah Shore and du Maurier Classic. Inkster won the last two in her rookie year in 1984 and captured the Dinah Shore again in 1989.

After nearly retiring a year earlier to spend more time with her husband and two young daughters, the 39-year-old San Jose State graduate became the first American to take the Open title since another former San Jose State golfer, Patty Sheehan, won it in 1994.

The three big wins were Inkster's first in major tournaments in 10 years and gave her enough points -- based on tournament victories -- to move into the Hall of Fame, where Sheehan has resided since 1993. Sheehan won the Open twice, the LPGA three times and the Dinah Shore once, but never took the du Maurier.

Inkster's Open win erased the bitter memory of her defeat in the same tournament by Sheehan in 1992. She had led by two strokes with two holes to play, only to lose to Sheehan in a playoff.

The two former Spartans ranked among the top all-time women money-winners as 1999 ended, Sheehan with $5.3 million in earnings and Inkster at more than $4.3 million. Sheehan had won 35 LPGA events and the Safeway win gave Inkster 22 career victories.

■ YEAR OF THE WOMAN

San Jose sports promoters liked to call 1999 "The Year of the Woman" and there were few arguments about that phrase as a marketing slogan.

If there were a Year of the Woman player of the year award based on the most thrilling moment involving a local athlete, it surely would have gone to Brandi Chastain. The former Mitty High and Santa Clara University soccer star rocketed the deciding penalty kick into the back of the net at the Rose Bowl to gave USA a 5-4 shootout win over China in the World Cup soccer final.

"I thought, "My God, this is the greatest moment of my life on a soccer field,' " Chastain said after the game.

The year began early when 15,367 came to Spartan Stadium to see the USA women's soccer team lose to an international all-star squad, 2-1, on the night the Women's World Cup tournament draw was held.

The USA team, with Chastain, Lorrie Fair (Los Altos) and Julie Foudy (Stanford) among its players, was one of the favorites. Games were played at venues across America during the summer, with the USA drawing huge crowds and entertaining large national television audiences.

USA beat Denmark, 3-0, on opening day in New York before 78,792. Mikka Hansen (Presentation, SCU), started at forward for the Danes. On the same day at a Spartan Stadium twin bill, 23,289 saw Canada and Japan draw, 1-1, and China top Sweden, 2-1.

The women returned to San Jose for the quarterfinals and 21,411 paid $30 to $75 a ticket to watch China down Russia, 2-0, and Norway knock off Sweden, 3-1.

USA reached the Independence Day semifinal at Stanford by beating Germany, 3-2, in a Maryland game that saw Chastain surrender an early own goal, but redeem herself by tying the score with a second half goal.

The dream of a USA championship was kept alive at Stanford by Briana Scurry's brilliant goal keeping that preserved a 2-0 semifinal win over Brazil before 73,123. The crowd dwindled to 30,000 for a second game between pro teams and fell to about half that before the Clash defeated DC United, 2-1, in its eighth shootout win of 1999.

USA won the cup at Pasadena before a record women's event crowd of 90,185 while 40 million watched on TV. After a 0-0 draw in overtime, Scurry saved China's third penalty kick to open the way for Chastain to win it.

The year got off to a bad start when its first scheduled event, the American Basketball League All-Star Game, was canceled after the women's professional circuit filed for bankruptcy late in 1998.

Although Stanford wasn't in the field as hoped for by many local basketball fans, the NCAA women's Final Four brought its great show to the San Jose Arena in late March, featuring No. 1 Purdue, Duke, Georgia and Louisiana Tech. After an ugly first half, Purdue rallied from a 22-17 deficit to beat Duke in the final, 62-45, before 17,773 fans.

Women's soccer drew 14,006 at Spartan Stadium in December for the NCAA semis and 14,410 for the championship, where North Carolina topped Notre Dame, 2-0.

The year closed with the USA women's soccer team downing a world all-star team, 8-5, in an indoor exhibition match at San Jose Arena before 10,842 fans.

■ FOR THE RECORD

Bob Boone, Stanford's pitcher-third baseman in the late 1960s, established a major league record by catching 2,264 games in a 19-year career that ended in 1990.

Joe Nedney (Santa Teresa) set San Jose State's all-time mark in 1992, kicking a 60-yard field goal as time expired for a 26-24 victory over Wyoming.

Lucius Davis (Piedmont Hills) hit 19 against San Jose State in 1992 to set a University of California at Santa Barbara single season basketball record with 566 points.

In the county's first meeting between father and son varsity high school football coaches in 1993, son John Andree's Gunderson High team beat father Ray's Del Mar squad, 16-13.

Valley Christian High's Scott Reeves buried a record 17 treys on his way to a county record 58 points against Silver Creek in 1995. This tied the single game points mark set earlier in the year by North Valley Baptist's Moses Andrade against Liberty Baptist.

In 1996, David Jackson of Cupertino High rushed for a CCS record 417 yards in 41 carries and scored eight TDs in a 54-42 barn burner against Lynbrook.

Gilroy High fell to North Salinas, 8-4, in the county's longest softball game in 1997. The teams played 16 innings on April 15 and 18 more three weeks later. Pitchers Sarah Caudle of Gilroy and Jennifer Deering of North Salinas each pitched a state record 34 innings.

Brandi Chastain

Gunderson High set a county record for most points by a losing football team in 1997, falling to Woodside, 48-44. Lynbrook tied it in a 47-44 loss to Fremont a week later.

Baltimore's Mike Mussina (Stanford) struck out 15 Cleveland batters in seven innings to set the ALCS record in 1997, but the Orioles lost after his departure, 2-1.

Ex-SJS defensive back Bob Ladouceur coached De La Salle High of Concord to a national prep record of 100 consecutive football wins from 1992 through 1999. The remarkable streak was still alive going into the year 2000.

Senque Carey of St. Francis High, averaging 23.3 points, 10.6 rebounds and 6.2 assists as 1998's CCS player of the year, finished his career with a section record 2,113 points, 31 more than Monta Vista's Ron Reis (1985-88).

Notah Begay III, who tied the NCAA golf record with a 62 while at Stanford in 1994, became the third player in the history of the professional golf tour to fire a 59 in 1998.

Deonce Whitaker of San Jose State set NCAA records with 51 kickoff returns for 1,214 yards in 1998.

SJCC head basketball coach Percy Carr recorded career victory number 500 in a 69-63 in over College of Alameda early in the 1998-99 season. The Jags made the postseason playoffs for the 23rd time in 24 years under Carr.

In the county's longest unbroken on-the-field football rivalry dating back to 1928, Santa Clara High downed Mountain View, 42-7, on the last weekend of regular season prep football in 1999. Despite the defeat, the Spartans had a 39-28-5 record against the Bruins during the period.

■ TENNIS ANYONE?

Stanford tennis fans call their program the best in the country and who could argue. The Cardinal took 16 NCAA men's titles after 1973 and the women added 10 more.

Men's coach Dick Gould said the 1998 aggregation was, "without question the best team I've ever coached." The 28-0 Cardinal shut out 24 opponents including four in the NCAA tourney to stretch its winning streak to 39 straight matches.

Top Cardinal players included Bob and Mike Bryan, Paul Goldstein and Ryan Wolters (Leland). NCAA winners were Goldstein in singles and the sophomore Bryan twins, who turned pro a month later, in doubles.

Wolters won the 1999 Pac-10 singles title and paired with K. J. Hippensteel for the NCAA doubles crown, but the team was upset by Baylor in the NCAA's first round.

Earlier in the decade, Stanford men won the 1990 team title and individual crowns in singles, Jared Palmer (1991), and doubles, Alex O'Brien and Chris Cocotes (1992).

Stanford women took NCAA championships 10 times since it first was contested in 1982. The 1990 team won its fifth consecutive NCAA with a second straight 29-0 record. Four-time All-America Teri Whitlinger and Meredith McGrath took the doubles and Debbie Graham won the singles.

Sandra Birch was the NCAA singles champ in 1991 and freshman Lilia Osterloh took the 1997 title. In 1998, Julia Scott won the indoor collegiate singles and Annica Cooper took the outdoor championship. Marissa Irvin led the Cardinal to the 1999 Pac-10 title and coach Frank Brennan's team made a record 18th straight NCAA appearance and won its second crown in three seasons.

■ HONORS

Kathy Stahl, an area player of the year in basketball, softball and field hockey while at Mitty High, accepted a softball scholarship to Oregon in 1993. Twice named All-American, she set many of Oregon's career records, including batting average (.381) and home runs (31).

Chicago White Sox pitcher Jack McDowell (22-10) won the American League Cy Young Award in 1993. He had led Stanford to its first NCAA baseball title in 1987.

Pitcher Mark Langston (Buchser, SJS) won his seventh American League Gold Glove Award for fielding in 1995.

George Hinaga, Henry "Lefty" Honda and Shigeo "Jiggs" Yamada, who starred with San Jose teams between 1917 and 1946, were among 46 Nisei baseball legends honored at a San Francisco Giants game in 1996.

San Diego third baseman Ken Caminiti (Leigh, SJCC, SJS) won the 1996 National League MVP award after batting .326 with 40 home runs and 130 RBIs.

Wes Terrell (Gunderson) was a first team Division II All-America tight end at UC-Davis in 1997.

1990s Hall of Fame inductees included Joe Leonard, the only American to win U. S. motorcycle and auto racing titles (motorsports); Cal QB Craig Morton, Stanford end Chris Burford, Stanford and SJS coach John Ralston and BYU QB Jim McMahon (college football); Butch Krikorian of SJS and Stanford's Jack Douglas and John McEnroe (college tennis); 49ers coach Bill Walsh (pro football); Patty Sheehan of SJS (LPGA); Stanford coach Payton Jordan and Francie Larrieu, Fremont High and UCLA distance champion (track and field).

Pat Burrell (Bellarmine) won the Golden Spikes Award as America's top college baseball player in 1998.

Cal's Deltha O'Neal (Milpitas) and Stanford's Troy Walters were football All-Americans in 1999. Walters also won the Fred Biletnikoff Award as the nation's top receiver after setting Pac-10 career marks for receptions (298) and yardage (3,995). Defensive back O'Neal captured the Mosi Tatupu award as the top special teams player in the nation.

■ IN PASSING

After lingering 15 months in a coma, motorcycle racer Steve Eklund of San Jose, 36, died in 1990 from head injuries received in a racing accident at Albuquerque, N.M.

Karl Ekern, 36, who went from San Jose State to a 13-year career as a Los Angeles Rams linebacker, was killed in a single vehicle crash in the Mojave Desert in 1990.

Frank Volpi, 83, minor league catcher and Municipal Stadium concessionaire for two decades, died in 1997. He hit Municipal Stadium's first home run in 1942.

Alan Simpkins, 74, who donated millions of dollars to San Jose State University and its athletic program and campaigned for Spartan Stadium expansion and the school's admission to the WAC, died in Santa Cruz in 1997.

Dan Fukushima, Lick High basketball coach for 22 seasons (353-198), founder of Northern California's oldest prep hoops tourney at Lick in 1955, and long-time assistant at Piedmont Hills and Independence, died at age 77 in 1998.

Ray Goni, 55, a Saratoga High School teacher and coach, died of cancer in 1999. He was an assistant football coach for five section championship teams in 31 seasons and head coach of three CCS girl's soccer champions.

John "Paddy" Cottrell, 87, baseball coach of Santa Clara University's 1962 College World Series finalists, died in Santa Clara in 1999. His 10-season record was 178-90.

Pioneer High School junior varsity football player Joseph Barajas, 15, died in 1999 after suffering a traumatic brain injury during a game against Piedmont Hills.

■ PARTIAL RETURNS

Stanford's 1999 football team (8-3-0), which combined a point-a-minute offense with a porous defense, was poised to meet Wisconsin in the Rose Bowl on Jan. 1, 2000.

The Cardinal gained its first Pasadena appearance since 1972 with a 31-13 win over Cal despite Deltha O'Neal's (Milpitas) 100-yard kickoff run back and 58-yard punt return for the Golden Bears' only scores.

Cardinal Casey Moore had a Big Game record 94-yard TD run and wide receiver Troy Walters grabbed six passes for 126 yards to set Stanford's season record.

Some seasons overlapped 1999 and 2000. At millennium's end, hoops leaders were No. 1 Stanford (11-0), West Valley College (15-1), SCU women (9-2), St. Francis (9-1) and Saratoga (14-1) boys and Mitty girls (9-2). In soccer it was Bellarmine boys (10-0-1) and Mitty girls (8-0-0).

San Jose's Sharks had their first winning October but fell to 19-18-4 and were second in the Pacific Division.

■ 1990 ■

Piedmont Hills High's Derek Meonske pumps in 42, but Pirates fall to Leland in OT, 89-86 . . . St. Francis High girls defeat Lynbrook, 60-53, behind Christy Stevens' 35 . . . 98-pound Sue Roshanzamir of Independence High wins more than she loses wrestling boys . . . San Jose High topples Gunderson, 89-81, as Jason Pierce buckets 37 . . . Monta Vista High crushes Cupertino, 82-58. Greg Siwek's 41 leads winners . . . Leland High tops

Pioneer, 4-0, ties state soccer record of 60 straight matches without loss. Bellarmine stops streak at 65 in CCS semis, 3-0, then earns Div. 1 crown with 2-1 OT win over Monta Vista . . . Lynbrook High (17-0) captures seventh CCS field hockey title. Vikings' Kristie Schneider is state player of the year . . . Stanford tops UCLA down south for first time since 1952. Andrew Vlahov's 20 points pace 87-79 win . . . USSR downs USA in soccer at Stanford, 3-1 . . . Jason Townsend of Fremont High converts steal into basket at buzzer to win CCS Div. 3 title over Yerba Buena, 50-48. Fremont loses state title to Artesia of Lakewood, 57-50, despite Townsend's 21 . . . Stan Spencer of Stanford fans 15 Arizona batters in 8-2 win . . . Hawaii dumps Stanford in NIT, 69-57. Adam Keefe's 31 leads Cardinal . . . SJS baseball win streak ends at 16 in 17-11 loss to UCSB . . . Milpitas High's Jason Tyrus belts three homers, bats in seven runs in 12-8 win against Gunn . . . California Angels' Mark Langston, Mike Witt combine for 1-0 no-hitter over Seattle . . . Matt Rice of Bellarmine wins 100, 200, anchors winning relay, high jumps 6-10 against St. Ignatius . . . Homestead High's unseeded Brandon Moglen wins CCS tennis over Tran Nguyen of Los Altos . . . State track and field champs: Craig Magness (Santa Teresa) in 800 in 1:51.89, Rocky Morris (Hill) in 300 hurdles in 37.46, Ed Lasquete (Mount Pleasant) with 15-10 pole vault . . . Bellarmine's 37 wins (37-1) sets state water polo mark . . . Monta Vista High (state No. 1 at 27-3) wins CCS Div. 1-4A baseball title over Leland, 3-0. Area players of year are Matadors' pitcher Ryan Hancock (13-0), Leland infielder Jason Hardtke (.507) . . . Mitty High (28-2) stops Gunderson in CCS Div. 1 softball, 5-0 . . . Casey Boyns repeats as county golf champ . . . Olympic Festival gold medals go to Meiling Okuno of Sunnyvale (tennis), Marco Sanchez of San Jose (wrestling) . . . Future Cal stars QB Dave Barr, wide out Sean Dawkins (Homestead) hook up for 18-yard TD pass as North downs South, 19-14, in prep classic . . . Pat Hurst (SJS) tops Stephanie Davis (Stanford) on extra hole for U. S. women's amateur golf title . . . After taking four previous no-hit bids into ninth inning before yielding hit, Toronto's Dave Stieb (Oak Grove) pitches no-hitter against Cleveland . . . Soph Bill Oliver throws for 412 yards, six TDs in Monta Vista High's 48-17 win over Montgomery of Santa Rosa . . . Robert Gooden's 312 yards on ground, four scores, lead Oak Grove High over Monta Vista, 37-15 . . . De Anza dedicates 5,000-seat stadium with 17-14 victory over Allan Hancock . . . PattiSue Plumer's 4:16.68 breaks record in New York's Fifth Avenue Mile . . . Land-air battle sees Wilcox High's Shon Lewis race for 193 yards, three TDs as Chargers top Gunn, 54-21. Titan QB Jason Sanborn hits 25 of 46 for 359 yards, all three TDs . . . Portland stops 38-game SCU unbeaten soccer streak, 1-0 . . . "Touchdown Tommy" Vardell lives up to nickname, scoring four Stanford TDs on one-yard runs in 36-31 upset of Notre Dame. Loss is first at home for a No. 1 Irish team since 1954 . . . Trevor Wilson's 320 yards rushing, seven TDs leads Los Gatos High over Monta Vista, 49-35 . . . Mike Ichiyama runs for 204 yards as Del Mar High tops Branham, 28-14, for Don's first grid title . . . Fremont High all-state running back Willie Harper grinds out 2,086 yards, scores 28 TDs, sets county career record of 4,539 yards . . . SJS tallies record 21 points in 1:24 during 42-7 win over Fresno State . . . Bill Oliver passes for 3,226 yards, 35 TDs. All-state teammate Greg Siwek has 20 TDs with state receiving yard marks 1,560 (season), 3,498 (career) . . . Pioneer High lineman Steve Hoffman is all-state . . . Big Game decider is last second John Hopkins 39-yard field goal as Stanford bumps Cal, 27-25 . . . Stanford's Glyn Milburn leads NCAA in all-purpose yards with 2,222, edging Sheldon Canley of SJS, who has 2,213 . . . TCU's Reggie Smith (Leland) scores 27, picks off 12 rebounds in 66-49 win over SJS . . . John Charles passes for 367 yards to set state JC yardage record as Foothill bows to Hartnell, 31-29 . . . Top U. S. soccer player Brandi Chastain (Mitty) scores 22 goals, leads SCU women (18-1-1) into NCAA playoffs . . . Al Morton hits 41 as St. Francis High tops Woodside, 90-67 . . . Santa Clara High drops Blackford, 82-57, aided by Huy Do's nine treys, 33 points . . . Juli Inkster is first woman to win Spalding Invitational coed golf, shooting 284 to edge Mark Brooks by stroke . . . Player of the year Staci Wolfe leads St. Francis to state volleyball final where Lancers bow to Corona Del Mar . . . Top county hoops player Kevin Dempsey's 42 gives Santa Teresa High 79-75 OT win over Valley Christian.

■ 1991 ■

Stanford swimmer Janet Evans wins two gold medals at world championships . . . SCU women set record, thumping Portland, 106-42, as Julie Lienert tosses in 31 . . . Branham High's Amy Cook scores 39 in 81-71 OT victory over Del Mar . . . Mitty High girls nip Monta Vista in CCS hoops final, 51-50, lose to Berkeley for Nor Cal title. Mitty's Kathy Stahl joins Monta Vista's Melissa Wuschnig as top area players . . . Mark Mirizzi scores 17 in Leigh High's 15th straight win. Longhorns take CCS Div. 3 from San Mateo, 66-56, fall to Washington of Fremont . . . Santa Teresa High's Chris Hightower is Parade All-America soccer goalie . . . Pair of 1-1 OT draws produce CCS boy's soccer co-champs: Bellarmine, Pioneer High (Div. 1), Gilroy, Santa Cruz (Div. 2). Santa Teresa girls topple Homestead in Div. 1 . . . Tennessee women dump Stanford five from NCAA tourney, 68-60 . . . Cupertino High wrestler Aki Yoshikawa wins U. S. title . . . Behind two homers by Billy Owens (Bellarmine), Arizona drops Stanford from Six-Pac race, 21-11 . . . Darin Brassfield of Los Gatos wins third straight Trans-Am Classic auto race at Sears Point . . . USA soccer squad gains respect in 1-0 loss to Argentina at Stanford . . . Willy T. Ribbs first black driver to qualify for Indianapolis 500 . . . Gunderson High 33-2 as freshman Jennifer Mallon (25-1) throws 6-0 win over Los Altos for CCS Div. 1 softball title. Serra High rocks Bellarmine, 12-1, in CCS baseball Div. 4A. In final season, Blackford takes Palo Alto, 3-2, for Div. 3A crown . . . County golf winners: John DeSantis (men), Roger Pineda (juniors) . . . 20 baseball no-hitters reported in CCS. Monta Vista's Ramiro Garcia has two . . . Tracy Hanson of SJS wins U. S. women's amateur public links golf title . . . Stanford gymnast Jair Lynch captures five Olympic Festival gold medals . . . Kristi Devert hits school record four goals as SCU women down Oregon State in soccer, 7-1 . . . QB Mike Morales throws Gunderson High record four TD passes to beat Lick, 34-0 . . . Aaron Wise sets SCU mark, rambling for 245 yards in 31-16 win over San Francisco State . . . Independence High trips Homestead, 34-20, as Allen Anderson connects on five TD passes . . . George Archer retains Senior Gold Rush golf title . . . Piedmont Hills High's Patrick Yun catches eight passes from Brad Quinet for school record 240 yards in 55-6 blowout over Pioneer . . . In high octane 64-47 grid win over Pacific, SJS gains 616 yards, Tigers 603 . . . John Brodie ends seven winless years on PGA Senior Tour with playoff birdie putt to win at Los Angeles . . . After four scoreless OTs, SCU's Craig Hampton knocks in goal to give Broncos 2-1 NCAA soccer win over

Stanford. Broncos lose title game to Virginia on penalty kicks after four OT draw . . . Chris Stone, who racked up 290 yards earlier against Gunn High, carries ball 29 times for 273 yards, seven TDs as Santa Clara topples Los Altos, 54-21 . . . Top county player Michelle Wagner leads Lynbrook to Div. 3 volleyball title . . . No. 8 seed St. Francis upsets Bellarmine, 35-14, in CCS Div. 4A final on R. J. Hackett's four TD tosses . . . Kathy Stahl has 22 as Mitty High tops Lynbrook, 60-54, in own hoops tourney final. Michelle Wagner of Vikes hits 35.

■ 1992 ■

Bill Walsh quits NBC-TV to coach Stanford football . . . WVC tips SJCC, 75-72, behind Tony Block's 21 for 20th straight win . . . Doug Louthan has 41 as Piedmont Hills drops Oak Grove, 69-63 . . . Jamie Sepeda, Willie Adams combine for first Stanford no-hitter in 11 years, downing UOP, 6-0 . . . On way to 28.6 average, Willow Glen High's Brad Quinet becomes first county player to score 50 or more twice in season with 51 against San Jose, Burlingame . . . Mark Mirizzi of Leigh High hits 11 treys on way to 33 points in 90-69 win over Mount Pleasant . . . Palo Alto (30-0) dunks Gunn, 13-8, to win CCS water polo . . . Homestead girls dedicate CCS soccer title game to John Reilly, boy's co-captain who dies in his sleep, take Div. 1 over Leigh on Amy Hargrove's OT goal, 1-0 . . . Live Oak High's one-legged wrestler Donnie Keller loses in state final . . . Monta Vista High girls win Nor Cal hoops crown over Berkeley with 19 from Melissa Wuschnig, who shares area top player award with Westmont's Suzanne Ressa . . . WVC (31-3) falls to Cerritos, 89-87, in state JC final. Mustafa Hoff scores 32 . . . Atlanta Hawks' No. 1 pick Adam Keefe ends Stanford career with 23 as Cardinal bows to Alabama in NCAA . . . Jenny Thompson, Summer Sanders, diver Eileen Richetelli lead Stanford to NCAA swim crown. Sanders, NCAA 1991, 1992 swimmer of the year, quits school to train for Olympics, where she wins three medals, including 200-meter butterfly gold . . . Eric Wynalda scores twice as USA soccer team blanks China at Stanford . . . San Jose Oaks soccer squad captures U. S. Open Cup . . . Dana Lofland (SJS) grabs first LPGA title at Las Vegas . . . NFL top draftees: Stanford tackle Bob Whitfield (Atlanta), fullback Tommy Vardell (Cleveland) . . . Stanford men win NCAA gymnastics, women take NCAA volleyball . . . Scott Parker tops San Jose Mile motorcycle field for seventh straight year . . . UCLA's Iwalani McCalla (Mountain View), partner win NCAA tennis doubles . . . Tracy Hanson, Ninni Sterner lead SJS women to NCAA golf title . . . Richard Dupree (relay, 100, 200), Terry Fulton (relay, both hurdles), pace Mount Pleasant High to CCS win . . . Wilcox High's Susie Bugliarello (27-7) out pitches Jennifer Mallon of Gunderson as Chargers win CCS softball title in 14 innings, 1-0. Mount Pleasant High nine (21-5) tops Serra, 2-0, in CCS Div. 1. Top county players: Roberto Lopez of Wilcox (9-2, 119 Ks) in baseball, Whitney Floyd of Lynbrook (28-2, 352 Ks) in softball . . . Jeff Alkire (Bellarmine) is winning pitcher as USA nine downs Spain, 4-1, in Olympic Games opener . . . Laura Charameda of Mountain View wins $2,000 in women's pro division of San Jose Grand Prix bike race . . . Blackhawks top Club America, 2-1, before 25,400 at Spartan Stadium, but fall from Cup of Champions . . . SCU wins 12th straight grid opener, 35-25, over Chico State. Aaron Wise extends school record with 35th TD . . . Lincoln High ends 28-game winless streak with 17-6 victory against Westmont . . . On way to becoming first county back to top 5,000 rushing yards in career (5,005), Shon

Wilcox High's Shon Lewis was the first county prep to rush for more than 5,000 career yards.

Lewis of Wilcox High rambles for 218 yards, six TDs in 55-0 romp over Los Altos . . . Live Oak High coach Norm Dow calls it, "my first miracle win," after beating Independence, 29-26. With fourth and 25 on own eight yard line with no time outs near game's end, Keith Rogers tosses to Justin Jacobs, who goes 92 yards for winner . . . Doug Walt, DeAnna Monahan win world roller skating dance title . . . Marquis Jessie runs for three TDs, scores two more on 92-yard kickoff run back, 65-yard fumble return as St. Francis High tramples Mitty, 48-24 . . . Oak Grove High trips Leland, 25-24. Eagles' Jack Belony rushes 190 yards for three TDs, Chargers' Brian Vye passes for 308 yards, two scores. Eagles' tackle Todd Skyberg knocks down two-point conversion pass with 18 second left to ice win . . . Glyn Milburn of Stanford returns punts for TDs against UCLA (75 yards), Oregon State (79), Cal (76) . . . Sister act sees Gunn High's Vedica Jain top Gitenjali Jain in CCS tennis final . . . North Carolina shuts out SCU women in NCAA soccer semi-final, 3-0 . . . Stanford falls to unbeaten Cal in NCAA water polo title match, 12-11, in OT . . . David Vedder of San Jose loses to Jeff Hardin in WBC light-heavyweight bout in France . . . Monta Vista High QB Bill Oliver finishes career with 87 TD passes, state's second best all-time . . . SCU's John St. Jacques has 7,968 yards passing, 68 TD tosses after last game . . . Wendy Kaup of Los Altos tops Juli Christopher of Saratoga for state women's golf title . . . All-America Sean Dawkins sets Cal season marks for catches (65), yards (1,070) . . . In rare daylight sellout at Toso Pavilion, flu-stricken Jason Kidd bags 17 for Cal in 80-73 win over SCU . . . All-state honors for Los Gatos High QB Tom Krug, St. Francis linebacker Nick Watts.

■ 1993 ■

On way to becoming SCU top women's hoops scorer, Melissa

Ken Caminiti (left) of Leigh High was the National League MVP for 1996 and Scott Erickson of Homestead High pitched an American League no-hitter in 1994.

King has career high 33 in 69-66 loss to Texas . . . Valley Christian High girls whip Notre Dame, 83-46, behind Shannae Castellanos' 21 points, 10 boards, 13 assists, 10 steals . . . Parade soccer All-Americas: Mikka Hansen (Presentation), Jen Renola (Saratoga), Seiji Sato (Prospect), Albertin Montoya (Los Altos) . . . Brian Tanger's 42 can't prevent Willow Glen High's defeat by Gunderson, 62-56 . . . State wrestling champs: Tracy Brown (Santa Clara), Eric Guerrero (Independence) . . . Molly McEnery hits 19 as Mitty High defeats Notre Dame of Belmont, 58-51, in CCS Div. 4 hoops final . . . NFL No. 1 draftees: Cal's Sean Dawkins (Indianapolis), Stanford defensive back Darrien Gordon (San Diego) . . . Under new coach Dick Davey, SCU upsets No. 5 Arizona, 64-61, in NCAA regional, then falls to Temple . . . Monta Vista High's Kristin Clark averages 17.5 points, is CCS girl's player of the year, state's top soph . . . Third straight NCAA fencing title for Stanford's Nick Bravin . . . Santa Clara High's Chong Yi is U. S. wrestling champ . . . Willow Glen's Mike Barbara has consecutive no-hitters against Gunderson, San Jose . . . Palo Alto High claims third straight CCS tennis title, runs match win streak to 71 . . . Wilcox High's Susie Bugliarello drives in game-decider, fans 23 Aragon batters in 1-0, 10-inning softball playoff win . . . Lynbrook High softball pitcher Whitney Floyd ends career with county record 1,056 Ks . . . Gunderson High softball pitcher Jennifer Mallon falls to Los Gatos High in CCS Div. 1 final, 2-1. Mallon, whose 109 career wins misses state record by two, is top county player . . . Greg Galasso tops Randy Haag second year in-a-row for county golf title . . . Patty Sheehan wins third LPGA title for largest career payday, $150,000 . . . Karen Kurreck of Cupertino, Inga Thompson tie for U. S. cycling road race title . . . Leland High's Scott Slover tops state pole vault at 16-2 . . . Juli Christopher grabs county women's golf . . . New Jersey Nets take Kansas guard Rex Walters (Piedmont Hills) as No. 1 pick . . . San Jose's Randy Hannagan is Speedway points king . . . Ken Nash, 65, of San Jose wins age group U. S., world triathlons . . . Jorge Salazar's goal for Blackhawks beats UNAM Pumas, 4-3, for San Jose Cup soccer crown . . . Stanford tips SJS, 31-28, in aerial duel between Jeff Garcia (380 yards, 1 TD), Steve Stenstrom (330 yards, 4 TDs). Stanford relies too much on Stenstrom's record-setting arm (300 completions, 455 attempts, 3,627 yards), finishes 4-7-0 . . . Milpitas High ends Palma's 37-game win streak, 31-28, as David Perotti throws pair of late TD strikes to Lenzie Jackson . . . Pat Tillman leads Leland High over Mount Pleasant, 52-13, scoring four TDs, one on 88-yard kickoff return, plus 12 tackles, sack, fumble recovery . . . Nevada-Reno defeats SJS, 46-45, when Joe Nedney's 62-yard field goal try fails . . . Buck Shaw Stadium record soccer crowd (3,457) sees SCU blank Stanford, 2-0, on Sarah Rafanelli's two goals . . . Stanford wins gymnastics, water polo crowns . . . St. Francis, Mitty, Los Gatos take state volleyball titles. Lisa Sharpley of Los Altos High is top CCS player . . . Gavilan (9-2-0) wins third straight league title, has 48-15 postseason win over Merced behind Josh Wallwork's 337 yards passing, five TDs . . . San Jose Roughriders whip Dallas in Pop Warner Bowl at Townsend Field, 8-0 . . . Vincent Barnett of SJCC scores 55 against Santa Rosa . . . World soccer champ Germany blanks USA, 3-0, before 52,397 at Stanford . . . Hullet Brooks sets SJS women's basketball record with 41 points against Sacramento State . . . De Anza's Johnny Harper makes JC All-America team as corner back.

■ 1994 ■

Jeff Garcia (Gilroy, Gavilan, SJS) throws three TD passes in fourth quarter, runs for winning conversion as West downs East in Shrine game, 29-28 . . . Jason Allen's 22 points propel SJS to first win over UNLV in 26 tries, 92-77 . . . Prospect High's record falls when Sheri Hiraki chalks up 44 in 75-73 OT loss to Presentation . . . Renzo Furlan, No. 69 in world, stuns Michael Chang in San Jose Open tennis final . . . IBF world title bout at Event Center draws fewer than 2,000 as bantamweight Orlando Canizales stops San Jose's Geraldo Martinez in four rounds . . . Troy Thompson hits 38 for Gunderson High, outdoing Oak Grove's Jamaal Sanford's 34, in Grizzlies' 91-84 OT win . . . CCS player of the year Lloyd Pierce of Yerba Buena High gets 33 points, 13 rebounds, 11 assists in OT win over Oak Grove, 80-78 . . . In JC playoffs, SJCC defeats Shasta for school record 30th win, 88-76. Brad Quinet's 27 leads WVC to 90-83 victory over Hartnell . . . Mitty High downs Novato for Nor Cal hoops crown as Kerri Walsh hits 20. Monarchs lose to Brea-Olinda in state final . . . Rare home loss to Purdue in regionals, 82-65, knocks Stanford women from NCAA . . . Minnesota's Scott Erickson (Homestead) no-hits Milwaukee . . . De Anza nine takes third straight league title with 2-1 win over Canada . . .Stanford's Jason Middlebrook no-hits UCLA, 3-0 . . . SCU wins first league title since 1978, stops Jackson State in Municipal Stadium twin bill to enter NCAA playoffs. Lou Donati sets NCAA career hit by pitch record (60) . . . Karch Kiraly, Kent Steffes win first San Jose pro volleyball title . . . After transferring from Gunderson High, Leland's Jennifer Mallon appears in fourth straight CCS Div. 1 softball final, pitching one-hit, 5-0, win over former Grizzly teammates . . . Bellarmine nine (28-5), nation's No. 20, upset in CCS semis by eventual champ Serra . . . Scott Slover of Leland High wins state pole vault at 17-0 3/4 . . . SCU pitcher Jennifer Acord (Los Gatos) goes 12-52, sets NCAA softball records for appearances (63), complete games (62) . . . Steve Woods of SJS tops former Spartan Ed Cuff Jr. for state amateur golf crown, 5 and 3 . . . San Jose cyclist Seana Hogan is first three-time Race Across America winner . . . Catholic nun Virginia Dennehy, 60, becomes oldest county women's golf champ . . . Ron Reis, 7-foot-2, 360-pound ex-SCU hoops star, holds International Wrestling Federation heavyweight crown . . . Patty Sheehan captures U. S. Women's Open . . . Cupertino Magic, Sunnyvale Roadrunners win U. S. girl's soccer titles . . . Bad snap, worse hold causes Stanford's Eric Abrams to miss 23-yard field goal try with six seconds left in 41-41 tie with Northwestern . . . Milpitas High's Deltha O'Neal has 85-yard kickoff return for TD, scores four more on runs of 28 to 53 yards in 55-32 win over Gunn . . . Fred Jackson tallies four TDs, two on 99-yard kickoff returns, another on 71-yard pass interception, as Piedmont Hills High clubs Dublin, 28-7 . . . Chris Cohan, ex-Los Gatos High student, buys Golden State Warriors . . . Lynbrook High's Jason Balkman, only four-time CCS champ, first county cross-country runner to win state boy's title . . . Stanford clips USC, 14-10, in NCAA water polo final . . . St. Francis High, Mitty retain state volleyball titles. Mitty's Kerri Walsh is All-American . . . Shawn Rodriguez scores four TDs as St. Francis High takes 23rd straight, blisters formerly unbeaten Los Gatos in CCS grid final, 34-7 . . . Pepsi Pinnock of De Anza (19-0-2) has both goals in state soccer title OT win over East Los Angeles, 2-1. De Anza women (18-1-1) repeat champs over Santa Rosa, 1-0, on Lisa Best's goal . . . Gary St. Claire of SJS (15-4) is U. S. soccer coach of the year . . . Oak Grove Rhinos win 41st straight Pop Warner game, over Wahiawa of Hawaii, 18-0 . . . Steve Nash has 34 as SCU hits first 12 shots to nip Oregon, 88-83 . . . Stanford women (32-1) overcome 46 errors, top UCLA in NCAA volleyball final.

Seven-footer Ron Reis became a pro wrestler after graduating from Santa Clara University.

■ 1995 ■

SCU's Steve Nash buries record 21 straight free throws against St. Mary's, then pops 40 points against Gonzaga . . . Willow Glen High's Scott Andrews hits 42 in 74-68 loss to Overfelt . . . Matt West delivers 46 as SJCC tramples De Anza, 94-46 . . . Bennett Davison collects 31 points, 16 rebounds in WVC's 132-114 win over Foothill . . . Andre Agassi whips Michael Chang for Sybase Open tennis title . . . Brad Quinet knocks in 34 points as SJS ends 13-game losing streak, 86-77, over Fullerton . . . Independence High's Eric Guerrero captures third straight state wrestling title . . . 1-0 soccer win over Leigh gives Bellarmine (19-0-1) CCS Div. 1 title, first unbeaten season. Led by Parade All-American Lorrie Fair, Los Altos defeats Presentation in girl's Div. 2 . . . John Maginnes shoots 11-under 277 to win Nike San Jose Open golf at Almaden . . . De Anza wins sixth consecutive league soccer title . . . David Weaver (Palo Alto) scores 16 as WVC loses to Ventura in state JC hoops final, 80-61 . . . Doug Swingley (Live Oak) captures Iditarod Trail sled dog race, covering 1,100 miles in record nine days, 2:42:19 . . . Mississippi State dumps SCU from NCAA, 75-67. Steve Nash scores 22 . . . St. Francis High boys upset Dominguez, 73-65, for state Div. 2 hoops crown. CCS player of the year Jack Kavanaugh scores 21. Mitty girls top Newbury Park, 64-56, for state title behind Reyna Fortenberry's 18 . . . Jenny Thompson's three wins help Stanford women take fourth straight NCAA swim crown . . . Isiaha Yacap hits three-run homer, grand slam in 12-2 Milpitas High win over Cupertino . . . San Jose Ice Centre sellout crowd watches USA women fall to Canada, 2-1, in OT shootout . . . Susan Rea starts at second base for Gunn High's boys team . . . WVC's Angela Weir takes three events, named state JC swim meet's top competitor . . . Sacred Heart Cathedral High nine snaps Fremont's 22-game win streak in CCS playoffs, 3-1 . . . Leigh High hands Westmont only loss after 23 victories, wins CCS Div. 1 softball, 1-0 . . . De Anza's Tyrenda Stamps (Mount Pleasant), takes state JC discus, shot put . . . Michael Johnson runs 19.99 in Jenner meet, fastest 200 meters ever at SJCC . . . State prep shot put title goes to Presentation's Rebecca Morrison at 47-6 3/4; other champs are Jason Balkman of Lynbrook in 3,200 at 9:05.31, Joe Naivalu of Fremont in 110 hurdles at 14.33 . . . Stanford ties Oklahoma State in NCAA golf, loses title playoff . . . Greg Galasso (SJS) first to take four straight county golf titles . . . Top CCS diamond stars: Sabrina Quintero of Los Altos (29-4, 307 Ks, 23 shutouts), Pat Burrell of Bellarmine (.369 average, 11 homers) . . . Holly Nybo of Mountain View, Cupertino native Scott Smith take San Jose Triathlon . . . Barbara Vandeweghe rallies from three down, wins third county women's golf title . . . Samantha Wagner's goal gives Central Valley United 1-0 win over Memphis in U. S. Youth Soccer final . . . Stanford plays first football game in San Jose in 95 years, tops Spartans, 47-33, before 28,467 . . . Filling in for injured Doug Flutie, QB Jeff Garcia throws for 546 yards, team record six TDs in Calgary's 51-26 victory over Edmonton . . . Del Mar High's

Santa Clara University stars of the 1990s included Mike Frank (left), regarded as the Broncos' greatest all-around baseball player, and Steve Nash, third on the all-time basketball scoring list.

Damien Brown runs for 298 yards, three TDs in 26-14 win over Santa Clara . . . Skyline tops St. Francis, 12-6, to end Lancers' 26-game victory skein . . . Joe Furlow's 42-yard field goal gives SJS 32-30 win over Utah State with 18 ticks on clock . . . Jason Sinatra of Silver Creek High opens game with 70-yard TD run, chalks up 212 more yards, two scores in 41-20 win over Santa Teresa . . . On way to school record 31 TD passes, Jon Crosswhite's 32-yard scoring strike to Kelly Edwards with 10 seconds left gives Foothill 32-25 upset win over CCSF, ends Rams' 29-game win streak . . . Mikka Hansen scores sudden death goal in 139th minute for 3-2 SCU win over Stanford in NCAA soccer. North Carolina beats Lady Broncos, 2-0. SCU men ousted by Portland, 2-1 . . . Leland High's Emily Allison wins third straight CCS cross-country crown . . . Sub QB Tom Krug (Los Gatos) rallies Notre Dame to 35-17 win over Navy . . . Behind Marlon Garnett's 21, SCU cuts UCLA's 19-game victory string with 78-69 victory in Hawaii . . . Pat Hurst (SJS) top LPGA rookie . . . Oscar Johnson runs for one, passes for two TDs as San Jose High keeps Big Bone with 33-14 win over Lincoln . . . Five Tim Garner TD runs give Leigh High come from behind win over Woodside, 44-37 . . . Kerri Walsh has 36 kills, 16 digs against St. Mary's High of Stockton as Mitty takes state volleyball title. Del Mar, St. Francis state runners-up . . . Div. 2 All-American back Steve Papin (Piedmont Hills, WVC) scores 21 TDs for Portland State . . . Top CCS gridder Manuel Austin scores on 60-yard punt return as Los Gatos High beats Mountain View, 34-27, for Div. 3 crown. St. Francis takes Bellarmine for fifth straight Div. 1 title, 21-17 . . . Willow Glen High's Scott Andrews has 43 in 66-61 win against Wilcox . . . Khoa Nguyen of Santa Clara, partner win U. S. table tennis doubles . . . Four players hit 20 or more points (Loneal Hampton, 20; John Smith, 26; Adam Sepulveda, 26; Tory Woodward, 36) as Santa Clara High riddles Lincoln, 116-68 . . . St. Francis High's record 22-game hoops win skein clipped by Northgate of Walnut Creek, 75-63.

■ 1996 ■

Kate Starbird sets Stanford basketball record with 44 against USC . . . Rain cuts Nike San Jose Open to 54 holes at Almaden where ex-SJS golfer Larry Silveira holes 48-foot putt on first extra hole for $36,500 . . . Cops escort Cal, Stanford mascots from Maples Pavilion after Oski and The Tree mix it up . . . Westmont High hoops coach Gary Brinck (402-338) ends 30 years in post after Warriors lose to Granada of Livermore in Nor Cal tourney . . . Steve Nash, SCU's third best career scorer (1,689 points), goes to Phoenix Suns in NBA draft's first round . . . Independence High wrestler Oscar Gonzales is state 171-pound champ . . . Pete Sampras defeats Andre Agassi before 10,172 in Sybase Open tennis final . . . Andy Newman's 28 with seven treys can't save WVC from 82-81 loss to Ventura in state JC final . . . Bellarmine's 45-game undefeated soccer streak ends with 1-0 loss to St. Ignatius in WCAL playoffs . . . Los Altos High's Lorrie, Ronnie Fair make Parade All-America soccer team. Homestead's Regina Holan joins them on A-A squad . . . Janice Moodie of SJS becomes first Big West three-time golf champ as Spartans win 10th straight team crown . . . Stanford's Ian Bachrac (floor exercise), Jamie Ellis (parallel bars) take NCAA gymnastic championships . . . Tiger Woods of Stanford breaks Pac-10 golf record at 270, captures NCAA title despite 80 in last round . . . Kyle Peterson pitches no-hit ball into seventh as 3,324 see Stanford defeat Cal State Fullerton, 5-0, in first Sunken Diamond night game . . . SCU's twin wins over St. Mary's takes WCC title. Cal State Northridge tops Broncos (40-21) in playoff for NCAA spot . . . WVC's Chantiel McDonnell (.542, 79 steals) is state JC softball player of the year . . . Live Oak High's Maggie Del Rio tosses one-hitter to top Leland, 2-1, for CCS Div. 1 softball title . . . SJS women's golf team ties Arizona, loses NCAA championship in playoff . . . Miami's Pat Burrell (Bellarmine) leads nation's batters, is top NCAA freshman . . . Jae Jean Ro of Valley Christian High wins second CCS girl's golf title, takes Nor Cal . . . Dan Sikiric (Leland) sets 1,600-meter record of 4:14.66 at SJCC . . . Joe Naivalu of Fremont High repeats as state 100 hurdles champ in 13.68; Del Mar's Tisha Ponder takes 300 hurdles in 42.22 . . . Top CCS baseball player is John Gall of St. Francis High (.483 average) . . . Gilroy's Joey Garcia wins dirt bike jumping in ESPN's X-Games . . . Tom Watson ends nine-year PGA victory drought, winning $324,000 in Memorial tourney . . . Swimmer Janet Evans (Stanford) passes Olympic torch to Muhammad Ali, who lights Olympic flame. Trinidad sprinter Ato Boldon (Piedmont Hills, SJCC, UCLA) captures two bronze medals. Gymnast Amy Chow (Castilleja, WVC), USA synchronized swim team, including county residents Suzanne Bianco, Becky Dyroen-Lancer, Heather Simmons-Carrasco, Jill Sudduth, takes team gold. Stanford basketball coach Tara VanDerveer guides USA women to title over Brazil. Stanford athletes collect 16 team, relay gold medals, plus Jeff Rouse's individual gold in swimming . . . Arena sellout hockey crowd sees USA ice Canada, 7-5 . . . Paul Ugenti plows for 284 yards in 37 carries as Leland High dumps Live Oak, 35-32 . . . As clock ticks toward minute mark, Carl Dean to Windrell Hayes 19-yard TD pass gives SJS 26-25 win over UNLV . . . QB Adam Perez goes 20 for 25 for 362 yards, five TDs in Milpitas High's 46-41 win over Newark-Memorial. Ruben Ortiz grabs 12 passes for 186 yards . . . Overflow crowd at SJCC sees Bellarmine down St. Francis, 20-13, on Tom Gutto to Tim Foley 20-yard TD toss 14 seconds before final whistle . . . No. 2 Santa Clara women beat No. 1 Notre Dame before record 3,714 Buck Shaw Stadium soccer crowd, 3-1 . . . Kevin Atherton takes Speedway's San Jose Mile motorcycle race . . . Jerrick Powell grinds out 318 yards on ground for three scores in Fremont High's 18-0 romp over Mountain View . . . Brian Vye (Leland) hits 21 of 26 passes, for five TDs as Gavilan tops Monterey, 42-16 . . . Golden State Warriors move to San Jose Arena during Oakland Coliseum renovation, opening with 97-85 loss to Los Angeles Clippers. Crowd of 15,593 is 3,000 short of capacity, ending home sellout streak at 311 games. Fans stay away as NBA team scores fall into the 80s, Warriors (30-52) reside in division cellar . . . Hill High's 260-pound Mike Jeeter racks up 344 yards, four TDs in 21 carries in 27-14 victory over Prospect . . . Stanford men, women take NCAA cross-country . . . Brian Jones sets SCU freshman mark with 34 in 79-72 basketball win over Marquette . . . CCS volleyball champs St. Francis High, Mitty lose regionals, but section's top player Annie Pogue leads Del Mar to Div. 3 state final, where Dons fall to Torrance Bishop Montgomery . . . North Carolina beats SCU women (18-4-2) in NCAA soccer semifinal, takes title with 1-0 win over Notre Dame in games at Buck Shaw Stadium . . . Oak Grove High defensive end Andre Carter makes Parade All-American . . . SJS (4-8-0) gives up 448 points, finishes 110th out of 111 Div. IA football teams on defense . . . Defensive end Alex Munro of Monta Vista High has 24 sacks, four shy of 1995 state record set by Oak Grove's Andre Carter . . . In CCS Div. 3, Del Mar High wins first grid title over Gunderson, 16-15, on Peter Salazar to Chris Underwood scoring strike . . . USA tops Costa Rica in soccer before 40,500 at Stanford . . . Stanford women rout Hawaii for NCAA volleyball crown . . . Olivier Saint-Jean, Thomas Lowrey hit 16 each as SJS stuns No. 19 Alabama in Cable Car Classic in OT, 60-59.

■ 1997 ■

SJS receives rude welcome to WAC hoops from New Mexico, 71-63 . . . Mike Holmgren, Oak Grove High's offensive coach in 1975-80, guides Green Bay to Super Bowl win over New England . . . Santa Clara High's Tory Woodward buries 46 as Bruins lose 69-68 thriller to Los Gatos . . . County player of the year Senque Carey of St. Francis High hits 45 against Leland, averages 23.4 points, 11.3 rebounds . . . Tennis star Pete Sampras wins Sybase Open at Arena when injury sidelines Greg Rusedski . . . Bellarmine wins seventh CCS soccer title in eight years . . . SCU ties St. Mary's for first, loses WCC hoops tourney opener for fourth straight year . . . SJS only 13-14, but Olivier Saint-Jean tops WAC scorers (23.8) . . . Fourteen years after setting county girl's hoops records at Westmont High, mother of four Jane Morgan Riley stars for De Anza . . . SJCC (32-5) bows to Los Angeles City College in state JC hoops final at the Event Center, 67-62 . . . Oklahoma State's Eric Guerrero (Independence) wins NCAA 126-pound wrestling title . . . Stanford fencer Alden Clarke is NCAA men's epee champ . . . Santa Teresa High's Mike Nunez fans 16 Leigh batters in win . . . Jenner meet at SJCC is canceled for lack of sponsor, another victim of decline in track and field interest . . . Paul Chiffredo (Leland) smacks two homers, bats in nine against St. Mary's in SCU's ninth straight win, 26-15 . . . Bellarmine captures 13th consecutive CCS swim title, breaking Santa Clara's record 12 straight (1966-77) . . . Mitty High pitchers Jaime Forman-Lau, Niki Stemberger toss back-to-back perfect softball games against Oak Grove, Gunderson . . . SCU's Tobin Lanzetta KOs 17 St. Mary's batters in 4-1 win clinching second straight WCC baseball title. Gaels later stop Mike Frank's 23-game hitting streak. SCU nine beats Southern University in playoff for NCAA berth, bows in regionals . . . Modesto 100-meter winners: Ato Boldon in 9.89, ex-Stanford coach Payton Jordan, 80, tops age-group in 14.35 . . . Western Division baseball champ SJS falls in WAC playoffs . . . Palo Alto High takes sixth straight CCS team tennis title . . . Stanford frosh Lilia Osterloh turns pro after winning NCAA tennis singles . . . SCU baseball coach John Oldham (433-326-6) retires . . . Pat Hurst grabs first LPGA win, edging Juli Inkster by stroke in Oldsmobile Classic . . . Stanford's Brevin Knight is Cleveland Cavaliers' No. 1 pick . . . Dick Vermiel (SJS) quits broadcast booth, returns to pros as St. Louis Rams coach . . . Kara Giannetto wins county golf in playoff against Lyn Nelson . . . Martina Hingis downs Conchita Martinez in straight sets for Bank of the West tennis title . . . Palo Alto's Kurt Grote wins two gold medals in U. S. swim championships . . . Victory over Houston in national under-17 soccer title match puts Central Valley Mercury (48-0-1) of San Jose's photo on Cheerios Team cereal boxes . . . San Jose cyclist Seana Hogan tops women, is fourth overall in Race Across America . . . Swimmer Jenny Thompson (Stanford) sets world record in 100-meter butterfly in Sweden, takes three gold medals in Pan-Pacific meet . . . Gunn High's She-Rae Chen ends prep gymnastics career with 13 of 15 CCS titles in three years. Gunn captures fifth straight team crown . . . San Francisco Bay Seals upset Clash in U. S. Open Cup soccer, 2-1 . . . Joel Kribel of Stanford loses 2 and 1 to Matt Kuchar for U. S. amateur golf title . . . Craig Smith of San Jose wins 50-lap Key Classic sprint car race. Speedway points title goes to Charlie Caraccilo . . . Wisconsin's Ron Dayne rushes for 254 yards in 56-10 victory over SJS, one yard shy of most by an opponent . . . Richard Tillman of Leland High passes for 321 yards, three TDs in 38-22 win over Leigh . . . Prospect High wide out Matt Heling snares eight passes for 201 yards, four TDs in 43-20 romp over Mount Pleasant . . . In first national TV appearance in 10 years, SJS upsets No. 24 Air Force, 25-22 . . . Prospect tops Willow Glen, 28-20, for league title as Justin Williams completes 19 of 37 for 234 yards . . . Third string QB Craig Whelihan (Santa Teresa) debuts with San Diego Chargers, hits 17 of 29 passes in 37-31 loss to Seattle . . . Stanford nips Cal in 100th Big Game, 21-20 . . . Although game produces 1,139 offensive yards, SJS defense stops UNLV at two-inch line for 55-48 OT win . . . Brian Martin of Palo Alto, partner Mark Grimmette, take World Cup luge title . . . Mitty High wins seventh straight CCS girl's Div. 1 volleyball title, falls to Marina of Huntington Beach in state tourney. St. Francis takes third straight CCS Div. 2, wins state over Santa Margarita . . . Stanford cross-country teams defend Pac-10 titles. Men win NCAA . . . Arizona State linebacker Pat Tillman (Leland) is Pac-10 defensive player of the year . . . Burlingame High beats Willow

Glen, 42-41, in CCS football on tie-breaker . . . Enrique Tovar's goal, assist lead De Anza (22-2-2) to state JC soccer title over Rio Honda, 3-1 . . . Ryan Sorahan, missing from lineup when Los Gatos High (10-3-0) drops first three games, passes for three TDs as Wildcats batter Mitty, 28-14, for CCS Div. 3 championship . . . Undefeated North Carolina knocks SCU (20-3-1) from NCAA women's soccer tourney third year in a row . . . D'Shaun Crockett runs for 206 yards, Jamar Julien intercepts two passes in Oak Grove's 21-0 CCS final victory over six-time Div. 1 champ St. Francis. During season, Crockett rushes for 1,696 yards, 22 TDs, Julien for 1,270 yards, 30 TDs. Loss ends Lancers' CCS playoff win streak at 20 dating back to 1990 . . . Troy Walters bright light for Stanford (5-6-0), setting season marks for pass receptions (98), yards (1,206) . . . Stacie Savage, ex-De Anza soccer All-America, scores 15 goals for SJS, named NCAA All-West . . . Ryan Berry's 21st goal gives SJS 4-3 ice hockey win over Stanford . . . San Jose Oak Grove downs Jacksonville, Fla., 12-0; Sunnyvale Micro Rockets clobber Garner, NC, in Pop Warner Super Bowl, 52-0 . . . Hector Lizarraga of San Jose whips Welcome Ncita in 10 rounds for IBF featherweight title . . . Penn State snaps Stanford 50-game home volleyball winning streak, but Cardinal women later defeat Nittany Lions for record third NCAA crown in four years . . . St. Francis High's Senque Carey ties Oak Grove with two seconds left, gets 46 points, 17 boards in Lancers' 72-66 OT victory . . . Canada ends SJCC 17-game win streak in OT, 82-80.

■ 1998 ■

Four gold medals for Jenny Thompson (Stanford) at world swim championships . . . Milpitas High gives state hoops coach of the year Steve Cain 500th career win, edging Palo Alto, 56-54. Others with 500-plus wins, not all at county schools: Ray Snyder (Fremont, Monta Vista), 562, Dave Morgan (Del Mar), 703 . . . Fresh from volleyball squad, Kristin Folkl scores 36 as Stanford women stop Washington in basketball, 90-70 . . . Tacky Stanford "Sixth Man" rooters taunt Mike Bibby with, "your father hates you," while Arizona fans chant "overrated" as defending NCAA champ Wildcats humble Stanford, 93-75. Loss is Cardinal's first in 18, ends 20-game home win streak . . . Nate Morrow of The King's Academy delivers 21 points, 20 rebounds, 13 assists, 10 steals in 94-60 win over St. Lawrence . . . Myreen Tan of Oak Grove High knocks down five treys, 20 points in 53-46 victory ending Del Mar girl's 19-game win streak . . . NHL takes 16 days off for Winter Olympics. Sharks playing in Japan: Marcus Ragnarsson (Sweden), Marco Sturm (Germany) . . . El Nino storms wash out soccer schedule, force Lincoln High girls to play five straight days. Tracy Hess scores 10 goals as Lady Lions win four to clinch playoff spot . . . Andre Agassi prevents Pete Sampras from winning third straight Sybase Open tennis, stopping world's No. 1 in straight sets . . . Triple double time for Lick High's Anthony Elias, who averages 37 points, 11 rebounds, 12 assists in consecutive wins over Overfelt, Silver Creek, Pioneer . . . Kacey Scheppler's seven treys in Pinewood School's 110-59 romp over Fremont Christian gives her state career mark 381 . . . Presentation High's Aly Wagner, Danielle Slaton, Krista Boling, St. Francis' Anna Kraus make Parade soccer All-America. Wagner, Slaton become first girls to make all-CCS soccer team four straight years. Wagner, U. S. girls's co-player of the year, scores twice as Panthers take CCS Div. 2 title from Mitty, 3-0 . . . Isaias Bardelas of Leland High is boy's soccer All-American . . . Senque Carey buries 43 with seven treys against West High of Tracy to propel St. Francis into Nor Cal final, where "Q" hits 29 more as Lancers fall to Montgomery of Santa Rosa, 63-57 . . . Balanced scoring by Kristie Reed (16), Cortney Keegan (15), Arbatisha Kitchen (14), plus MVP work by Natalia Jonas gives SJCC women (34-2) state JC hoops title against Ventura, 83-69. WVC (30-4), SJCC (31-5) men lose in quarterfinals. State co-player of the year Jane Morgan Riley leads De Anza (29-8) to women's semis, where Dons fall to Ventura, 73-70 . . . Led by MVPs Chuck Jefferson (four-time champ), Amy Tong, SJS wins NCAA men's, women's judo . . . Stanford sweeps three NCAA swim crowns. Misty Hyman wins three races as women capture sixth title in seven years. Tom Wilkens takes three for men. Olympic gold medalist Heather Pease leads synchronized swimmers to first title . . . Oklahoma State's Eric Guerrero wins second straight NCAA wrestling crown . . . Phil Johnson takes over SJS men's hoops. Spartans were 3-23 in Stan Morrison's last year, 10th losing season in last 11 . . . Led by Steve Lee's 54-hole total of 216, SCU wins first WCC golf title . . . Pat Hurst wins first major LPGA title, taking Dinah Shore Classic's $150,000 prize money . . . Mitty High's Melissa Glazebrook, Mount Hamilton division co-MVP with Molly Shanley of Presentation, is CCS hoops player of the year . . . Piedmont Hills freshman Jessica Busick tosses fourth softball no-hitter of season in league opener against Willow Glen . . . Lick High's Brian Pino mows down 17 San Jose batters in 6-1 win . . . Ato Boldon runs 100 meters in 9.86 at Mt. SAC Relays, .02 off world record . . . Trying to discover if life begins at 40 after five years away from game, former big league pitcher Dave Stieb compiles 7-4 mark in minors, returns to majors with Toronto, ups lifetime record to 176-137 with win, two losses . . . Manuel Medina regains IBF welterweight crown, capturing unanimous decision over Hector Lizarraga at Arena before disappointing crowd of 2,895 . . . USA women crush Argentina, 7-0, in first soccer game on widened Spartan Stadium turf . . . Pitcher Javier Pamus of SJS leads NCAA Div. 1 with 13 wins . . . Wilcox High scores three runs in last inning, to end Valley Christian's unbeaten streak (one tie) at 22 games, 4-3 . . . Anna Kozlova leads Santa Clara to sweep of all events for sixth straight national team synchronized swim title . . . Central Valley Mercury, 76-0-2 since last loss in 1995, drubs San Juan, 5-0, for Northern California under-18 soccer title . . . Suzy Nicoletti wins fourth straight 100 breaststroke, accounts for majority of Mitty High's points as Monarchs take first CCS crown . . . Silver Creek High outfielder Alan Dunn hits grand slam, three-run homer for eight RBIs in 19-9 win over Lincoln . . . Los Gatos High's Marcia Wallis retains CCS golf title . . . Philadelphia makes Miami infielder Pat Burrell (Bellarmine) No. 1 selection in draft. Stanford pitcher Jeff Austin (12-4), Baseball America's player of the year, goes to Kansas City as No. 4. Austin holds out, signing with Royals for $2.55 million bonus in 1999 . . . Mitty High's Niki Stemberger (18-1), Jaime Forman-Lau (12-2) combine for five-hit, 5-0, victory over Carlmont for CCS Div. 2 softball crown . . . Stanford's Brian Hauser, twin brother Brent, Nathan Nutter finish 1-2-3 in NCAA 10,000 meters, while Toby Stevenson takes pole vault at 18-2 1/2 . . . Darren Marble of Los Altos High captures state high jump at 6-8 . . . John Ellis wins county golf title . . . Iran, coached by Palo Alto resident Jalal Talebi, whips USA, guided by former SCU mentor Steve Sampson (Homestead, SJS), in World Cup soccer match, 2-1. Sampson (26-22-4) resigns after USA finishes last among 32 teams . . . Stanford freshman Gabe Jennings wins unprecedented double in 1,500, 5,000 at U. S. championships . . . Led by tourney MVP Niki Hartley (St. Francis), Kaepa City Beach wins national junior volleyball crown . . . Cinnabar Hills opens near Calero Reservoir. Fees to play San Jose's first new public golf course since 1968 are $50 weekdays, $75 weekends . . . Santa Clara Aquamaids Bill May, first male synchronized swimmer, partner Kristina Lum take duet silver medal at Goodwill Games . . . Four goals by Marcia Wallis pace Central Valley Mercury to third straight national soccer title with 6-0 win over Columbus, Ohio, in under-18 girl's final . . . Defending league champion San Jose Spitfires has 7-9 record when six-team Ladies Professional Baseball League folds for lack of attendance . . . Lindsay Davenport tops Venus Williams for Bank of the West Classic title . . . QB Steve DeBerg (SJS), starter, super sub for 16 years, returns to NFL as backup at Super Bowl-bound Atlanta after five years away from game. When starter is hurt, throws first TD pass since 1993, leads Falcons to 31-23 win over New Orleans . . . Nathan Fast hits 13 as SCU opens European tour with loss to Turkish team, 75-68 . . . Rap star running back Carlos Meeks races 129 yards in 22 carries as 18-point underdog SJS blasts Stanford, 35-23, in opener. Casey LeBlanc (Bellarmine) returns onside kick 45 yards for TD . . . St. Francis rips Hollister, 41-7, with Ronald Nunn scoring two TDs on 15-carry, 258-yard night . . . Santa Teresa High's Manny Rios runs for 272 yards, 5 TDs in 35-0 win against Lick . . . Subbing for injured QB Todd Husak, Joe Borchard races 41 yards on first play to set up Kevin Miller's 20-yard field goal as time expires for Stanford's 37-34 victory over North Carolina . . . Charlie Caraccilo (Oak Grove) repeats as San Jose Speedway points champ, finishing seventh in 45th annual Johnny Key Classic, oldest West Coast racing event . . . Willow Glen High's David Macchi tosses five TD passes, but Rams fall to Saratoga, 42-34, as backs Jason Choe (139 yards), Brent Coleman (135), Ryan Bernard (126), Daniel Goni (103) all rush for more than 100 yards . . . SJS loses to Fresno State, 2-1, ending school record soccer winning streak at nine . . . St. Francis becomes 80th victim in De La Salle of Concord's U. S. record prep football win streak, 21-0, but holds Spartans to lowest total points . . . QB Jason Dent explodes for 176 yards in seven carries, three TDs including 94-yard scoring sprint, as Wilcox High tramples Los Gatos, 37-7 . . . Robin Freeman's four-foot putt on fourth extra hole gives him $40,500 Nike San Jose Open win over Sean Murphy, Tom Scherrer at Almaden . . . Stanford's Todd Husak hits 26 of 48 passes for school record 450 yards, but Oregon State wins, 30-23 . . . Juli Inkster shoots back-to-back 66s to defend World Championship of Women's Golf title, moving her into LPGA's top 10 with $3.7 million in earnings . . . Cal officials threaten to bench mascot Oski after Bear backers steal The Tree's costume from Stanford. Tree later returned unharmed . . . UCLA defender causes Jeff Allen fumble at 1-yard line in fourth quarter to preserve UCLA's 28-24 win over upset-minded Stanford . . . Newport Harbor snaps St. Francis' 54-match volleyball winning streak in Santa Barbara tourney finals . . . Willow Glen High drops Pioneer, 32-19, as David Macchi hits 19 of 20 for 327 yards and five TDs, four to wideout John Fernandez . . . Ryan Bernard rushes for 257 yards, three TDs, adds 14 tackles as Saratoga ambushes Wilcox, 28-6 . . . Stanford's Carey Cloyd is MVP as Cardinal tops Southwest Missouri, 3-2, for Nor Pac field hockey title . . . St. Francis rallies for two TDs to win WCAL title over St. Ignatius, 28-25 . . . Tony Oka runs for two scores, passes for third in Westmont High's 18-12 win over Yerba Buena for first league title since

Olivier Saint-Jean was one of San Jose State's most spectacular basketball players.

1981 . . . Santa Clara High's 34-14 win over Fremont gives Panthers first league grid crown in 41 seasons . . . Richard Tillman's five TD tosses lead Leland High to upset 35-31 victory against Overfelt . . . Juan Miramontes of WVC takes Nor Cal cross-country . . . Andrew Hill of Los Altos first runner since 1987 to break 15-minute mark at Crystal Springs, winning Div. 3 CCS cross-country in 14:52 . . . Back-to-back soccer crowds of 15,000-plus see USA and Australia in 0-0 draw and Clash fall to Toluca, 2-0 . . . Five-foot-six Jeremy Jones rolls for 203 yards, six TDs as Bellarmine Prep beats Milpitas, 54-33, in CCS playoffs . . . Own goal, three overtime loss to Stanford, 3-2, ends San Jose State's hopes in first NCAA soccer appearance since 1978 . . . Behind Sasha Maese, WVC beats Golden West, 13-7, for state JC water polo title . . . Playing in 10th straight NCAA soccer tourney, SCU women (22-1-1) whitewash Connecticut, 1-0, for NCAA record 16th consecutive shutout, but fall to Florida in semis, 1-0 . . . St. Francis High boys win state Div. 3 cross-country . . . Fernando Palazzo scores 31, grabs 19 rebounds to tie Gary Hopkins' 1980 school record, leads Milpitas High to 56-55 win over Irvington . . . Overfelt High's Larry Morris racks up more than 400 yards total offense, scores four TDs in Royals' 34-20 CCS semifinal win over Serra. Royals whip Wilcox for title as Joe Cattolico (Leigh), 24, becomes youngest coach to take CCS crown . . . CCS player of the year Staci Millichap leads St. Francis girls (40-1) to second straight state Div. 2 volleyball crown . . . St. Francis High (10-3) avenges early season loss, edging Oak Grove (12-1), 14-13, for 13th CCS football title. Oak

Grove linebacker Marcus Reese ends year with 110 tackles, 19 sacks, Mercury-News CCS top player, Parade All-America honors . . . Stanford, SCU men reach NCAA soccer semifinals. Broncos (15-5-2) fall to Indiana, 4-0, as Cardinal nips Maryland, 1-0. Hoosiers top Stanford (18-5-2) in final, 3-1 . . . Jeff Garcia leads Calgary to Grey Cup win, is Canadian Football League MVP . . . Lick High's A. J. Williams scores 33, 35 with 21, 22 rebounds in back-to-back losses to Gilroy, Santa Teresa.

■ 1999 ■

George Brett, an infielder with San Jose's California League team in 1972, is elected to Baseball Hall of Fame . . . Beating coach Jerry Tarkanian for only second time in 37 tries, SJS stuns highly regarded Fresno State, 91-64. Terrence Richmond leads Spartans with 21, adds 16 in next outing, an 82-81 loss to No. 16 New Mexico . . . Rometra Craig, Kerri Nakamoto each hit 25 as Mitty girls destroy future Div. 3 state champion Acalanes of Lafayette, 93-50 . . . State freshman player of the year Brandon Worthy's 27 points propels Mitty to 70-63 win at St. Francis . . . Live Oak High's Kristi Robles sets school girl's hoops mark with 48 against Alisal . . . Cecil Mamiit tops Mark Philippoussis for Sybase Open tennis crown after Andre Agassi is ejected for cursing, Pete Sampras drops out with ankle injury . . . Fernando Palazzo hits 20 points, grabs 16 rebounds as Milpitas High trips Palo Alto 64-56 to take De Anza title . . . Lick High's A. J. Williams blasts school record 46 points with 22 rebounds in 71-67 win over Silver Creek . . . Donnie Guerinoni swishes eight treys as WVC captures conference title with 82-72 victory over Chabot . . . SJS downs BYU on OT, 76-74, as Michael Quinney pops in 26 with six three-pointers . . . San Jose Clash midfielder Eddie Lewis scores winning goal in 2-1 USA win over Chile . . . Milpitas' run of CCS soccer upsets ends in 3-0 loss to Div. 1 champ Bellarmine (22-0-3). Mitty (20-0-2), led by CCS player of the year Kate Morgan, St. Francis (20-1-3 with 18 shutout wins), Cupertino (14-3-5) grab girl's playoff titles . . . Misty Hyman, Elin Austevoll win titles to lead Stanford women to Pac-10 swim championship . . . 18 points by WCAL player of the year Jeb Ivey paces Bellarmine to 59-48 upset of state's Number 1 St. Ignatius for CCS Div. 1 hoops title. Bells (23-7) lose to Oakland Fremont in NorCals . . . In girl's CCS play Homestead (28-3) topples Leland, 45-43 on Julie Randall's final shot for Div. 2 crown . . . Lauren Smith-Hams sets state title game records with seven treys, 31 points as Pinewood girls (31-1) take Div. 5 crown, 61-45, over Palos Verdes Chadwick . . . Oklahoma State's Eric Guerrero wins third straight NCAA wrestling title . . . Brian Sager tosses three-hitter, Josh Hochgesang blasts two homers in 9-0 rout of Washington State as Stanford gets off to best league start (9-0) in school history . . . Juli Inkster moves past $4 million career earnings mark and to within five points of spot in LPGA Hall of Fame with four-stroke win in Longs Drug Challenge tourney . . . Silver Creek High's Kevin Rose fans 17 on way to 1-0 no-hit win over Lick . . . Making debut after transfer from Los Gatos High, Valley Christian soph Casey Neale blasts three homers in 6-2 win over Del Mar . . . Santa Clara captures U. S. synchronized swim championship as Anna Kozlova takes solo title, pairs with Tuesday Middaugh in duet victory . . . WVC takes conference men's, women's swimming titles behind Greg Drysdale, Tracy Kinsch . . . Stanford topples Princeton, 42-31 in overtime, to win inaugural national women's college rugby championship . . . Monta Vista High's Kim Stocklmeir goes five for five in second straight week to elevate softball batting average to .533 . . . Catcher Darrel Jacks of Prospect High is seven for eight, picks off five runners in pair of late season games that include Panthers' victory over previously unbeaten Leigh . . . Gilroy's Eric Rossi drives through cloud of dust to capture 46th Johnny Key Classic sprint car race over Ronnie Day at San Jose Speedway . . . Santa Clara nine (20-36) drops final game to LMU, 12-3, ends year with most losses in school history . . . San Jose State (30-26-1) finishes third in WAC, is ousted from league baseball playoffs by losses to Rice, TCU . . . Jessica Busick of Piedmont Hills tosses 11th softball no-hitter of year, fans 16 in 4-0 win over Independence . . . Los Gatos High's Marcia Wallis wins third straight CCS golf title . . . Cincinnati's Jeffrey Hammonds (Stanford) blasts three home runs against Colorado . . . Bellarmine nine ties school record set in 1964, winning 29th game of season with 10-4 CCS Div. 1 final victory over Oak Grove. Saratoga's 6-2 win over Burlingame gives Falcons Div. 2 championship. CCS co-player of the year Sarah Caudle (22-3) pitches Gilroy to Div. 1 softball title victory against Piedmont Hills, 2-1 . . . Ronnie Grant wins both hurdle races to lead Mount Pleasant High to CCS track crown. Silver Creek is third behind long jump, triple jump victor Vincent Ibia . . . In feat unprecedented in NCAA history, Stanford sweeps 10,000 meter race second straight year. Nathan Nutter wins race over Jason Balkman (Lynbrook), Brent Hauser. Cardinal's Tracye Lawler takes NCAA heptahlon with school record 5,855 points . . . County golf title goes to Brady Stockton . . . San Jose among 13 cities considered for franchises in spring pro football league planned to open in 2000 . . . David Esquer, shortstop on Stanford's 1987 national champion team, becomes Cal's head baseball coach . . . St. Francis High first baseman Garrett Cook (.528 batting, 8-4 pitching) is tops in CCS . . . Swimmer Jenny Thompson wins five events at Santa Clara International Invitational . . . Regina Jacobs (Stanford) wins seventh U. S. 1,500 race plus 5,000-meter title at U. S. outdoor championships . . . Santa Clara's Gina Kehr tops women in San Jose Triathlon . . . Stanford's Tim Young goes to Golden State in NBA draft's second round . . . Ato Boldon keeps winning on international track circuit with 100 meter victory in 9.86 at Athens. Same time earlier gave him second behind Maurice Green's world record 9.79 . . . Tricia Martin captures county women's golf title with rounds of 77, 74 . . . Clash players Mauricio Wright, Ron Cerritos score as West beats East, 6-4, in MLS All-Star game. Ex-San Jose Grizzly star Preki is game's MVP . . . Marcia Wallis (Los Gatos) blasts three goals as USA dumps Trinidad and Tobago, 9-1, in Pan American Games . . . In repeat of 1998 Bank of the West Classic tennis final, Lindsay Davenport defeats Venus Williams . . . Paul Bravo (Santa Teresa, SCU) scores goal in USA's 2-0 soccer triumph over Saudi Arabia in Pan American Games third place contest . . . Dino Quintero pounds two first inning homers in Santa Clara's 15-2 victory over Lansing, Mich. for Palomino World Series title . . . Jenny Thompson sets world record in 100-meter butterfly at Pan Pacific Games . . . SJS basketball coaching job goes to Steve Barnes after Phil Johnson (12-16) quits to become Chicago Bulls assistant . . . Oak Grove High rallies from 10-point fourth quarter deficit, beats Bellarmine, 35-31, in game dedicated to former QB Brent Evans, who has battled brain cancer for four years. Evans, 28, (Gavilan, SJS) dies seven weeks later . . . Cal's Deltha O'Neal (Milpitas) intercepts two passes, returns one 75 yards for TD against Rutgers . . . Top ranked St. Francis High nips No. 2 Oak Grove, 15-14, when QB Pat Dillingham hits Chase Lyman for 27-yard score plus two-point conversion with 1:06 left . . . Modesto outfielder Eric Byrnes (St. Francis) leads California League batters with .345 average . . . 5-foot-6 Deonce Whitaker returns opening kickoff 86 yards for score, rushes for 203 yards, scores SJS record five TDs in 38-3 rout of St. Mary's . . . After 13 straight losses to North Carolina, Santa Clara's top ranked women's soccer team defeats Tar Heels, 1-0, on Nikki Serlenga's goal . . . Oakland Skyline High takes lead with 18 seconds left, but St. Francis wins, 19-16, on 51-yard scoring pass from QB Pat Dillingham to Forrest Mozart . . . Stanford's Troy Walters grabs nine passes for 278 yards, including Pac-10 record 98-yard TD catch, sub QB Joe Borchard throws for 324 yards, five TDs in 42-32 victory over UCLA . . . Leigh High posts 20 unanswered fourth quarter points to down San Lorenzo Valley, 26-24, on three-yard Ricky Wester to Danny Malloy TD pass . . . Brandon Simmons cruises for 174 yards, four TDs in 15 carries as Wilcox High crushes Homestead, 41-8 . . . St. Francis High dumps teams ranked second, fifth in U. S. to win Mitty Invitational girls volleyball tournament . . . QB Chris Kasteler passes for 386 yards as wideout Steven Pulley catches school record 15 for 255 yards in SJS upset win over Stanford, 44-39 . . . Making first NFL start as sub for injured Steve Young, QB Jeff Garcia completes 21 passes for two TDs, scores another as 49ers trip Tennessee, 24-22 . . . Oak Grove High's Nick Gardiner carries 24 times for 231 yards, four TDs in a 36-7 victory over Leland. CCS player of the year Gardiner chalks up 1,821 yards, scores 31 TDs . . . Mandy Clemens has goal, three assists to become all-time women's soccer points leader (167) at SCU . . . SJS women's volleyball team (18-1) downs Rice for school record 14th straight win , but streak ends with loss to Cal . . . Los Gatos High's Justin Narragon plows for 194 yards, two TDs in 45 carries while Tab Perry of Milpitas racks up two scores on 71 yards rushing in seven carries, 103 more on pass receptions as Wildcats edge Trojans in league crucial, 18-13 . . . Auto racing fans mourn for Speedway, set to be eliminated from Fairgrounds under year 2000 renovation . . . Pro golfer Casey Martin (Stanford), allowed by court to ride in cart because of circulatory disorder in right leg, qualifies to play on PGA tour . . . Paced by Saladin Washington's 232 yards, four TDs, Prospect High tramples Independence, 43-20 . . . San Jose State cancels SMU game after Spartan Stadium electric transformers explode . . . Pioneer High's Mike Weins rushes for 251 yards, scores four TDs on runs of 7, 51, 55, 78 yards in 53-0 rout of Independence . . . Michael Collins of Milpitas High has 255 yards on ground, TD runs of 20, 46, 58 yards and 67-yard punt return as Trojans crush Cupertino, 50-23 . . . St. Francis High's girls volleyball team loses to Newport Harbor in Santa Barbara Tournament of Champions, ending 37-match win streak . . . Christina Kim of Oak Grove High shoots record 72 for CCS girls golf crown . . . Stanford frosh point guard Jamie Carey has 11 points in impressive debut in 101-58 loss to USA national women's team . . . Ryan Nelsen's headed goal gives No. 17 Stanford 1-0 OT soccer win over No. 9 Santa Clara . . . Valley Christian, Oak Grove Highs hit with one year probation for violating CIF's "undue influence" recruiting rule in case involving former player Ben Fritz . . . County passing champ Andy Heiser runs 66 yards for one score, throws for 276 yards, four more TDs as Santa Clara High defeats Gunn, 47-27, to clinch league crown . . . Despite scoring 34 last quarter points, SJS loses to Hawaii, 62-41, after surrendering 545 yards, 138 penalty yards, seven turnovers . . . Playing college hoops first game of season at Madison Square Garden, Stanford tops Duke in OT, 80-79, as David Moseley scores 20. Next night, twins Jason, Jarron Collins combine for 35 points, 22 rebounds in 72-58 win over Iowa . . . Pac-10 defensive player of the year Deltha O'Neal of Cal sets NCAA mark with season's fourth TD on interception return against Oregon. Score gives him record-tying career five TDs on interceptions . . . Eric Hayes' 10-yard TD catch with 1:12 on clock gives No. 8 Piedmont Hills High to 21-18 victory over top ranked Santa Clara in opening round of CCS Div. II playoffs . . . St. Francis High girls (31-1) takes ninth CCS volleyball championship in 10 years, downing Lynbrook in Div. II behind Becky Biniek's 15 kills,10 digs. Lancers top Rio Americano of Sacramento for NorCal title . . . Notre Dame ousts Stanford women (15-5-1) from NCAA soccer tournament, 1-0 . . . After four scoreless OTs, SCU goalie Rusty Johnson saves penalty kick for 3-2 NCAA soccer win over Stanford . . . Leland High scores include Nate Ramezane's punt return (42 yards), kickoff runback (52), Kevin Ernst's punt returns (48, 31), scoring pass (63) as Chargers top Monterey, 49-28, in CCS playoff opener . . . WVC retains state water polo title with 13-8 victory over Citrus . . . Joe Kelly's 34 points with eight treys leads WVC to 89-65 win over Cuesta . . . Sasha Spalding has16 as SJS women beat Sonoma State, 68-62, end 24-game hoops losing streak . . . Mike Biselli's 22-yard field goal as time expires gives Rose Bowl-bound Stanford 40-37 victory over Notre Dame . . . No. 1 St. Francis High fails to reach CCS grid final for first time in 11 years after 39-34 loss to Hollister . . . Three interceptions, fumble recovery by Andy Hoover help Mitty upset undefeated Los Gatos, 34-6, in CCS Div. 3 semifinals . . . SJS tops Northern Arizona, 49-46, for first 3-0 hoops season start since 1973 . . . Bellarmine beats Live Oak, 8-5, for 14th straight CCS water polo crown . . . Ill with flu, Nick Gardiner runs 92 yards for clinching TD as Oak Grove High holds off Hollister, 28-20, in Div. 1 title game. In Div. 3, Mitty's Kevin May rolls for 202 yards, four TDs as Monarchs snuff Jefferson, 49-6 . . . Micah Weber's 36 points leads Saratoga High to win over Menlo School, 86-81 . . . Mitty High girls' 35-game hoops win streak ends with 89-55 loss to Canyon of Texas . . . 1999 awards go to Lorrie Fair (NCAA women's soccer player of the year), Tiger Woods (AP male athlete of the year).

Bibliography

Books

Andrada, Randy, *They Did It Every Time, The Saga of The Saint Mary's Gaels*, self, 1987

Benson, Michael, *Ballparks of North America*, McFarland & Co., Inc., 1989

Brodie, S. Dan, *66 Years on the California Gridiron*, Olympic Publishing Co., 1949

Cavalli, Gary, *Stanford Sports*, Stanford Alumni Association, 1982

Church, Seymour, *Base Ball, The History, Statistics And Romance of the National Game From Its Inception to the Present Time*, facsimile reproduction, The Pyne Press, 1974

Clark, Dick, and Larry Lester, editors, *The Negro Leagues Book*, The Society for American Baseball Research Negro Leagues Committee, 1994

Cohen, Richard M., David S. Neft and Roland T. Johnson, editors, *The World Series*, The Dial Press, 1976

Considine, Bob, *The Unreconstructed Amateur, A Pictorial Biography of Amos Alonzo Stagg*, Amos Alonzo Stagg Foundation, 1962

Dickey, Glenn, *The History of Professional Basketball Since 1896*, Stein and Day, 1982

Dickson, Paul *The Baseball Dictionary*, Facts on File, 1989

Dobbins, Dick, and Jon Twichell, *Nuggets on the Diamond, Professional Baseball in the Bay Area from the Gold Rush to the Present*, Woodford Press, 1994

Finch, Robert L., L. H. Addington and Ben M. Morgan, editors, *The Story of Minor League Baseball*, The Stoneman Press, 1952

Gipe, George, *The Great American Sports Book*, Doubleday & Co., 1978

Greenberg, Stan, *Olympic Games, The Record*, Guiness Books, 1987

Grothe, Peter, *Great Moments in Stanford Sports*, Pacific Books, 1952

Guzman, Fred, *The Great San Jose Earthquake of 1974*, self, 1975

Hession, Joseph, *Forty Niners, Looking Back*, Foghorn Press, 1985

Hession, Joseph, and Steve Cassady, *Raiders*, Foghorn Press, 1987, 1991

Hildebrand, Chuck, *Bronco Sundays*, Columbia Printing, 1999

Hollander, Zander, editor, *The American Encyclopedia of Soccer*, Everest House, 1980

-----, *The Modern Encyclopedia of Basketball*, Four Winds Press, 1973

Karst, Gene, and Martin J. Jones, *Who's Who in Professional Baseball*, Arlington House, 1973

Liebendorfer, Don, *The Color of Life is Red, A History of Stanford Athletics, 1892-1972*, Department of Athletics, Stanford University, 1972

Lyttle, Richard B., *A Year in the Minors, Baseball's Untold Story*, Doubleday and Co., Inc., 1975

Maher, Tod, *The All-Time United States Football League Register*, Professional Football Researchers Association, 1986

Mallon, Bill, *The Olympic Record Book*, Garland Publications, 1988

McCallum, John D., *Pac-10 Football, The Rose Bowl Conference*, The Writing Works, 1982

McCarty, Bernie, *All-America, The Complete Roster of Football's Heroes*, self, 1991

Merrick, Fred, *Down on the Farm*, The Strode Publishers, 1975

Migdol, Gary, *Stanford, Home of Champions*, Sports Publishing, a division of Sagamore Publishing, 1997

Morse, C. R. "Brick," *California Football History*, self, 1937

Neft, David S., Richard M. Cohen, Rick Korch, *The Sports Encyclopedia: Pro Football, The Modern Era*, 1972-1996, St. Martin's Griffin, 1997

Neft, David S., Roland T. Johnson, Richard M. Cohen, Jordan A. Deutsch, *The Sports Encyclopedia: Pro Football*, Grosset & Dunlap, 1974

Owen, V., *The Adventures of A Quiet Soul, A Scrapbook of Memories*, The Rosicrucian Press, 1996

Peters, Nick, *100 Years of Blue and Gold*, JPC Corp. of Virginia, 1982

Spalding, John E., *Always on Sunday, The California Baseball League, 1886 to 1915*, Ag Press, 1992

-----, *Pacific Coast League Stars, 90 Who Made It in The Majors*, Ag Press, 1997

Stiles, Maxwell, *Football's Finest Hour, The Shrine East-West Game*, Nashunal Publishing Co., 1950

Sullivan, John, *California vs Stanford, The Big Game*, Leisure Press, 1982

The Associated Press and Grolier, *Pursuit of Excellence, The Olympic Story*, 1979, Grolier Enterprises, Inc.,

1979
Thorne, John, and Peter Palmer, editors, *Total Baseball*, Warner Books, fourth edition, 1995
Whalen, James, *Gridiron Greats Now Gone*, McFarland & Co., 1991
Walsh, Christy, editor, *College Football and All America Review*, Murray & Gee., Inc., 1949

Articles in Periodicals
Four Minutes of Fame, Sports Illustrated, Aug. 7, 1997
The Hal Chase Case, Robert C. Hoie, The Baseball Historical Review, 1981
The O'Connell-Dolan Scandal, Lowell Blaisdell, The Baseball Research Journal, 1982

Game Programs
Basketball programs, numerous colleges, high schools, junior colleges
Football programs, numerous colleges, high schools
California Interscholastic Federation, state basketball
California Interscholastic Federation, state track and field
Central Coast Section playoffs, baseball, basketball, football
Peninsula Basketball Tournament
San Jose baseball teams in the California League
Tournament of Champions (basketball)

Media Guides
San Francisco 49ers
San Jose Clash
San Jose Earthquakes
San Jose Sharks
San Jose State University, baseball, basketball, football
Santa Clara University, baseball, basketball, football, soccer
Stanford University, baseball, basketball, football
University of California, baseball, basketball, football
University of Pacific, basketball, football

Newspapers
Los Angeles Times
Los Gatos Mail-News
Mountain View Register-Leader
Oakland Tribune
Palo Alto Times
Peninsula Times-Tribune, Palo Alto
San Francisco Chronicle
San Francisco Examiner
San Francisco Nichi Bei Times
San Jose Daily Mercury
San Jose Mercury-Herald
San Jose Mercury-News
San Jose News
Santa Clara News
Spartan Daily, San Jose State University
Sunnyvale Standard
The Normal Times, San Jose Normal School
The Santa Clara, Santa Clara University
The Sporting News, St. Louis

Periodicals
Illustrated Football Annual
National Hockey League Yearbook
Street and Smith Football Pictorial Year Book

Record Books
California League Record Book
ESPN, Information Please Sports Almanac
North American Soccer League Guide
NCAA Basketball, The Official 1998 College Basketball Records Book, National Collegiate Athletic Association
NCAA Football, The Official 1997 College Football Records Book, National Collegiate Athletic Association
Official Collegiate Basketball Guide, National Collegiate Athletic Association
Official Collegiate Football Guide, National Collegiate Athletic Association
Official Olympic Companion, Atlanta Edition, 1996, International Olympic Committee
Pacific Coast League Record Book
Reach Official Baseball Guide
Spalding's Official Baseball Guide
Spalding's Official Basketball Guide
Spalding's Official Football Guide
Sporting News Official Baseball Guide
Sporting News Baseball Register
Sports Illustrated Sports Almanac
The Baseball Encyclopedia, The Macmillan Co.

Yearbooks
La Torre, San Jose State College
The Bell, San Jose High School
The Redwood, Santa Clara University

Unpublished material
Delphia, Tracy Ann, *A History of Bicycle Track Racing in San Jose; The Burbank Velodrome Years: 1935-1941*, 1994 master's thesis on file in the Clark Library at San Jose State University
Nash, Don., Santa Clara County high school football results, 1928-1999
Nash, Don, and John E. Spalding, Central Coast Section playoff results for 26 boy's and girl's high school sports, 1968-1999
Rogers, Chris, *CRAB -- Chris Rogers' All-Bay*, an on-going study identifying the high schools attended by outstanding athletes in the nine counties of the San Francisco Bay Area through 1999
Spalding, John E., Santa Clara County high school football results, 1895-1927
-----, Santa Clara County high school basketball results, records and other information, 1932-1999

Index